I'm The Greatest Star

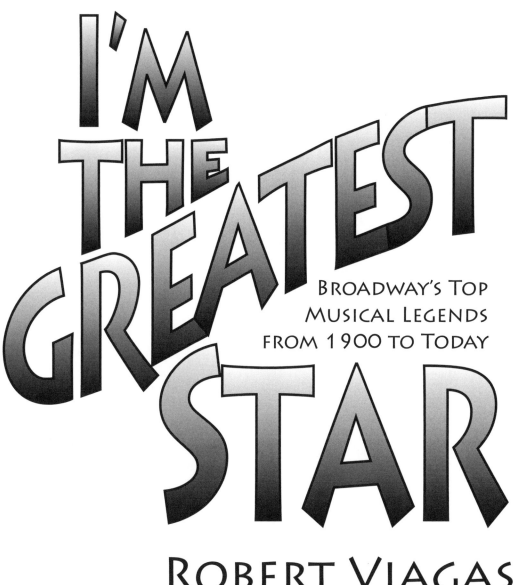

I'M THE GREATEST STAR

BROADWAY'S TOP
MUSICAL LEGENDS
FROM 1900 TO TODAY

ROBERT VIAGAS

APPLAUSE
THEATRE & CINEMA BOOKS

An Imprint of Hal Leonard Corporation
New York

Published in 2009 by Applause Theatre & Cinema Books
An Imprint of Hal Leonard Corporation
7777 West Bluemound Road
Milwaukee, WI 53213

Trade Book Division Editorial Offices
19 West 21st Street, New York, NY 10010

Printed in the United States of America

Book design by Bob Antler

Library of Congress Cataloging-in-Publication Data

Viagas, Robert.
  I'm the greatest star : Broadway's top musical legends from 1900 to
today / by Robert Viagas.
     p. cm.
  ISBN 978-1-55783-727-1
  1. Singers–United States–Biography. 2. Actors–United States–Biography. 3. Musicals–New York (State)–New York–History and criticism.
I. Title.

  ML400.V48 2009
  782.1'409227471–dc22
  [B]
  2008050402

www.applausepub.com

For my father, Anthony Viagas,
the best Tony Award anyone could want

Contents

Preface

A star is a brilliant light in the darkness far above us.

The five-pointed image of a star was used to draw the eye's attention to the presence of a popular performer on a crowded vaudeville bill. A star was hung on backstage doors to indicate the biggest, best-appointed, or most convenient dressing room, which was usually claimed by the performer with the most clout at the box office.

It didn't take much to make the leap from "starred" dressing room to "star's" dressing room. Thus was born the modern concept of stardom, which has metastasized into superstardom and megastardom as the art of public relations has continued to develop it in other lands and other fields of endeavor. We now have star athletes, star politicians, even Wall Street stars, however dimmed.

But stardom in the modern sense was born on Broadway and came to its first flower there, with many of the individuals in this book. Starting with Bert Williams and George M. Cohan and continuing through the eras of Gwen Verdon, Zero Mostel, Patti LuPone, Nathan Lane, and Kristin Chenoweth, stardom on Broadway has come to be defined as a mixture of high achievement, sustained achievement, extraordinary achievement, unique achievement, achievement despite personal adversity, and achievement through personal charisma. Each star has had his or her own special DNA mixture of those qualities.

Having observed many of the stars in this book up close, I have noticed one more quality that's subtle but the watermark of a true star, like the pea that keeps the princess awake under thirty mattresses in the fairy tale: Stars attract the eye. They could be dressed in a sack; when they walk into a crowded room there is something in their bearing that causes everyone to *watch*. Something in their very breathing fascinates us.

Stage stars have a unique quality that no other stars can boast. They're here with us, up close. We're not watching images of them or listening to electronic reproductions of them. They share the same space with us and, for a few hours, breathe the same air. We see them struggle, see them sweat. They are gods come down from Olympus to go about their business alongside us.

Acknowledgments

Special thanks to the staff at the New York Public Library (Theatre Collection, Billy Rose Collection), the Goodspeed Musicals Library, Michael Messina, John Cerullo, Bernadette Malavarca, Charles Rodriguez, Catherine Ryan, Amy Asch, Lillian Viagas, Keith Viagas, Nicholas Viagas, Ben Viagas, and the many fine biographers, historians, and journalists whose books and interviews formed the basis of so much of my research, notably Gerald Bordman, Louis Botto, Kurt Ganzl, Herbert G. Goldman, Ethan Mordden, and Steven Suskin. Special thanks, also, to the stars themselves, who shared their talent in performances—and sat down with me for interviews—over the past three decades.

I'm The Greatest Star

the homeland, with the inevitable comedic clash of cultures. The show was so well written (for its time) that some whites complained to theatre owners that the blacks were failing to stick to their stereotypes.

The show also produced what became Williams's signature song, "Nobody," which he cowrote. The song has a blues feeling, if not structure. Over the course of eleven verses, Williams lists all the nice things that could be happening to him, but the catch is when he asks who is doing those nice things, back comes the glum answer: "Nobody."

The song became a mixed blessing, earning him tens of thousands of Teddy Roosevelt-era dollars and identifying him indelibly as "That 'Nobody' Guy"—but also forcing him to sing it almost every time he made an appearance.

Walker and Williams made one more Broadway bow, in the February 1908 musical *Bandana Land*. For this one, Walker's fast-buck scheme involved selling half a plot of Williams's land to the railroad at a low price, then building a "black man's park," Bandana Land, on the other half and threatening to disrupt the railroad unless they buy the other half of the land at a grossly inflated price. Walker and Williams celebrated the success of their scheme with a reprise of their famous cakewalk. Audiences—with the exception of some black critics, who had begun to object to the stereotypes—loved the show, and it seemed to be building into their biggest hit yet.

Then, at the peak of their success, came a sudden end to the team of Walker and Williams. Walker began suffering from the effects of a chronic disease identified as syphilis and had to leave the cast of Bandana Land, bringing it to a premature closing in April 1908 after a run of just two months. Walker lingered for two years, eventually succumbing to paralysis and death in 1911.

The Ziegfeld Follies

Meanwhile, Williams tried performing solo, even starring in another all-black Broadway musical, *Mr. Load of Kole*, in 1909. But he found his warmest welcome on the vaudeville stage. And there he was scouted by master showman Florenz Ziegfeld, who was assembling the fourth edition of his increasingly sumptuous *Ziegfeld Follies* revues. The 1910 edition also saw comedienne Fanny Brice make her *Follies* debut.

It's a measure of Ziegfeld's openness to pure talent that he took the step of hiring Williams. He was aware that it was the first time a black man had starred alongside white performers in a major Broadway musical. He expected trouble, and he got it. Ziegfeld had planned to roll out Williams with a major set piece for the 1910 *Follies*, but some of the white cast members threatened to strike if a black man were placed on the same footing as they. Ziegfeld compromised by keeping Williams but having him do his sure-fire vaudeville routine instead. As soon as Williams got in front of an audience, however, his artistry was apparent to all. Ziegfeld biographer Marjorie Farnsworth wrote in *The Ziegfield Follies*,

"Williams had only to come on-stage wrinkling his eyebrows and balancing on one foot when he reached the edge of the stage to send audiences into a paroxysm of joy."

In the end, the cast accepted Williams, and his new material was restored, though it included playing a blackbird in one of the comedy sketches.

Things improved the following year when Williams was paired with comedian Leon Erroll, whose specialty was playing drunks. In the sketch "Upper and Lower Level," Williams played a worker giving Erroll a tour of the New York Central Depot, then under construction. The intoxicated Erroll kept having close brushes with disaster while the exasperated Williams kept saving him at the last minute. Their perfectly timed physical comedy sent audiences into hysterics, so, during tryouts in Chicago, they kept trimming down the dialogue and adding to the acrobatics until the act consisted of four spoken lines and twenty-two minutes of mimed tomfoolery. The company manager wrote to Ziegfeld in New York to complain that they weren't sticking to the script. When Ziegfeld came out personally to Chicago to get the funnymen under control, he was so delighted with the audience reaction that he allowed them to keep the changes.

Williams stayed with the *Follies* for ten years, missing only the 1913 and 1918 editions. Rival producer David Belasco tried to hire him away, but Williams felt he owed a debt of loyalty to Ziegfeld.

Among highlights of these years: A 1912 skit in which Williams played a taxi driver, with Errol as his impatient passenger, stuck behind a stubborn horse. A 1914 sketch, the "Darktown Poker Club" routine, in which he pantomimed an entire poker game on a dark stage with only a spotlight on his head, shoulders, arms, and hands. Also that year, he was teamed again with Errol in a sketch that had Williams as a golf caddy, trying to teach the game to Errol's duffer. Williams played a harried hotel switchboard operator in the 1915 edition and played a parody of Shakespeare's *Othello* in 1916.

Williams was one of the performers most closely associated with the *Follies* in its heyday. Ziegfeld billed him just as prominently as any white star, which caused the usual objections. When the *Follies* toured, Williams often had to enter hotels through a service entrance or stay in segregated accommodations. Many audience members who applauded him onstage refused to ride with him in an elevator car or on public transportation. Small wonder he began to drink. Backstage he was not chummy with many of his coworkers, either (with a few notable exceptions), and would often retire to this dressing room when not actually performing. Nevertheless, by the late 1910s Williams was earning more than $50,000 a year in the *Follies*, a huge paycheck by the period's standards.

One of Williams's closest professional and personal relationships was with white comedian Eddie Cantor, who joined the *Follies* in 1917. Together they performed one of that's year's most famous skits. The now portly Williams played a railway redcap whose educated son (Cantor in blackface) is constantly trying to correct his grammar and comportment—

though dad does win the day in the end. Also that year, in the midst of World War I, Williams earned applause singing Ring Lardner's "Home Sweet Home (That's Where the Real War Is)."

Cantor would later write about Williams, "As a natural black face comedian he was far superior to any of us who put on burned cork. But as an actor, Williams was far more than this. . . . very frequently during moments in odd scenes Williams dipped into the great realm of the fundamental art of acting and gave us emotion or comedy which was as universal in its appeal as the very writings of Shakespeare himself. Bert Williams had a natural aptitude for acting . . . which he cultivated industriously all the years of his career."

In his final *Follies* appearance in 1919, Williams brought his career full circle with "I Want to See a Minstrel Show," a parody of then-passé minstrel shows, performed with a blackfaced Cantor.

Cantor helped Williams bankroll his first post-*Follies* shows, in a bid to set him up at last on his own two feet. The two men partnered with George LeMaire for the *Broadway Brevities of 1920*, starring both Cantor and Williams. They hoped to make the *Brevities* into their own annual series like the *Follies*, but it lasted only 105 performances, and there was no sequel.

Under the Bamboo Tree

By late 1921, Williams's heavy drinking and smoking began to catch up with him. His diet was poor, and he suffered from circulation problems in his extremities. In the two years since he'd left the *Follies*, his recording career was booming, but he just hadn't had the big stage hit of his dreams. So a lot was riding on his next show, *Under the Bamboo Tree*, which took its name from the standard by Bob Cole and J. Rosamond Johnson. The tryout tour, which continued into early 1922, revealed that the only thing about it drawing good reviews was Williams himself. He was carrying the entire show, employing dozens of people who depended on him, and protecting his friends' investments. He was determined to make *Under the Bamboo Tree* a success even if it killed him.

And then he began to get ill. It was pneumonia, with symptoms including complete physical exhaustion. He kept driving himself night after night, feeling worse and worse, until finally, on February 27, 1922, he collapsed onstage in Detroit. As he was carried off, the audience was in stitches, thinking it was part of the act. "That's a nice way to die," he's reported to have said, by Tim Brooks in *Lost Sounds: Blacks and the Birth of the Recording Industry*. "They was laughing when I made my last exit."

In the days before antibiotics, the infection killed him five days later, at age forty-six, despite a transfusion of blood from his business partner William Voederey. So many showed up for his funeral that police were hired to keep the crowd under control. A throng estimated in the tens of thousands lined the streets of Harlem to watch his funeral procession pass by.

But in death, he still couldn't escape the racism of even his closest friends. Ziegfeld himself issued the quote, "Bert Williams was one of the greatest comedians I ever employed.

In fact, he was one of the greatest in the world, and the whitest man I ever had the honor to deal with," which he obviously intended as the highest compliment.

W. C. Fields was perhaps more to the point, writing, "He was the funniest man I ever saw; the saddest man I ever knew."

Ben Vereen was attached to historian Loften Mitchell's planned Broadway musical about Williams, to be called *Star of the Morning: Scenes in the Life of Bert Williams*, but the project fell through. Williams is still waiting for someone to bring him back to life, as Barbra Streisand did for Williams's *Follies* costar Fanny Brice.

George M. Cohan impersonates Franklin D. Roosevelt in *I'd Rather Be Right* (1937). PHOTOFEST

GEORGE M. COHAN
The Man Who Owned Broadway

Only one showman has a statue in the middle of Times Square, and that's George M. Cohan.

The bantamweight author/composer/singer/dancer/producer/superpatriot/huckster represented the upbeat, polymath talent of Broadway at its cockiest.

And you would know all that because he'd tell you so himself, probably by shouting it right in your face. Cohan didn't suffer from any self-esteem problems. He turned chin-up, cocked-hat, blustering swagger into an art form, and audiences loved him for it, though it was apparently fairly hard for those offstage to endure on a daily basis. Cohan was a royal pain in the neck.

In the two decades before World War I, Cohan had a hit or two or three each year, first in vaudeville with the family act the Four Cohans, then as a songwriter, playwright, and producer on Broadway. He would write, direct, and star in his own shows, then tour them and write more while he was touring.

His first big Broadway hit, *Little Johnny Jones*, opened in 1904, the same year that the New York subway system opened its first station in Longacre Square, and the same year Longacre Square was renamed Times Square. The hit song of that show was "Give My Regards to Broadway," which became the anthem of showbiz—although it mentions only Herald Square ten blocks south, then the center of the theatre industry. Cohan wrote melodramas, comedies, and thrillers, but he was best known for his jaunty musicals, which departed sharply from the overproduced, slow-moving European-style operettas that were standard musical comedy fare of the time and created a template for snappy, light musical comedy that became the standard for decades to come.

It became a cliché that at some point in his shows, a giant American flag would appear and the stage would explode in bunting as Cohan sang "Yankee Doodle Boy" or one of his other ultrapatriotic tunes.

Broadway, America, and George M. Cohan were all one entity, indivisible, to him, though in later years he started to have some doubts about the Broadway and America. In his self-regard he rarely wavered.

and in a clear, clarion tenor without the vocal frippery that had been popular until that time. Although there was more than a little Irish in his delivery, his unembellished, to-the-point style was seen as very American. The same was true of his dancing: a crisp, straight-backed strutting style bursting with vitality. He would dance back and forth across the stage like a tiger in a cage, executing graceful turns or sometimes leaping up on the prosce-nium and kicking off from it, like a swimmer at the end of a lap, then heading back in the other direction.

His patriotic songs, like "It's a Grand Old Flag" and (later) "Over There," helped make Americans proud of the nation they were building. He helped define Americans as en-thused, straightforward, extroverted, unabashedly sentimental, and proud of their families and flag.

Similarly, Cohan helped define what it was to be a New Yorker and a denizen of Broad-way. "Give My Regards to Broadway" remains the anthem of the Great White Way more than a century later. His shows over the next two decades includes *45 Minutes from Broad-way, The Man Who Owns Broadway, Broadway Jones,* and *Hello, Broadway!* Less famously, he also wrote *Fifty Miles from Boston, Los Angeles,* and *American Born.*

The Plays

Many of Cohan's greatest successes involved no music at all. *Get-Rich-Quick Wallingford* (1910) was his adaptation of Randolph Chester's *Saturday Evening Post* series about a young man involved in a scheme to create covered carpet tacks that will match your carpet. This celebration of American guile and gullibility ran a phenomenal 424 performances, longer than any of his musicals.

In 1913 he wrote a stage adaptation of Earl Derr Biggers's popular mystery novel *Seven Keys to Baldpate*, about a writer who takes a room at the Baldpate Inn in hopes of finding a quiet retreat to finish his new crime novel. But it's soon apparent that the Baldpate is any-thing but quiet, and the author is drawn into a web of mysteries. He thinks he has the only key to the place, but strange characters keep showing up, each claiming he or she has the only key. In a final surprise twist, it's revealed that the whole play has been taking place in-side the mind of the author and that the play itself is the crime story he has written at the inn.

The show had 320 performances, a handsome run for the period, and was revived periodically. It was filmed a startling seven times (so far), mostly under its original title, but also as *Haunted Honeymoon,* starring Gene Wilder in 1986.

Cohan was also revered as a play doctor, punching up other authors' work. Biographer John McCabe quotes critic George Jean Nathan summing up the "Cohanization" formula by saying it involved "prefixing to each of the author's original speeches such phrases as 'By gosh,' 'Gee whizz,' 'I say, kid,' 'Oh baby,' 'I'll tell the world,' and 'You said a mouthful' . . . and of writing in at least one mention of a million dollars and one cheer for the United States."

Despite his nonstop writing, directing, producing, and performing, Cohan remained close to his immediate family. Cohan's beloved sister Josie married Fred Niblo, scion of the theatrical Niblo family. She died of heart disease when barely forty years old in 1916. His father, Jeremiah "Jerry" Cohan, died in 1917, and his mother, Helen "Nellie" Costigan Cohan, lived until 1928, leaving George M. as the last of the Four Cohans.

George's marriage to fellow vaudevillian Ethel Levey ended in divorce after just a few years. She wasn't prepared to be such a distant number two to her powerhouse husband. Together they had a daughter, Georgette. His second marriage was to Agnes Nolan, a dancer he met while casting *Little Johnny Jones*. She was much more content with her supporting role. Cohan wasn't always faithful to her, but he appears to have had a genuine love for her, and their marriage lasted until his death. They, too, had a daughter, Helen F. Cohan, named for her grandmother, and a son, George Jr.

ASCAP and Equity

In addition to his many other talents, Cohan was also a hardheaded businessman. As such, it pained him to see his songs played and sung by other performers and sometimes even used by other managers in their shows without a penny being paid to the creator. In 1914 he became one of the cornerstone members of the American Society of Composers and Publishers (ASCAP), a songwriters' union that looked after members' rights, arranged licenses for performing works, collected and disbursed royalties, and prosecuted pirates. The organization still exists today, facing the challenges presented by the Internet and other electronic sound-copying and -distributing issues.

The creation of ASCAP helped change songwriting from a craft into a business. Composers could now make a living just writing songs and not having to perform them, as well, if they didn't have the talent or desire to do so. Songwriting became lucrative and thereby respectable—yet another way in which Cohan helped transform American entertainment as it headed into the broadcast age.

Cohan's fervent patriotism blossomed anew during World War I and found a receptive ear with the public. In response to the war declaration, Cohan sat down and wrote the song "Over There," which became one of the anthems of the doughboys in the trenches and among their families back home. The song and its sentiment earned Cohan a congressional medal, which was handed to him years later by President Franklin D. Roosevelt.

Cohan was at the peak of his popularity in 1919 when he wrote the operetta spoof *The Royal Vagabond*, which ran 348 performances. He felt he was, at last, on top of the world. And that's why he was stunned when the Actors' Equity Association, the fledgling actors' union, called a strike against theatrical managers, including him, on August 7, 1919.

Cohan, who was both actor and manager, came down firmly on the side of the managers. While he believed songwriters needed a strong trade guild like ASCAP, he just as firmly believed that actors had no right to one. Cohan had always been very generous with his brother actors; he paid actors well and fulfilled many of the conditions Equity was fighting for. He was openhanded to a fault and often personally aided actors who had fallen on hard times. Cohan felt, however, that such generosity should be an option, not a requirement. Cohan, who was abbot of the Friars Club, a fraternal organization for actors, resigned from that post after the strike was called.

By speaking out against the strike, Cohan became identified as the poster boy for rapacious managers. He was vilified in print and to his face, and bullets reportedly were fired at his home. The four-week strike ended in victory for the actors, who won nearly all their demands. Bitterness between Cohan and Equity persisted the rest of his life. He refused to join the union, and on those increasingly rare occasions when he returned to the Broadway stage, Equity made an exception for him and allowed him to perform without a union contract.

Later Career

During the 1920s, Cohan's pace began to slow down. He started to focus more on writing than on performing, and on comedies and mysteries at the expense of his musicals. One of his hits from this period was *The Tavern*, a 1920 melodrama about a mysterious traveler called only "The Vagabond," who gets involved in solving a mystery at a roadside inn in colonial-era America. Dramatic moments were punctuated with claps of thunder, a device that became a cliché of bad mystery movies but that thrilled audiences when first used by Cohan. Though the main character was originated by Arnold Daly, the play enjoyed a long life on tour and in revivals with Cohan in the role.

The public still clamored for his musicals, as well, even as they were starting to look a little old-fashioned. He continued to write, produce, and sometimes star in musicals throughout the 1920s, including in *The Merry Malones, Little Nellie Kelly*, and *The Rise of Rosie O'Reilly*.

Movies barely attracted Cohan's interest. In 1917 he appeared in silent-movie versions of *Broadway Jones* and *Seven Keys to Baldpate*, but a silent Cohan was an emasculated Cohan. He waited until 1932 to try again, playing the dual roles of a crook and a presidential candidate in Rodgers and Hart's *The Phantom President*, which was performed, for some reason, entirely in verse. With oddly matched costars Claudette Colbert and Jimmy Durante, Cohan offered the public a rare glimpse of his dancing, singing, and blackface (!) skills.

Cohan returned to Broadway in October 1935 when he agreed to star in *Ah, Wilderness!*, written by the man who had become recognized as the foremost playwright of the age, Eugene O'Neill. Like many O'Neill works, *Ah, Wilderness!* dealt with the stresses within a close-knit New England family very similar to the playwright's own. But, for once, O'Neill showed the warm and humorous side of his memories. Cohan played Nat Miller, a newspaper publisher who is father to the central character, a teenager whose coming of age serves as the play's plot. Nat is a firm but loving father, filled with wisdom and common sense.

Everyone expected the star to Cohanize the piece, but—surprise—Cohan stuck to the master's script and gave a surprisingly affecting performance. In a 1933 *New York Times* article, critic Brooks Atkinson wrote of Cohan, "The jaunty mannerisms and the mugging have disappeared. For the fact is that *Ah, Wilderness!* has dipped deeper into Mr. Cohan's gifts and personal character than any of the antics he has written for himself. Ironic as it may sound, it has taken Eugene O'Neill to show us how fine an actor George M. Cohan is."

Sadly, *Ah, Wilderness!* opened a door for Cohan that he declined to pass through. He found himself increasingly lost in the world of 1930s America. In the booming 1900s and 1910s, he reflected a pride and confidence that went into eclipse after the stock market crash of 1929. In the sober, pessimistic, self-critical, and often desperate days of the Depression, Cohan increasingly seemed jarringly out of place. In typical style, he sneered right back, regarding his countrymen as crybabies and defeatists. Without an America to celebrate, Cohan became a crabby and querulous old man, pining for the good old days.

I'd Rather Be Right

No fan of President Franklin D. Roosevelt, Cohan nevertheless agreed to play him in the 1937 Rodgers and Hart musical *I'd Rather Be Right*, a gentle parody of the New Deal (more of an homage, actually) and Roosevelt himself. Though Rodgers and Hart had been one of America's leading songwriting teams for more than a decade, Cohan was unimpressed with them and their work. At times he was openly contemptuous, calling them "Gilbert & Sullivan." In truth, *I'd Rather Be Right* was one of their weakest scores (with the exception of "Have You Met Miss Jones?") and the book by George S. Kaufman and Moss Hart lacked satirical bite. The production achieved a run of 290 performances, largely thanks to older Cohan fans and folks curious to see what their parents had been raving about.

Though convinced that Broadway was no longer interested in him, Cohan tried one more time. His final Broadway show was *The Return of the Vagabond*, a sequel to his perennial crowd-pleaser *The Tavern*. Despite the presence of ingenue Celeste Holm (three years before *Oklahoma!*), audiences weren't interested; it ran just seven performances. But it was unmistakably a Cohan show: written by Cohan, produced by Cohan, and starring in title role . . . Cohan!

Cohan died of intestinal cancer, on November 5, 1942. Although he'd lived through so many eras, he was only sixty-four. A showman even in death, he starred in one of the most opulent funerals ever held at St. Patrick's Cathedral in New York.

Even then, his public wasn't quite ready to let him go. As he was dying, he had gotten an advance peek at *Yankee Doodle Dandy*, a film biography starring James Cagney, which was released shortly after Cohan's demise. Cagney loping back and forth across the stage like a rooster while singing Cohan's "Yankee Doodle Boy" became one of the iconic images of film history and fixed Cohan's persona in the wide public's mind. Cagney won the Oscar as Best Actor for his impersonation of Cohan.

In 1958, Oscar Hammerstein II spearheaded a drive to erect a statue to Cohan in the middle of Times Square. The statue, with the titles of Cohan's greatest hit songs engraved on the pedestal, still stands at the foot of a traffic island at Forty-sixty Street and Broadway, looking downtown toward both Forty-second Street and Herald Square beyond.

Others hitched themselves to Cohan's persona. Mickey Rooney played him in the 1957 TV special *Mr. Broadway*, and in 1968 Joel Grey brought His Jauntiness back to the stage in the 1968 revue *George M!*

Cohan survives today as more of a presence, a bright red-white-and-blue ghost, than as an actively produced and recorded writer. The last time one of his shows was revived— *Little Johnny Jones* in 1982 with Donny Osmond—the production closed on opening night. Broadway had grown up, and one of its favorite childhood toys no longer seemed fun. Cohan continues to be honored and remembered by Broadway, but rarely performed.

Fanny Brice as Baby Snooks (circa 1938). PHOTOFEST

FANNY BRICE
The Terrible Tot

Fanny Brice offers a classic ugly-duckling-becomes-a-swan story that's also a classic American tale: A child from a lower-middle-class family, whom everyone derided as homely, used raw talent and determination to raise herself up to become the wealthy and admired star of the *Ziegfeld Follies* who could call her own career shots—but whose happiness was always tempered by a disastrous love life.

Her life would later be memorably outlined in the musical *Funny Girl*, but the real story had far more twists, turns, triumphs, and sorrows than that show had time to tell. Brice was the first female star hired for the *Follies*, slaying audiences with her homely-girl clowning and Jewish-dialect comedy, but she could also turn around and break hearts with a sobbing torch song.

Which brings us to a startling Fanny Brice factoid: She came from a family of Hungarian and French Jews who didn't speak Yiddish. She never knew more than one hundred words of Yiddish, and those, plus her hilarious trademark Yiddisher accent, she picked up from friends. How's that for acting?

Fania Borach was born October 29, 1891, on the Lower East Side of Manhattan into a family of Jewish immigrants (mom from Hungary, dad from the Alsace region of France), who soon resettled to Newark, New Jersey. There the child, soon nicknamed Fanny, spent most of her formative years. Like the terrible-tot character of Baby Snooks she would later create, Brice was a mischievous child, constantly playing tricks on the other kids, disobeying her parents, and even stealing from them and from local merchants—though her larceny often had a Robin Hood aspect to it. She often used her ill-gotten gains to help the poorer children in her neighborhood.

Her parents' marriage was not a happy one. Brice's mother, Rose, had married her father (variously nicknamed "French" Charlie and "Pinochle" Charlie Borach) largely because he was making good money as a bartender. After their marriage, however, he proved to be something of a bum, drinking and gambling until he was no longer able to work. Fortunately, Rose proved to be smart, tough, and capable. She learned the tavern-keeping business and bought a bar, then more bars. She soon was supporting the family as her husband sank into an alcoholic haze.

One of the few ways young Fanny could command her father's attention was to dance, sing, and clown for him. He would applaud and give her coins that he had gotten from her mother. A lot of her acting (and acting out) seems to have grown at least partly from this urge to get male attention, and this need may have been the source of much of her later heartache, as well. Biographer Herbert G. Goldman observed that she loved her father but didn't respect him, and she respected her mother but didn't love her. The problem only increased when her parents separated and her father moved out (though he stayed in contact with her).

Fanny loved going to the theatre from her earliest days. After her mother moved the family to Brooklyn, the adolescent Fanny took a series of crazy jobs, including Christmas present wrapper, to earn ticket money.

And that's how Brice backed into showbiz one night at Keeney's Theatre in Brooklyn. She went with a friend to one of the raucous amateur nights, expecting to pay twenty-five cents a ticket. When they arrived, they discovered tickets were fifty cents, so Fanny bluffed her way backstage, saying she was going to perform. Her intention was to sneak out before her turn came, but the manager changed the order of the acts, and Brice found herself pushed out onstage.

She had to sing something the band already knew, so she picked a then-current hit, "When You Know You're Not Forgotten by the Girl You Can't Forget," and launched into it with a strong voice and a funny way with the lyric. She had had no formal training but used her natural extroversion to her advantage. The audience, which had catcalled when she first came out, threw money onto the stage. She got laughs by breaking into the song to say "thank you" when a coin landed, ringing, on the boards and she bent down to pick it up. In all, they threw about four dollars on the stage, and Fanny won the nightly prize, another ten dollars.

She decided then and there that she'd be back. At age fourteen, Fanny Borach was in show business (actually, she was "Fannie" at first but changed the spelling some years later).

She started traveling around to amateur nights at various Brooklyn theatres, often winning, until she was offered regular work in burlesque. Burlesque is associated with strippers today, but in the first decade of the twentieth century it was a little bit more like *Saturday Night Live*, a place for not-ready-for-prime-time humor, making fun of people, show business, and social pretensions. It bore little resemblance to 1970s Times Square burlesque, or even to the musical *Gypsy*, which showed burlesque in its degenerated form of twenty years later.

Nowadays, sexual humor is everywhere but ethnic humor is considered deeply offensive and sometimes even career-ending. All of that was exactly reversed during Brice's heyday. Sexual humor, except for the most allusive, was considered in the worst taste, but stereotyped ethnic comedy–known as "dialect" comedy for the broad accents employed by the performers—was hugely popular. This was also the age of minstrel shows and black-face. Al Jolson did much of his act as a black dialect comedian (singing what were known as "coon songs"). Others included Gallagher & Shean (Irish and "Dutch" [German], respectively) and, later, Chico Marx of the Marx Brothers as an alleged Italian. There were dozens, if not hundreds, more.

Brice was not the first "Jewish" dialect comic (meaning one who employed a cartoonish Yiddish accent), but she quickly established herself as the top. She learned (or "loined") the accent ("hexent") from listening to older masters of the art like Harry Delf.

Brice's first success in vaudeville came with a number she bought from a young Tin Pan Alley song plugger named Irving Berlin, then also at the dawn of his career. Titled "Sadie Salome, Go Home," it was a parody of "The Dance of the Seven Veils" in the form of a thickly accented Jewish friend urging Salome to stop the dance because "Dot's not a business for a lady."

But Brice didn't just sing the song with an accent. She illustrated each line by rolling her shoulders, snaking her hands and arms, and, especially, pulling all sorts of droll and suggestive faces. She was an inveterate "mugger," using her expressive lips and eyes to add a coquettish flip to each line. But her gawky homeliness turned it all into a joke. The sexy/funny alchemy, coupled with the cartoonish Yiddish inflections and body language, became her trademarks. Debuting in a touring burlesque show called *The College Girls*, she learned the show business ropes, quickly picking up all the little ways a performer could "play" an audience. She kept adding material to her act until she became a headliner.

Men assumed that because she was homely, she was also "easy." They were wrong. She was worldly-wise for her age and defended her virtue capably. She had many persistent fans and stumbled into an ill-advised marriage with one, a barber named Frank White, just after her eighteenth birthday. It was a disaster from the start. They separated after three days and quietly divorced.

Brice even tried out for the legitimate stage and was cast in the chorus of George M. Cohan's *The Talk of New York*, but she proved so inept a dancer that she was fired after the first rehearsal by Broadway megaproducer Sam Harris. Back to burlesque she went. That kind of backhand treatment would have demoralized many performers. But throughout her life Brice drew on a deep well of confidence, not only in her own talent, but in the audience's love for her. Offstage she would always find love hard to come by. But onstage, it flooded her like a waterfall.

How self-confident and assertive was she? This title of this book comes from a song in *Funny Girl*, the show based on Brice's life.

Others agreed with the self-assessment.

Brice had once gotten a letter from a music publishing house, Joseph W. Stern & Co., signed by secretary Helen Ziegfeld. She jokingly showed it around the burlesque theatre, proclaiming "Ziegfeld wants me."

The joke was that she was pretending it was from another Ziegfeld—Florenz Ziegfeld, the

the way—she had become embittered. Onstage she was still a sprite, but offstage, friends found that she had acquired a hard edge.

Brice's marital heartbreak played out in the press, as well, which added to her distress. Audiences came to see her clowning but were all too aware of how difficult her offstage life was becoming. It was Ziegfeld who found a way to capitalize on this quandary, in the process delivering one of her greatest hits: Channing Pollock's English translation of Maurice Yvain's French torch song "Mon homme"—"My Man." It was a raw cry of pain from a woman who loves a man despite his neglect and abuse. It might as well have been custom written to describe Brice and Arnstein. Brice didn't want to perform it at first. It wasn't the least bit funny and gave her no accent to hide behind. Would audiences object to seeing their funny girl sad?

The against-type casting was a stroke of genius. The song, which she always sang with her eyes closed, became her signature piece, and audiences demanded to hear it again and again over the next decade, to the point where she finally refused to sing it anymore—or resisted, at any rate.

There were other songs, too. The word *rose* recurred again and again in her life. Her mother's first name was Rose, and her second husband's surname was Rose. Among her greatest song hits were "Rose of Washington Square" and "Second-hand Rose," both of which were introduced in Ziegfeld shows.

Movie Career

Brice was so popular in the late 1920s that after Al Jolson appeared in the first widely released sound film, *The Jazz Singer*, she was among the first stage stars producers sought out. Brice holds a little-known place in Hollywood history as the first woman to star in a talking film. *My Man* was rushed into production by First National Films and released before the end of 1928. The story of a plain Jane who gets her heart broken by a heel not all that different from her real-life husband Arnstein, the musical showcased some of her best-known stage routines and included performances of "I'm an Indian," "Second-hand Rose" and, of course, "My Man."

However, her movie stardom didn't last long. After the flop of her next two top-lining vehicles, *Night Club* and *Be Yourself!* (which preserves her performances of several Billy Rose songs, including "Cooking Breakfast for the One I Love" and "When a Woman Loves a Man"), producers turned to other stars. Brice's film career was limited to cameos and specialty appearances thereafter.

Meanwhile, in her personal life, Brice finally had enough of Nick Arnstein. The serial infidelities, the constant arrests, the numerous pending court cases for fraud and theft, and the constant male preening finally became too much even for the ever-patient Brice. She demanded and was granted a divorce in 1927 and got sole custody of their children.

In 1929 she took up with another flashy character who would break her heart. Billy Rose was a Broadway and nightclub songwriter with dreams of being a big-time producer.

Brice admired his moxie, he admired her talent and her ability to bring in the crowds. Though they were never really in love, they married in 1929. It turned into more of a business arrangement than a romance, but it served them both well in the darkest days of the Depression. He wrote comedy material for her, including the hilarious "Sascha, the Passion of the Pasha," in which she happily related life as a nice Jewish girl who is drafted into a sultan's harem, and "Is Something the Matter with Otto Kahn (or Is Something the Matter with Me)?," in which she played an aspiring opera singer who can't get a break.

The Late *Follies*

When Fanny Brice returned to the *Follies* for its 1934 edition, many things had changed. She had been eighteen when she did her first *Follies* in 1910 and was now past forty. Instead of sitting on top of the world, Ziegfeld had died broke, and the new show had been organized on behalf of his widow, chirping-voiced actress Billie Burke. The general taste level of the audience had moved on, too. Ziegfeldian opulence looked vulgar to Depression-era audiences, who had come to appreciate personal wit and ability over simple excess. Nevertheless, critics complained that there was a certain expectation of lushness associated with the Ziegfeld name that went unfulfilled.

Fortunately, the 1934 *Follies* had plenty of talent. The cast featured Eve Arden, the dance team of Buddy and Vilma Ebsen, and comedians Willie and Eugene Howard. Brice sang three songs by Ballard MacDonald and her husband, Billy Rose: "Soul-Saving Sadie" (a parody of evangelist Aimee Semple McPherson), "Countess Dubinsky" (about a former Russian noblewoman who now stripped for Minsky), and a send-up of the nudism fad, "Sarah, the Sunshine Girl."

At Rose's urging, Brice performed a sketch written by David Freedman in which she played a mischievous baby. She had played baby characters from time to time throughout her career, though she had avoided doing so for some time because another *Follies* comedienne, Rae Dooley, also did a baby act.

But Rose saw that, offstage, Brice would sometimes use babytalk when she was angry, to take the sting out of the words. Freedman created a character called "Babykins," who had debuted in the 1930 revue *Sweet and Low*, and was an immediate hit.

In the *Ziegfeld Follies of 1934* Brice resurrected the character and gave her a name, "Baby Snooks," after a friend's term of endearment. The character would, in time, become the mainstay of Brice's career. The *Follies* sketch was a classic bit of Snooks shtick. She listened carefully as her daddy told the story of George Washington and the cherry tree, then proceeded to turn around and lie straight to his face.

Brice brought Baby Snooks back to the Winter Garden for the *Ziegfeld Follies of 1936*, which costarred Bobby Clarke, Josephine Baker, Eve Arden, Bob Hope, Harriet Hoctor, Judy Canova, and the Nicholas Brothers, with staging by John Murray Anderson and choreography by George Balanchine.

The Snooks skit was "Baby Snooks Goes Hollywood," in which she wreaked her trademark brattiness on a film executive played by Bob Hope. Brice supplemented it with another David Freedman skit, "The Sweepstakes Ticket," in which she played a woman who learns that her husband has lost her winning lottery ticket and goes to comic lengths to get it back. She also poked fun at her own image, singing a parody of the overexposed "My Man" titled "He Hasn't a Thing but Me," in which the lamppost she was leaning against came alive and walked off in disgust at her lugubriousness.

The overstuffed show was a huge hit and charged along well for 115 performances, until Brice fell ill with what was described as neuritis of the spine. It was the first time in her long and grueling career that her health began to break. The producers felt that the show, even with that stunning supporting cast, couldn't go on without her. After a summer hiatus, it returned in the fall, but by then its golden supporting cast had mostly been snapped up elsewhere.

In the midst of all this, Brice learned that her husband, Billy Rose, was leaving her for a girl he had met in *Aquacade*, another of his extravaganzas, this one set on water.

The collapse of her third marriage, especially on such humiliating terms, put an end to what was left of her romantic vulnerabilities. The divorce was finalized in 1938. She never remarried.

In *Funny Girl*, the character of Fanny Brice sings about how "People who need people are the luckiest people in the world." But her real life illustrated exactly the opposite point. Fanny needed people, especially a reliable man, in her life. But nothing about what happened as a result made her feel remotely lucky.

All Snooks, All the Time

Brice headed back to Hollywood. In 1938, the year before Judy Garland achieved immortality in *The Wizard of Oz*, she and a number of other contract players, including Brice, appeared in the film *Everybody Sing*, a thing of rags and patches that showcased yet another of Brice's ballet parodies, "Quainty Dainty Me."

Brice and Hollywood had an unpleasant run-in in 1939. She was startled to learn that a movie titled *Rose of Washington Square* not only used one of her signature songs as its title, but told the story of a plain girl named Rose (Alice Faye) who becomes a *Ziegfeld Follies* star but has her heart broken by her criminal heel of a husband (Al Jolson). The story was so close to that of Brice's life that she quickly sued the studio and settled out of court.

Brice made only one more movie, *Ziegfeld Follies*, in 1946. Billed as "The greatest production since the birth of motion pictures!," the film sought to re-create the glorious excesses of the old *Follies* (Ziegfeld himself having died fifteen years earlier). Producers found it surprisingly hard to get any of the actual *Follies* alumni to take part. Surrounded by movie stars like Fred Astaire, Lucille Ball, Judy Garland, Lena Horne, Gene Kelly, Esther Williams, and Red Skelton, Brice was the only one on hand to re-create some of her classic Ziegfeld-related material, including the "Sweepstakes Ticket" sketch and the songs "Yiddle on Your Fiddle," "Queen of the Jungle," and the inevitable "My Man."

Toward the end of Brice's long, successful career, it was all Snooks all the time. The *Follies* had become defunct, and her wacky acting style was considered passé. Snooks was the last of her characters who appealed to the general public. Week after week, radio audiences heard her merrily sass her mother, torment her brother Robespierre, and drive her "daddy" crazy with her never-ending responses of "Whyyyyy?" when he would answer one of her questions, followed by yet another "Whyyyyy?"

Also, as her health declined and her age increased, the minimal demands of radio became more and more appealing. Her successful "Snooks" radio show was heard on CBS from 1945 to 1948 and then spent two seasons on NBC, in 1949-50 and 1950-51.

There was some talk of moving Snooks to television. But whereas seeing Brice dressed as a baby onstage was funny and absurd, and hearing her on the radio allowed listeners to imagine Snooks as a tot, the prospect of a woman in her late fifties in the Snooks getup on TV was actually a little bit creepy. In 1950, with radio itself in decline, Brice decided she'd had enough and planned to retire at age 60. Brice also planned to finish her memoirs, but fate didn't allow her a retirement. On May 24, 1951, with five shows left on her final contract, she suffered a cerebral hemorrhage and died five days later without regaining consciousness.

Aside from older folks who may remember Baby Snooks, most people today form their image of Brice from one source: *Funny Girl*, the stage and screen musical biography which starred Barbra Streisand. Her performance was so definitive that no one has ever attempted a Broadway revival.

Produced by Brice's real-life son-in-law, Ray Stark, it was originally envisioned as a nonmusical film. But Isobel Lennart's screenplay immediately suggested treatment as a stage musical.

Streisand, who had done some memorable club work and had stolen the Harold Rome musical *I Can Get It for You Wholesale* with a single song, "Miss Marmelstein," was eagerly drafted to play Brice. It was a perfect match. People made much of both performers' perceived Semitic features, and both were wildly talented anomalies who shot to the top from seemingly nowhere. Songwriters Jule Styne and Bob Merrill managed to capture Brice beautifully in show-off pieces like "I'm the Greatest Star," which gives this book its title, and "His Love Makes Me Beautiful." Even the plaintiveness of "My Man" was suggested by "Who Are You Now?" and the show's iconic hit, "People." Streisand would later sing "My Man" itself in the sequel, the film *Funny Lady*, about Brice's years with Billy Rose.

But there's something a little sad about the stupendous success of *Funny Girl*. When people think of Brice, they see Streisand. One vivid personality has virtually been erased by another vivid personality. Streisand and company did well and got very close to Brice. But the original was unique and defies duplication.

The classic Al Jolson in blackface for *The Singing Fool* (1928). PHOTOFEST

AL JOLSON
You Ain't Heard Nothin' Yet

Al Jolson earned his place in history by starring in the first successful "talkie," or sound film, *The Jazz Singer*, in 1927.

But he made that film after nearly a decade as the single biggest star in American show business. Seeing clips of him today, that may be hard to imagine. There he is, down on one knee grotesquely made up in blackface, white-gloved hands outstretched imploringly, sobbing, "Do ya hear me, Mammy?" How could something so offensive and excessive have been so massively popular?

But in his day, the folks just couldn't get enough of "Jolie." Over the course of a dozen Broadway musicals and thousands of vaudeville dates, they would stomp and roar after a big number, and Jolson would step down to the footlights and shout to the back wall, "You ain't heard nothin' yet!" and then top himself.

Broadway theatres were big and had no amplification of any kind other than acoustically astute architectural designs that helped as much as they could. A performer who wanted to break the heart of the person in the last row had to make big movements and big sounds. At this, Jolson was the master. Photographs show him up close, but that's not how most people saw and enjoyed him. He looked much better from the rear mezzanine.

One of the things that enabled Jolson to cut loose was his ability to hide behind a mask. In his case, the mask was a coating of burnt cork. He adopted (from minstrelsy) the meta-persona of a black man who has come north but who proudly misses the old days on the plantation. He sang about missing the Swanee River, about missing his dear old mammy. It's hard to say how many actual black people found anything nostalgic in this. But it was Jolson's power to enable general audiences, many of them European immigrants (like Jolson himself) or children of immigrants, to share his simple and profound emotions and remember their own homes, their own mothers.

And yet there is always what historian Ethan Mordden, in his book *Make Believe: The Broadway Musical in the 1920s*, has called "the question of Jolson": Jolson was a stupendous pain in the neck to those who worked with him and to anyone who tried to get close to him. He could seem obsessed to the point of mental illness. As Mordden put it, "He was a troll, his voice itself lacked beauty, his persona was that of an aggressive know-nothing urban opportunist, his casting couch made Ziegfeld look like Squirrel Nutkin, he blackmailed songwriters into giving him author credit (and therefore royalties) for the privilege of having Jolson introduce their song, and his bedazzled media contacts perforce advertised him as 'The World's Greatest Entertainer,' the press release as mythopoeia."

For all his self-mythmaking, he lived up to the "greatest entertainer" sobriquet all his life.

★

Asa Yoelson was born in Lithuania. He later gave the date of his birth as May 26, 1885, but that may have been a guess. His Jewish parents emigrated to the United States in 1894 and settled in Washington, D.C., where his father worked as a *shochet*, or kosher slaughterer of meat animals, and sometimes acted as *mohel*, or ritual circumciser, for the Talmud Torah Synagogue in that city.

The expectation was that Asa would become a *cantor*, or religious singer at the temple, but after the death of his mother when he was ten, Asa became hard to control and frequently ran away from home. As Herbert G. Goldman wrote in his book *Jolson: The Legend Comes to Life*, "Jolson, for all his tough, earthy exterior, would remain an emotional child for the rest of his life—a self assured braggart who was terrified of being alone, a sentimentalist with a heart of gold who made life miserable for those around him, and a lothario who chased, conquered, and in turn ignored young women. In short, a man-boy, full of seeming contradictions and haunted by the specter of his mother's death."

By the time of his bar mitzvah in 1898, Jolson was already singing and dancing for money on street corners. When he was fourteen he tried to enlist to fight in the Spanish-American War, and while the army rebuffed his offer, it did permit him and his brother to entertain the troops.

To their religious father's great distress, Asa and his brother Hirsch decided to run off and start a vaudeville act, in the process anglicizing their names to Al and Harry Jolson.

Their vaudeville act, Jolson, Palmer and Jolson, gave Al his first opportunity to "black up," or color his face with burnt cork, in the style of minstrel shows that had been one of America's most popular forms of mass entertainment for more than a half century. Minstrelsy was just beginning to die out, not so much because it had become worn out, or even because it was racist. The all-male minstrel shows just couldn't compete with burlesque and vaudeville, which featured pretty girls in abundance. Still, Jolson was able to continue performing in his signature blackface well into the 1930s.

Jolson spent ten years in vaudeville gradually developing his distinctive shtick. He was a highly animated performer who swayed his body with the music, clapping, snapping his fingers, jerking his thumb, and throwing out his arms to emphasize a point. He was a champion eye roller and sometimes would start batting his eyes and perform a few lines with a cartoonishly effeminate lilt. This led some to believe he was gay or at any rate bisexual, and apparently the latter was true, which did not help his relationships with his (eventually) four wives.

When he was in blackface, which was most of the time, Jolie adopted an accent that probably sounded very little like any actual southern black. It was Jolie's own personal accent. He also developed a distinctive way of talk-singing, which he used for interludes in nearly every song he did. He would let the line of music play, then would speak the line over the end of it. His voice could also rise to a plaintive shriek when he was feeling strongly about something he was singing.

It was an oddball mix of traits that somehow touched something deep in American audiences at the dawn of the twentieth century. He became one of the top draws in vaudeville during the years 1900 to 1910.

La Belle Paree

Trying to compete with Florenz Ziegfeld Jr.'s opulent *Follies* revues, the Shubert brothers assembled their own variety show, *La Belle Paree*, hiring Jolson for his Broadway debut on March 20, 1911.

La Belle Paree was an overstuffed Frankenstein of a show, stitched together from bits and pieces of vaudeville acts edited to conform to the vague Parisian theme. Jolson appeared in blackface as Erastus Sparkler, an expatriate southern African American who gratefully sings "Paris Is a Paradise for Coons," a number that would kill a career today but made Jolson's in 1911. Applause was sparse on opening night, and Jolson afterward went out and got drunk, thinking he'd be fired the next day. But most of the reviews lauded him as a firecracker. He was moved to a better spot on the bill and started putting his whole crazy heart into the performance. He attracted loyal fans from the first. Mesmerized by his sheer extroversion, they would come back to see him again and again. The Shuberts noticed, ensuring that Jolson would get to do the same for years to come.

La Belle Paree also marked the debut of the newly built Winter Garden Theatre, which would become Jolson's second home and lucky charm, the site of many successes in the two decades ahead.

In the years before World War I, the Shuberts or their associates starred Jolson in a series of musicals—*The Whirl of Society*, *Vera Violetta*, *The Honeymoon Express*, and *Dancing Around*—all forgotten today. None of them had much in the way of a story, a score, or even a cast. Jolson deliberately surrounded himself with second- and third-rate performers. If any of them somehow got a rise out of the audience, Jolson would fire them, as he did dancer George White, who later became the major domo of *The George White Scandals*. "There's only one star in a Jolson show," Jolie famously explained, "and that's Jolson."

Was that confidence or insecurity? While the very image of brash self-confidence on stage, Jolson had such anxiety about performing that he kept buckets in the wings so he could vomit when he came off. But the applause kept drawing him back to the spotlight.

Robinson Crusoe, Jr.

Most of these shows were performed in blackface, and Jolson eventually evolved an entire alter-ego character for this parallel self: Gus Jackson, a scheming, girl-chasing scamp. Gus reappeared in the 1916 Shubert musical *Robinson Crusoe, Jr.*, about a Long Island million-aire who falls asleep and dreams that he's stranded on a desert island. Gus is his faithful (or, actually, not so faithful) chauffeur, along as his man Friday. The show ostensibly had this plot, and ostensibly had a score by Sigmund Romberg. But Jolson very quickly took control of things and began interpolating barely relevant songs like "Where Did Robinson Crusoe Go with Friday on Saturday Night?" and completely irrelevant ones like "Yaka Hula Hickey Dula" and "Where the Black-eyed Susans Grow."

There were times when he'd be in the middle of a dopey scene and would break char-acter. He'd walk down to the footlights and ask if the audience wanted to hear more of the show, or if they just wanted to hear him sing. He knew exactly what the roared answer would be. The next minute the rest of the cast might as well have gone home, because *Robinson Crusoe, Jr.* would go out the window and the evening would turn into a Jolson solo concert.

Jolson sang these songs because the audiences loved them, but he also sang them be-cause they sold records and sheet music—which is where the real money was. He was one of the first recording stars, and even in the earliest days of the recording industry with the most primitive of formats, Jolson recordings sold hundreds of thousands of units—some-times millions. Like big rock 'n' roll acts of later years, he would appear in shows and tours to publicize his recordings as much as to connect personally with his fans. He would take a percentage both as performer and as coauthor, a credit many songwriters were grateful to give him, even when he hadn't actually written a note. A small percentage of a Jolson hit was far more lucrative than a hundred percent of almost any other kind.

Sinbad

Jolson's biggest Broadway success came in 1918 with the costume extravaganza *Sinbad*, in which he played the blackface mischief-maker Inbad. Historian Gerald Bordman called it "the quintessential Jolson show." The composer of record was Sigmund Romberg, but the show is remembered today for four songs by other composers interpolated into the score as specialty material for Jolson: "Mammy," "Swanee," "'N Everything" and "Rockabye Your Baby with a Dixie Melody." To bring Jolson closer to his fans, the Shuberts built a ramp down the center of the Winter Garden. For his big solos he would come down the ramp and sing right into people's eyes.

"Mammy" was the song in which he went down on one knee and opened his heart to the house. The show ran 404 performances and toured, etching itself into the memories of any who saw it.

In an essay titled "The Daemonic in the American Theatre," on Jolson and Fanny Brice, critic Gilbert Seldes wrote, "His generosity is extravagant; he flings into a comic song or three-minute impersonation so much energy, violence, so much of the totality of one human being, that you feel it would suffice for a hundred others. . . . His galvanic little figure, leaping and shouting—yet always essentially dancing and singing—upon it was the concentration of our national health and gaiety."

Personal Life

Jolson was married four times; three marriages ended in divorce, and the last one ended only with his death. Women were attracted at first by his stunning vitality and power and glamour. But when they got him home they realized they had married the all-time black hole of ego. One story will illustrate what that meant and will reveal all that was magnificent and frightening about his personality.

Jolson's third wife was dancer (and later *42nd Street* star) Ruby Keeler. There was considerable friction in their marriage over Jolson's obsessive need to be the center of attention. But he promised her he would attend the opening night of her new show, *Show Girl*, on July 2, 1929, and would sit back and applaud her like the rest of her fans.

Keeler had just launched into her big number when she suddenly noticed her husband standing. Not only was he standing, he was approaching the stage. Jolson jumped in front of her and took up her song, then completed it to thunderous if confused applause. Jolson had literally been unable to control his urge to seize the spotlight from his wife on her big night.

The 1920s

Jolson's blackface alter ego Gus Jackson reemerged after World War I in the 1921 extravaganza *Bombo*, in which he played the wayward servant of Christopher Columbus in his journey to the New World. As usual, this plot quickly walked the plank so Jolson could introduce some of his hits, "April Showers," "Toot Toot Tootsie, Goodbye" and, added for the subsequent tour, "California, Here I Come!"—all of which he would sing and record countless times for the rest of his life. The show opened at a theatre the Shuberts built specially for him, Jolson's 59th Street Theatre.

Though *Bombo* was a success, Jolson returned to his beloved Winter Garden for this next show, *Big Boy* (1925). In this incarnation, Gus was a stable boy at an English stable, and the title referred to a racehorse. Through a series of comic complications, Gus defeats a malevolent English jockey and winds up riding Big Boy to victory in the derby. Increasingly often, Jolson dropped the show and sang—among the new numbers were "Keep Smiling at Trouble" and (for the first time in New York) "California, Here I Come!" He didn't get to sing them long. Severe bronchitis caused Jolson to withdraw, closing the show after just two months.

Jolson was under a lot of stress. His second wife had succumbed to alcoholism, even in the midst of Prohibition, and members of the cast saw him strike her backstage when she came to his workplace drunk.

Whatever else might be said about Jolson—and over the years, people who knew him have said plenty—Jolie delivered the goods. Biographer Herbert G. Goldman unearthed an illustrative anecdote. In *Jolson: The Legend Comes to Life*, Ralph Reader, a British producer, remembered his first time seeing Jolson when he was a young man, just arrived in America, who wanted to sample the performer so many were buzzing about. For the final Saturday performance for *Bombo*, June 9, 1923, he arrived for the matinee only to find a sign stating that the performance was canceled because Jolson decided to take the entire company to watch his beloved ponies run at the track. Reader was able to get a ticket for the evening show but was still fuming at what he saw as a profoundly unprofessional act.

"I walked into that theatre absolutely hating the very name of Jolson," Reader huffed, and his mood was not helped by the fact that it took twenty minutes of set-up plot before the blackfaced man of the hour made his entrance. "Being the favorite he was, the whole house cracked with applause. He hadn't opened his mouth, but there was nobody in that theatre applauding . . . more than I was.

"I sat through that performance; I still regard it as the most moving night of my whole life. When the performance ended, I couldn't go home. All I could see was . . . a wonderful 'magic man,' who hadn't been singing and talking to anybody in the theatre but me. . . . I have never been so emotional about anything, anybody, in my life."

The Jazz Singer

And it was for this reason—Jolson's magical ability to connect with audiences—that the manufacturers of the Vitaphone system and their partners at Warner Bros. sought him out to star in the very first commercial talking feature film in history.

Jolson wasn't the first star to make a sound picture. Eddie Cantor and others had made experimental shorts with various sound formats earlier in the 1920s. But Vitaphone was the first format to be used widely in cinemas, and *The Jazz Singer* was the first talking film that most members of the public had ever seen or even heard of. The first voice they heard from a screen was Jolson's.

There is a fascinating and intimate scene in which Jolson is in his dressing room in the process of blacking up. He played Jack Robin, son of a deeply religious Jewish cantor. Jack is drawn into the world of secular show business by the lure of demon jazz. His father, who expected him to use his voice for the praise of God, is horrified.

The film actually is mostly silent. Jolson's voice is heard only in the musical sequences. The first words he speaks in the "first" talking picture are "Wait a minute, wait a minute, you ain't heard nothin' yet!," and he launches into "Toot Toot Tootsie," clapping his hands, snapping his fingers, wiggling his hips, shaking his head, and rolling his eyes. Then, in a completely surreal development, he sticks his fingers in his mouth and begins whistling like a songbird as the camera zooms in for a close-up. In this first sound film scene, Jolson does pretty much everything except set his hair on fire.

Jolson had used the line "You ain't heard nothin' yet!" previously on Broadway, but it became closely associated with *The Jazz Singer*. In the twenty-first century it was voted number seventy-one of the one hundred greatest movie quotes by the American Film Institute.

Later in the film Jolson sings Irving Berlin's "Blue Skies" to his "mamma" (he barely resists saying "mammy"), who fairly squirms with delight. He then delivers a monologue promising all the things he's going to do for her if his new show is a hit. He follows this speech with an uptempo verse of "Blue Skies" until his dour father bursts in and shouts, "Stop!"

Jolson and Warner Brothers quickly followed *The Jazz Singer* with *The Singing Fool*, a far superior film and a huge box office success. Jolson played a waiter who works his way up to becoming a professional songwriter and marrying the girl of his dreams, only to have it all fall apart when the girl loses interest and leaves him, taking his beloved son. It was chock full of De Sylva, Brown, and Henderson songs that became Jolson standards, including "I'm Sitting on Top of the World," "There's a Rainbow 'Round My Shoulder," "Sonny Boy," and "Keep Smiling at Trouble."

The best of his movies was *Hallelujah, I'm a Bum!* (1933), in which he played the "mayor" of a merry band of homeless people living in New York's Central Park who are mainly delighted with their status and actually consider work to be a crime. Jolson saves a young woman from suicide and finds she's suffering from amnesia. As he nurses her, they fall in love, though it's soon revealed that she is the mistress of the actual mayor of New York. Much of this underrated Rodgers and Hart musical was (like their 1932 George M. Cohan film *The Phantom President*) rendered in spoken and sung verse.

Jolson performed without blackface and in a much more naturalistic style than previously. Putting aside the film's absurdly chirpy view of homeless life, it showcases one of Jolson's most appealing performances, at least to the modern eye.

Many treasured obsessions of the 1920s went out of style in the 1930s. Among them was Jolson. This is not to say he didn't retain devoted followers in large numbers. But that amazing spark quickly dimmed. Eddie Cantor and Fanny Brice were able to reinvent themselves for the new era, often by finding a new way of relating to the more sober and political 1930s audiences on Broadway, or by transposing their shtick into radio or film. Jolson tried and failed. Ultimately, film diminished him, which is ironic, considering his place in movie history.

When Jolson returned to New York in 1931 to star in an Americanized version of a lukewarm German musical *The Wonder Bar*, he found the city uncongenial. The show closed after just seventy-six performances, though he did make a movie version, which became notorious for its finale, "Goin' to Heaven on a Mule," a Busby Berkeley production number with every racist black cliché from fried chicken to dancing watermelons. Jolson continued throughout the 1930s to make movies, though with gradually dimming success.

When Jolson announced in 1940 that he was returning to Broadway, fans were surprised to realize it had been nearly a decade since the onetime king of Broadway he had trod

Marilyn Miller in toe shoes in *Sunny* (1930). PHOTOFEST

MARILYN MILLER
Look for the Silver Lining

No performer ever had a more perfect signature song than Marilyn Miller. She is forever identified with Jerome Kern's "Look for the Silver Lining," a sweetly optimistic paean to hope, sung by one of Broadway's most universally cherished elfin blond sweethearts.

She specialized in the sweet but plucky Cinderella-like heroines that abounded in the early 1920s, when American women were widely coming out in the world by themselves for the first time. She always rose above any sort of adversity through the incorruptible purity of her soul, as expressed externally in her plain but not showy beauty.

Many years later, a successor blond goddess would rename herself Marilyn Monroe because someone said she reminded him of Marilyn Miller. Like her later namesake, the original Marilyn flew a little too high and perhaps believed her own legend a little too much. In the golden age of the *Ziegfeld Follies*, she was the ultimate ingenue. In 1925 she was the highest-paid performer on Broadway. But by 1936 she died more or less broke at age thirty-seven, unable to find a silver lining no matter how hard she looked. She became the sad prototype for many young stars who followed her: too much fame and too much fortune too young.

But it sure didn't start that way. She was born September 1, 1898, into a family similar to the one depicted in the musical *Gypsy*: a family act in the small time, forever touring the boondocks, dreaming of the big time. Miller was born Mary Ellen Reynolds (later changed to "Marilynn"; though she'd eventually drop the extra "n") in Evansville, Indiana, but her biological father objected to his children being in showbiz. He gave her Mama Rose–like mother an ultimatum: showbiz or their marriage. She sent him packing. After that, it was Mama, her brother, and her two older sisters. Marilynn was the baby and—at first—too young to perform.

Mama got remarried, but Marilynn's stepfather was no sweet-tempered Herbie. Caro Miller was an abusive taskmaster who would rehearse the children for hours, beating them with a stick when they failed to meet his exacting standards. But the Five Columbians, as they billed themselves (later the Columbian Trio as the older siblings fled), were never anything special and seemed doomed to the five-a-day circuits.

That all changed in 1903 when they performed at an amusement park in the Midwest. While the family was working, four-year-old Marilynn's nanny took her to see the latest wonder—a nickelodeon. These small protocinemas played short films for a five-cent admission. Baby Marilynn fastened on one that showed a ballerina pirouetting across a stage. She insisted on seeing the same one over and over and that evening entertained the family with her imitation of the pretty lady on the screen.

Her performing instinct had awakened, but her stepfather still vehemently opposed her joining the act. Marilynn stole onstage one night during curtain calls, and when the curtain rose, the audience saw the family joined by this tiny blond child in an improvised tutu. Responding to their applause, she rose onto her toes and spun in the spotlight. Did any child star ever have a more magical debut? The crowd went wild, and before long, there was a new Columbian. She was dubbed "Mademoiselle Sugarlump," which led to her life-long nickname (used only by her nearest and dearest): "Lumpy."

Because Mademoiselle Sugarlump was under the age of sixteen, her presence in the act violated child labor laws in many parts of the United States at the time. Caro Miller tried to pass her off as older in tours that crisscrossed the country, but after the act incurred ruinous fines, he decided to the take the Columbians to Europe.

From 1911 to 1913 the Columbians traveled wherever they could get work. While booked at London's Lotus Club, they changed their name to The Millers to sound less "vaudeville." Marilyn, now billed as "Baby Miller," would do her ballet passage, then move on to pint-sized impressions of current stars. Marilyn quickly became a favorite of the regulars—including the Prince of Wales (later King Edward VIII).

Word of this prodigy got back to the United States. Lee Shubert, one of the legendary theatre-owning and producing Shubert brothers, paid a visit to the club in January 1914 and promptly signed her for the Shuberts' annual *Passing Show* revues, designed to compete with Florenz Ziegfeld's *Follies*. Marilyn was still a few months shy of her sixteenth birthday at this point—a detail Caro Miller neglected to mention to Shubert but that had enormous subsequent significance. Caro was offered a job by the Shuberts as a deal sweetener.

Miller made her Broadway debut June 1, 1914, in *The Passing Show of 1914* at the Winter Garden Theatre. Like the *Follies*, it had comedians, spectacle, and a chorus line of pretty girls. This edition marked a change in the public's notion of female beauty. The Junoesque Lillian Russell figure was giving way to a slimmer look, possibly inspired by the kind of girls who tended to show up in the nickelodeon movies. *The Passing Show* chorus girls emphasized this new trim look. The adolescent-thin Miller fit right in and, as a featured performer, got to dance, sing (songs by operetta king Sigmund Romberg), and do parodies. A favorite from this edition was her impression of female impersonator Julian Eltinge.

Miller went on tour with the *Passing Show* and returned for the 1915 edition, which first placed her front and center as star. During this period she suffered an onstage injury to her nose that doctors promised would heal completely. They were wrong. Miller began to experience chronic sinus infections and migraine headaches that would afflict her the rest of her life.

After appearing in the Shuberts' *The Show of Wonders*, she returned to *The Passing Show* in 1917, boosting World War I audience morale and cementing her position as one of the chief gems in the Shubert crown. But she wasn't destined to stay there. Ziegfeld swooped down and carried her off for his *Follies*. The Shuberts waved their contract, but Ziegfeld had learned that Marilyn was underage when it was signed, and he declared it void. The Shuberts were so enraged at Caro Miller that they fired him and made it difficult for him to find work. Here was the beginning of Marilyn's emancipation.

Ziegfeld was the master showman of his era. He spared no expense on his annual *Follies* revues, variety shows inspired by the *Folies Bergère* of Paris but hugely expanded to lengths bounded only by his ego and fortune, both of which were considerable. Comedy sketches would be followed songs by the top talents of the day, then by sumptuous dance routines with dozens of young women either in the most extravagant of costumes or virtually nude. Ziegfeld was known for hiring bouquets of pretty girls, some who could sing, some who could dance, some who just knew how to wear a dress—glorified models.

And for a time around the end of World War I, Marilyn Miller became queen of this entire entertainment phenomenon. Her every glance, gambol, and warble were considered so delicious to gaze upon, so heavenly to hear, that her entrance was the climax of a show (*The Ziegfeld Follies of 1918*) that also starred Eddie Cantor, W. C. Fields, dancer Ann Pennington, Will Rogers, and the Fairbanks Twins on the same bill.

A lot of her buildup was Ziegfeld hype, of course. Only Barnum outdid him there. But a substantial part of her charm must have been real. When I first began writing about theatre in the 1970s, I would interview old-timers who would still sigh at the memory of her beauty. "That new girl is pretty enough, but she's no Marilyn Miller!"

Pictures don't do her justice. The tiny eyes, the cloud of blond hair, the moon-shaped face are very pleasant indeed, but they don't depict a traffic-stopper by twenty-first-century standards. She was neither the world's greatest dancer nor singer. But Miller's charm was more than the sum of her parts. Her movements were animated by a girl-woman joy, verve, and vividness. The greatest aphrodisiac is enthusiasm. Miller burst with enthusiasm whenever she stepped on the stage. Marjorie Farnsworth wrote that Miller was "the twinkle-toed, dainty darling of a gaudy, poignant era that defied rationalization, caricature and prohibition."

Her reign over the *Follies* lasted for two editions, 1918 and 1919. After that, Ziegfeld had even bigger plans for her.

But first she had some personal business to attend to. Marilyn had at last turned eighteen in 1916 and, though she still lived with her mother and taskmaster stepfather, she began to defy their wishes and keep company with a handsome young *Follies* actor named Frank Carter. They married in late spring 1919, just before rehearsals were to start for the way. To top things off and rub Ziegfeld's nose in his triumph, Dillingham booked the New Amsterdam Theatre and kept it occupied from September 1925 to December 1926.

The show put Miller in a ridiculous story about a circus bareback rider/dancer who finds herself stuck aboard an ocean liner and forced to marry one of the passengers to avoid being arrested as a stowaway. But the premise gave her ample opportunity for gorgeous costumes, wild acrobatics, nutty comedy songs, and big production numbers. The hit song, which became Miller's other signature song, was the coquettish "Who (Stole Your Heart Away)?"

Another monster hit (and one that she accomplished without Ziegfeld's hand), the show solidified her reputation. For the first time she was being called "the Queen of Broadway."

Offstage, however, her semi-open marriage with Pickford simply wasn't working. Pickford was an arrested-development party boy who would never make a satisfactory husband. He was suffering the results of drug addiction and also showing symptoms of advanced syphilis. She divorced him in 1927 on grounds of desertion and neglect.

Miller eventually kissed and made up with Ziegfeld, who promptly found her an all-star vehicle in the operetta *Rosalie*, which had music by George Gershwin and Sigmund Romberg, with lyrics by Ira Gershwin. It was a typical 1920s social fairytale, except this time Miller was the princess instead of Cinderella, trying to marry a dashing commoner over the objections of her royal parents. It ran ten months and, aside from introducing the Gershwins' "How Long Has This Been Going On" and "Oh Gee! Oh Joy!," it has been forgotten.

The same thing happened to an even higher-profile Ziegfeld-produced project, *Smiles*, about a French war orphan who is adopted by some American soldiers and brought back home, where she grows into a Salvation Army beauty and falls in love with one of her rescuers. Despite having sets by Urban, a score by Vincent ("Tea for Two") Youmans, and costars in the form of Fred and Adele Astaire, the show simply didn't hold together and closed after just seven weeks. If an alliance of Ziegfeld, Youmans, Urban, the Astaires, and Miller couldn't produce a hit, perhaps things were worse than anyone thought.

Miller was already looking west for salvation. She had arrived in Hollywood just in time for the 1929 stock market crash. But if she was hoping to sit out the Depression making hit after hit, she was to be disappointed. Hollywood, which had discovered sound just two years earlier, had seemed a boomtown for musicals. Within a year of her arrival Miller had filmed versions of her two biggest hits, *Sally* (1929) and *Sunny* (1930), though by the time they came out, the public was beginning to be gorged on musicals and both had their scores severely truncated. Neither was a success. Miller was one of the first Broadway stars to discover that stage personas don't always come across on the screen.

Nevertheless, the two films (plus the flop *Her Majesty, Love*, with master comedians W. C. Fields, Leon Errol, and Chester Conklin), leave twenty-first-century audiences with their only samples of Miller's performing skills. *Sunny* offers a wonderful tap interlude, which Miller performs in baggy pants in a single take, fluffy blond curls bouncing. Her hips were perhaps a little wider than in her willowy heyday, but you might never guess she was over thirty by the way she performs her complicated steps so crisply, making high kicks effortlessly, taking little-girl-like leaps, and ending with a big grin.

She's in formal attire and deploying a broad French accent in the *Sally* number "I'm Just a Wild Rose," which ends with about fifty chorus boys in formal wear chasing her around a vast, opulent set. Film archivists recently did a heroic job rescuing this sequence from oblivion after it had been unceremoniously lopped from the film—such was the disrespect Miller's megahit was getting just six years after she created it.

Miller's movie career was short-lived, perhaps because it started so late and her hard living was beginning to show. She made only those three films, all failures, and then Warner Brothers bought out her contract and she returned to New York. She visited Ziegfeld, who was putting together one more *Follies*, but he was nearly broke, and his grandiose plans sounded more like a folly than a *Follies*. Ziegfeld died July 22, 1932.

Miller kept getting offered work, including a featured spot in the Cole Porter musical *Gay Divorce*, but she kept holding out for another star vehicle, which never came along. She was unable to adapt gradually to her age and to the changing times, as Patti LuPone would do in later times, and unable to transform herself into something new, as Barbara Cook would. Without those guiding examples, she was trapped inside being Marilyn Miller the cute little thing. And this limitation eventually helped to kill her.

Miller had one last hurrah. Writer Moss Hart, who had watched her as a fan during her *Sunny* era, was working on a new kind of revue. He ran into her at a dinner party and was struck by her beauty and vivacity. Her name had come up when planning the show with composer Irving Berlin, but they had ruled her out as a "has-been." Yet now, seeing her in person, Hart saw there was still some magic left.

As Thousands Cheer is still considered among the most successful (and the longest-running) topical revues ever mounted. As staged by Hassard Short, it was presented in the form of a newspaper, with a political skit, a sports skit, even a sequence incarnating some of the famous comic strips of the era. There was plenty of comedy, but this show produced in the darkest days of the Depression also had a sharp political edge. Ethel Waters, for instance, got to report the weather in the dance number "Heat Wave" but also mourned the absence of her husband, who has been lynched, in "Supper Time."

For her part, Miller got to impersonate Joan Crawford, dress as Alice in Wonderland for the funnies section, take part in a wedding sequence that was part of the society page, and, most memorably, introduce (with costar Clifton Webb) Berlin's "Easter Bonnet" in the sequence that served as the rotogravure (color magazine) section.

Audiences who could afford tickets loved the show. While it wasn't a star vehicle, Miller was very happy to be back in the spotlight once again. She also fell in love with a dancer and assistant stage manager named Chet O'Brien. Then suddenly, everything went south at once. Miller's sinus infections flared up, she began to quarrel with Webb, and O'Brien got fired from the show after he allowed a wealthy friend to appear unexpectedly onstage in the middle of a skit.

Miller married O'Brien that fall, but it was to be her last happy time. She lived less than two years after the final performance of *As Thousands Cheer* and never appeared on Broadway again. Her health compromised by alcoholism, she found herself unemployed, unemployable, and less and less able to fight off her chronic, agonizing sinus infections.

Not long afterward she underwent surgery for the infections, but in the days before antibiotics, there was little the surgeons could do once complications set in. Miller died at age thirty-seven with little remaining of her fortune or her looks. It was a desperately sad ending for Mademoiselle Sugarlump, who had once seemed to be fashioned out of sunshine.

Marilyn Miller was supposed to be perfect, and nobody's perfect.

A superficial, highly sanitized version of Marilyn's life appeared in the form of the biopic *Look for the Silver Lining* (1949) with June Haver starring as Marilyn. Let's just say that it didn't do her justice. Judy Garland played her in *Till the Clouds Roll By*, but there was little of Miller's essence in her performance.

It's been said that George M. Cohan's statue is the only statue in Times Square, and that is technically true. But just a few steps east of Times Square on Forty-sixth Street, partly hidden by a sign for T.G.I. Friday's restaurant, are four small statues set in faded gilt niches at the second-floor level. These were placed on the side of what was then a theatrical shoe shop. They are the figures of the four "greatest actresses of the age" as determined by a 1920s poll of the readers of *Playbill*. The four are Ethel Barrymore as Ophelia, Mary Pickford as Little Lord Fauntleroy, opera singer Rosa Ponselle as Norma . . . and Marilyn Miller as Sunny.

Who knows how long they will remain?

Eddie Cantor in *Strike Me Pink* (1936). PHOTOFEST

EDDIE CANTOR
Banjo Eyes

Alot of the great stars of Broadway history were also great archetypes of one kind or another. Eddie Cantor was the wily little Bugs Bunny–like guy who somehow or other always managed to outwit those stronger and handsomer and richer than he. He also sometimes was the schlemiel who beat them by pure luck. He didn't have to go far for inspiration; that was pretty much his life story.

He had a classic shtick and a classic look. His narrow, hawklike face and jug ears were topped by a pair of wide eyes that he would pop and roll constantly. "Banjo Eyes" was a nickname that became the title of one of his musicals. Cantor was a favorite with balcony crowds, because they could always read his expressions from way in the back row.

His voice was a clarinet-like tenor, which he could pinch up into a squeak, remedied by a timely clearing of the throat. When happy, Cantor would start clapping his hands in a unique fingertips-upward way and prance around from foot to foot. He called this prancing his "stage walk," but it looked like a kind of dance. You always wanted something good to happen to Cantor, because then he'd do his crazy little dance. People of his era would sometimes do a little Eddie Cantor dance when they felt happy, like a choreographic catchphrase.

His colossal peepers looked even better when he was in blackface, which was most of the first half of his career. Like Jolson, Cantor counted blackface among his specialties, though he didn't do it exclusively.

Considering that Cantor's shtick was so minimal (or perhaps *because* it was), it's perhaps surprising to see how readily he adapted it from vaudeville to Broadway, from Broadway to radio and films, and from radio and films to the earliest days of TV. Cantor did it all.

★

Like Al Jolson and Ethel Waters, Cantor had a traumatic childhood. He lost both his parents before he was three. He was born Israel Iskowitz on January 31, 1892, on the Lower East Side of Manhattan to a pair of Russian-Jewish immigrants who were having a very hard time getting their feet on the ground in America. His mother died of lung disease. His violinist father, he was told, also died, though biographer Herbert Goldman believes evidence shows that his father may have simply abandoned the motherless boy.

In any case, Itchik, as he was known, was raised by his maternal grandmother, Esther Kantrowitz, who had also emigrated from Russia to help her penniless daughter and shiftless son-in-law, and wound up serving as surrogate mother to the scrawny, malnourished orphan. When she signed him up for school, the administrators assumed he was her child and logged him with her last name. She raised him to be proud of his Jewish faith, and when he later decided to shorten the name for marquee purposes, he deliberately avoided anglicizing it. "Cantor" was as far as he'd go.

One of the few bright spots in Cantor's Dickensian childhood was being sent to Surprise Lake Camp in New York's Putnam County through the offices of the Henry Street Settlement. It had been founded by the Educational Alliance to give Jewish kids from New York tenements a chance to breathe some fresh air, see trees and flowers, and get three square meals a day. It was one of the formative experiences for the boy, partly for how it affected his body (he was suffering from malnutrition when he first arrived), but also for his social life. He was the classic weakling who is protected by the tough boys because he entertains them.

As an adult, Cantor demonstrated an extraordinary social consciousness. He joined every union (often rising to board membership or even the presidency) and lent his name and fund-raising efforts to numerous worthy charities. His pet charity, however, remained the Surprise Lake Camp. As of 2009, the camp was still in existence.

Like Fanny Brice, Cantor got his first stage recognition and earned his first showbiz money at one of the innumerable amateur contests held off-nights at vaudeville theatres in New York. Today they survive in open-mike nights at comedy clubs and, on a much larger scale, in the *American Idol* TV show and its imitators. In the first decade of the twentieth century, nearly every local theatre gave neighborhood talent a chance with these performances. Cantor made his stage debut in 1908 at Miner's Bowery Theatre, telling jokes and doing impressions, and won the ten-dollar prize plus picked up two more dollars' worth of coins that were tossed on the stage by fans.

He entered small-time vaudeville that fall, appearing in Frank B. Carr's *Indian Maidens*. Over the next few years Cantor's career as a professional actor ebbed and flowed. At one point he worked as a singing waiter at Coney Island, with a young Jimmy Durante as his accompanist. Like Bert Lahr, Cantor also was one of the child performers discovered and showcased by legendary impresario Gus Edwards. He popped Cantor into the basket of wildflower talent he called *Kid Kabaret*, and off he went on another cross-country tour. Cantor was then a teenager, but he was so undersized that he fit right in.

Cantor had been in love with his childhood sweetheart Ida Thomas since they met in a schoolyard. Their crush later turned serious, and they wanted to wed. But Ida's father in no way wanted an impecunious small-time actor as a son-in-law. The only way Itchik could win Ida was to prove that he could be a success. Cantor labored six years before he finally won her hand. In later years he would credit her for helping to tame him and set him on the path to a professional career. Answering his father-in-law's challenge eventually took him to the pinnacle of show business.

Itchik Cantor would do almost anything for his Ida. When she told him she liked the name of one of her friends' beaus, he immediately adopted it at his own, and henceforth he became "Eddie." Like Tevye in *Fiddler on the Roof*, they had five daughters: Marilyn, Marjorie, Natalie, Edna, and Janet. The youngest gave birth to composer Brian Gari, keeping showbiz in the family.

Cantor also put his family in showbiz, and not in a way they always liked. Many of Cantor's comedy routines involved insult humor directed at his wife and daughters. He insisted it was just in fun, but it produced some tension in the Cantor household. Theatre historian Marjorie Farnsworth described their relationship as "one of the great, inspiring stage marriages of our time," though she allowed that they had their "squabbles." She said that whenever things got tense between them Ida would hand him one of the children and say, "Here Eddie, hold the little girl for a while."

To support his growing brood, the vaudevillian Cantor moved from Gus Edwards to two-man comedy teams and revues. Here Cantor developed his specialties for blackface and physical humor, for rolling his eyes, for singing mildly salacious songs that were often built on puns, for always being chased by girls despite his nebbishy look, for his little clap of delight, and for pulling a white handkerchief out of his pocket and waving it as he made his exit. He was a Jewish comedian at a time when ethnic comedians were kings, and he tapped into that rich heritage of humor.

He became part of that suite of comedians known for bold facial features. Jimmy "Schnozzola" Durante had the big nose. Joe E. Brown had the big mouth. Groucho Marx had the big black moustache. These devices were part of what enabled pretelevision audiences to remember and recognize a favorite performer from way back in the cheap seats.

Things began to pick up in 1914. Cantor was traveling as a double act with Al Lee. Songwriter (and future producer) Earl Carroll saw their act and decided he wanted Cantor to appear in Carroll's touring musical *Canary Cottage*, as a blackface chauffeur who does a specialty dance. He found himself up against stars Charles Ruggles and Trixie Friganza, who did not welcome the competition from this newcomer.

After getting his part cut down, "as is not unnatural" among stars, Cantor wrote, he lay low until opening night, then cut loose with ad-libbed clowning that stopped the show. The nominal stars were furious and threatened to quit, but the material was the best thing in the show, and producer Oliver Morosco stood by him.

As Cantor put it in his autobiography, "In the limited domain of *Canary Cottage*, I had made a rash but successful coup d'etat." Word of Cantor's success filtered up to the highest levels of pre–World War I showbiz. They next thing he knew, Cantor had a telegram from Florenz Ziegfeld Jr., producer of the *Ziegfeld Follies*, to come to New York.

Over the next decade and a half, Ziegfeld and Cantor would have a strange father-son relationship, with each struggling to gain respect and the upper hand from the other. Ziegfeld produced many of Cantor's best shows, but Cantor never hesitated to tear up a Ziegfeld contract and jump to his competitors Lee and J. J. Shubert. Soon, however, Cantor would be back. They went through several of these breakups and reconciliations.

Their first meeting set the tone. Cantor arrived at the theatre and introduced himself to the great man, who asked what he did. "Oh, I'm marvelous," Cantor replied. When Ziegfeld pressed the question, Cantor coolly replied, "I don't ask you what you do!"

Ziegfeld was amused enough to put Cantor in the 1916 edition of his *Midnight Frolic*, which had songs and skits like the *Follies*, but with a more adult and night-clubby feel. Cantor brought the house down by pretending to do a magic trick. He asked three of the era's biggest swells sitting stageside to take a card from a deck and hold it over their heads. He then proceeded to continue with his act, after which he thanked them and took back the cards.

Ziegfeld promoted him to the *Follies* proper in 1917, putting him at last on an equal footing with the era's showbiz titans, W. C. Fields, Fanny Brice, Will Rogers, and Bert Williams, all of whom appeared in the glittering 1917 edition—one of the greatest in a great series. Ten years after he won the Bowery amateur night, Cantor had risen as high as it was possible to rise, at last in the eyes of his in-laws, who would announce his growing salary to anyone who would listen.

One of the high points of the 1917 *Follies* was a sketch in which Cantor (in blackface) played the sissy son of master comedian Bert Williams (also in blackface, though he was already black himself).

Cantor's up-and-down relationship with Ziegfeld hit its most serious pothole in 1919 when Cantor led his fellow actors in walking out of the *Follies* in the first strike by Actors' Equity Association, of which he was a board member. The union had many serious gripes with management. In his memoirs he lists the long unpaid rehearsal periods and extra performances (beyond the customary eight weekly) as the main issues. He asserted that Ziegfeld was not guilty of the more extreme abuses, but because Ziegfeld stood with his fellow producers, Equity shut down his shows, as well.

The strike was settled in just a few weeks with a victory for the actors, and Cantor resumed playing in the *Follies of 1919*. But Ziegfeld refused to speak to Cantor for a long time, and he canceled a promised musical comedy with Marilyn Miller.

Cantor responded by going across the street to Ziegfeld's main competitors, the Shuberts, who featured Cantor in *The Midnight Rounders* and then *Make It Snappy*. Though he was making double or triple the salary he'd earned with Ziegfeld, he longed to return. "Mr. Ziegfeld was class," he wrote. "The Shuberts were just show business." All feelers to Ziegfeld were rebuffed.

Cantor's opportunity came when the *Make It Snappy* tour played Chicago across the street from the tour of *Sally*. A local critic wrote, "Eddie Cantor at $3.30 a seat is better entertainment value than Marilyn Miller and Leon Erroll at $4.40." Cantor reprinted the quote as a large-print ad in *Variety*, hoping to catch Ziegfeld's eye. Within days, Ziegfeld called and asked Cantor if had plans for the following season. The 1923 edition of the *Follies* once again starred Cantor.

Also in 1923, Cantor agreed to appear in an experimental feature by DeForest Phonofilms, one of the first sound movies ever made, four years before Jolson's *The Jazz Singer*. Titled *A Few Moments with Eddie Cantor*, it was never released commercially, but it offers a vivid portrait of Cantor at the peak of his early fame. Tipping his bowler, he enters an empty space and addresses the camera as if it were an audience member. He tells some jokes, recites a punning poem, and sings a naughty ditty with the lyric, "The dumber they come, the better I like 'em, 'cause dumb ones know how to make love." He then tells a funny story about "a gentleman of Hebraic faith" and ends with, "Oh, gee, Georgie!" topped with the handclap and prance.

Kid Boots

Ziegfeld was finally ready to give Cantor his wish, a musical comedy of his own. The resulting show, *Kid Boots*, formally subtitled "A Musical Comedy of Palm Beach and Golf," quickly made the showman glad he did. The show was a popular success, playing 489 performances on Broadway, the longest run of any Cantor show.

Kid boots were a stylish item of footwear, but writers William Anthony McGuire and Otto Harbach used the term as the nickname of the central character, Samuel "Kid" Boots, an insouciantly corrupt caddymaster who sells both crooked golf balls and bootleg booze. Both activities make him very popular—and get him into all kinds of trouble—at the Everglades Club in Palm Beach, Florida.

The score by Harry Tierney and Joseph McCarthy wasn't much to cheer about, though Cantor had fun with the interpolated hit "Dinah." Instead, the main fun in *Kid Boots* was its comedy set pieces. Cantor gives a nonsensical golf lesson early the show, and in one scene he undergoes a near-murderous massage in the club spa.

A silent 1926 film version of *Kid Boots* retained little but the title and Cantor, and instead tried to make Cantor into an action star, surviving a landslide, being dragged by a horse, driving an out-of-control car, and, at one point, literally hanging from a cliff.

Whoopee

Of the hundreds of nightclub, vaudeville, film, radio, recording, Broadway, and benefit appearances he made during the 1920s, a few stand out. In 1925 he had one of the top-selling records of the year with "If You Knew Susie (Like I Know Susie)," a number that had been passed on to him by Al Jolson. In 1927 he cowrote the book for the *Ziegfeld Follies of 1927* and costarred with Ruth Etting, Claire Luce, and Cliff Edwards ("Ukelele Ike"). The score included Irving Berlin's "Shaking the Blues Away" and "It All Belongs to Me." One of his routines made fun of the Hollywood practice of using stunt doubles for dangerous scenes. Cantor played a man pursued by a jealous husband. Just as he was about to be walloped, he called for a double, who came in and took the punch for him.

Perhaps Cantor's best-known musical comedy was 1928's *Whoopee*, produced by Ziegfeld after burying the hatchet with Cantor following yet another feud. Set in the cowboy era, this Wild West musical involved a young woman who rushes the nervous Cantor into an elopement, so she can escape the local sheriff, who wants to force her to marry him. It seems she really loves a third man, a half-breed Indian. Everyone heads off to the local Indian reservation, where things heat up and then are sorted out.

A sample of the humor: When the vengeful sheriff descends on the reservation and surrounds Cantor's hiding place, he admonishes his posse, "Don't let a white man get by you." In response, Cantor strolls out—in his old blackface.

To the 1920s audience the show's title was a wink and a nudge. "Whoopee" was a popular cheer, but it was also jazz slang for sex and may still be heard today in a joking way. *Whoopee* was actually able to squeeze past moralists with this flimsy ploy. Cantor sang the title song, "Makin' Whoopee," to a bevy of chorus girls, rolling his big eyes suggestively whenever he came to the word *whoopee*.

The show was a huge hit—and one of the last of the nutball 1920s musicals.

The Crash

Cantor was a great believer in the stock market and bought stocks with every penny he could lay hands on. He also evangelized Wall Street to all his showbiz friends, including Ziegfeld. When the markets collapsed in 1929, Cantor was wiped out. Just about every nickel he'd made from smart negotiations on *Whoopee* and *Kid Boots* and everything else for the previous fifteen years of hard work went out the window, along with so many stockbrokers.

But Cantor didn't go with them. He was down, but he wasn't out. He still had his talent and his popularity, and as the Great Depression gathered force, he was still able to make a living. And he figured that if he could make one fortune, he could make another.

His first instinct, as always, was to fight disaster with humor, and he quickly put together a book of gallows humor about the crash, "Caught Short: A Saga of Wailing Wall Street." He claims in his autobiography that it sold a half million copies and helped put a big dent in the $285,000 he owed his bank for loans to buy stocks that were now worthless.

Cantor relocated to California so he could pursue the movie and radio business, and he excelled at both. He had already appeared in a hit, *Kid Boots*, and returned in triumph when

Sam Goldwyn plucked the rights to *Whoopee* from the financially stricken Ziegfeld and turned it into a hit sound film in 1930. Cantor enjoyed hit after hit in his film career, including *Roman Scandals, Kid Millions*, and *Tickle Me Pink*, which carried on the various personas he'd developed onstage.

Along the way, the piano-string-thin Cantor began to fill out a little bit and not look quite so starved as he traditionally had. He enjoyed tremendous success on the radio in the golden age of that medium. Starting in 1931 he was featured on a series of variety shows, usually named for their sponsors, including *The Chase & Sanborn Hour, The Camel Caravan, Time to Smile, The Eddie Cantor Pabst Blue Ribbon Show*, and others.

He came into conflict in the mid-1930s with anti-Semitic (and anti- a lot of other things, too) Father Charles E. Coughlin, who got one of Cantor's shows pulled off the air, though Cantor popped right back up again elsewhere. It took a long time for Cantor to rebuild his fortune, but there was still Ida and the girls to provide for. Working on film, radio, stage, and concert productions simultaneously, he made the most of his fame and connections and was soon back in the money again.

Which led to one of Cantor's saddest duties. His old friend/enemy Ziegfeld had proven unable to adapt to the new financial environment and just kept spending on lavish, hopeless productions until he was deeply in debt. The crisis arrived in spring 1932 when Ziegfeld came to Cantor, hat metaphorically in hand, and asked for money to save his latest production, *Hot-Cha!*, which starred Bert Lahr. Cantor wrote out a check for $100,000, but the show flopped, and by midsummer Ziegfeld was dead.

Cantor was never very good with money, but he made plenty of it and was generous with it when he believed in the cause. Knowing the value of a dime, he organized a charity called the March of Dimes to help battle polio, a disease that killed, paralyzed, or otherwise disabled thousands in the years before the Salk vaccine was developed. Starting in 1938 he used his radio show to ask people to send dimes to help support the National Foundation for Infantile Paralysis, and fans responded with more than a quarter of a million dollars' worth of the coins. He made a personal trademark of ending every radio show with a plug for one of his charities.

During World War II, he also helped sell war bonds in a personal crusade to help crush Hitler's genocide against the Jews.

Always a union man from his Equity days, he also served as president of its sister union, the NVA, the National Variety Artists (the vaudevillians union), and then, after his move to California, as president of the Screen Actors Guild (SAG) from 1933 to 1935.

After a long and successful career out west, later including the films *Show Business* and *If You Knew Susie*, Cantor made one last return to Broadway.

Banjo Eyes opened on Christmas Day 1941, just weeks after the Japanese attack on Pearl Harbor. It was based on George Abbott's racing comedy *Three Men on a Horse*, about a horse (the "Banjo Eyes" of the title, and *not* Cantor) who appears in Cantor's dreams and tells him who will win horse races–but only if he doesn't bet on them. Things naturally get complicated.

The weak score by Vernon Duke and John La Touche produced no hits for Cantor–though audiences cheered the hastily assembled finale, "We've Done It Before and We'll Do It Again" ("It" being understood by everyone to mean "beat the Germans"). After a disappointing five-month run, Cantor returned to Hollywood and never sang on Broadway again.

In 1950 he moved into his newest medium, television. His *Colgate Comedy Hour* was a variety show that reunited him with many of his old showbiz comrades like Jimmy Durante and Ed Wynn, and lots of new ones like Sammy Davis Jr. and Milton Berle. Cantor made a special point to champion a young comic and dancer named Joel Grey, future star of *Cabaret, George M!*, and *Wicked*, in whom Canter saw something of himself.

Partly in response to the great success of *The Jolson Story* and *Jolson Sings Again*, Hollywood followed with *The Eddie Cantor Story*, with Keefe Brasselle. It wasn't as successful as the Jolson films, but it made money. Cantor himself was less sanguine. He's quoted saying as he emerged from the premiere, "If that was my life, I didn't live."

Cantor suffered a severe heart attack in 1952, which forced him to give up the TV show, though he returned with a more modest half-hour format that ran in 1954-55 before he retired. He lived quietly in California–emerging in 1956 to accept a special Academy Award for "distinguished service to the film industry"–until a second heart attack claimed his life in 1962.

Fred and Adele Astaire in their final show together, *The Band Wagon* (1931).

FRED AND ADELE ASTAIRE
You Irreplaceable You

More than any of the other great 1920s Broadway musical comedy stars, Fred Astaire was able to translate his virtuosic stage grace to the screen. And that's possibly why he's not only still remembered, but his name serves as a catchphrase for "great dancer" decades after his death.

The fact that Astaire often played a Broadway star or Broadway hoofer in his films was an allusion to an earlier career that is nearly forgotten today. Before going to Hollywood, Astaire spent nearly a quarter century working his way from the small time to the big time of vaudeville and then into a series of frothy Roaring Twenties revues and musicals by the likes of Irving Berlin and the Gershwins.

And throughout that first career his constant companion and costar was his older sister, Adele. For much of the first two decades of their collaboration it was Adele who was considered the bigger star, the prima ballerina of their brother–sister pas de deux. The two modeled themselves on husband–wife dance team Vernon and Irene Castle, and the Astaires (everyone knew them just as "Fred and Adele") introduced new steps, new sounds, and new musical styles at what was then the pinnacle of American pop culture.

The world thinks of Fred and Ginger (Astaire and Rogers, of course) as the ultimate dancing pair. If you created a museum of Hollywood icons, Fred and Ginger would have a statue in the front hall. But Ginger was only a replacement. For Broadway in the 1920s, it was Fred and Adele.

They were born twenty months apart, Adele Austerlitz on September 10, 1897; Frederick Austerlitz on May 10, 1899 in Omaha, Nebraska. Their father, also named Frederic (without the "k") Austerlitz, was a brewer who emigrated from Vienna, Austria, where he had been a music aficionado. Their mother was Ann, née Gelius, a local schoolteacher whose family had come from Alsace-Lorraine. She enrolled Adele in a local dancing school and brought toddler Fred along because there was no one to leave him with.

From the start, the star of the family was Adele. Her facility with dance impressed all her teachers, who encouraged Ann's aspirations to head to New York and get her prodigy some serious training. Upon arrival, Ann enrolled Adele in dancing school and enrolled Fred, as well, partly, again, to keep Fred busy. It succeeded. Fred danced amazingly well for a five-year-old. Dancing as a pair, the two Austerlitz children won the schoolwide competition their first year at the school. They danced, they sang, they played instruments. They were a two-man band. The headmistress advised Ann that her children would likely have success in vaudeville, then the dominant form of American mass entertainment.

The siblings now began one of the greatest training programs for entertainers ever devised. They grew up on the vaudeville stage, sharpening their skills night after night in front of live audiences with no chance for a reshoot or a second take. Fred and Adele Astaire were a combination kid act, family act, and dance act, which made them easy to book. They performed a series of increasingly sophisticated "bits" from 1905 to 1917. Their mother traveled with them and "homeschooled" them, though "home" was a series of theatrical hotels and dressing rooms.

By all accounts they got along well throughout their long years together. Fred was all work until he discovered horses and golf in the early 1920s. Adele was a social butterfly who whose looks and charm attracted a long series of boyfriends. She sometimes exasperatedly called Fred "Moaning Minnie" because he was always after her to rehearse. He called her by the affectionate family nickname "Delly."

Whatever positive reviews they got, the lion's share of the praise always went to Adele.

"One of the best brother-and-sister acts seen here in a long time," said an unnamed Washington, D.C., critic in 1915. "The girl is superior to the boy."

In 1916 the *Detroit Free Press* critic wrote, "Anyone who can watch Adele for more than ten seconds and not like her had better get terms from the nearest undertaker."

The Astaires had a unique chemistry. *New York Times* critic Brooks Atkinson would later write, "With them, dancing is comedy of manners, very much in the current mode. Free of show-shop trickery, they plunge with spirit into the midst of the frolic. . . . [T]hey give dancing all the mocking grace of improvisation with droll dance inflections and with comic changes of pace. Adele Astaire is also an impish comedian; she can give sad lines a gleam of infectious good-nature. Slender, agile and quick-witted, the Astaires are ideal for the American song-and-dance stage."

Broadway and the West End

The Astaires finally broke through to Broadway on November 28, 1917, with the Shuberts' revue *Over the Top*. Adele was twenty and Fred eighteen. It ran less than three months, but the Shuberts liked their work enough to put them almost immediately into another revue, *The Passing Show of 1918*, which gave them the chance to resurrect a tango that had been added to their vaudeville act. In one of the first Broadway reviews that mentioned Fred by name, Alan Dale of the *New York Journal* wrote, "Fred Astaire, with Adele of the same name, danced all evening in knots, and it made one swelter to look at them. Fred is an agile youth, and apparently boneless, like that nice brand of sardines." The show subsequently toured.

Next, under the management of Charles Dillingham, Fred and Adele appeared in the operettas *Apple Blossoms* in 1919 (with George Gershwin as rehearsal pianist) and *The Love Letter* in 1921. The latter gave them a chance to introduce a piece of material that became their signature dance: the Runaround, also known as the Oompah Trot. It formed the finale of a number called "Upside Down," and is hard to describe because it was so silly. As the orchestra played an oompah beat, Adele would trot in a circle with her arms up, miming that she was riding a bicycle. Fred would follow along and the number would go faster and faster, clowning all the way, until they disappeared into the wings. The virtuoso piece was so popular it would draw numerous encores, which was a challenge because they had to start back at low energy again and build to a frenzy.

They appeared in two quick flops, *For Goodness' Sake* and *The Bunch and Judy*. They thought they'd blown their chance at stardom, but their luck changed when they embarked on a London run of *For Goodness' Sake*, retitled *Stop Flirting*. They packed up their surefire Runaround number and boarded the *Aquitania* for Europe. *Stop Flirting* opened in February 1922 and, contrary to the tepid response in New York, proved to be a smash. Sydney Carroll in the *Sunday Times* wrote, "They typify the primal spirit of animal delight that could not restrain itself . . . They are as lithe as blades of grass, as light as gossamer, and as odd as golliwogs."

Audiences loved the Runaround so much they would chant along with the oompahs in one encore after another. The *Pall Mall Gazette* observed, "Their final should-to-shoulder gallop . . . not only brings the house down, but is one of the funniest things I remember. It makes you laugh, without extravaganza or burlesque, but a wit of its own—a triumph of mind over matter."

Edward, Prince of Wales, gave his imprimatur to the young American hoofers by attending the show repeatedly, and soon the Astaires' social card was full. The fact that they were embraced by British high society, even by royalty (encouraged by their early fan Noël Coward, who had seen them in New York), added to their cachet and made them even more fashionable in anglophile New York.

Despite their Omaha birth and upbringing in fleabag hotels, the Astaires quickly cultivated aristocratic tastes. Fred was always the quieter, more intense and studious of the two. He developed a superb judgment for fine things, especially English-tailored clothes, and was always elegantly turned out. It was the beginning of the bon vivant image he'd later display to perfection in his films.

His slim form seemed made for top hat and tails, and this became his image, especially after *Funny Face*. But it is a matter of record that Astaire didn't much like the outfit for dancing. "They were difficult to wear," he later said. "If you're working in a picture under all those hot lights, you simply wilt in a heavy, stiff shirt. It shows up badly, and you have to stop, dry off, change, come back and get all sweated again."

Adele was more the flapper, but never in a vulgar way. She tended to hobnob with high society and thus avoided some of the pitfalls that snared show-business girls of the era, especially some of the *Follies* girls who rose rapidly on their good looks—and fell rapidly from the same cause. She sniffed in print that British manners were superior to those of Americans and went out of her way to praise all things English.

Lady, Be Good! and *Funny Face*

The Astaires returned to New York in 1924 in triumph, with the public eagerly awaiting their next show. The Gershwin brothers were engaged to supply virtually a full score for the project, titled *Lady, Be Good!* Astaire and the Gershwins inspired one another, and they worked together often. Astaire provided them with some of their earliest song hits, and one of the last things Gershwin wrote before he died in 1937 was the score to an Astaire film, *Damsels in Distress*.

With a book by Guy Bolton and Fred Thompson, *Lady, Be Good!* tells the story of down-and-out brother and sister Dick and Susie Trevor, who help each other unravel the hidden identities of the two people with whom they are in love. Along the way the Astaires got to introduce two songs that became standards, "Oh, Lady Be Good!" and the syncopated "Fascinating Rhythm." The show ran 330 performances in New York, then transferred to London, where their cult awaited them. Once again they were the toast of two continents.

Fred and Adele's mid-1920s successes also show that the Astaires were developing as actors and singers as well as dancers. Adele had always had a gift for comedy. Her piping singing voice had been considered too light for the operetta-like songs popular a decade earlier. But it was just right for the jumpy, lyric-intensive tunes being written by the Gershwins.

Fred's bearing had always been slightly withdrawn and serious. That worked well when roles called upon him to be suave and elegant, the 1920s answer to "cool." He began to translate that quality into high comedy and even showed he could be easygoing and down-to-earth. When he was playing a society man, he was never a snob. When he was playing a beggar, he always had dignity.

Master choreographer George Balanchine would later call Fred "the greatest dancer who ever lived." Lesser authorities often shared the sentiment. But now Astaire was starting to get encomiums for singing and even for his acting, whereas such praise formerly had gone exclusively to Adele. Songwriter Irving Berlin later proclaimed, "I'd rather have Fred Astaire introduce one of my songs than any singer I know—not because he has a great voice, but because his delivery and diction are so good that he can put over a song like nobody else."

Fred and Adele returned to New York in 1927 for their next Gershwin musical, *Funny Face*, which topped even *Lady, Be Good!* Adele played a flapper whose guardian (Fred) has locked up both her diary and her valuable pearl necklace to keep them safe. Adele and her boyfriend scheme to break in and steal the items, only to find themselves competing with a pair of real burglars.

Never mind the plot—the key things in *Funny Face* were the Astaires' dances (again culminating in the Runaround) and of course the glittering Gershwin score full of gems like "'S Wonderful," "My One and Only," "High Hat," "He Loves and She Loves," "Tell the Doc," and the satirical "The Babbit and the Bromide," in which Fred and Adele sang entirely in clichés. "High Hat" was notable because it was the first time Fred performed in top hat, white tie, and tails backed by a male chorus that wore the same. The number, and many others like it in various films, would prove to be one of the lasting images of Fred's career.

Ray Harper of *The Dance Magazine* tracked down the sibs in their dressing room before a performance of *Funny Face* in 1927. He found them barely able to sit still and concentrate long enough to answer his questions. Fred had come to the theatre an hour and a half early to practice his steps and see if he could come up with something fresh.

Adele startled Harper by proclaiming, "I positively hate dancing." She elaborated, "To watch my brother and myself go through our dances, one would think that we both enjoyed dancing better than anything in the world. Well, that's all wrong—that is, inasmuch as I'm concerned. As for Fred,—well, he's the dancer of the family. His perfection hides a multitude of sins in my own dancing."

She was being humble, but even at that point she was beginning mentally to detach herself from showbiz life.

They took *Funny Face* to London, where once again, they triumphed. It was the height of the Roaring Twenties, and the Astaires had become icons of the era in both Europe and America. It was a sweet time for them and for their long-suffering mother, who got to see all her dreams for her children come true.

But the team was running into a problem unique to their situation. The plots of their shows always had to be convoluted and improbable because the public knew well that the two stars were siblings and thus could never play lovers. There were only a limited number of stories that could be built around that fact.

The Later Years of Fred and Adele

Florenz Ziegfeld stepped in to produce their next musical, *Smiles*, with a score by Vincent Youmans of *No, No, Nanette*, and, as costar, one of the most luminous stage personalities of the 1920s, Marilyn Miller.

In this show Astaire introduced another one of his best-known dance novelties, which he said came to him in a dream. Dressed in top hat, white tie, and tails, he sang "Say, Young Man of Manhattan," accompanied by a mass of chorus boys dressed exactly the same. At the climax of the number, Astaire wielded his cane like a rifle and "killed" the entire chorus by "shooting" them one by one. It was bizarre, but audiences found it fascinating.

Astaire later used the concept in one of his most popular films, *Top Hat*, partly because so few people got to see it on Broadway. Ziegfeld's *Smiles* proved to be a folly of a different kind, running just 63 performances. The failure of *Smiles* made January 1931 seem that much colder to the Astaires, who had been able to float along above on champagne bubbles of their celebrity without being affected by the economic collapse that brought on the Depression.

The Band Wagon

The Astaires were riding high again, but one member of the team was starting to get restless. Adele had turned thirty in September 1927. Just a few months later she was involved in a boating accident that burned her face, neck, and shoulders. She made a full recovery, but in a world that valued looks so highly, it was too close a call.

"I'm tired [of] having to go to parties," she told a reporter. "Just think of being able to go to Europe when I want to instead of traveling only to fulfill a contract."

The final performance of *Funny Face* in London in 1929 had been a sold-out high-society event. One of the guests, Prince Aly Khan, introduced the Astaires to a friend of his, Lord Charles Arthur Cavendish, scion of an ancient noble family. The second son of the Ninth Duke of Devonshire, Lord Cavendish fell in love with Adele and managed over the ensuing year to pull to the head of the pack of her scissor-tailed would-be beaux. He stood by her in November 1930 when *Smiles* flopped. Being thirty-three in the midst of the worsening Great Depression and watching your big musical project go belly-up may have influenced her. Perhaps she was intrigued by the prospect of marrying a title, though it was scarcely the first she'd been offered. Perhaps Cavendish was just a sweet guy. In any case, one night at the 21 Club in New York, Adele proposed to Cavendish, and he held her to it.

The only catch was that becoming Lady Cavendish meant that her career as an entertainer would have to come to an end. She assented, with just one reservation: she wanted to go out with a hit. And she did. The Astaires were delighted when producer Max Gordon called to say that Arthur Schwartz and Howard Dietz were writing a new musical called *The Band Wagon*, to which George S. Kaufman was writing the sketches. (The Broadway version is very different from the later movie, which retained only a few of its songs.)

When *The Band Wagon* opened in June 1931 it was hailed as the finest revue of its kind ever mounted, a good mixture of witty skits like "The Pride of the Claghornes," pretty or funny songs like the Astaires' "Sweet Music (to Worry the Wolf Away)," and that ode to beer and buxom fräuleins "I Love Louisa," plus ample opportunities for Fred and Adele to trot their stuff, like "The Beggar Waltz." In the latter, Fred played a homeless man who is given some coins by a beautiful rich lady (Adele), then falls asleep and dreams that the two of them are doing an elegant pas de deux. It was storytelling in dance, and it became a template for the kind of dance Fred later explored in his movies.

The show also introduced the Dietz and Schwartz standard "Dancing in the Dark," originally sung by John Barker for dancer Tilly Losch. In later years, Astaire made this number his own.

Adele played her final performance onstage at the Illinois Theatre in Chicago on March 5, 1932, and hung up her dancing shoes forever. Her wedding to the patient Lord Cavendish came just two months later, and Adele withdrew with her nobleman to sit out the Great Depression in his ninety-three-room Lismore Castle in County Waterford in Ireland on thirty thousand acres of the auld sod.

Fred himself married in July 1933, to Phyllis Livingston Potter. They had two children, Fred Junior and Ava, and remained married until her death in 1954. Potter had a son, Eliphalet ("Peter"), from a previous marriage.

With Adele retired, Fred was now at a crossroads. He clearly had no intention of giving up performing. On the contrary, it was his life. He plunged right back into work, appearing in December of that same year in Cole Porter's musical *Gay Divorce* (later filmed under the slightly altered title *The Gay Divorcée*). Finally freed from the need for a plot that explained the presence of his sister, Astaire played an American writer in France who gets involved in a scheme to help a woman (Claire Luce) obtain a divorce from her fuddy-duddy husband, only to find he's in love with the woman himself. The score included the delightful "After You, Who?" and the sublime standard "Night and Day."

Though *Gay Divorce* opened in one of the darkest stretches of the Great Depression, it managed a six-month run on Broadway and a further five months in London, concluding in early 1934. At age thirty-four, after a quarter century as a professional dancer, Fred saw his Broadway career come to a close—or, at any rate, his Broadway career on Broadway itself.

Hollywood

In a break between the two productions, Fred had made his film debut in *Dancing Lady*, playing a well-known Broadway dancer named Fred Astaire. He was already a brand name, though at least one studio executive was less than impressed. RKO Studio boss David O. Selznick gave Astaire a screen test in 1933 that became infamous when another, unnamed executive summed up his reaction with an immortal dismissal. In a 1980 interview on ABC-TV's *20/20*," Astaire said the comment was, "Can't act. Slightly bald. Also dances."

Among those whose opinion of Astaire was somewhat higher was producer Pandro S. Berman. He created a film unit within RKO to tailor movies specifically to Astaire's strengths. Over the next three years, Astaire, Berman, director Mark Sandrich, and choreographer (and Astaire alter ego) Hermes Pan created not just a series of film musicals, but a series of icons that permanently etched in the public's mind for generations what film dancing and, indeed, Broadway dancing, were supposed to look like. In *Top Hat, Swingtime, Shall We Dance*, and other films, he epitomized the dapper elegance of 1930s dancing and made it seem effortless, though it took countless hours of rehearsal.

However, Astaire's most visible collaborator in the series was the female dancer chosen to replace Adele—Ginger Rogers. She brought out a sexy side that Astaire could never fully explore when his partner was his sister. Katharine Hepburn reportedly said, "He gives her class and she gives him [sex appeal]."

Over the years he danced with many others, including Eleanor Powell, Jane Powell, Cyd Charisse, Lucille Bremer, Betty Hutton, Vera-Ellen, Leslie Caron, Debbie Reynolds, Paulette Goddard, Gracie Allen, and Judy Garland. Some may have been technically better dancers than Rogers, but none had the same chemistry with him.

Movies also gave Astaire the chance to keep doing something new—once he had perfected a dance and frozen it forever on film, he could move on to something else relatively quickly. He restlessly sought novelty and new places where dance could be inserted into everyday life. He danced on the roof of a skyscraper in *The Belle of New York*, in street traffic in *Damsels in Distress*, and seemingly on the walls and ceiling of a room in *Royal Wedding*. In the film *Blue Skies* he used camera magic to levitate his cane and tap with a mob of Astaire clones in perhaps his most iconic number, "Puttin' on the Ritz," which was parodied so successfully in Mel Brooks's film and stage musical *Young Frankenstein*. The monster's strangled cry of the title and fumbling steps were the comic antithesis of Astaire's cool precision, virtuosic grace, and crisp persona.

Film proved to be the perfect medium for Astaire, though in many of his thirty-plus movies he played some variation on what he had once been: a Broadway song and dance man. Astaire's reputation earned him references in the lyrics of songs by such writers as Cole Porter ("You're the Top") and Lorenz Hart ("On Your Toes").

Fred Astaire's star on the Hollywood Walk of Fame was laid in front of 6756 Hollywood Boulevard. But there was no star for Adele. While Fred was ascending into the Hollywood pantheon, things were not going well at Lismore Castle. Adele gave birth to a daughter in 1933 and then a set of twins in 1935. All three infants died shortly after birth. Lord Cavendish developed a liver ailment and became an invalid before dying in 1944. There was hopeful talk of Adele returning to show business and joining her brother in the movies, but it turned out to be nothing more than talk. The closest Adele came to showbiz was volunteering as a hostess at the Rainbow Corner, a morale-boosting canteen for off-duty servicemen in London, similar to the Stage Door Canteen in Times Square. Adele did everything from chatting with the soldiers, to writing letters for them, to guessing their weight. She even danced with a few.

One of the men she met at the Rainbow Corner was American Kingman Douglass, whom she married in 1947. An investment banker from Arizona, he went into government for several years, rising to become assistant director of the Central Intelligence Agency before retiring to Scottsboro. The Cavendishes generously allowed Adele to continue using the castle as she wished, and she visited every year from Scottsboro to reenter the social whirl she liked so much.

Later Career

By the mid-1950s, the public's taste began to change and the gaps between Astaire pictures got longer and longer. He made one last musical movie in 1968, agreeing to play the title role in Francis Ford Coppola's adaption of the Broadway musical *Finian's Rainbow*, which had not previously been touched by Hollywood, owing to its political content. By the late 1960s, the time seemed right for this wacky fairy tale about an Irishman who has stolen the leprechauns' crock o' gold. He flees to America and takes refuge in the hills of "Missitucky" where his daughter uses one of the crock's wishes to turn a racist senator black.

It was the first time Astaire had danced on film since *The Pleasure of His Company* in 1961 and the first time he'd been in a full-scale musical since *Silk Stockings* in 1957. His eyes were a little crinklier, but the technique was still all there. Astaire made a classy and, as ever, graceful refugee, especially on the number "When the Idle Poor Become the Idle Rich," but he told the press that this was the last film in which he would dance. And he kept his word, except for a few nostalgic steps with Gene Kelly in the introduction to *That's Entertainment* (1974). He appeared in a few more nonmusical films, notably *Towering Inferno* (1974) and *Ghost Story* (1981, his last film). On TV, he lent his voice and image to the holiday perennial *Santa Claus Is Coming to Town*. A chain of dancing schools that bears his name was still operating in 2008.

Fred died on June 22, 1987, of pneumonia, and the newspapers and airwaves were filled with salutes and memorials. With him at his death was his second wife, retired jockey Robyn Smith, forty-five years his junior, whom he had married in 1980. In 1999 the American Film Institute named Fred number five on the list of all-time greatest male movie stars, behind only Humphrey Bogart, Cary Grant, James Stewart, and Marlon Brando. By contrast, Adele's death on January 25, 1981, after a stroke, was barely noticed. What obits she got treated her as little more than another celebrity sibling. Fred had earned his immortality, but Adele didn't deserve her oblivion.

For more than a decade, Fred and Adele Astaire—as a team—represented the highest tradition of dance on Broadway. That's the way they should be remembered.

Bobby Clark with several of his signature props, in *Jollyanna* (1952).

BOBBY CLARK
Bugle Boy

Here's what you need to know about Bobby Clark: short, bandy-legged, a too-tight coat, a too-short cane, a nutty hat, a wiggling cigar, and a wide pair of "glasses" drawn on his impish face with burnt cork or an eyebrow pencil. Often seen playing a bugle.

With partner Paul McCullough, he got into every sort of mischief and escaped through slapstick of a seemingly quantum precision. He started his career as a silent acrobat and wound up a star of musical comedy, introducing songs by Cole Porter, Vernon Duke, and the Gershwins.

Everything else is footnotes.

★

Robert Edwin Clark was born June 16, 1888, in Springfield, Ohio. He learned to play the bugle so he could signal folks on his paper route when he delivered their papers. When Clark was six years old his father, a Pullman car conductor, was killed in a gruesome accident involving the coupling pin then used to hold railroad cars together. It's tempting to draw a straight line between this tragedy and Clark's later immaculate care about timing, measurement, and safety.

In any case, young Bobby's replacement father figure was his grandfather, a devout Mason, who wore the robes and insignia of the mysterious group every chance he got. Bobby found this very entertaining.

When he was twelve, Clark was transferred to a new school, where he met Paul McCullough, a boy four years older than himself. They became friends through their shared love of doing complicated acrobatic stunts in McCullough's back yard. This was 1900, and they would romp together nonstop for the next thirty-six years.

They started performing at ages fourteen and seventeen, respectively, at the local YMCA and fraternal lodges. While still in their teens they began working professionally in one of the dominant and most popular mass entertainment forms of the period, the minstrel show. As part of Culhane, Chace & Weston's Minstrels, the boys would "black up" with burnt cork to do their dancing and acrobatics after corny joke sessions between Mr. Interlocutor and Mr. Bones. When the manager of the show failed in the little matter of paying them, Clark & McCullough fulfilled a kid's dream to run off and join the circus. They joined several in succession, including the Hagenbeck-Wallace Circus, the Sells-Floto Circus, and, finally, in 1906, when Clark was just turning eighteen, the Ringling Brothers Circus, which was then king of the West and Midwest.

They were hired as clowns and buglers and over the next five years developed their signature look. McCullough always wore a shaggy raccoon coat or a dog-skin coat, a derby hat, and a toothbrush moustache.

A legend holds that Clark began wearing horn-rimmed glasses but couldn't find them one night and so he just drew them on. More likely, it was simply easier to do his acrobatics without having to worry about real eyeglasses falling off or getting broken. The short cane, similarly, was a practical consideration; a cane was a versatile prop, but a full-length one was just too unwieldy. He used the cane as a weapon, as a golf club, as a drum major's baton. He once even brought on a cane covered in fur and informed the audience that it had just won first prize in a dog show.

Clark and McCullough made their New York debut with Ringling Brothers at Madison Square Garden. By 1912, he and McCullough developed a vaudeville act that seemed the essence of simplicity: two boobs trying to lift a chair onto a table. From this premise they spun fifteen minutes of physical comedy, punctuated now and again by a joke. Though they continued in their first love, circus tumbling, during the summer months they spent their winters touring the B. F. Keith vaudeville circuit. They soon found they could make good money without constantly worrying about getting injured. Though the elder McCullough got the lion's share of laughs from their silent comedy, once they began speaking—and even singing—the spotlight began to shift to Clark. His reedy voice was funny all on its own, and Clark would break the fourth wall to tell the audience, "I can sing even higher, but my eyes would pop out."

A Comedy of Millimeters

Still, physical comedy always remained the duo's strongest suit. They toured in both vaudeville and burlesque, gradually expanding their repertoire of comedy "bits."

Their signature bit involved Clark's cigar. Clark would make his entrance puffing his cigar like a steam locomotive. The cigar would then pop out of his mouth (the end had been treated with Vaseline so it would slide out easily), and Clark would catch it and toss it back into his mouth. He'd do this a few times until it fell to the stage. McCullough would go to retrieve it for him, but Clark, in a sudden spasm of anger, would whack his knuckles with his cane. The pouting McCullough would retreat, leaving Clark alone with the fallen cigar. Clark would then kick the still-lit cigar into the air and catch it. There followed a veritable juggling act, with the cigar bouncing through the air from hand to foot to mouth.

Clark was a very precise man, very scientific about his comedy. He traveled with a tape measure and carefully gauged the precise dimensions of his props and the proper placement and arrangement of the pieces on his set. His was a comedy of millimeters, and his experience as a juggler and acrobat made him fastidious about the fine points.

In one scene he needed to roll a gold coin across a stage. When the producer suggested he use a lesser-value coin for the scene, Clark explained that a gold coin made a certain sound and rolled a certain way that was required for exactly the effect he wanted.

He had strong opinions about his ubiquitous cane. When he used it as a weapon, he always brandished the curved handle, because he believed that threatening people with the pointed end wasn't funny.

Elliott Norton of the *Boston Globe* was fascinated with Clark and described how Clark would time jokes to the burning of the cigar until the ash was long enough to flick: "In rehearsal he determines just how many jokes he must tell, how many paces he must walk or sprint before that ash will have grown long enough to be amusing."

Clark was also a student of the comic potential of dust. "Whacking a dowager with a board is funny, he thinks, but it is much funnier if a whiff of dust is raised at the point of contact," reported Robert Lewis Taylor in *The New Yorker*.

He experimented with different types of tiny sacks of flour that he would conceal in his jacket so that when he slapped himself, not only would he get a small cloud of dust, but exactly the right amount of dust to create the maximum comic effect.

Clark's comedy was visual, rather than verbal. Sight gags were very important to him. The magazine reported, "One good prop, he feels, is worth a thousand words."

As Clark traveled around the country with Ringling Brothers, he amassed a collection of oddments that simply struck his fancy as potentially funny props. At one point Ringling complained about the fact that they had to haul sixteen pieces of luggage containing "stovepipe joints, false teeth, buggy whips, ladders, corsets, embalming fluid, mustard plasters, fire tongs," not to mention Clark's French horn, his fox-hunting coat, and a cuspidor.

He'd find ways to work them into his act.

In addition, Clark loved silly hats. His standard hat was a beat-up derby, but he was never afraid to experiment with the millinery and would often rotate through a half-dozen different hats in a single show, again seeking maximum comic effect.

As a result, his material is endlessly imitated and referenced in movies, sitcoms, and cartoons and by stage comedians. His material has become so pervasive that people reference it without knowing Clark's name. Among his most direct spiritual heirs is New Vaudeville clown Bill Irwin.

The Big Time

By 1917, Clark and McCullough were reportedly the highest-paid comedy act in burlesque. With Jean Bedini's burlesque troupe, they made their London debut in the revue *Chuckles of 1922* and were drafted for Broadway that same year by producer Sam H. Harris for

Irving Berlin's *Music Box Revue*, in which another future Broadway star, William Gaxton, made his debut. Clark & McCullough were invited back for the 1924 edition of *Music Box*, as well.

The two were a smash, reimagining some of their classic routines for the high-profile, big-time show, which eventually would feature some of the best-written sketches in the history of revues, including Robert Benchley's "Treasurer's Report" and George S. Kaufman's "If Men Played Cards as Women Do." Clark and McCullough got to create their usual tumult, and Clark got to do some sketches with veteran funny lady Fanny Brice. Clark and Brice performed a pas de deux in "I Want to Be a Ballet Dancer" and played a scene as Adam and Eve.

Clark and McCullough finally got to topline their own Broadway production in the thoroughly nutty Harry Ruby and Bert Kalmar musical *The Ramblers*, in which they played a pair of traveling con men posing as mystics who somehow get involved in a film shoot in Mexico and need to save the leading lady from a kidnapper. It ran 289 performances, a respectable number for the 1920s; they became Broadway stars only a quarter century after they formed their partnership.

In his book *Movie Comedy Teams*, Leonard Maltin wrote, "For several years they rivaled the Marx Brothers in popularity in New York, and even when they had to support weak material, they captured the hearts of the Broadway critics, who admired their madcap sense of fun and their boundless energy."

Over the next decade they moved easily back and forth from Broadway to burlesque to vaudeville. They made their film debut in W. C. Fields's silent feature *Two Flaming Youths*, playing circus performers, which led to a contract to make a series of shorts. Unfortunately, most of Clark & McCullough's films have been lost; otherwise, the team might have had a TV resurgence like the Three Stooges did in the early 1960s. As a result of the films' loss, plus the fact that Clark made no more features after McCullough's death, he is barely remembered by the public today.

Among their stage musicals were *Here Goes the Bride* (1931), *Walk a Little Faster* (1932) with Beatrice Lillie, and *Thumbs Up!* (1934). But their greatest musical comedy success by far came in 1930, when Edgar Selwyn chose them to star in the satirical *Strike Up the Band*, with a libretto by Morrie Ryskind and a score in Gilbert and Sullivan style by George and Ira Gershwin.

A satire on American business in wartime, the show's absurd plot reveals the behind-the-scenes shenanigans as the United States prepares to go to war with Switzerland over cheese. The show had failed in its first incarnation in 1927, closing in Philadelphia. Rewritten and restaged in the early days of the Depression (when the public was more in the mood to see incompetence in the worlds of government and finance), the show was a big a hit as the era could muster. It didn't have a bad orchestra, either. In the pit were future swing masters Benny Goodman, Glenn Miller, Jimmy Dorsey, Jack Teagarden, and, on drums, Gene Krupa.

The End of Clark and McCullough

In the darkest days of the Depression, people considered themselves very lucky to find work. They were grateful for what they got, and Clark and McCullough took all they could find. They were lucky enough to find plenty—perhaps too much.

Possibly, then, the disaster came because of overwork. Or maybe it arose from the fact that critics always praised Clark at McCullough's expense. In any case, after making thirty-four short films re-creating many of their vaudeville and burlesque bits in the years 1929 and 1935, along with appearing in four Broadway musicals and just finishing a road tour of *George White's Scandals*, McCullough was hospitalized in Massachusetts in early 1936 for "nervous exhaustion."

In a family history by Michael D. Brick, McCullough's great-nephew, it was recorded that McCullough was being driven to another sanatorium by a longtime friend and member of the board of directors of the Circus Fans Association, Frank T. Ford. Brick writes that McCullough "asked to stop for a shave in Medford, MA. . . . While there, and while the barber was distracted, Paul apparently grabbed a straight razor, and before he could be stopped he slashed his throat and wrists. Paul was hospitalized, and had surgery to save him, but he died two days later."

Clark hadn't just lost his closest childhood friend, his road buddy of three decades, and his closest collaborator. He also lost the center of his showbiz identity: the entity of Clark and McCullough. Who was he without his partner?

As it turns out, he was a lot. It's not an exact comparison, but, in the end, Clark losing McCullough was like Groucho, Chico, and Harpo losing Zeppo (in that case, to retirement). If anything, as Norton pointed out, Clark became an even bigger star without McCullough. But it should be noted that aside from a brief appearance in *The Goldwyn Follies*, Clark never appeared in another film.

Going Solo

Like Zeppo, McCullough was the straight man, and Clark had plenty of others lining up to feed him straight lines. These included, in *Mexican Hayride*, June Havoc and, in his biggest post-McCullough hit, *Star and Garter*, Havoc's sister, Gypsy Rose Lee.

Lee and Clark were first paired in a revised version of the *Ziegfeld Follies* of 1936, and Lee not only served in the foil role as well as McCullough, but she looked better, too. The pair stopped the show with the Vernon Duke number "I Can't Get Started," in which Clark complained about his lack of success in his efforts to court her.

They were paired again in producer Mike Todd's 1942 *Star and Garter*, which was essentially an upmarket burlesque show (perhaps the high tide of the form), with Lee as the star stripper and Clark as top banana in sketches "For a Quarter" and "Turkish Oomph."

Clark also appeared with fellow burlesque alumni Abbott and Costello in the 1939 revue *Streets of Paris*.

As successful as some of these pairings were, Clark was now essentially a solo act and worked with new partners only on a show-by-show basis. This gave him a chance to pursue a lifelong dream: to play the classics. He finally appeared onstage without his signature drawn-on glasses in Richard Brinsley Sheridan's *The Rivals* (as Bob Acres), directed by Eva Le Gallienne; in William Congreve's *Love for Love* (as Ben); and in Molière's *The Would-Be Gentleman*, which he adapted himself.

In the script for the Molière he wrote, "At this point, I throw a snuff box across the stage and it falls into the valet's pocket." In a footnote for director John Kennedy he added, "This can be done. I have practiced it."

In his review of *The Rivals,* *New York Times* critic Brooks Atkinson described how Clark developed a scene in which the self-important country bumpkin Bob Acres attempts to write a letter: "Mr. Clark attacks the scene with unexampled ferocity—throwing his legs over the back of a chair, burrowing into the writing paper, tossing pens around the room like darts, shaking ink into a drawer for no logical reason and writing like a house afire. His excitement is a legendary. . . . Mr. Clark's acting in *The Rivals* is a masterpiece."

Clark alternated these classical roles with more traditional high jinks. Cole Porter wrote the score for Clark's 1944 musical *Mexican Hayride*, another lighthearted gags-and-gals show from Todd, though with a much bigger budget than usual. Clark made his entrance puffing his traditional cigar and carrying a papoose on his back. The bundle was rigged so it looked like the baby was puffing on its own little cigar, which gave off real smoke. Clark played an American crook on the lam in Mexico. He and George Givot introduced Porter's cheerily suggestive "Count Your Blessings" with costar June Havoc. Clark appeared in two more Todd burlesque shows, *As the Girls Go* (1948) and *Michael Todd's Peep Show* (1950), but neither had the pizzazz or success of the early ones. *Peep Show* was Clark's final Broadway appearance.

In 1947 Clark starred in a rare revival of Victor Herbert's operetta *Sweethearts* and managed to build it into a hit—reportedly the first Broadway revival to outrun its original production.

Clark's last stage role came in a late-1950s national tour of the musical *Damn Yankees*, in which he played the devilish Mr. Applegate, earning rave reviews around the United States. By this time he used actual glasses because, at his age, he needed them.

The tour proved to be his farewell. Clark died February 12, 1960, at his Manhattan apartment of what was described as a heart spasm, perhaps brought on by a viral infection. Broadway had lost her master clown technician.

Robert Garland of the *Journal American* once wrote, "Every drama critic has a pet. And every drama critic's pet is Bobby Clark . . . he can do no wrong."

No one has ever written a biography of Clark, and while his spirit infuses many movies, films, and TV shows, he's rarely depicted. Even the massive PBS *Broadway* series included only the briefest of clips of him. He did appear as a character in a musical, the short-lived

Mike Todd bio *Ain't Broadway Grand*, in which he was capably impersonated by Gerry Vichi, who got Clark's bawdy spirit right, if not his physical comedy.

Though he's barely remembered today, Clark once was synonymous with Broadway. Historian Harry Turtledove, in his epic alternate history of America speculating how life would have been different or the same had the South won the Civil War, wrote a scene in which one of his characters went to see a Broadway show. "When Daisy June Lee was on stage the orchestra could have been playing kazoos and bazookas for all Sam cared. And even when she wasn't, the comic with the painted-on spectacles kept him laughing."

Even in an alternate universe, Bobby Clark is still getting the yocks.

William Gaxton (left) with frequent costar Victor Moore in *Leave It to Me!* (1938). PHOTOFEST

WILLIAM GAXTON
You're the Top

Few men looked as good in a top hat as William Gaxton. Fred Astaire may be more closely associated with that distinctive piece of headgear, mainly because he starred in a film titled *Top Hat*. But, next to Gaxton, Astaire looked like a kid playing dress up in his dad's closet.

Unlike Astaire, however, Gaxton was not loved by the camera. Among his few films was 1943's *Best Foot Forward*, made when he was in his early fifties, by which point his time had essentially passed. As a result, Gaxton is barely remembered today.

And that's too bad, because from the mid-1920s to the mid-1930s, Gaxton was the leading man of choice for Broadway musicals. He had the magic tall, dark, handsome looks, he had a gift for smart-aleck comedy, and, while his singing wasn't technically sterling by any means, he had a snappy, jazzy way with a song—enough to satisfy the likes of George Gershwin, Cole Porter, and Richard Rodgers, all of whom turned to Gaxton to introduce some of their best-known songs just as they were reaching the peak of their songwriting powers. When Ethel Merman sang "You're the Top" in *Anything Goes*, it was Gaxton she sang it with. At a time when many performers were losing their livelihoods on the stage because of the Great Depression and fleeing to California, Gaxton thrived, finding some of his best Broadway roles. In 1931 he set the record as the performer who had played the most consecutive weeks—ten—at the apex of vaudeville, the Palace. People eagerly paid their Depression dollars to see him. But who was he?

Gaxton was born Arturo Antonio Gaxiola on December 2, 1890 (1893, by some accounts), in San Francisco, a scion of the Carillo family, one of the clans of local aristocrats called "hidalgos" who settled in California on what is today some of the most valuable land in North America. His father was a real-estate agent and manager in the booming former gold-rush metropolis.

So Gaxton might have settled into a comfortable upper-middle-class life if the silver spoon hadn't been jarred from his mouth by the 1906 San Francisco earthquake. In forty-five seconds of vibration, a huge part of his father's inventory crumbled into dust. Most of what didn't crumble burned in the ensuing fire. Gaxton recalled years later helping his family and neighbors to survive by digging canned food out of the rubble. His family was crowded into temporary shelter at Lowell High School with Chinese and Japanese boys, from whom he picked up the rudiments of their languages, used later to surprising effect in *Anything Goes* and other shows.

Gaxton's upbringing made him aware of the finer things in life, but this early privation, though it turned out to be temporary, also helped him to appreciate them. He used his money to keep himself impeccably dapper and well dressed—an instinct that served him well in the top-hat-and-tails era of showbiz glamour—but he always kept a sense of proportion about it.

His father's fortune recovered, just like San Francisco itself, and young Arturo was sent to Santa Clara College, though he was still unsure whether he should pursue medicine or the law. Arturo had always enjoyed visits to the local vaudeville theatres, but one of the priests at Santa Clara unintentionally nudged him into his eventual career by asking him to take part in a variety show for the students. Gaxton later told the *New York Herald Tribune*, "I was entranced. I hadn't expected to make them laugh like that. . . . From that time on I knew what I wanted to do."

In the days before television, radio, and even the movies, entertainment meant the stage. And for those far beyond New York, the stage meant vaudeville. He made his debut as a "super" in the Alcazar Stock Company, earning fifty cents a performance playing the role of an ocean wave in *The Count of Monte Cristo*, and broke into small-time eight-a-day vaudeville at the Dewey Theatre in nearby Oakland with an act called "Stories, Songs and Stuff." It wasn't much of an honor: he was considered the cleanup act—an act so bad it would drive stragglers out of the house so the next performance could begin. But he watched and learned, and soon was earning a dollar a performance at Tony Lubelski's Novelty Theater, again singing, telling jokes, and dancing.

Gaxton—he now adopted a more easily pronounced version of his name—was playing at the cramped Riverside Theatre when he found himself sharing a dressing room with an old comedian named Nat Goodwin (1857–1919), who immediately took the young man under his wing. Goodwin taught Gaxton the subtler points, like how to stand still on the stage and still command the audience's attention. "It was from Goodwin that I learned to be fussy about my dressing and diction."

Gaxton partnered with Rudy Cameron (1894–1958) for a song-and-dance act in which Gaxton played the violin. All vaudevillians have war stories, and one of Gaxton's favorites was claiming that he was frightened into become a comedian in Leadville, Colorado. Arriving at the town's saloon early in the day, Gaxton claimed a local gunslinger asked what their act would be. When he replied that it was a musical act, the gunman warned, "You'd be funny if you know what's good for you."

Gaxton told the *New York Post* that the man attended the makeshift theatre that night and trained a pistol on Gaxton, who then told every old vaudeville chestnut he'd ever heard.

The audience reportedly howled in response—so satisfyingly that Gaxton started looking for comedy material for his act.

He found it in a sketch titled "Kisses," written by S. Jay Kaufman, about a modern-day Casanova who pursues four different women. It earned him his first coveted "New Act" review in *Variety* in 1916 and was to become Gaxton's signature piece, performed thousands of times over the next two decades, across the United States and even eventually in London. Entrepreneur Al H. Woods saw his act and decided it was time to bring Gaxton to New York. Gaxton married Madeline Cameron (no relation to Rudy), half of the dancing Cameron Sisters, later to be featured in the *Ziegfeld Follies*. The marriage lasted until Gaxton's death in 1963. After a stint in the navy during World War I, Gaxton found himself playing "Kisses" at the pinnacles of vaudeville, the Palace in Times Square and the Palladium in London, earning himself a reputation as a matinee idol the ladies would pay top dollar to see.

Broadway Debut

Gaxton attracted the notice of legendary producer-director Charles B. Dillingham, who was then helping Irving Berlin and Sam H. Harris cast a second edition of the *Music Box Revue*, a Broadway variety show inspired by the *Follies* but presented in the more intimate precincts of the custom-designed Music Box Theatre and emphasizing relaxed wit and melody over opulence. Gaxton made his Broadway debut on October 23, 1922, singing a Berlin comedy number, "Pack Up Your Sins."

Gaxton was then cast in a series of national tours of third-rate musicals. When none led to further Broadway work, Gaxton returned to vaudeville with a new sketch, "Partners." He even traveled to his home state in the mid-1920s to make a short silent film, *It's the Old Army Game*, with W. C. Fields and his old partner Rudy Cameron.

In her 1971 essay "The Other Face of W. C. Fields," Louise Brooks recalled working on the film with Gaxton, who played the romantic lead. Off camera, "He and Rudy Cameron did their old vaudeville act, singing and dancing and telling bum jokes with violent self-approval. Then Gaxton appeared alone playing the violin. This was even worse than the vaudeville act. Trying to recapture the essence of Gaxton's impromptu comedy, I realize now that it was born of despair because he was funny every day too . . . I knew that our parts as the 'love interest' in a Fields comedy meant nothing, but Gaxton had convinced himself that this first job in films would launch him on a successful new career allowing him to escape from years of mediocre vaudeville sketches. At best it was a mistaken act of friendship, Eddie's giving the part of a boy to a sophisticated actor of thirty-four. Billy Gaxton was so vulnerable, so proud of his good looks, his Spanish ancestry, his acting ability. When he became a great Broadway star in George Gershwin's *Of Thee I Sing* (1931), the deadly bitterness of this failure [in movies] was exposed by the fact that he refused fabulous contracts, never making another film."

In fact, he did make another film, but more on that later.

At the time, producer Lew Fields was casting about for a handsome leading man who could also play comedy in a new musical by the young songwriting team of Richard Rodgers and Lorenz Hart. Based on Mark Twain's novel *A Connecticut Yankee in King Arthur's Court*, the musical bore the abbreviated title *A Connecticut Yankee*.

The 1927 smash became one of the most successful musicals of the 1920s. Gaxton played Martin, a man who dreams he travels back in time to Arthurian England after being clocked with a champagne bottle by his bossy fiancée (Nana Bryant) at his bachelor dinner. Martin, now known as "The Yankee," uses his knowledge of modern technology and business practices to convert the Round Table to something of a corporate boardroom before a plot by Morgan Le Fay (Bryant again) sends him hurtling back to 1927.

Gaxton got to introduce Rodgers and Hart standards "Thou Swell" and "My Heart Stood Still" and to perform choreography by Busby Berkeley. Gaxton finally was getting the "A" material he craved. All his qualities came into play: his looks, his ability to dance, his flexible if unexceptional voice, his skill with comedy.

Gaxton had the right look at the right time. He could fulfill the lacquered playboy image of a square-jawed, tall, dark, handsome macho man, all the while managing a layer of comedy that took off just enough of his sexual edge to make him nonthreatening. He looked completely competent and in control, but when he spoke, you could perceive that he was just a little dim. He excelled at non sequiturs and off-center cockeyed observations that sounded authoritative and plausible . . . until you thought about them a little. He was a more stolid edition of the Valentino Latin lover type, much valued at the time, with just enough winking self-awareness to set him apart.

When the stock market crashed in 1928–29, Gaxton claimed to have lost $100,000, a huge sum in those days. But he soldiered on with preparations for his next show. Having piloted a Richard Rodgers musical and an Irving Berlin revue to hit status, Gaxton now had Cole Porter knocking on his door. The project, titled *Fifty Million Frenchmen*, was set in Porter's beloved Paris.

Wealthy playboy Peter Forbes (Gaxton) bets his friend $25,000 that he can win the heart of visiting American beauty Looloo Carroll (Genevieve Tobin) without flaunting his fortune at her. He assumes the persona of a tour guide and discovers that her parents have promised her hand to a Russian grand duke. The plot chronicles Forbes's various attempts to win her heart, and along the way she wins his. Gaxton shone in two Porter tunes, "I Worship You" and the soon-to-be standard "You Do Something to Me." The show ran eight months and replenished both Gaxton's bank account and his self-confidence.

He returned briefly to vaudeville—but this time as the headliner at the Palace. His engagement of ten consecutive weeks there in the depths of the Depression established a house record that was never broken while that theatre maintained a vaudeville-only policy.

Of Thee I Sing, Baby

Gaxton was contentedly slaying them at the Palace when he received a call from producer Sam H. Harris, who was now representing a property being assembled by a high-octane creative team. Playwrights George S. Kaufman and Morrie Ryskind, who had written some of the Marx Brothers' most beloved hits, including *Animal Crackers* and *The Cocoanuts*, were turning their satirical sights on no less than the presidency of the United States, and they wanted Gaxton to play the commander in chief. The score was supplied by the champagne team of George and Ira Gershwin. *Of Thee I Sing* opened the day after Christmas, 1931, with Gaxton playing candidate John P. Wintergreen.

At the time, Herbert Hoover's White House was complacently promising, "Prosperity is just around the corner" even as millions of Americans lost their jobs, homes, and futures. Once-mighty politicians and industrialists seemed impotent or unwilling to do anything about the disaster. The time was ripe for a show that painted them all as incompetent boobs. And *Of Thee I Sing* did that with brio. Wintergreen runs on the slogan "Love Is Sweeping the Country."

Of Thee I Sing brought Gaxton one of the most enduring collaborations of his life in the person of round-faced, piping-voiced comedian Victor Moore, who played mousy vice president Alexander H. Throttlebottom. As the *Boston Evening Transcript* put it, "Everyone could see at once that there was something uncanny in the partnering of the voluble, breezy Gaxton style and the shy, hesitant diffidence of Moore. Each had appeared without the other in half a dozen musicals, but now they belonged together."

And indeed they stayed together for eight shows, from the triumphant *Of Thee I Sing* in 1931 to the catastrophic *Nellie Bly* in 1946. They weren't formally a team—their managers booked them separately. But the Gaxton and Moore chemistry was so perfect for the period that they took their place alongside the likes of Laurel and Hardy and the Marx Brothers in audience affection. Why aren't they similarly honored today? Like Gallagher and Shean, and Clark and McCullough, they made few recordings or films and thus live only in the memories of those lucky enough to have seen them.

The sharp-nosed Gaxton was always a little more worldly-wise and usually got the girl. The snub-nosed Moore was the slightly ditzy naif. Both were loopy in their own special ways, but the two found common ground, each serving as both comic and straight man in different scenes, with Gaxton a little more the singer and romancer, Moore a little more the funnyman. Dean Martin and Jerry Lewis offered a more extreme version of this formula. But Broadway didn't see anything like their pairing again until Nathan Lane and Matthew Broderick teamed up in 2001 for *The Producers*.

At an eventual 441 performances, *Of Thee I Sing* turned out to have the longest run of any book musical of the 1930s. The first eleven months of the show's run coincided with the 1932 presidential election campaign, which ended in Franklin D. Roosevelt's crushing victory over Hoover. Gaxton later played a command performance for Roosevelt himself. Roosevelt's vice president, John Nance Garner, attended the show and gave Gaxton a photo signed, "To a 'president' who never applied the veto to the joys of life."

It was an appropriate sentiment. Gaxton invested in fine clothes and perfume companies, and he became a real-life Connecticut Yankee when he bought a home for himself and Madeline in Connecticut, where he spent the rest of his life.

In contrast with Merman, who was known to "freeze" her performance and do it exactly the same way night after night, Gaxton was famous, or perhaps infamous, for allowing his performances to get broader and broader as runs continued. Perhaps this was inspired by his vaudeville training. If something didn't get a laugh, you'd cut it. If it got a laugh, you'd do a little more of it next time. Such a policy could snowball, and not everyone appreciated the result.

One of prickly playwright George S. Kaufman's most famous poisoned barbs was launched at Gaxton. Late in the run of *Of Thee I Sing*, Kaufman returned to the Music Box to find that Gaxton had generously supplemented Kaufman's Pulitzer-winning dialogue scenes with beaucoup ad-libs. In the era long before cell phones and texting, the author fired off a telegram from the back of the house to be delivered to Gaxton backstage. It sniped: "I am watching your performance from the rear of the house. Wish you were here."

Zinger notwithstanding, Kaufman wrote two more librettos for Gaxton, *Let 'Em Eat Cake* and *Hollywood Pinafore*. Perhaps coincidentally, both cast Gaxton as a scoundrel, though a usually loveable one.

Let 'Em Eat Cake, which opened just a few months after *Sing* closed in 1933, proved to be an ill-advised sequel to the previous show. In it, Throttlebottom rises up and overthrows Gaxton's presidency and establishes a dictatorship. It was intended to satirize events in Europe, such as Hitler's and Mussolini's rise to power. But most people found nothing funny in those developments. Despite Kaufman, Ryskind, and the Gershwin brothers (adding "Mine" to their, and Gaxton's, roster of hits), the show bombed. Gaxton later called *Let 'Em Eat Cake* "a sad mistake." His next show would be anything but.

Anything Goes

Gaxton's luck returned with his next project, the one of his shows perhaps best known today: Cole Porter's *Anything Goes* (1934), one of the iconic shows of the 1930s (its 420-performance run was the second-longest of the decade for a book musical). In Howard Lindsay and Russel Crouse's book, which is not all that different from that of *Fifty Million Frenchmen*, Gaxton played Billy Crocker, a young man who goes to the quay to see his sweetheart (Bettina Hall) off on a cruise to Europe, where her parents have arranged for her to marry an English nobleman. He just can't stand to let her go, so he stows away and is forced to adopt a series of silly disguises and accents to pass as a legitimate passenger. He is assisted by nightclub singer Reno Sweeney (Ethel Merman), who gets sweet on him.

He also gets a hand from Reverend Doctor Moon, actually aspiring gangster Moonface Martin (Moore), who is only public enemy number thirteen and is trying to work his way up. Amid the shipboard shenanigans, Gaxton sang the sultry love song "All Through the Night" to Hall and duetted with Merman on what is perhaps his best-known hit, "You're the Top," a classic Porter list song in which each compared the other to great things, like "the steppes of Russia" and "the pants on a Roxy usher" (which, in New Yorkese, rhymes beautifully).

Brooks Atkinson wrote in the *New York Times*, "Following the lead of a madcap book, [Gaxton] is in and out of all sorts of disguises—a sailor, a Spanish nobleman with false whiskers just clipped off a Pomeranian, a fabulous public enemy. Through the show he fairly dances with enjoyment and high spirits, making every song sound good on his old Gaxiolaphone. When he sings with Miss Merman the composer ought to be very grateful for a pair of performers who can make every note burst with vitality and every line sound like a masterpiece of wit."

Later Career

Gaxton had no way to know that *Anything Goes* was to be his last smash. He turned down a chance to pair with Merman again in Porter's 1936 show *Red, Hot and Blue!* (the role went to Bob Hope) and probably regretted it. Instead, he appeared in Ralph Benatzky's operetta *White Horse Inn*, imported from Germany. It was an odd choice for Gaxton, whose zippy musicals had helped to kill audience taste for the old operettas. Gaxton played a waiter named Leopold, in a huge fake mustache. His love interest was Kitty Carlisle, but the production, which opened in October 1936, lasted only six months.

Leave It to Me! (1938) was a subpar effort by Cole Porter, in which Gaxton played a snide newspaperman who tries to sabotage the central romance. He'd always played charlatans of one type or another, but this was his first actual villain role. If the show is remembered at all today, it's not because of Gaxton. A newcomer named Mary Martin stopped the show with "My Heart Belongs to Daddy," with another future star, Gene Kelly, in the chorus.

Gaxton marked his fiftieth birthday in 1940. He was still considered something of a fashion plate by many, but his meal ticket, his famed looks, had begun to deteriorate. Theatrical historian Ethan Mordden describes him in this period as "seedy."

Gaxton again teamed with Moore for his last musical success, *Louisiana Purchase*, in May of 1940. Morrie Ryskind's latest political-satire libretto had Gaxton playing another villain, scheming lawyer Jim Taylor, a cat's-paw of a Huey Long–like corrupt Louisiana politician. His job was to finagle investigating Senator Oliver P. Loganberry (Moore) into compromising positions with smoky vamps Vera Zorina and Irene Bordoni, but Moore proved impervious to their charms. Even with a second-class Irving Berlin score, the show ran more than a year. But Gaxton and Moore's luck had finally run out.

They collaborated on organizing a 1942 revue called *Keep 'Em Laughing*—but it didn't, even with Hildegarde, Paul and Grace Hartman, the Jack Cole Dancers, and, in a minor comic spot, a young Zero Mostel making his Broadway debut. At this point, Gaxton decided to give Hollywood one more chance. He accepted a secondary role in *Best Foot Forward*, an adaptation of a second-rate musical known mainly for the college fight song "Buckle Down, Winsocki." It remains Gaxton's most notable film appearance but reflects little of the suave charm that had once made him a star.

Gaxton and Moore's other *Of Thee I Sing* librettist, George S. Kaufman, tapped them for major roles in his next Broadway satire, *Hollywood Pinafore*, which used Gilbert and Sullivan's *H.M.S. Pinafore* as a template to poke fun at the excesses of the movie capital, with revised lyrics by Kaufman himself. Gaxton played aggressive talent agent Dick Live-Eye (based on *Pinafore*'s Dick Dead-Eye) to Moore's dictatorial head of Pinafore Studios. Critics faulted the parody as scattershot and unoriginal, and the show folded after just two weeks.

The Gaxton–Moore partnership came to an end the following year, with the failure of *Nellie Bly*. After three flops in a row, Gaxton played his last performance on a Broadway stage on February 2, 1946.

Gaxton spent his later years living in Connecticut, traveling with his wife, working on behalf of the Lambs Club, and making occasional guest appearances. He appeared several time on *Toast of the Town* (aka *The Ed Sullivan Show*), including one in which he sang "You're the Top" with Dolores Gray, proving that he still had a lot of zip and stage presence (if an uncertain hold on the beat), clapping and shouting, "Oh, yeah!" as she sings her lines. It is one of the few surviving recordings of him performing.

Moore died July 23, 1962. Gaxton, who by then was feeling the effects of cancer himself, followed him on February 12, 1963, at the age of sixty-nine.

Ray Bolger leaps into his starring role in *By Jupiter* (1942). PHOTOFEST

RAY BOLGER
Life Would Be a Ding-a-Derry

Fred Astaire may have been the king of Broadway's elegant dancers in the 1920s, but in those days dance had many specialties, including what was known as "eccentric" dancing—acrobatic and comic footwork.

The crown prince of the eccentric hoofers was Ray Bolger. Bolger transcended his niche in the dance world to become one of the icons of twentieth-century mass entertainment when he played the Scarecrow who longs for a brain in the 1939 film musical classic *The Wizard of Oz*.

But he got to play the role only after a skyrocketing, decade-long career on Broadway, kicking, wiggling, bounding, and sometimes apparently floating in a half-dozen musicals, notably Rodgers and Hart's *On Your Toes*, in which he danced literally for his character's life in the "Slaughter on Tenth Avenue" ballet.

Bolger's career continued on to even greater heights after *Oz*, especially his showstopping performance in *Where's Charley?*, leading the audience-participation number "Once in Love with Amy."

Lanky, hawk-nosed, and rubber-limbed, Bolger could be testy and pugnacious on stage, but he always radiated an inner sweetness that won audiences to his side. Singing, acting, and dancing with a distinctive physical style, Bolger was sometimes imitated by others but never equaled in his comic panache.

★

Bolger danced around the house when he was a child, but he began to develop a mature interest in the subject when his family began taking him to vaudeville shows. Born January 10, 1904, into a Portuguese-Irish family in Boston's tough Dorchester neighborhood, Raymond Wallace Bulcao grew up determined to succeed in business and get himself out.

At this formative moment, the future Ray Bolger had one of those thunderbolt life-changing experiences. It was 1920 and he was 16 years old when he saw the comedian Fred Stone at a matinee of *Jack O'Lantern* at a Boston theatre. Stone played a scarecrow in the piece—to older theatergoers, this was obviously just a thinly-disguised opportunity to clone his most famous performance, that of the Scarecrow who wishes for a brain in the original 1903 Broadway operetta production of *The Wizard of Oz*, cowritten and supervised by *Oz* creator L. Frank Baum himself.

Stone's concept of the Scarecrow was to define him by the way he moved. A dancer by training, who would later organize his family into the dance group the Stepping Stones, Stone created a Scarecrow who truly seemed to be made of nothing but straw and rags. He was always stumbling and tumbling, giving the impression that he had no bones at all. The illusion, in various forms, had been delighting pretelevision audiences for seventeen years.

For a while, Ray Bulcao seemed doomed to a civilian life. He tried some terribly earnest jobs, working as a bank clerk, a vacuum cleaner salesman, and an accountant. But a different future kept drawing him on. He took dancing lessons and appeared with local amateur shows.

Legend tells that he was fired from an insurance company after he was caught practicing dances when he was supposed to be working. It was now the mid-1920s, the late golden age of vaudeville, and Bolger decided to take the plunge, going to work for legendary talent-finder Gus Edwards and changing his stage name to Ray Bolger.

He loved to tell this fiction story about his origins, as quoted in the *New York Times* in 1987: "I became a dancer in self-defense. I was doing a comedy monologue and didn't know how else to get off, so I danced off. I've been dancing ever since, but I'm still a comedian."

Bolger presented an Ichabod Crane figure: big nose and spidery legs jutting out from a body as thin as a pipe cleaner. He could kick his huge feet high over his head or leap and draw his knees up almost to his ears. In one of this signature bits, he would fall into a full split, then rise out of it by jerking his body upward bit by bit.

He was a mime in dance. He invested his moves with all sorts of emotions. He would dance up brashly to the audience, then recoil in mock fear while skipping backward. While doing an amazing crisp and precise tap dance he would make it look like he was forever losing his balance, staggering stage right, then swerving, seemingly out of control, back stage left, often teetering at the edge of the stage before stumbling backward.

He would pretend to fall behind the beat, then, in a panic, rush to catch up. He would execute wild spins and then pretend to be dizzy or lost and unable to find the audience, and then, with an expression of gratitude and relief, notice where they were and head into the next turn.

Sometimes he'd dance as a street tough, sometimes as a scaredy-cat. He could mince effeminately, cavort like a child, or promenade like an English lord. Sometimes he made it seem like his legs or hands had acquired a life of their own and he'd struggle to get them back under control.

He'd often end his act with a full feet-in-the air pratfall that could turn into a backward somersault; then he would leap back to his feet. Ta-dah!

Bolger made his Broadway debut in the short-lived revue *A Night in Paris* and got to work in his first real musical comedy in 1929 when he had a featured spot in *Heads Up!*, starring Victor Moore. Moore was unable to disguise the fact that the show closely resembled the far better earlier musical *Oh, Kay!* Over its 144 performances, Bolger got to know the show's songwriting team, Richard Rodgers and Lorenz Hart, who would later write him two of his biggest hits.

As the Depression wrapped itself around showbiz, Bolger's skill enabled him to keep getting bookings in clubs and what was left of vaudeville. In 1929 he married Gwendolyn Rickard, and their marriage lasted the rest of his life.

Having tasted Broadway, he returned as often as he could. His next appearance was a featured spot in the musical revue *George White's Scandals of 1931*, billed alongside Ethel Merman, Rudy Vallee, and Willie and Eugene Howard.

But his first real starring role came in *Life Begins at 8:40*, a sumptuous variety show that tried to recapture the sparkle and glamour of the *Ziegfeld Follies*, and did so while poking fun at Broadway institutions and clichés. The show gave Bolger seven numbers, which showcased his singing as well as his dancing, including one that had him impersonating New York's onetime playboy mayor Jimmy Walter in "Life Begins at City Hall." *Life Begins at 8:40* also gave Bolger the chance to originate his first standard, "You're a Builder-Upper," with costar Dixie Dunbar. Songs were by Harold Arlen and E. Y. "Yip" Harburg (among others), who would go on to write the score for *The Wizard of Oz*. *Life Begins at 8:40* featured one scene in which Bolger played Boccaccio to the Balzac of future *Oz* costar Bert Lahr.

On Your Toes

Having proved he could act and sing just as well as he could dance, Bolger inspired his old *Heads Up!* pals Rodgers and Hart to craft a role that would use all his skills. *On Your Toes* (1936) was the story of a university music teacher named Junior Dolan who persuades the director of a Russian ballet company to stage a new American ballet he's written, called "Slaughter on Tenth Avenue," at the school. The ballet tells the tawdry story of a barroom brawl between two men over a woman (danced by Tamara Geva) and the death of the woman and her lover.

After numerous plot twists, Junior winds up having to dance the main role on opening night—only to learn that some gangsters have come to rub out the guy he's replacing at the end of the ballet, and the only way he can avoid being shot is to keep dancing.

Broadway had never seen anything like the seventeen-minute "Slaughter on Tenth Avenue" scene. Choreographer George Balanchine combined elements of jazz, ballroom, and classical dance to tell a dramatic story wordlessly and bring the book of an otherwise traditional musical to its climax.

For Bolger's part, the marathon dance called on him to increase his energy and tension level again and again until he was in danger of collapsing . . . just as the cops arrived and saved him. Bolger reportedly had to be rubbed down after each performance.

In its unbylined 1936 review, *Time* magazine called the show "a definite milestone in the U.S. musical theatre" and called "Slaughter" an "impressive theatrical miracle," adding, "Bolger has his first chance to establish himself as a definite stage personality rather than a funny Broadway tap dancer. Called upon to impersonate a WPA music teacher who winds up as a master of ballet, his genuine charm and humor are instantly apparent."

Hollywood and *The Wizard of Oz*

Bolger had made his film debut in 1924 in a silent short called *Carrie of the Chorus*, but after *On Your Toes* he was able to command $3,000 a week as a contract player at MGM. Among his 1930s assignments were performing dance interludes in *Rosalie*, *Sweethearts*, and *The Great Ziegfeld*.

One of the projects MGM put on his plate was an epic musical of L. Frank Baum's classic American children's novel *The Wonderful Wizard of Oz*, which would get all the resources of costume, set, and special effects design that MGM, the home of musical film, could muster.

Bolger was delighted to appear in the story that had provided such a signal role for his terpsichorean idol, Fred Stone. At first, however, MGM wanted him to play the Tin Woodman. It took some hard campaigning to swing the role of the Scarecrow, but generations have attested that it was a role he was born to play. His costars included Lahr as the Cowardly Lion, Jack Haley as the Tin Woodman, Margaret Hamilton as the Wicked Witch, Ziegfeld's widow Billie Burke as the Good Witch, and, in the central role of Dorothy, Judy Garland, with whom Bolger became close friends.

Bolger's fatherly warmth toward the teenage Garland is evident in the final film. He's the first of the remarkable creatures she encounters along the Yellow Brick Road to Emerald City. A scarecrow who is unable to scare crows, he blames his failings on the fact that his head is stuffed with straw and he can't think. "If I Only Had a Brain" is his lament, as written by Arlen and Harburg, and it's so clear and emotionally affecting that Dorothy invests herself completely in helping him ask the Wizard for a brain—as Bolger does with her goal of getting back home to Kansas. Although Bolger played the role in a rubber face and neck prosthesis that took an hour to apply each day, he was able to project a tenderness and empathy that helps glue the whole film together. His Scarecrow may have been frail and may have had trouble standing upright, but he was steadfast and true, exactly the sort of friend you'd want to have if you were heading into the unknown.

The boneless physical vocabulary Bolger brought to the role was his personal homage to Fred Stone's Broadway Scarecrow of nearly forty years earlier. Bolger also found that bits of eccentric dancing sharpened over years in his old vaudeville act lent themselves perfectly to the perpetually unsteady Scarecrow.

Years later, Bolger told the *New York Post*, "I knew I was taking part in a strange kind of adventure. Everything had to be invented for that picture—the effects, the sound, the Technicolor—it was all new. But when the reviews came out it was a terrific disappointment. The picture got terrible notices.

That's an exaggeration, but the reviewers seemed to see no blockbuster, let alone a classic. Though today the movie winds up on virtually every list of greatest Hollywood films, in fact it was deemed a disappointment if not an outright flop at the time. It was nominated for an Oscar as Best Picture but in the end won only two Oscars, both for music, including the song "Over the Rainbow." "It was only when *The Wizard of Oz* came into the home with television [in the 1950s] that it redeemed itself," Bolger said. "It was no longer a picture—it was an institution."

In 1939, however, *The Wizard of Oz* seemed to be just an "oh, well" in Bolger's career. He went right back to working in films and in Broadway. He completed *Sunny* (1941) and the wartime hit *Four Jacks and A Jill* (1942). He even reunited with Judy Garland for 1946's *The Harvey Girls*, dancing with her in the film's signature number, the Oscar-winning "The Atchison, Topeka and the Santa Fe."

Back to Broadway

In his first visit to Broadway after *The Wizard of Oz*, Bolger was one of a half-dozen stars (also including Jimmy Durante and José Limon) clustered by producers Lee and J. J. Shubert in *Keep Off the Grass* (1940), an unpromising title for a revue that turned out to be fairly thin soup. Choreographer George Balanchine gave Bolger a comic turn as an over-the-hill dancer trying to stay hep in "The Old Jitterbug," plus more traditional dances in "A Latin Tune, a Manhattan Moon and You" and "Raffles." *Keep Off the Grass* wilted after just forty-four performances.

Bolger found much better material in Rodgers and Hart's next show, *By Jupiter* (1942). Based on Julian Thompson's play *The Warrior's Husband*, *By Jupiter* extracted a brief episode from classical history and turned it into a satire on society's gender roles. It's set in the land of the Amazons, where women are the rulers and warriors and men stay home, take care of the children, and knit. Bolger played Sapiens, a classic example of one of these Amazonian men, happy to be ruled by the stern Queen Hippolyta (Benay Venuta).

The plot gets rolling when a Greek army invades and each side is dumbfounded by the gender roles the other finds perfectly normal. But each side learns something from the other, and soon romance is in bloom. The epicene role gave Bolger license to be even lighter and freer than usual, and while the romantic plot took up a lot of the show, he got the best of the comedy songs and plenty of chances to show off his dancing chops.

The score offered such Rodgers and Hart gems as "Nobody's Heart," "Ev'rything I've Got," and "Careless Rhapsody," but they were hard-won. In the brief years since *On Your Toes*, lyricist Hart had gone steadily downhill, falling ever more firmly into the grip of alcoholism. Rodgers reported in his autobiography that the only times they were able to work in concentrated fashion on *By Jupiter* was when Hart was hospitalized and Rodgers talked the staff into letting him move a Steinway piano into the hospital room. The *Christian*

Science Monitor later reported that Bolger himself wrote much of the show's second act without credit.

By Jupiter opened to enthusiastic reviews and ran 427 performances, more than a hundred performances longer than the better-known *On Your Toes* and the longest run of any Rodgers and Hart original production. It was also the last original work from the team. Rodgers became fed up with Hart and ended the long and fruitful partnership, moving on to an even more fruitful collaboration with Oscar Hammerstein II. Aside from a few new songs for the 1943 *A Connecticut Yankee*, this Ray Bolger show was their farewell.

Three to Make Ready

In 1946 Bolger entertained the postwar crowds with a John Murray Anderson Broadway revue titled *Three to Make Ready*. *Time* magazine said, "Bolger, to be sure, is a pretty great fellow, and seems an even greater one by contrast—fair as a star when only one is shining in a show. He repeats his floppy *Wizard of Oz* scarecrow dance; he wickedly burlesques ballroom dancers; and in the show's and the season's most fetching solo act, he does a perfect soft-shoe routine while poking delightful fun at it." Otherwise, however, "*Three to Make Ready* is a very wet box of matches."

Bolger's personal appeal kept this middling showcase running for 327 performances, but he was looking for something with a little more meat on its bones. He thought he'd found it when tyro producer Cy Feuer and his partner Ernie Martin approached him with the idea of a musical based on George Gershwin's concert piece *An American in Paris*. They weren't able to come up with a satisfactory story (Alan Jay Lerner and Vincente Minnelli later made a classic film musical of this idea for Gene Kelly), but now that they had a star of Bolger's caliber on their hook, Feuer and Martin devised a project they thought would be just as good.

Where's Charley?

Brandon Thomas's play *Charlie's Aunt* had been around since 1892 and had settled into the comfortably profitable status as a staple of amateur theatres and stock companies in Britain and the United States. The farce tells the story of two college boys who want to have their sweethearts stay over for a school event but naturally couldn't think of doing so without a chaperone. One of the fellows, Charley Wykeham, gets his elderly aunt to serve in that office. But when she drops out at the last minute, Charley—desperate for some social time with his beloved girlfriend, Amy Spettigue—turns to a neighbor, who happens to be going to the soiree in drag as a dowager, to impersonate the aunt.

Feuer claims he was the one who hatched the idea to change the plot slightly, compounding the farce by combining Charley and the neighbor into one character. In the plot of the new musical, aptly retitled *Where's Charley?*, Charley uses quick-change skills to juggle being himself and his own aunt at more or less the same time. Frank Loesser, composer of "Praise the Lord and Pass the Ammunition," made his Broadway songwriting debut on the show, which was directed by George Abbott and choreographed by Bolger's "Slaughter on Tenth Avenue" collaborator George Balanchine.

In his autobiography, *I've Got the Show Right Here*, Feuer wrote of Bolger, "He didn't have the charm or smooth, graceful form of Gene Kelly, or the elegant style of Fred Astaire. But he always had a lot of energy. . . . He'd do all these 'rube' moves that you might expect to see in a cornball country fair, but he did them with a tuxedo on and it worked."

Bolger worked so hard on the dizzying costume changes, door slamming, and general running around that he had to be hospitalized during the show's tryout.

The show opened on Broadway October 11, 1948, to the by-now familiar reviews: Bolger dynamite; show so-so. It was only on the show's first post-opening matinee that it figured how to ascend from the commonplace into the rare. The show had two standout tunes, the infectious march "The New Ashmolean Marching Society and Students' Conservatory Band" and the adorable ballad "Once in Love with Amy." As Feuer tells it, Bolger went up on the lyric to the latter song and broke out of character to ask if anyone in the audience knew the words. Feuer's seven-year-old son Bobby, who had been watching rehearsals and tryouts for weeks, shouted out that he knew the words and proceeded to feed them to Bolger until he was back up to speed.

The audience was delighted with this bit of audience participation, and Bolger figured out how to make it a permanent part of the show. Instead of someone from the audience teaching him the lyrics, he would use the rests Loesser wrote at the end of each line to teach the lyrics to the audience and have them sing along.

The trick became the talk of the town and helped power the show to a two-year run, earning Bolger the Tony Award as Best Leading Actor in a Musical. Obeying his trouper's instinct, he had saved the show and turned it into a hit. Bolger even re-created the effect on the show's cast recording. Bolger also appeared in a 1951 revival and a 1952 film version of *Where's Charley?* It remains his most popular single stage work.

Last Musicals

Stage roles began coming less frequently as Bolger moved into his fifties. He had his own show on television in 1953, *The Ray Bolger Show*. But he hoped for one more Broadway hit. Sadly, that wish was denied him. In the 1962 musical *All American*, he played Professor Fodorski, a European teacher who comes to the United States and learns the ways of American college life. He wins notoriety when he teaches advanced physics to boneheaded athletes by using examples from football games. The show had a spritely score by Charles Strouse and Lee Adams, who were then still in the glow of their first hit, *Bye Bye Birdie*. It also had a book by onetime *Your Show of Shows* writer Mel Brooks, who appeared to have been in over his head. He later used part of his experience on *All American* for his Oscar-winning film script to *The Producers*.

Bolger got to sing the bittersweetly nostalgic Strouse and Adams duet "Once Upon a Time." At the end he sighs over lost love, "Where did it go?" He might as well have been talking about his stage success.

After several years in Hollywood, Bolger in 1969 ventured back to a Broadway that had changed a great deal in the twenty-one years since *Where's Charley?* Bolger had changed, too, and was no longer the grinning bedspring he once had been. His chosen vehicle was *Come Summer*, a gentle little musical that marked the passing of an era. Bolger played Phineas, a nineteenth-century New England peddler making his last circuit of little towns before the freight railroad puts an end to his way of life.

The show offered two great opportunities for collaboration. First, it represented a reunion with Margaret Hamilton. More importantly, it gave Bolger a chance to work with master choreographer Agnes de Mille (*Oklahoma!*), who also directed. The show proved to be a final Broadway effort for both de Mille and Bolger, who produced surprisingly few fireworks.

Critics clobbered the show for its weak book and score, and for being so old-fashioned in its construction. On the sixty-three-year-old Bolger the critics were divided, with Richard Watts Jr. of the *New York Post* saying, "He can make every step seem a marvel of grace, agility and humor." But Martin Gottfried of *Women's Wear Daily* complained that his performance "made me wonder why he ever was a star. As singer and as dancer I find him a man with neither grace, style nor a musical sense."

A week later, at the conclusion of the seventh performance, Bolger gave a curtain speech striking back at the critics and announcing that the show had just closed.

According to Ken Mandelbaum's *Not Since Carrie*, the audience wailed, "Oh, no!"

"Oh, yes," Bolger replied. It was his last starring role in a Broadway musical.

In between those shows he made a memorable appearance in Disney's rather flat-footed film remake of *Babes in Toyland*, starring teen idols Frankie Avalon and Annette Funicello. He played the villainous Barnaby, complete with a ridiculous mustache, a towering stovepipe hat, and a disconcertingly evil mien. It was a poor fit for the loveable Bolger.

In his seventies, Bolger made his peace with television and took occasional roles in shows as diverse as *Little House on the Prairie, Diff'rent Strokes, The Love Boat, The Partridge Family, Fantasy Island,* and even *Battlestar Galactica*, usually playing a feisty or whimsical grandpa figure who has showbiz in his background. He even danced one more time, in a commercial for the soft drink Dr Pepper. Audiences were always happy to see him.

He took one serious role, as an elder bishop in the film version of the Broadway drama *The Runner Stumbles*, and had more than sufficient gravitas for the serious role. In 1985 he and Liza Minnelli hosted the compilation film *That's Dancing!*, introducing clips from great dance movies of the past. It was his final film appearance.

Many also thought he was taking the roles more or less for fun, incorrectly assuming that *Oz* had left him financially set for life. It was an impression he was always quick to correct. For example, he told the *Christian Science Monitor* in 1980, "People ask if I still get residual payments for showings of that movie. My wife has the best answer to that question. She says I don't get any more money for it. Just immortality."

Of the leading players in *The Wizard of Oz*, Bolger was the last survivor. He died of bladder cancer on January 15, 1987.

Ethel Waters in *As Thousands Cheer* (1933). PHOTOFEST

ETHEL WATERS
Sweet Mama Stringbean

Ethel Waters came from the same line of female jazz singers as Billie Holiday, Bessie Smith, and Ma Rainey, but she could act as well as sing, so she was the one who succeeded on Broadway.

Brought up in poverty, with a mentally ill mother and an absent father, the illegitimate child fought her way through a maze of racial prejudice to achieve stardom, breaking down one locked door after another. Even then, many of those out front who applauded and cheered her and paid top dollar to see her wouldn't have sat next to her on a bus.

Waters was at her best singing the blues—the old blues of the 1910s and 1920s when she was growing up—rooted in the constant miseries and disappointments she suffered in the long years before the civil rights movement. But she had a sweet and quiet way of singing them that became her trademark. That sweetness came out mainly onstage; off-stage she fought for every advantage and earned her stardom the hard way.

She rose to stardom after the decline of the old minstrel shows, in which blacks almost never performed. Cartoonish black characters like Mr. Bones and Mr. Interlocutor were played by whites in blackface in most companies. Waters gave stage audiences a startling dose of the real thing. Gershwin brought jazz to Broadway; Waters brought the blues. In venting her sorrows she voiced the sorrow of her people and helped a wide audience to grasp and taste it.

Black shows were often as segregated as public accommodations. She performed in some of these blacks-only revues, because that's where the work was. She was sometimes held up as an example of a positive black role model, and sometimes excoriated for taking roles seen as stereotypes. The truth is, she widened the scope of roles it was accepted for blacks to portray. She played her share of maids and hookers—but also working mothers and wives just trying to survive. She opened field after field to black women. She was a pioneer, not only in the recording business, on the concert stage, and on Broadway, but in radio, movies, and even television late in her long career. She was the first black woman to be billed over the title in a drama in Broadway history, and for a brief time in the late 1930s she was one of the highest-paid women of any race in show business.

A few understood her talent and helped her. When her costars in *As Thousands Cheer* protested against taking curtain calls with her, composer/producer Irving Berlin said that then there would be no curtain calls at all for anyone. The stars relented, and they took their bows as a company.

But mainly it was Waters herself who served as her own best advocate. She fought for every penny of compensation and for every scrap of professional recognition of her talent, and she rarely compromised.

It would be pleasant to think that such a person was saintly and noble, but Waters had a reputation for being tough and mean. And her meanness was often directed at her sister black performers. She jealously guarded her hard-won perks and especially resented other black female stars as a threat to the tiny patch of turf she'd carved out for herself.

Nevertheless, in her greatest moments, such as when she was singing "Suppertime" in *As Thousands Cheer* or "His Eye Is on the Sparrow" in *The Member of the Wedding*, she could radiate vulnerability, inner strength, and a kind of patient peace. She was strongly religious and became more so as she got older. Her faith helped her survive her many hard times and also helped keep her successes from going to her head too much.

Which Waters was the real one? Both, of course. She was a complex individual—and, more than most in this book, a truly self-made star.

Ethel's precise date of birth remains a question mark. She firmly claimed October 31, 1900, though researchers have found that this date doesn't jibe with public records and put the true date as 1896. "Conceived by force" is the way one newspaper delicately put it. Waters's mother, Louise, was raped at knifepoint by John Waters when she was just twelve years old. No charges were brought, but he was known to her family, who thereafter shunned him. He died when was Ethel was three, poisoned by a jealous lover, by Ethel's own account. Louise married and started a family, leaving Ethel to be raised mainly by her maternal grandmother (her paternal grandmother, a white woman, refused to see Ethel until the older woman was approaching death) and two alcoholic aunts.

Waters opened her autobiography, *His Eye Is on the Sparrow*, (named for her favorite hymn) with the words "I never was a child. I never was coddled, liked, or understood by my family. . . . I was always an outsider."

She wrote that she never minded being illegitimate. "If I wanted pity, I got it. . . . When I didn't want it and was mean and nasty I could always say: 'Well, what can you expect of an old bastard like me?'"

They lived in extreme poverty, and with her maternal grandmother working to bring in what little they had, Ethel grew up among criminals, prostitutes, alcoholics, and drug addicts, living in a series of "rat-infested, bedbug-plagued shanties" in the toughest neighborhoods of Philadelphia.

There were only two wholesome influences beside her grandmother: the church and music. Both her aunts could sing, and they put Ethel in a church show when she was still just a child, billing her as "Baby Star." She recited and sang a ditty about "dying for someone to love me." The church audience brought her back for encore after encore, and she made what she called "a sensational success" in her first appearance.

When Ethel was twelve she had a profound religious experience at a revival meeting and became a devoted Catholic for the rest of her life, though she respected Protestant denominations, especially the Methodist and Baptist churches.

Breaking into Vaudeville

Waters didn't originally want to go into show business. Though she sang and danced and loved attending local black vaudeville and club shows whenever she could, her original aspiration was much humbler: "I dreamed of . . . becoming the lady's maid and companion of some wealthy woman who was traveling around the world and would take me with her."

She worked throughout her teens as a chambermaid, washerwoman, and waitress and seemed destined to settle into domestic work. But her life changed on her birthday in either 1914 or 1917 (depending on the source), when she sang at a Halloween party at Jack's Rathskeller in Philadelphia. She went over so well that the vaudeville team of Braxton and Nugent, who happened to be in the house that night, told her they could get her a booking at a theatre in Baltimore.

She was billed as "Sweet Mama Stringbean" because she was so tall and skinny. This will surprise those who know only her later work, when she had put on a great deal of weight and adopted Earth-mother roles. She brought the house down singing W. C. Handy's "St. Louis Blues," to the point where the paying audience would throw money on the stage when she was she was done. "Low and sweet" is how she described her sound, which was something new in a time when audiences were used to hearing the blues shouted. With this new singing style, coupled with her big eyes and long, lean blossoming figure, Waters presented an appealing novelty.

She later signed with the Theatre Owners Booking Association (T.O.B.A.), known derisively by its poorly treated clients as "Tough on Black Asses." The T.O.B.A. booked black acts into vaudeville houses mainly in the Jim Crow–era South. The shabby theatres, bare-bones accommodations, low pay, and persistent racism by both the managers and the (white) man on the street were balanced by the steady work and the wildly appreciative audiences—not to mention the generous and persistent stage-door johnnies.

Waters made her New York singing debut in 1919, and it led to her cutting some of the earliest recordings of the blues. Edmonds's Cellar in Harlem became her artistic headquarters, and news began to spread of the super-skinny, snake-hipped girl with big eyes, crisp enunciation, and sexy, teasing delivery.

Waters appears to have been bisexual, though she tended to keep her preferences under wraps. For several years in the 1920s she lived with another dancer, Ethel Williams, and they participated in the sub rosa homosexual world of Harlem at the time, becoming known to gay friends as "the two Ethels." However, Waters also married—four times, the first when she was just thirteen—though none of the men proved to be a satisfactory husband.

She continued in the early 1920s to be in demand as a club singer, fronting Fletcher Henderson and Duke Ellington's bands at various times. But she made it her goal to break into the higher-paying "white time" vaudeville venues, as several top-tier black acts had done.

In 1925 she was invited to replace the popular black performer Florence Mills at Sam Salvin's Plantation Club "downtown" at Fiftieth Street and Broadway. On her first night playing to a white audience, Waters was shocked by their muted reaction—at least compared to the noisy appreciation expressed by the black audiences she was used to. She thought she had bombed, but the applause was genuine.

Her understudy was a stylish and ambitious young singer named Josephine Baker, with whom she was constantly in conflict. According to Stephen Bourne's biography *Ethel Waters: Stormy Weather*, Baker spurned Waters for doing what she called "mammy from Alabammy" songs—not the last time she'd be criticized by other blacks for buying into what were considered stereotyped images. Both women chafed under the restrictions of American show business. In 1925, Caroline Dudley Reagan came to Waters with the idea of organizing an all-black revue in bohemian Paris. When Waters demanded too high a salary, Baker jumped at the opportunity, leading to her starmaking role in what became *La revue négre*.

Glenda Eloise Gill observed, "At no point in her career did Waters have the adulation given to Baker and Mills. Nor was she as beloved as Lena Horne. But she appealed to a multiracial audience."

Waters eventually made her own trips to Paris and London in the late 1920s, enjoying tremendous success at the London Palladium. But first, Broadway had finally beckoned.

Broadway and Film

Waters appeared in several all-black revues, *Africana* (1927), *Lew Leslie's Blackbirds* (several editions, 1927–30), and *Rhapsody in Black* (1931), singing her blues and dancing. During this period she also made her movie debut in the film musical *On with the Show!* (1929), singing "Am I Blue?" and "Birmingham Bertha" while wearing a bandanna and literally carrying a basket full of cotton. Opportunities and offers poured in from every direction, but during the early years of the Depression she settled in Harlem and made the Cotton Club her artistic home.

Waters's club career reached its zenith with the 1933 *Cotton Club Parade*, in which she introduced the Harold Arlen/Ted Koehler torch song "Stormy Weather." Swells lined up outside the Harlem nightspot to see her, and the club even relaxed its whites-only policy so her friends could attend. Standing under a blue-lit lamppost, Waters put her heart into the song about how it "keeps raining all the time" since her man went away. Twelve encores greeted the number, which Waters recorded just a few weeks later, earning herself a rare crossover hit. In the ensuing years many other singers interpreted the song, one of Arlen's best-known aside from "Over the Rainbow." It later became associated with Lena Horne, who sang it in the movie of the same title. But it was written for Waters.

As Thousands Cheer

Among those who flocked to Ethel Waters's shows was Broadway composer Irving Berlin. He resolved to write her a part in his new Broadway revue, *As Thousands Cheer*. This was easier said than done because the stage in the early 1930s was still largely segregated. A few black performers appeared side by side with whites over the years, notably Bert Williams in the *Ziegfeld Follies*. But that was only because someone in power, like a Ziegfeld, had the clout to decree exemptions to the taboo. Berlin resolved to do the same. On those terms Waters agreed to leave the Cotton Club and join him at the Music Box Theatre, though she was billed beneath the three white stars, Marilyn Miller, Clifton Webb, and Helen Broderick.

As Thousands Cheer was envisioned as a "living newspaper," with different scenes bringing to life the fashion section, the comics section, et cetera.

One of Waters's assignments was the weather page, under the headline "Heat Wave Hits New York," for which Berlin wrote another classic, "Heat Wave." The number gave Waters a chance to lead the chorus in a Caribbean ode to hot weather (and hot blood). She was also assigned some international news, playing a Josephine Baker–like expatriate black performer in Paris who misses her home and sings the bluesy "Harlem on My Mind."

But Berlin and librettist Moss Hart resolved to break with tradition and confront some of the serious news of the day in the scene headlined "Unknown Negro Lynched by Frenzied Mob." With the song "Supper Time," Waters played a mother who is going through the motions of serving dinner to her children with no idea how to tell them, or how to deal with the fact, that her husband has been murdered. Berlin and Hart came under intense pressure to cut the inflammatory scene, which was considered inappropriate for a Broadway musical revue. The writers insisted that it stay in, and Waters poured into it all the pain and injustice she'd ever seen or felt.

"Supper Time" proved to be a sensation and became one of Waters's signature songs, one that was demanded at concert after concert for the next two decades. It was a high point, not only of musical theatre, but of American drama in the 1930s. Unlike Hart's previous work, it dealt with a serious subject in a serious way, without a wink or a silly name. It was drama, and Waters proved she was not just a singer, but a fine actress.

Mamba's Daughters

One of Waters's greatest successes—and the one that apparently gave her the greatest satisfaction—was a nonmusical drama called *Mamba's Daughters* (1939), by Dorothy and DuBose Heyward. *Mamba's Daughters* tracks the tribulations of three generations of black women, focusing on the character of Hagar, a hulking, inarticulate woman single-mindedly devoted to her daughter, Lissa. The play's villain rapes and then tries to blackmail Lissa and destroy her singing career. In the climactic scene, Mamba confronts the attacker and uses her physical power to strangle him to death.

Waters wrote in her autobiography, "In Hagar was all my mother's shock, bewilderment, and insane rage at being hurt and her fierce, primitive religion. . . . She was all Negro women lost and lonely in the white man's antagonistic world."

Mamba's Daughters was staged by Guthrie McClintic at the top-line Empire Theatre, where Waters became the first black woman to be billed over the title on a Broadway marquee for a drama. On opening night, she wrote in *His Eye Is on the Sparrow*, she sat in the star dressing room, in the place where giants like Helen Hayes, Lynn Fontanne, and Ethel Barrymore had sat, and she thought, "That was the night of my professional life . . . the night I'd been born for, and God was in the room with me."

When the show earned raves from all but the *New York Times*, Waters's show business friends took out a full-page ad in that paper and extolled the brilliance of her performance. It ran 162 performances on Broadway and enjoyed a successful tour.

Mamba's Daughters was never filmed, but Waters played the mother of a light-skinned girl trying to pass as white in the film *Pinky*.

Cabin in the Sky

Of all Waters's musical theatre projects, the one best remembered today is 1940's *Cabin in the Sky*, partly because it was turned into a popular wartime film by MGM.

Waters played Petunia Jackson, long-suffering wife of Little Joe Jackson, an inveterate drinker, gambler, and all-around sinner whose transgressions make her fear for his very soul. As it turns out, she has good reason. Satan is personally working overtime to lead him into temptation. Answering Petunia's prayers, God Himself steps in to even things out. The musical was set in the Deep South and had an Uncle Remus folktale quality, reflecting the fact that the whole action takes place in one of Little Joe's dreams. Once again, though, these were black characters created mainly by white writers and supervised by white directors. Waters acted it with as much legitimacy as she could muster, which was plenty.

Cabin in the Sky opened October 25, 1940, and ran six months, one of the biggest successes for composer Vernon Duke and lyricist John La Touche (with Ted Fetter). The best-known song from the show is the swinging "Taking a Chance on Love," but audiences also got to enjoy such southern-style melodies as "Honey in the Honeycomb," "Love Turned the Light Out," and the title song.

The 1943 film version was the first movie musical directed by Vincente Minnelli, who threw in nearly every major black star the studio had under contract, including Lena Horne, Louis Armstrong, John "Bubbles" Sublett, and Butterfly McQueen, plus Duke Ellington and his Orchestra! Despite that competition, Waters more than held her own and is remembered best from the film, mainly for her widely smiling performance of "Taking a Chance on Love" punctuated by an endearing little kiss when she sings "Mr. Rabbit, of course you better kiss your foot good-bye!"

She also sang the interpolated Harold Arlen song "Happiness Is a Thing Called Joe," which was nominated for an Oscar.

Talent and Temper

A word should be said here about Ethel Waters's fearsome reputation, especially with other black female performers. Her backstage clashes with Billie Holiday, Lena Horne, and others became legendary. Waters had a trip-wire temper that could explode at the slightest gesture of disrespect, real or imagined.

Waters always spoke her mind, something many people in positions of power in that period found hard to take from a black woman. Her talent earned her many friends, and her attitude earned her a fair number of enemies. People thought they could abuse her with impunity but then discovered they'd swatted a hornet's nest. Waters always believed that the one in the position of power was she, because she had the talent. It's a lot easier to get money than to get talent.

She always found a better range of interesting projects on the stage, and she returned to it again and again.

The Member of the Wedding

Waters struggled to find work of any kind for most of the late 1940s. She often dashed off for brief bookings far from New York when she could get them.

This long dry period came to an end in 1950 when Waters played her last and greatest Broadway role, Berenice Sadie Brown in Carson McCullers's *The Member of the Wedding*. Berenice is a domestic who cares for two children, volcanic twelve-year-old Frankie (Julie Harris) and her bespectacled and bullied cousin John Henry (Brandon DeWilde). There isn't much plot—Frankie's emotions have been thrown into turmoil by the impending marriage of her older brother, who, of course, won't allow her to come on the honeymoon.

Part of Frankie's upset comes from the simple change in her family's routine as her brother departs. But the play touches on deeper concerns. It illustrates Frankie's first rush of understanding about the transitory nature of life. Waters, on the other hand, is the symbol of calm wisdom, of profound inner peace. Her suffering, especially from the death of her beloved husband, has burned away all the nonsense inside her and left her soul clear.

The play's climax comes when Berenice is comforting a sobbing Frankie after an outburst. She begins to sing the hymn "His Eye Is on the Sparrow," which would seem to come out of left field but which is actually sublimely perfect for the scene. The song is saying that God is not just watching everything, but that everything happening in the world is actually important to God and worthy of his attention. It can be a very comforting notion. And Waters conveys the sense that she knows this fact firsthand.

It became Waters's new signature song. She used it as the title of her autobiography published the following year. And it's all the more remarkable that it came from a person who, at that point in her life, was anything but peaceful and patient. But the record shows that as she aged, Ethel Waters transformed into someone resembling Berenice.

Despite a luminous performance that was (luckily) captured in the Oscar-nominated 1952 film, Waters never got such a strong property again.

Just as her stage career was coming to an end, she had one more brief, bright moment in the public eye, achieving stardom in the new medium of television. From October 1950 to April 1952, Waters became the first black woman to star in a TV sitcom, playing the title role in *Beulah*, chronicling the domestic adventures of a white family and their sassy black housekeeper. Waters was almost immediately criticized for embracing one of the archest of stereotypes, especially given her history of groundbreaking roles. Once again she mitigated some of the worst aspects of the character and situation, but people saw only what wasn't done.

After she left *Beulah* she continued to do guest appearances on television and in concert halls, and she even made one third-rate film, *Carib Gold*, with the young Cicely Tyson. But Waters had grown tired of fighting for increasingly scarce bookings. Still only in her late fifties, she had entered the long twilight of her career.

In its place, she turned more and more to religion, and in 1957 she joined the Rev. Billy Graham's crusades and spent most of the turbulent 1960s singing in gospel choirs behind him as he preached.

"The stage was my livelihood," she said in a recorded interview. "But the Lord has made me rich since then. I'm not talking about financial. . . . I have found in Him everything I need."

After she was diagnosed with uterine cancer in 1976 she was cared for by friends until her death on September 1, 1977, at age seventy-six, eighty, or eighty-one, depending on whose count you believe.

Leaving a crowd in Chicago in the mid-1970s, she told them, "I want to see you all in heaven. I'll be looking for you."

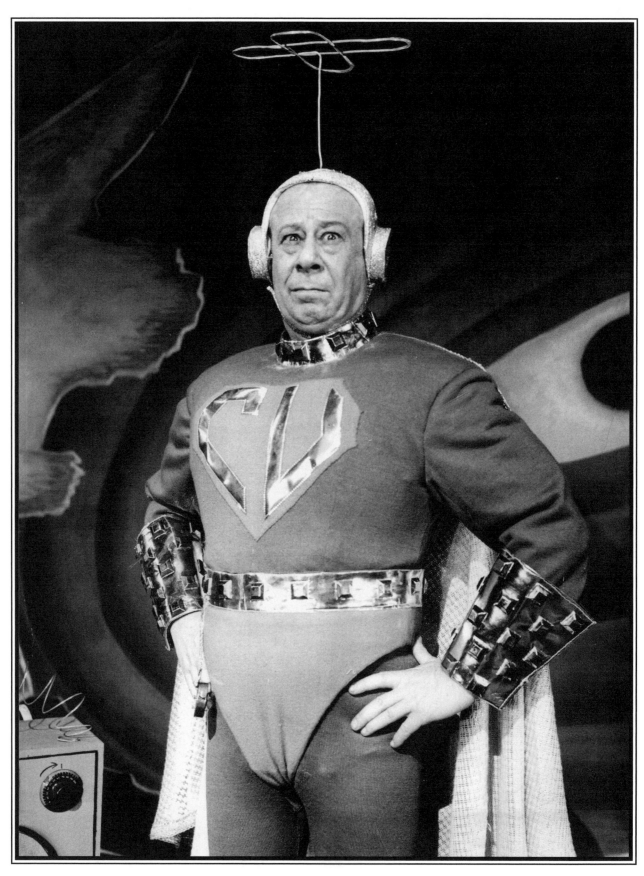

Bert Lahr as Captain Universe in *Two on the Aisle* (1951). PHOTOFEST

BERT LAHR
Be a Lion, Not a Mowess

Bert Lahr had nothing and everything going for him, as far as looks were concerned. He was short, with a mass of unruly hair (later he was completely bald), an impossible accent, and a goofy, almost deformed face led by a nose like a meatball. Yet with the help of a voice that he could twist into a hundred bizarre shapes, Lahr spun all his minuses into pluses. Still, he was a sui generis comedian who found himself unable to make the transition to film and TV like so many of his contemporaries, and he struggled to stay fully employed in a business that was never quite sure what to do with him.

Most people who had been in a hit as big as the film of *The Wizard of Oz* wouldn't have had that problem. But Lahr, who was immortalized by his role as the Cowardly Lion, was also unrecognizable under all that makeup. Other movie stars were mobbed by adoring fans. Lahr could hobble down the street or stand in a bus stop and no one suspected they were in the presence of one of history's great clowns.

Onstage, Lahr exploded in a trademark series of accents, faces, and voices, howling, screeching, barking, and growling his way through a series of comedy parts that made him the top baggy-pants comic of his time, which was saying a lot. However, his offstage apparently involved intense insecurity, bouts of deep depression, marriage to a woman who wound up in a mental institution, and perpetual financial problems. We know about all the latter mainly because Lahr was also the subject of one of the best showbiz biographies ever written, *Notes on a Cowardly Lion*, by his son, John Lahr, who became a theatre critic and writer of considerable skill for *The New Yorker* magazine.

For the rest of Lahr's career, people would criticize him for making his roles sound too much like the Cowardly Lion. They had it backward, of course; the Lion's "Puddem up! *Puddem up!*" argot was just the way Lahr always sounded.

He evolved a whole repertoire of strange noises and gestures that were uniquely his own. When playing at being hoity-toity he would adopt a twittery British accent, rolling his r's and batting his eyes. When singing a note he wanted to embellish, he would deploy a comically exaggerated vibrato that could shake his entire upper frame.

When feeling bellicose, he would snarl and woof like a cornered dog, a bit of shtick he used, incongruously, when playing the Cowardly Lion, in the scene where he chases Toto.

When frightened (by danger) or amazed (by female pulchritude), he would emit half-strangled gurgles of terror: "Gnong! Gnong! Gnong!" In fact, comic terror became his métier. Casting him as the Cowardly Lion was a stroke of genius, because he spent the entire first half of his career honing every bit of business that he would use to such perfect effect on the Yellow Brick Road.

★

Irving Lahrheim was born August 13, 1895, in the Yorkville section of Manhattan, then a working-class neighborhood. His parents were poor German-Jewish immigrants, and his father worked as an upholsterer and interior designer. The family moved to the then-bucolic Bronx around the time he reached puberty, but he had already become addicted to going to see vaudeville shows whenever he could scrape together twenty-five cents for a balcony ticket. He was a poor student and often delinquent. His only happy memory of his school days was an eighth-grade class show in which he sang and imitated his father's German accent, which was known in vaudeville as a "Dutch" accent—very popular at the time.

Lahr later told his son and biographer John that after the show a teacher predicted, "If you don't go on the stage, you'll probably go to jail."

When low grades caused school officials to hold him back, he abandoned school (at age fifteen) and went to work in a series of low-level jobs as errand boy or stock clerk. Life outside school was tougher than he'd imagined.

At this crossroads moment in his life, a friend alerted him that he'd heard a producer was organizing an all-kids vaudeville act. Lahr scampered down to auditions, and he was hired to play the "sissy" in an act called the Seven Frolics (though still using his "Dutch" accent), which toured the Loew's circuit of vaudeville theatres starting in 1910. He worked in a series of these "school" acts with names like Nine Crazy Kids, May Party, the Boys and Girls of Avenue B—which showed unruly kids acting out in class. His son wrote, "On stage, Lahr was the most frivolous of all, the loudest howler, the wildest acrobat, the merriest Merry Andrew." When he got too old to play a kid any longer, he tried establishing himself as a solo act, though without much luck.

In 1914 he was scouted by the Columbia Burlesque Wheel and spent most of the next few years in a thick mustache and putty nose. As Green put it, "he scampered, snorted, bellowed, growled, tumbled, ogled and grimaced his way from one end of the country to the other." He was especially adept at taking "bumpers"—pratfalls in which he would slap the stage as he fell to make it sound like he'd hit much harder than he had. A 1951 *Time* magazine profile reported that his left wrist was permanently enlarged from the effects of this activity. "And though he remained a loud, low comedian," *Time* said, "he labored for the sympathy of the audience and concentrated more and more on perfecting an air of bewilderment and insane incompetence, the eternal fall guy with one foot in his mouth and the other poised over a banana peel."

This was showbiz university, and Lahr graduated summa cum laude, rising to the enviable position of "top banana," the star comedian.

It was during this period that his eye fell on a pretty dancer named Mercedes Delpino. At first they ran into each other only when they were booked at the same theatre. Then they tried getting bookings together and soon were living together. Lahr was terribly insecure about his grotesque looks, especially compared with the soubrette's radiant beauty.

In 1922 they formed the team of Lahr and Mercedes and graduated to vaudeville's Orpheum Circuit, performing a classic beauty-and-the-beast act called "What's the Idea?" for most of the next five years. The act, which was constantly honed and perfected, consisted of Mercedes standing on a street corner performing a fetching dance. She's interrupted by a red-nosed and apparently soused police officer (Lahr), who proceeds to berate her in comic fashion while clearly appreciative of her finer points: "Shtopppppp! What's the idea? What's the idea of massagin' the atmosphere? . . . The second I saw ya I said to myself, 'This has got to stop at once!' So I watched ya for ten minutes."

She demands to know what she's doing wrong, and he replies that she's breaking the law. "Nineteenth Amendment, Section Six, Upper Seven, which says it's a public nonsense to shimmy or vibrate any part of the human astronomy. And it's punishable by the fine of one year or imprisonment for two years of E Pluribus Aluminum."

The act degenerates into a scuffle, dancing, and a duet before he discovers that she's actually his long-lost niece.

Broadway Debut

In 1927, fellow variety performer Harry Delmar organized *Harry Delmar's Revels*, another of the myriad *Follies*-inspired revues, showcasing the best acts he knew from vaudeville. Now in his early thirties, Lahr at last made his Broadway debut, performing "What's the Idea?" and some of his classic bits, plus a ridiculous song composed for him by the team of Harold Arlen and E. Y. "Yip" Harburg, who would later write *The Wizard of Oz*. Called "Song of the Woodman," it had Lahr in a lumberjack shirt waxing philosophical about his chosen profession in exaggerated macho style. Once in a while, from the wings, he would take a blast of wood chips in the face. It was so nonsensically funny that it became one of his signature pieces. *The Revels* lasted just four months, but it was enough to get Lahr noticed on the Mainstem.

Hold Everything!

Legendary 1920s producers Alex Aarons and Vinton Freedley, who had showcased Fred and Adele Astaire and other major talents, concluded that Lahr's pug-dog face, wiry body, and gift for physical comedy made him the perfect candidate for a musical comedy they were marshalling to take advantage of the prize-fighting craze inspired by the 1927 Jack Dempsey/Gene Tunney bout.

Hold Everything! was the story of broken-down fighter Gink Schiner, who somehow actually wins a championship bout, even though he has bet against himself. Lahr opened in front of a celebrity-packed crowd and afterward wandered around backstage with typical insecurity, wondering whether his first starring role on Broadway would also be his last. As *Time* magazine later told it, "[The] next day gritty, garish, gold-lined Broadway was Bert Lahr's street. Lahr was a smash. Lahr was a sensation. NEW COMEDY KING CROWNED, read a *Journal* headline. Suddenly the headwaiters, the cabbies, the reporters, the speakeasy bartenders all knew Bert Lahr."

After the show's 409-performance run, Lahr went back to playing his drunken-cop act in vaudeville, but now he was playing the Palace for $4,500 a week.

Lahr married Mercedes in 1929, over the objections of his parents because she wasn't Jewish. It wasn't a happy marriage. Their son, Herbert, was born the same year as their marriage, but Lahr's budding Broadway career had meant the end of Mercedes and Lahr, and he wasn't around much. Delpino's eccentricities soon descended into obsessive jealousy and then into mental illness. Lahr eventually had to have her institutionalized.

Flying High

One of Lahr's biggest musical comedy hits was the De Sylva, Brown, and Henderson musical *Flying High* (1930), which capitalized on the airplane craze that followed Charles Lindbergh's historic first solo flight across the Atlantic Ocean.

Lahr played hapless airplane mechanic Rusty Krause, who wins a transcontinental flying race when one of the experimental planes he's working on takes off with him aboard and he's forced to pilot it himself, with the help of costar Kate Smith, who climbs out on a wing and makes repairs in flight! It seems he doesn't know how to land the darn thing, and pure comic terror keeps him flying to victory. He was able to "Gnong! Gnong! Gnong!" to his heart's content, and the audience adored it. *Flying High* ran 355 performances.

One of the funniest scenes in *Flying High* took place in a doctor's office, in which the Prohibition-era Lahr is asked to give a specimen but apparently has never heard that expression before. He thinks the doc wants some bootleg hooch from his hip flask. He fills the specimen jar and hands it to the startled medic, apologizing, "Here ya go, Doc. I could only spare a quart."

The show was filmed in 1931. Lahr had made his first comedy short in 1929, but *Flying High* was his first comedy feature in the starring role, with comedienne Charlotte Greenwood replacing Smith as his wing person.

The advent of inexpensive entertainment mass media like radio and talking pictures in the late 1920s meant the death of vaudeville. Many of the old vaudeville theatres were converted to show movies—and many of the old vaudeville performers became film actors. The exodus to Hollywood was spurred by the onset of the Great Depression. Lahr went in the 1930s, as well. Between Broadway assignments he made films from time to time throughout the 1930s, including a series of comedy shorts from 1933 to 1937, often paired with petite starlet Sally Starr.

The late 1930s saw him back in features, including a 1938 Shirley Temple musical, *Just*

Around the Corner, and Universal's *Merry Go Round of 1938*, re-creating his classic "Song of the Woodman," one of his best non–*Wizard of Oz* film performances. In *Merry Go Round* he played one of four crusty vaudevillians who promise a dying trapeze artist that they will raise her young daughter.

Hot-Cha!

By 1932, master impresario Florenz Ziegfeld Jr. was at the end of his rope, his fortune decimated by the 1929 stock market collapse and public taste having turned against his immoderate style of show business. Deeply in debt, he decided to roll the dice once more for a hit on Broadway. He gathered the best talent he could muster, including songwriters Lew Brown and Ray Henderson, *Follies* set designer Joseph Urban, costume designer Charles LeMaire, comedian Buddy Rogers, and dancer Eleanor Powell. Set mainly in Mexico, *Hot-Cha!* was designed as a vehicle for sultry singer/dancer Lupe Velez, but Lahr quickly stole what there was of the show. This wasn't a *Follies*-like revue; it was a musical comedy with a libretto by Mark Hellinger and H. S. Kraft, along with Brown and Henderson. It looked great but told a nonsensical story about Alky Schmidt (Lahr), a waiter in a speakeasy who somehow finds himself south of the border trying to break in as a bullfighter. The latter profession gave Lahr ample opportunity to cross his eyes and "Gnong" in terror, but the story and songs were weak.

When the show failed to come through as a smash, Ziegfeld sent Lahr one of his famous backstage telegrams: "Dear Bert, Can't understand why you let show down in second act bull fight scene which cost me fifty thousand. You ruined me completely."

The missive reveals more about Ziegfeld's state of mind than it does about Lahr's performance. The show ran three months and lost more than $100,000. Just over one month later, Ziegfeld was dead, leaving his widow, Billie Burke, a Himalaya of debt. Burke spent the next decade working her way out of that debt, including taking an acting gig alongside Lahr in *The Wizard of Oz*.

In the 1930s, Lahr found his home in the topical musical revues of the time. The best of them was the 1934 show *Life Begins at 8:40*, which had a score partly by Arlen and Harburg, partly by George and Ira Gershwin. Lahr played a half-dozen roles, including "a pompous tea-concert singer gushing at the 'utter, utter, utter loveliness of things,' and getting as a reward a pie in the face." "Chin Up" poked fun at "stiff-upper-lip" British aristocrats (a favorite Lahr target). In crisply spoken lines, an entire manor-born family reveals disgrace over gambling debts, infidelity, and illegitimacy, and each member calmly commits suicide for "honor of family," including Lahr himself, until no one is left but the butler.

Also in the cast was the limber "eccentric" dancer Ray Bolger. The next time the two of them sang an Arlen and Harburg tune together, it would be five years later and they would be heading "off to see the Wizard."

The Wizard of Oz

In 1939 Lahr was cast in the role of his career—the Cowardly Lion in a musical adaptation of L. Frank Baum's children's classic *The Wizard of Oz*. Though not strictly a Broadway show, the film was written mainly by Broadway talent and populated mainly with Broadway and vaudeville actors, right down to the Munchkins. The film proved to be a touchtone for everything else that happened in Lahr's career.

He created a richly detailed character who demonstrated aggression, then terror, then sorrow, then loyalty and resolve, and finally, indeed, courage. He also deployed a detailed inventory of odd sounds, physical tics, and strange little habits—some from vaudeville, some new. He compulsively pets the tuft at the end of his tail and uses it to dab his tears when he weeps, which is plenty. Then there's the wruffing noise he makes when he's first trying to frighten Dorothy and her friends. He sounds more like a Pomeranian puppy than a lion. There's also his machine-gun vibrato on "If I were King of the fore-e-e-e-e-e-est," which was a beautifully tailored specialty number by his old *Harry Delmar's Revels* pals Arlen and Harburg. Harburg filled the song with Lahr-esque turns of phrase and accommodated his New York accent in "If I Only Had the Nerve," making his quest not for courage per se, but instead for "da noive."

Making the film was physical torture for Lahr, whose entire leonine head, face, and shoulders had to be constructed anew each morning by the makeup staff, making it impossible for him to eat a normal meal between dawn and dinner. That face-obliterating makeup job was his fortune and his curse. As mentioned previously, everyone in Hollywood knew who the Cowardly Lion was, but nobody there seemed to know who Bert Lahr was. He was both too familiar and not familiar enough. It became difficult to build a movie career because no one could recognize him from his greatest role.

DuBarry Was a Lady

The Wizard of Oz was released in August 1939. On December 6 of that same year, Lahr was back on Broadway with his biggest musical yet, *DuBarry Was a Lady,* with a score by Cole Porter and a top-drawer costar, Ethel Merman. Lahr played a men's room attendant having trouble with his girlfriend (Merman), a nightclub singer who's been flirting with another guy. When he accidentally downs a drugged drink intended for his rival, he winds up in an elaborate musical fantasy where he is King Louis XV of France and Merman is his mistress, Mme. La Comtesse du Barry. Lahr got to do his patented hoity-toity accent and generally have a ball lampooning royalty and all its trappings. His songs included the absurdly prim "It Ain't Etiquette," the mildly salacious "But in the Morning, No," and the showstopper of the evening, "Friendship," in which he and Merman pretend to pledge amity forever while actually insulting each other extravagantly. It's one of the most elegantly passive-aggressive songs ever written.

Lahr would often look back on *DuBarry Was a Lady* as the kind of show he did best but that became harder and harder to find.

In 1940 Lahr took the painful step of divorcing his institutionalized wife (though he continued to support her) so he could marry Mildred Schroeder, with whom he had been in love for several years. They would have two children together, John and Jane.

Trying in vain to cultivate a movie career, Lahr made only two Broadway appearances during the 1940s. *The Seven Lively Arts* (1944) was Billy Rose's attempt to stage a big all-star revue in the Ziegfeld tradition. The revue was thronged with talent, including Cole Porter writing the score and a cast that included comedienne Beatrice Lillie, singer Dolores Gray, and bandleader Benny Goodman. But critics found the show not quite lively enough, and it lasted just five months.

After the war, Lahr returned with *Burlesque*, a successful comedy about the offstage life of a "top banana," which ran a year.

Two on the Aisle

By the late 1940s, they just weren't writing stage revues like they did in the old days. In 1951, however, Lahr got to put on the baggy pants once more for *Two on the Aisle*, an old-fashioned comic revue with more or less topical skits (written by former members of the Revuers, Betty Comden and Adolph Green), pretty girls, bouncy songs, and specialty comedy spots, with the material tailored for his unique style, notably "The Clown," a mock-serious nonsense song that let him do his crazy vibrato, goofy laugh, and eccentric rhymes.

His costar was the glamorous Dolores Gray, who had hit stardom in London, originating *Annie Get Your Gun* there, and then had appeared with Lahr in *The Seven Lively Arts*. Unfortunately, each of them considered themselves the headliner of *Two on the Aisle*, and they clashed from the start. Despite their offstage animosity, they duetted amiably on "Vaudeville Ain't Dead" and "Catch Our Act at the Met," in which they summarized opera plots in two or three phrases.

The material was good but lacked the spark Lahr had hoped for. The kind of variety show represented by *Two on the Aisle* was already going out of style, or, at any rate, moving to television. *Two on the Aisle* opened July 19, 1951, and ran 276 performances.

Waiting for Godot

In 1956 Lahr, increasingly desperate for work, took on a hopeless project that, in retrospect, has come to be regarded as one of his greatest works of genius. He was engaged to play the neurotic but ever hopeful Estragon in the U.S. premiere of Samuel Beckett's existential masterpiece *Waiting for Godot*. It's set in a barren wasteland where two tattered men, Vladimir (Tom Ewell) and Estragon, are biding their time waiting for the arrival of a third man, named Godot. It's never explained who these men are, why they are waiting, or what Godot's arrival would mean to them. It's completely abstract; they're just waiting. And in doing so, their waiting becomes all the waiting ever done by anyone anywhere.

Lahr admitted that he really didn't know what *Waiting for Godot* was about. But on a certain level the classic clown in him responded to the play's spiritual desolation as clowns have always responded to darkness: with a raspberry.

New York Times critic Brooks Atkinson wrote, "Lahr is an actor in the pantomime tradition who has a thousand ways to move and a hundred ways to grimace in order to make the story interesting and theatrical, and touching, too."

The production debuted at the Coconut Grove Playhouse in Miami, to the utter confusion of Lahr's elderly fans who came to see him. The show's New York press agents glibly advertised it as Lahr's latest laff riot, which only made many audiences, unfamiliar with Beckett's minimalism, feel lost and tricked. Despite a rapturous opening night attended by cognoscenti—"It was the most satisfying moment on stage I ever had," he would tell his son and biographer—the production ran only fifty-nine performances on Broadway. But its reputation grew steadily through the 1960s as critics and audiences became more used to experimental plays, of which *Godot* was a pioneer.

The Beauty Part

S. J. Perelman was one of the legendary *New Yorker* magazine contributors, from the same generation as James Thurber and Dorothy Parker. He was witty and well educated, and his prose was the work of a master craftsman, arch and sarcastic but with an intense love for the absurd—and especially for funny-sounding words. He had written two of the Marx Brothers' most successful films, *Horse Feathers* and *Monkey Business*, and in 1962 he assembled a mélange of his crazy characters into a quilt of a play called *The Beauty Part*, about a young man who sets out in the world to become some kind of artist but who encounters one greedy, self-serving hypocrite after another—all of them played by Lahr.

Perelman's sense of the absurd and his perhaps excessive love of silly names did not translate well from the page to the stage. Scene after scene that "read" as hilarious in the script seemed inert when spoken by actors, even one as accomplished as Lahr.

Lahr struggled to spin flax into gold as he played multiple characters Hyacinth Beddoes Laffoon, Nelson Smedley, Judge Herman J. Rinderbrust, Harry Hubris, and Milo Leotard Allardyce DuPlessis Weatherwax—most of whose comedy began and ended with their monikers. Lahr's silly voices supplied much of whatever laughter there was, along with his bulldog-in-drag looks.

The Beauty Part lasted only eighty-five performances, much to the surprise of Perelman's fans, who concluded that it had been caviar for the masses. However, two off-Broadway revivals and a production at Yale in the 1980s all failed to make a successful stage comedy of the material, though there are still some devoted partisans out there who believe that a great definitive production will someday arrive.

Foxy

In 1962 Lahr was approached to star in what seemed like the perfect project, *Foxy*, a Broadway-musical updating of Ben Jonson's 1606 Jacobean comedy *Volpone*, about a con man who pretends to be dying so he can gain control of everyone's money by promising them to leave his own (nonexistent) fortune to them when he dies.

The location was moved to the Gold Rush–era Canadian Yukon, and Lahr should have sensed trouble coming when the producer, Robert Whitehead, announced that he would conduct the show's tryout at the Canadian Gold Rush Festival in the Yukon's Dawson City. The location made good press but little practical sense. Many audience members had never seen a musical before, and many had never heard of Lahr and didn't know what to make of his peculiar mannerisms—and that was when the show had any audience at all. There simply weren't enough theatergoers in Dawson City to support the planned seven-week tryout. Lahr was not helped by the weak book, courtesy of Ian McLellan Hunter and Ring Lardner Jr., and they objected strenuously when he tried to enliven the proceedings with ad-libs.

Lahr got to wear funny costumes and adopt silly accents, and, in the best-reviewed moment of the show, he appeared to shinny up the proscenium arch to escape a pursuer, with a bear trap on his leg. Howard Taubman in the *New York Times* asked, "Can more be asked for in this vale of crises than to have Bert Lahr back on stage, mugging shamelessly or being as delicate as a viscount at an unexpectedly rowdy lawn party?"

Apparently so. The parts of the show that weren't Lahr were a shambles.

By the time *Foxy* arrived at Broadway's Ziegfeld Theatre on February 16, 1964, it had a splashier design and a new producer (David Merrick), but many of the fundamental problems had not been solved. Merrick, who was mounting *Hello, Dolly!* at the same time, spent very little to promote the show, which closed after seventy-two performances and brought to an end one of the great comic careers on Broadway. As a parting gift, Lahr won the 1964 Tony Award as Best Leading Actor in a Musical.

After the flop of *Foxy*, Lahr never returned to Broadway. What work he found was on television. Two of his appearances were notable. In 1964 he appeared in *Hallmark Hall of Fame*'s hourlong TV adaptation of *The Fantasticks*, which was then in the fourth year of its landmark forty-one-year run. Lahr played Hucklebee, the Boy's father, and sang "Never Say No" with Stanley Holloway.

TV viewers from this period will also recall a series of amusing commercials he shot for Lay's potato chips, in which Lahr, appearing in various silly costumes, tried with a comic lack of success to eat only one of the snacks, thus illustrating the slogan "Betcha can't eat just one." The commercials nearly always ended with Lahr engulfing one of the chips with a thunderous crunch.

It's fitting that Lahr's last role had him in baggy pants once more. He played a burlesque top banana in the film *The Night They Raided Minsky's*. And it was while he was working late into the night in a cold, damp studio trying to finish *Minsky's* that he fell into his final illness, described to the public as pneumonia but, according to his son John, was the final crisis of cancer that had been eating at him for years. Lahr died at the hospital on December 4, 1967.

Ethel Merman as Edith in the film *We're Not Dressing* (1934). PHOTOFEST

ETHEL MERMAN
The Merm

And now, of course, the Merm.

There is no question that in her later years she became a very scary old lady. But put aside that image and meet the young Merman, the one who first became a star.

Imagine 1929 Ethel: slim and sparkly-eyed, like a living Erté drawing. But she was also tough and wiry and full of pep (a highly valued quality in the 1920s). Her bold voice became the voice of a generation of women who were cutting loose. It landed like a trumpet call for America's first generation of independent young urban females.

Nearly all of Broadway's great songwriters lined up to create material for this amazing creature. The Gershwins gave her *Girl Crazy*, Cole Porter gave her *Anything Goes*, Irving Berlin gave her *Annie Get Your Gun*, and Leonard Bernstein and Stephen Sondheim gave her *Gypsy*. And don't forget that the part of Dolly Gallagher Levi in *Hello, Dolly!* (by Jerry Herman) was written for her (though Carol Channing ultimately got to open *Dolly*).

Ergo, we can conclude that there was something in Merman that did not survive on television and in the movies—two media that just could never find a place for her.

Back again to that brass section of a voice. It was almost operatic in the amount of air it was able to set vibrating. Listening to her big notes was a physical experience. Merman may have emitted more vocal decibels than any human being who ever lived, auctioneers and hog-callers included. Opera singers took long rests. Merman played all eight performances week after week and then jumped to the next project.

Did her voice turn into a foghorn in later years? As we know, yes. Did she start to look like a creature from another planet? Harsh, but sadly accurate. Did she really do that disco album of her old hits? Let's just look away.

Some bright stars die young, like Marilyn Miller or George Gershwin. So tragic. But there's a separate kind of tragedy that accrues to the opposite, the star who outlives her or his era.

And how will some of our contemporary and recent stars look when they are seventy or eighty? Let's hope they look as human as Merman did.

★

Ethel Agnes Zimmermann was born in Astoria, Queens, on January 16. The month and day are not in question, but the year has been reported variously as 1908, 1909, 1910, and 1912. The earliest date appears to have been the correct one, and her centennial was celebrated in 2008. She lived with her folks, Edward and Agnes Zimmermann, in her grandmother's house on Fourth Avenue, which is significant because just two blocks away stood the Famous Players–Lansky studio, one of the world's first movie factories in the era before the American film industry fled the changeable New York weather for the steady sun of Hollywood. In the early years of World War I, Ethel was one of the neighborhood kids who used to gather at the studio entrance to watch the stars, mainly moonlighting from starring roles on Broadway, roll in and out in their fancy cars.

Ethel was determined to be a star, too. Her father, an accountant, would encourage her to sing and would accompany her on the piano. She did her first public singing in the church choir at Holy Redeemer Episcopal in Astoria. Her folks took her to the movies, and a family friend even took her to see vaudeville at the Palace Theatre in Times Square. She learned from the best performers of the day and tried to copy them when she got home.

Her self-taught extroverted singing style was evident from the start, as was demand for her services as a singer at her father's Masonic lodge, at neighborhood social events, and, after World War I began, for servicemen at army camps around the metropolitan area, escorted by her watchful mom. At age nine her specialty was a number titled "Since Maggie Dooley did the Hooley Hooley," and she became a favorite of the men in khaki. Soldiers appreciate firepower, and Merman had it. In the days before electronic amplification, a singer with a loud voice was appreciated all the way to the last row of the balcony because she could be heard clearly there.

How did she do it? Merman mastered the singing technique known as "belting." Most trained women singers have what's known as a "chest" voice or ordinary singing voice but then also have what's known as a "head" voice, similar to the male falsetto but with a great deal more power that allows them to hit those soaring ethereal high notes. Barbara Cook and Julie Andrews were justly renowned for the beauty and purity of their head voices. Merman, however, specialized in pushing her chest voice higher and louder than usual—a technique known as "belting" for the extra diaphragm power it requires.

In his memoirs, *Pavarotti: My Own Story*, opera singer Luciano Pavarotti had a technical analysis: "One of the things that makes Ethel Merman's voice so remarkable is that she has no *passagio*; her voice is all one register, she never has to shift gears, but can sing right to the top of her range in the exact same vocal quality that she has with the middle or lower notes."

Merman never fussed about such things. She just sang out. There was something about her brashness that audiences found very appealing. There was something very American about it, and in the years following World War I, when America was finding its voice for the first time in many ways, it seemed just right for the times. It wasn't an opera or operetta voice, which was the prevailing "approved" technique of the time. And Merman hadn't yet developed the wobbly vibrato of her later years. People compared her voice to a trumpet; later Cole Porter would write for her the song "Blow, Gabriel, Blow" to take advantage of the sound.

During her teenage years in the 1920s she began singing in nightclubs, and while her parents didn't object to the singing per se, they were wary of show business as a steady career for a respectable young lady and insisted she develop secretarial skills. Upon graduation from William Cullen Bryant High School in Long Island City, she worked for a time as a stenographer at a factory, taking singing gigs nights and weekends at clubs and speakeasies, gaining some recognition as the headliner at Les Ambassadeurs in Manhattan. She also dropped the first syllable and last letter of her last name so it would fit more comfortably on a marquee. Ethel Zimmermann had become Ethel Merman. She blossomed as a woman and as a performer. Added to her clarion voice were shapely legs that she displayed in daringly short skirts and an abundant bosom she displayed in low-cut tops. It was a package that bookers found hard to resist.

Helped by manager and music arranger Al Siegel, she moved into vaudeville work and in the fall of 1930, at the tender age of twenty-two, made a stunning trio of debuts that would be the envy of all the young performers of her generation. In September 1930 she took her first bow at New York's Palace Theatre, where she had gazed longingly at the stage from the other direction not so many years earlier.

At the time of her Palace debut, she was already in rehearsals for her Broadway debut, which came on October 14, 1930. Producer Vinton Freedley had caught her act earlier that year at the Brooklyn Paramount Theatre and had introduced her to the songwriting Gershwin brothers. They had just the part for her in their new musical, *Girl Crazy*.

In December 1930 she also made her film debut in the musical *Follow the Leader* with Ed Wynn and Ginger Rogers. But of the three close-packed debuts, *Girl Crazy* was one that opened the door to Ethel's future. It was one of the greatest single Broadway debuts by anyone ever, a beautiful collaboration of top talents. George and Ira handed her the trickily syncopated song "I Got Rhythm," and Merman wrapped her carbon-steel vocal cords right around it. If you look at the lyric on a page, it's just a list of good things in a young woman's life, things like romance, leisure, and dreams, capped by the phrase "Who could ask for anything more?" It looks like a gentle little feel-good ballad. But in George's and Ethel's hands, it turned into a rousing skyrocket of a song.

Merman's manager, Siegel, is credited with the career-making idea of her holding the "I" of the title phrase for the entire sixteen-bar second verse, a feat that seems scarcely credible today. By the time she'd finish belting the note, the audience was just as out of breath as she was. It was the biggest single note in Broadway history.

"I Got Rhythm" was Merman's second number in *Girl Crazy*. The first was the comic torch song "Sam and Delilah." As Merman biographer Bob Thomas observed in *I've Got Rhythm*, "'Sam and Delilah' drew a huge response. 'I Got Rhythm' brought down the house."

Audiences demanded encores, and Merman was happy to give them. Reviews the day after opening were ecstatic. It was clear that a new star was born and had demonstrated a lusty first cry. Merman soon parted ways with Siegel over money, but he had successfully put her right where she wanted to be: on top. She stayed there for the next thirty years.

Anything Goes

Broadway, however, still treasured Merman and was about to award her the starring role in one of the greatest musicals of the 1930s, Cole Porter's *Anything Goes*. Producers Alex Aarons and Vinton Freedley had been responsible for many of the great musical hits of the 1920s, showcasing and promoting the careers of the some of the era's biggest stars. By 1934, however, they were suffering financially along with the rest of the country. To improve their fortunes, Freedley conceived the idea of a show about a bunch of society swells aboard a luxury liner. P. G. Wodehouse was to supply the book and Cole Porter the songs. For stars, he and his partner rounded up the *Of Thee I Sing* team of William Gaxton and Victor Moore, plus Merman.

Librettists Howard Lindsay and Russel Crouse concocted a plot about a playboy (Gaxton) who stows away aboard a luxury liner to be with his sweetheart, who's been sent abroad by her parents, who disapprove of him. Merman played former holy roller Reno Sweeney, who now does rousing nightclub shows.

For many years Reno stood as Merman's definitive performance. On one hand she got to ring the rafters with the gospel number "Blow, Gabriel, Blow." She got to play comedy with one of Porter's best "list" songs, "You're the Top." She also got to introduce one of Porter's best-known torch songs, "I Get a Kick Out of You," which is both an ode to a handsome fella and a lament for a brassy gal, as the handsome fella is more interested in the more traditionally girly heroine.

The success of *Anything Goes* cemented a friendship and collaboration between Merman and Porter that would last a decade and produce one hit show after another. Though Porter was aristocratic where Merman was working-class, he admired the fact that she enunciated clearly and loudly, enabling even the folks in the cheapest seats to hear every word of his complex, tongue-twisting, and witty lyrics in an age before electronic amplification was permitted in legitimate theatres.

She liked the fact that he gave her plenty to play. His sly, bawdy double entendres were perfect for her style and suited her offstage sense of humor. He created for her a series of characters later described by John S. Wilson as "brassy, classy and tough as a nail."

It was a match born in practicality but made in heaven.

Red, Hot and Blue!

The success of *Anything Goes* tempted Merman to try for a repeat with more or less the same team. Gaxton and Moore were off to other projects, but Cole Porter again supplied the score for the new show, *Red, Hot and Blue!*

Russel Crouse's book seemed to work overtime to be quirky. The dingbat plot involved "Nails" O'Reilly Duquesne's (Merman's) search for a man's (Bob Hope, replacing Gaxton) lost childhood sweetheart, who can be identified by the mark on her bottom caused by accidentally sitting on a waffle iron. A subplot involved a convict (Jimmy Durante, replacing Moore) who is released from prison to aid in the search but who is miffed because he had made it to captain of the prison polo team. The Supreme Court (à la *Of Thee I Sing*) eventually gets involved to certify the waffle mark by observing it *in situ* through a cellophane skirt.

Porter's score yielded two hits, "It's De-Lovely," a comic duet for Merman and Hope, and Merman's torch song "Down in the Depths (on the Ninetieth Floor)," which obliquely acknowledged the recently opened Empire State Building.

Apart from the dynamic (if meaningless) title, there actually wasn't a whole lot to *Red, Hot and Blue!* from a contemporary audience's point of view. *Only* two great new Cole Porter songs. The book by Russel Crouse didn't crackle, despite the funny character ideas. They figured they'd probably see Merman, Durante, and Hope in something better soon. It ran only 183 performances and is remembered today primarily for its intractable battle over whether Merman or Durante should get top billing. Porter himself, probably in jest, finally suggested they crisscross the names and that's the way it appeared on posters, with "Ethel Merman" angling from top left to bottom right and "Jimmy Durante" angling from bottom left to top right.

By *Red Hot and Blue!* Merman had become more than a star, she'd become a brand. Through musicals like *Stars in Your Eyes* and *DuBarry Was a Lady*, she always appeared in outfits that showcased her curves, always made sure she had a number with a couple of huge notes in it, and always had plenty of comedy songs and scenes that let her exercise her wise-cracking comedy chops. She was usually the sexy dame with the pipes (vocal cords) and stems (shapely legs), and she was usually paired with a master comedian like Durante or Bert Lahr.

DuBarry was the unlikely story of a men's-room attendant who drinks a mickey finn intended for his rival, and dreams he's King Louis XV, with his nightclub-singer girlfriend (Merman) transformed into the royal mistress Madame DuBarry. Cole Porter was back in the composer's seat and gave her both the mildly smutty "But in the Morning, No," the comically inflated "Well, Did You Evah?" and the perky "Friendship," a classic Porter comedic list song in which Merman and Lahr insulted and imagined horrible accidents for each other under the guise of expressing their undying amity. The show ran a year and was a classic of a kind of suggestively screwball and tuneful musical comedy that seemed extinct for decades but has been making something of a comeback in the 2000s with shows like *Monty Python's Spamalot*, *The Producers*, and *Young Frankenstein*.

Despite its success, Merman once again was denied the movie, with her role going to Lucille Ball (opposite Red Skelton and Gene Kelly). Merman's rap is that she was always terrible on film; that her eyes looked "dead" in movies. Critics complain that she never looked at her costar, but only out at the place where the audience should be. But if you want to get a sense of what Merman was like in her 1930s prime and understand why she was so beloved as a performer, check out the film *You're the Top*, which steals its title song from the score of *Anything Goes*. With a lyric substantially different from the one used on Broadway, a trim and flirtatious Merman warbles Porter's (heavily edited) superlatives to a weirdly bearded Bing Crosby, who then returns the favor.

Nevertheless, the film was the exception to Merman's movie career, not the rule.

Back in New York, she was also developing a reputation as a performer very protective of her prerogatives. She would "freeze" her performances during the last week of previews and permitted no changes after that from either the authors or her fellow performers. Those who deviated in even small ways would witness Merman's escalating wrath.

Two major biographies of Merman were released within weeks of each other in November 2007, Brian Kellow's *Ethel Merman: A Life* and Caryl Flinn's *Brass Diva: The Life and Legends of Ethel Merman,* both of which were helpful in the preparation of this chapter. Flinn's, especially, was frank about Merman's high-handed mistreatment of her coworkers and especially her hired help.

Years later, responding to a question about her reputation as a *diva assoluta*, Merman said, "All my life, I've just wanted to treat people well and wanted them to treat me the same. But if you cross me or hurt me, that's when I'll get angry. I could never take people lying down on the show, if that's what you mean. Nobody in my shows ever, ever got away with coming in loaded or stepping on my lines. You want to know about my real professional reputation? Go to my union. Go to Actors' Equity. They'll tell you that I'm fair."

There were, nevertheless, employees who formed quite a different opinion.

Make It Another Old-Fashioned

By the late 1930s, Merman was a huge star on Broadway but was comparatively little-known in the rest of the country, partly because of her dislike of touring. That changed when her face appeared on the cover of *Time* magazine's October 28, 1940, edition. The story inside described her look and style in a way that piqued interest across the continent.

In October 1940 she opened her next Cole Porter musical, *Panama Hattie*, about Hattie Maloney, a brassy saloon singer (natch) in the Canal Zone. In this story, writers Herbert Fields and B. G. De Sylva had her in love with a divorced diplomat who has a little girl. Hattie needs to win over the little girl in order to land her father in marriage. She does so after uncovering a wartime plot to bomb the canal.

The second-drawer Porter score had her singing the cutesy "Let's Be Buddies" and the lachrymose torch song "Make It Another Old-Fashioned, Please," but the show was more than the sum of its parts. Audiences in the last days of relative peace before Pearl Harbor (and the last days for this kind of silly old-fashioned musical before *Oklahoma!* in 1943) had a ball.

One important distinction for *Panama Hattie* is that Merman's name appeared alone over the title for the first time. There was no high-octane Gaxton or Durante or Hope to help her (her supporting cast included the capable Arthur Treacher, Betty Hutton, and James Dunn). Was Merman star enough to carry a show on the strength of her name and abilities? At 501 performances, *Panama Hattie* was the longest-running show of all the Porter/Merman collaborations and indeed the longest-running Broadway musical to open since the boom years of the 1920s. It would have run longer still if Merman hadn't become pregnant with her daughter and namesake and had to withdraw. For all its success at the time, *Panama Hattie* was so carefully carpentered for Merman that it's never been revived on Broadway.

The final Merman/Porter show, *Something for the Boys* (1943), also had the most ridiculous plot yet, with Merman playing a Texas ranch owner who discovers that the material in her dental fillings is somehow able to pick up radio transmissions. This singular talent enables her to save a military plane in trouble and win a marriage proposal from her soldier boyfriend. Merman's best-remembered number is the comic duet "By the Mississinewah," in which Merman pretended to be an Indian maiden and hissed her way merrily through a chorus that required her to repeat the "sis" of the title eight times. They just had fun with a funny word.

The 1940s were perhaps the happiest time in Merman's life. She was at the top of her industry while at the same time bearing and raising her children in a second marriage that had equipoise if not exactly wild romance. Her country was at war, so she plunged into entertaining for the troops and giving benefit concerts to sell war bonds. She also was one of the many stars who made cameo appearances in the 1943 film *Stage Door Canteen*, about a soldier who falls for one of the hostesses at that famed wartime Manhattan landmark where servicemen could be entertained by the top stars on Broadway, who performed there for free.

Annie Get Your Gun

In the mid-1940s, Broadway was shifting gears and Merman had to find a way to shift hers. *Oklahoma!* showed the old-timers like Berlin and Porter that their whole way of writing shows had suddenly gotten a little harder, more professional, and more grown-up.

Berlin responded with a backstage musical about sharpshooter Annie Oakley, star of *Buffalo Bill's Wild West and Congress of Rough Riders of the World*, a touring show in the late nineteenth and early twentieth centuries that was part rodeo, part circus, part vaudeville show. Once again, Merman found herself playing a performer, but this time with a twist. Instead of a suave New York chanteuse or a worldly-wise nightclub belter, she played a naive hayseed with an amazing ability to shoot rifles instead of lift highballs. Her fans were delighted that the girl from Brooklyn somehow mastered (more or less) Oakley's country argot to sing lines like "Folks're dumb where I come from." But Annie was as brash as Ethel.

The spirit of Oakley and the spirit of Merman turned out to be very similar.

Annie Get Your Gun has gone down in history as one of the greatest Broadway scores ever, rolling out one standard after another. Berlin was inspired by the new form to write the lush ballad "I Got Lost in His Arms," the hillbilly-flavored "Moonshine Lullaby," and the mildly ribald comedy song "Doin' What Comes Natur'lly."

Berlin gave Merman the comic lament "You Can't Get a Man with a Gun," which contains the complaint that men "don't buy pajamas for pistol-packin' mamas."

She also got to share the perennial favorite can-you-top-this song, "Anything You Can Do I Can Do Better," which illustrates the clash of egos getting in the way of the romance between Oakley and fellow sharpshooter Frank Butler.

But Merman's greatest number in *Annie Get Your Gun* was a throwaway song for a trio to sing "in one" in front of the curtain while a big set change was going on behind them. It had to be bright and loud, to drown out any noise. So Berlin wrote a generic ain't-showbiz-great song . . . except it turned out to be the greatest of such songs—"There's No Business Like Show Business," which became the theatre's anthem.

Both the show and the song were the biggest hits of Merman's career and became forever identified with her.

Call Me Madam

Merman returned to Broadway in 1950 as another all-American type in *Call Me Madam*. She played Sally Adams, a wealthy society hostess and political fundraiser, who is appointed ambassador to a tiny European country. There, she strikes comedic sparks as her down-to-earth simplicity runs up against the hoity-toity ways of the continentals. She even gets to have a romantic adventure with a handsome nobleman—though one a little more age appropriate for the increasingly matronly forty-two-year-old Merman than the one in *Annie Get Your Gun* of four years earlier.

Despite program disclaimers to the contrary, librettists Howard Lindsay and Russel Crouse were writing a send-up of Washington, D.C., hostess Perle Mesta, who had recently been appointed ambassador to Luxembourg. Far from being insulted by the ribbing, Mesta hosted Merman on a visit to Europe and showed her how things were done around the embassy.

The project surrounded her with old pros, many near the peak of their powers. George Abbott was the director, Jerome Robbins the choreographer, and Mainbocher the costumer. The score was supplied by Merman's old friend Irving Berlin, on what turned out to be his last successful Broadway project.

Berlin supplied Merman with nine songs—another ironwoman challenge—including "The Hostess with the Mostes'" and "You're Just in Love," the latter a bouncy contrapuntal duet with the bespectacled Russell Nype that became yet another signature tune for Merman. Nype sang the first melody, complaining that there is something about a young princess he's met that gives him hallucinations and makes him feel odd. Merman comes in with the countermelody diagnosing his ailments, saying, "You're not sick, you're just in love!" The swaying tune was written late in the tryout process but proved irresistibly catchy in the patented Berlin way—and delightful fun both to sing and to watch.

Of all the amazing shows and roles Merman created over the course of her long career, she won the Tony Award for Leading Actress in a Musical only once, in 1951 for her performance in *Call Me Madam*. (She was also awarded a special Tony Award for lifetime achievement in 1972.) Owing to a contract dispute between record companies, no original cast album was made. Dinah Shore appeared with the rest of the original cast on one recording; Merman sang much of the score herself on a separately released disc.

The show was so closely tailored for Merman that it has never gotten a full-scale Broadway revival, though a 1995 "Encores!" production starred Tyne Daly in the Merman role.

Family

Overall, Merman married and divorced four times. The first marriage, to theatrical agent Bill Smith, lasted only from 1940 to 1941. This union came on the rebound from her breakup with the true love of her life, Stork Club owner Sherman Billingsley, who was already married. (His wife, Hazel, outlived them both.) Merman's second marriage, to newspaper circulation manager Robert Levitt, lasted the longest, 1941 to 1952, and produced two children, Ethel Levitt and Robert Levitt Jr. Her third, to airline executive Robert Six, lasted just seven years, 1953 to 1960. And her fourth marriage, to fellow actor Ernest Borgnine in 1964, was a legendary disaster, essentially over after a honeymoon quarrel. She filed for divorce after just thirty-two days. Following that, she'd had enough of the marriage business.

Happy Hunting

After *Call Me Madam*, Merman took a hiatus from acting, in an unsuccessful attempt to make her marriage to Six work. The hiatus ended in 1956 when she returned to Broadway in *Happy Hunting*, another musical with a book by Lindsay and Crouse and a score by first-timers Harold Karr and Matt Dubey. *Happy Hunting* told the improbable story of a Philadelphia society matron who tries to marry her daughter to the pretender to the Spanish throne, only to find herself falling for the nobleman instead.

The show's title turned out to offer a poor description of how things went backstage. Merman's ego collided with that of her costar Fernando Lamas from the first day of rehearsal to the final performance about a year later. In a notorious television interview with Mike Wallace, Lamas said that kissing Merman was "somewhere between kissing your uncle and a Sherman tank." Merman filed a complaint with Actors' Equity Association, which issue a reprimand to her costar. Merman also had trouble with the show itself, feeling that, except for the showstopping number "Mutual Admiration Society," the material was weak, which it was.

That's one of the reasons she balked when offered her next project, a musical about the life of stripper Gypsy Rose Lee, in which she'd play Lee's mother, Rose Hovick. It was to have had music and lyrics by another relative newcomer, twenty-nine-year-old Stephen Sondheim, who would be making his Broadway debut as a composer, having written only lyrics to his one previous credit, *West Side Story*, which wasn't Merman's kind of musical in any case. She wanted Jule Styne, veteran of *Gentlemen Prefer Blondes* and *Bells Are Ringing*, to write the music. Sondheim was ready to turn his back on the project but was persuaded that working with Merman and Styne would provide invaluable professional experience and, indeed, life experience.

Very few performers get to create timeless signature characters even once in their careers. For Merman, whose Hattie Maloney and May Daly faded quickly after the sets were hauled away, Rose, or "Mama Rose" as she's widely known, was her third opportunity for immortality, after Reno Sweeney and Annie Oakley.

Gypsy turned out to be one of the finest musicals in Broadway history. Though based on Gypsy Rose Lee's autobiography, the musical made Gypsy a supporting role. The central character was to be her mother, Rose Hovick, who pursued vaudeville stardom for her young daughters with an obsession bordering on monomania. "I had a dream" became her motif, and the ultimate stage mother uses it to bully them into the spotlight. She holds the family together despite providing no stable father figure. But along the way she sacrifices nearly everything else, including their childhoods and their dignity, until the daughters no longer feel her drive; they feel only driven. When the older daughter, June, finally runs away and vaudeville dies, Rose shifts the burden of her dreams to her hitherto neglected daughter Louise and vows to make a star of her—even if she's to be a star stripper.

In her now thirty-year career, Merman had put her stamp on so many classic songs. Now she was handed the resolute "Some People," the flirtatious "You'll Never Get Away from Me," and the chipper "Together Wherever We Go," which might have been enough in a 1930s show. But she also got the volcanic "Everything's Coming Up Roses," in context one of the most thrilling and horrifying anthems ever. Though it superficially sounds like a 1930s cheer-up song, it's actually something of a death march for her daughter, who will be forced to continue seeking stardom whether she wants to or not. Naturally, Louise isn't heartened by the song; she cringes through it. She just wants to retire and settle down and have a real family life for what's left of her childhood. "Everything's Coming Up Roses" is Rose's subconsciously self-referential denial of her daughter's dream.

That song ends Act I. Styne and Sondheim topped it with an eleven-o'clock number to end all eleven-o'clock numbers, a musical nervous breakdown titled "Rose's Turn," in which many of the show's musical themes collide as Mama Rose realizes that her daughters have grown up and left her behind, taking her dream with them. It was a mini opera, delivered by Merman standing alone at center stage.

Considering its current place in the pantheon of great musicals, *Gypsy* was not quite as well regarded when it first opened, and it managed to run a respectable but not extraordinary 702 performances. Part of the problem was that, for the time, it was considered a dark and unpleasant show, about a mother willing to sacrifice her own children to her relentless drive for "fame, that glittering bauble," as another Styne show put it. Merman lost that year's Tony Award to Mary Martin of *The Sound of Music*. And while the Best Musical Award was a once-in-a-history tie, the two winners were *The Sound of Music* and *Fiorello*, not *Gypsy*.

Still, Merman saw what others didn't and considered Mama Rose her greatest role. When Merman discovered that producer/director Mervyn LeRoy had handed the film role of Mama Rose to Rosalind Russell, she was so furious she fired her agent. Merman joined the sad list of Broadway stars, including Mary Martin, Carol Channing, Julie Andrews, and Angela Lansbury, who saw their signature roles go to less-qualified Hollywood names when the property was filmed.

Merman agreed to return to Broadway in a September 1966 revival of *Annie Get Your Gun*, at the City Center. Merman performed without a microphone and made herself heard to the back corners of that cavernous space. Merman had been nearing forty when she first played the teenage Annie Oakley; she was now nearly sixty and filled her costumes a lot more than she once did. But you'd be kidding yourself if you think most audiences cared (critics were another matter). They were just happy to see Merman in her most famous role—even if it had, like Mama Rose, been taken from her and assigned to someone else for the film version.

Hello, Dolly!

Some of Merman's wounds were self-inflicted. Merman had introduced so many great songs by Gershwin, Porter, and Berlin, but she passed up a prime chance to do the same for the next generation of greats.

One of Merman's biggest mistakes was turning down a show written expressly for her, *Hello, Dolly!* Her experience on *Happy Hunting* had been so negative she refused to once again take a chance on an "unknown" composer—this time one named Jerry Herman. Even the experience of working with Sondheim so fruitfully on *Gypsy* didn't sway her. So the role and the glory went to Carol Channing instead.

Late in the show's long Broadway run, Merman did finally consent to play the role of Dolly Gallagher Levi—an unprecedented step down for the great star who always originated roles and had never before deigned to be a mere replacement. Herman eased the pain by restoring two songs—"World, Take Me Back" and "Love, Look in My Window"—that had been customized for Merman's voice, then cut when Channing took the role. Merman played Dolly from March 28 to December 27, 1970. When she came down those stairs in that red dress for the last time, it was also the last time she answered a Broadway audience's applause in a regular role. Aside from two special onetime benefit performances, her Broadway career was over.

The era of television was in full swing, and while she made many appearances over the years, television regarded her increasingly as a curiosity, rather than a real star. She had enjoyed a triumph in 1953 when she and Mary Martin teamed for a special celebrating the fiftieth anniversary of the Ford Motor Company. Their medley of amazing hits, arranged and conducted by Jay Blackton, became a standard feature of such shows.

But when the 1960s rolled around and audiences' tastes changed, suddenly the show-biz world seemed to have no idea what to do with her. As she began to appear on talk shows and do cameos on shows like *Batman* (as guest villainess "Lola Lasagne") her odd looks and over-the-top singing style came to seem simply strange.

The problems started just a few years after *Gypsy* with the 1963 film *It's a Mad Mad Mad Mad World*, an all-star road-trip farce, in which a half-dozen carloads of people race to find a buried treasure. Among the cast were Jimmy Durante, Mickey Rooney, Jonathan Winters, Phil Silvers, and two dozen other comedy stars. Merman played the naggy in-law of Milton Berle, sporting a Marge Simpson–like pile of hair. Merman spent the entire film playing a giant pain in the neck very effectively. At one point she's holding a cactus and asks Berle, "Where should I stick this?" Berle does a take and murmurs, "Oh boy. . . ."

The film was an enormous success by contemporary standards and, for many people, this was the first they'd seen of Ethel Merman. It became lodged in the public's mind as her new persona.

As the years went on Merman seemed to have no self-awareness of how she was coming across. She had been queen of show business for most of her adult life and seemed to think audiences were still responding to her as they had in the 1930s. A low point came in 1979 with the release of *The Ethel Merman Disco Album*, Peter Matz's brainchild, in which Merman sang eight of her hits to a disco beat. "No Business Like Show Business" actually achieved a vogue as a novelty for a period of time. She continued to make concert and TV appearances, wearing garish outfits, her hair permed into a bizarre helmet, playing to camera close-ups with the same bombast she used to catapult high notes to the second balcony and her vibrato getting ever more shaky.

Everyone knew who she was, however. In one memorable segment of the sketch show *Saturday Night Live*, everyone onstage and backstage at the show was asked to "do Merman," and every single person was able to produce an impression instantly.

Merman finally became a parody of herself. Her final movie role came in the 1980 comedy *Airplane!* She did a cameo as a shell-shocked soldier, Lieutenant Hurwitz, who suffers from the delusion that he's Ethel Merman and tries to bark out a few lines of "Everything's Coming Up Roses" while wrestling sanitarium orderlies trying to administer a sedative.

Merman died in New York February 16, 1984, after surgery to remove a brain tumor.

In the years since, her image has improved a bit. She has remained a byword for Broadway brassiness, Broadway excess, and Broadway professionalism. Mel Brooks's 2001 musical *The Producers* had a Hitler parody doing a floor show and singing, "I'm the German Ethel Merman, don'tcha know!" The blog Mermaniac.com tracks developments in musical theatre.

The Tony-winning parody revue *Forbidden Broadway* often referred to Merman as the preferred model for Broadway performers. In one skit an actress playing Merman erupted from the audience to upbraid an actor (playing the Phantom of the Opera) on his breathy modern singing technique. To the tune of "You're Just in Love" she explained, "You just can't sing."

When Merman appeared onstage, she always gravitated to the zero spot, downstage center in the brightest point of light—as she had in the hearts of four generations of musical theatre fans.

Alfred Drake in *Kismet* (1953). PHOTOFEST

ALFRED DRAKE
Where Is the Life That Late I Led?

Alfred Drake was the very model of a Broadway leading man.

He was tall, sturdy, charming, and funny, with a devilishly handsome face and an athletic grace. He was an excellent actor in both romantic and comedy scenes. He deployed a lush, flexible baritone that gave life to some of the most beloved show tunes of the 1940s and 1950s, in shows like the original *Oklahoma!* and *Kiss Me, Kate*. Costumes looked great on him, and he wore hats with unparalleled panache.

He had an appealing persona, as well. He could play the egotistical rooster with ease, but with just enough self-parody to let people know he didn't take himself too seriously. He had so many things going for him that he could have been playing an insufferable egomaniac but (at least onstage) all the while project an underlying humility and goodness that excused any excesses in the part.

Drake also had the good fortune to make his entrance to the Broadway scene at just the right moment. He was there at the birth of the modern American musical, strolling onstage with no overture in the first moments of *Oklahoma!*, singing those first few words of "Oh, What a Beautiful Mornin'" to an old woman churning butter. From then on, he was in demand for the new kind of musicals that emerged in the 1940s.

He had his disappointments, too. After a disastrous attempt to break into film work, he confined himself mainly to the stage, seeing his greatest roles go to other actors when it came time to make his shows into movies. He was smart and creative, and he attempted to write and direct plays and musicals but had only modest success there, at best.

What he excelled at was being a Broadway leading man. He got to enjoy two decades of doing that before the rock revolution of the 1960s changed people's tastes in music, in singing technique, and in the kind of fellow they wanted to see as a leading man. But Drake was in his fifties by then and could confidently say that he'd had his day and made the most of it. Douglas Watt of the *New York Daily News* wrote, "Drake was the most versatile and dashing musical star of the mid-century. . . . Like any great star, Drake spawned imitators, but he was matchless."

★

Drake was born Alfred Capurro in Brooklyn, New York, on October 7, 1914. A large portion of his early life revolved around Our Lady of Good Counsel Roman Catholic Church, where his mother, a mezzo-soprano, sang in the choir and where young Alfred made his singing debut, along with his older brother, known professionally as Arthur Kent.

Alfred matriculated at Brooklyn College, where he studied to become a teacher of English and French. His interest in singing landed him in the college's glee club. In a typically grand gesture, Drake made his Broadway debut at age twenty in 1935 with not one show but six of them, simultaneously. While still a student, he was walking down a Manhattan street past the old Adelphi Theatre on Fifty-fourth Street when he spotted a sign advertising an audition that day for a planned season of Gilbert and Sullivan music. He walked in, sang, and was hired on the spot. He took his first Broadway bow on July 15, 1935, in the ensemble of *The Mikado*, closely followed by *The Gondoliers, The Yeomen of the Guard, The Pirates of Penzance, H.M.S. Pinafore*, and *Trial by Jury*.

He graduated with a BA and accepted an invitation by his older brother to come down to Atlantic City and join him in the Steel Pier Opera Company, a small troupe that brought Puccini and Verdi to the Boardwalk. Like Albert Peterson in *Bye Bye Birdie*, he left his career as an English teacher behind. When he heard the applause his voice engendered, he said, "My fate was sealed."

He returned to New York to audition for the operetta *The White Horse Inn* and was startled not only to be cast in the ensemble, but to understudy the lead, Broadway's premier leading man of the 1920s and 1930s, William Gaxton. When Gaxton fell ill at Christmastime 1936, Drake got his first Broadway leading role, at age twenty-two. In retrospect, it was a portentous passing of the torch. Drake was, at this point, entirely untrained as a singer. To keep from damaging what evidently was a fine vocal instrument, he was remanded to vocal coach Clytie Mundy for burnishing.

Rodgers and Hart saw him in the role and put him in the original cast of *Babes in Arms*, their classic let's-get-a-barn-and-put-on-a-show musical. In Depression-era America, the kids of a group of dispirited ex-vaudevillians all want to be on Broadway, so they put on their own musical in a bid to make their own luck. This let's-take-charge-ism was a hallmark of that entire generation. Drake was a part of Rodgers and Hart's vision for the kind of talent who would take over in the years to come, and they were right. The show's casting concept was to have no stars but to pack the cast with brightest young unknowns they could find. Leading man Ray Heatherton was twenty-six, and the principal female, Mitzi Green, was only sixteen. Among others featured in the show that produced "Where or When," "Johnny One Note," and "My Funny Valentine" were Dan Dailey, Robert Rounseville, and the Nicholas Brothers. Drake had two tiny roles and sang in the chorus, but from then on Rodgers kept an eye on him.

Drake worked steadily in the late 1930s and early 1940s, in Broadway and stock, in plays and in musical revues. There was the English operetta *The Two Bouquets* (in which he appeared with future *Kiss Me, Kate* leading lady Patricia Morison); John Murray Anderson's *One for the Money* (in which Drake lampooned Orson Welles, among others); *The Straw Hat Revue* (with future stars Danny Kaye and Imogene Coca); Anderson's sequel *Two for the Show; After the Ball*; and the comedy *Out of the Frying Pan*. Drake also got the chance to play Shakespeare, appearing as Orlando in a Broadway production of *As You Like It* opposite Helen Craig as Rosalind.

After the April 1942 flop of the Emlyn Williams's play *Yesterday's Magic*, despite the presence of Paul Muni and Jessica Tandy in the cast, fate tapped Drake on the shoulder. Richard Rodgers asked him if he would sing at backer auditions to raise money for their new project, a musical western being prepared with his new lyricist Oscar Hammerstein II for the Theatre Guild—a project that would eventually become *Oklahoma!* It took months of grueling performances for unimpressed money folks who had nursed their bankrolls through the Depression and were very choosy about where they were investing. Drake sang the role of the male lead, Curly, a cowboy in love with the farm girl Laurey in the territory of Oklahoma in the early days of the twentieth century, before Oklahoma was admitted to the union as a state.

Rodgers and Hammerstein were so impressed with Drake's voice and bearing that they told him the part was his. He had something else, as well. He understood the new kind of theatre song Rodgers and Hammerstein had written. Book musicals—that is, musicals with a fully developed story, as opposed to a revue—had always integrated songs into the plot and characters to a greater or lesser degree. But just as many of them inserted some songs more or less at random in an attempt to create a hit. Most of these latter kinds of songs could just as easily fit into another show, or no show at all. They could be sung by a radio or concert artist out of context and sound just generic enough to stand alone.

In *Oklahoma!*, Rodgers and Hammerstein tried to write songs that were very specific to the moment and the character they reflected. They were written as theatre songs for a particular context and no other. Drake got to sing "The Surrey with the Fringe on Top," a detailed description of the carriage he would use to take Laurey to the party; "People Will Say We're in Love," a flirtatious duet with Laurey; and the show's opening number, "Oh, What a Beautiful Mornin'," which recorded the sights, sounds, and sensations of Oklahoma farmland in the early hours. Drake "got" what the writers were trying to accomplish and approached Curly not as a joking caricature of a cowboy but as a fully realized dramatic character.

When the show opened on March 31, 1943, it changed the way musicals would be written henceforth. Drake was there at the birth of the modern American musical and sang its first words.

Elliot Norton wrote in *Christian Science Monitor*, "In that scene and song, American musical-comedy took a new turn away from stilted nonsense towards something like truth and beauty. And Alfred Drake, because he got all that into his manner, his bearing and his exuberant natural singing voice, became in effect the herald of a new era."

Over time, *Oklahoma!* has fallen to the status of a chestnut. Its innovations have been absorbed by the mainstream and now seem like clichés. So it's hard to imagine today the impact that show had on wartime New York. Servicemen on leave would come see the show (for free, as was the theatre's policy) and would leave with brimming eyes. This wholesome, big-hearted show reflected the vision of the America they were laying down their lives to protect. Drake was the embodiment of the all-American good guy they believed themselves to be.

The show transformed Drake's life and career. He went from struggling singer to what critic Brooks Atkinson hailed as "about the most valuable man in his field."

Offstage, Drake's marriage to Alma Tollefsen ended in divorce, and he married Esther Harvey Brown from the cast of *Oklahoma!* They remained together until his death forty-eight years later, and they had two daughters, Candace and Samantha.

Movies

After the success of *Oklahoma!*, Hollywood agent Harry Cohen lured Drake to Hollywood with promises of swashbuckling film musicals based on *The Three Musketeers* and *Robin Hood*. Instead, he got stuck in a third-rate 1946 film, *Tars and Spars*, with a nonsensical plot about a Coast Guardsman who spends three weeks on a life raft as part of a government test of vitamin gum. Drake got to sing two Jule Styne/Sammy Cahn songs, "I'm Glad I Waited for You" and "Love Is a Merry-Go-Round," but the film, such as it was, was stolen by Sid Caesar, doing some of the clowning he would later perfect in *Your Show of Shows*.

Drake was profoundly embarrassed by the experience, calling *Tars and Spars* in an interview "one of the worst movie musicals ever made . . . Don't ever see it."

Except for a few specialty appearances, that was pretty much the end of his film career. In the years to come, the role of Curly in the movie *Oklahoma!* went to Gordon MacRae, and both Fred Graham in *Kiss Me, Kate* and Hajj in *Kismet* went to Howard Keel; the latter two casting decisions must have been particularly galling, as Keel had been Drake's understudy in *Oklahoma!*

But Drake's public pronouncement on the movie business was unequivocal: "Hollywood was a prison" he said, "and I finally escaped."

Drake told Robert Wahls of the *New York News*, "I always feel terribly alive on stage."

He got the chance to do so in *Sing Out Sweet Land*, Walter Kerr's revue that showcased American folk and pop songs up to World War II. Produced by the Theatre Guild, it also starred Burl Ives. It ran three months. Drake also starred as amoral killer Macheath in *Beggar's Holiday*, Duke Ellington and John La Touche's musical adaptation of *The Beggar's Opera*. Kurt Weill's adaptation of the same material, *The Threepenny Opera*, had flopped in the 1930s but would return triumphantly in the 1950s and make everyone forget *Beggar's Holiday*, which had run 111 performances.

Drake also appeared in a 1947 revival of Marc Blitzstein's controversial agitprop musical *The Cradle Will Rock*, playing union organizer Larry Foreman. Produced in the days of the gathering anticommunist witch hunts, the anti-big-business, pro-worker musical stayed for just over a month.

Kiss Me, Kate

In the meantime, Drake and *Oklahoma!* had helped create a headache for another major Broadway composer, Cole Porter. Porter was one of the foremost practitioners and proponents of the old-style musical, and despite his genius with the show-tune form, the old dog knew he needed to learn some new tricks if he didn't want to wind up left in the past.

His response to the Rodgers and Hammerstein revolution was an original show based upon the legendary backstage bickering of the married stage couple Alfred Lunt and Lynn Fontanne during a production of Shakespeare's *The Taming of the Shrew*. In the cleverly constructed musical, to be called *Kiss Me, Kate*, the onstage story of *Shrew* would serve as a subtext to the offstage battles of characters Fred Graham and Lily Vanessi, a divorced acting couple forced by circumstances to reunite (at least onstage) in a musical adaptation of the Shakespeare comedy. The conflicts that ended their marriage are still very much in evidence, but so is their obvious love for one another. Much clowning in the way of a comic secondary couple, a pair of singing gangsters, and Lily's jealous Texan fiancé intervene before the two wind up where they obviously belong, in each other's arms.

Porter rose to the occasion, turning in one of the wittiest, most glittering scores in Broadway history, including the saucy "Always True to You (In My Fashion)," the brilliantly comic "Brush Up Your Shakespeare," and the frankly sexual "Too Darn Hot." Drake and costar Patricia Morison got to poke fun at old-time operettas in "Wunderbar" and shared one of Porter's most lushly romantic melodies, "So in Love." As a soloist, Drake (as Petruchio) got to recount his numerous romantic conquests in "Where Is the Life That Late I Led?" and to state his no-holds-barred intentions in "I've Come to Wive It Wealthily in Padua."

The show, one of the greatest of Broadway's golden age, was another triumph for Drake, as well as for all involved in the production. Drake proved again that the age of the quadruple-threat leading man (singer, dancer, actor, and comedian) was here to stay and that he was the master.

A decade later, Drake and Morison reunited for a television adaptation of the show. A kinescope of the "Wunderbar" scene shows the two stars playing to the TV camera, trying to upstage each other in character. At one point they come right up to the camera and try to elbow each other out of the frame. This bizarre and wonderful sequence demonstrates how relaxed Drake was in the part and how willing he was to accommodate the medium of television and make the camera part of the storytelling.

Immediately after he left *Kiss Me, Kate*, Drake tried branching out. He directed a musical, *Courtin' Time*, collaborating with dance master George Balanchine on a gentle story about a farmer courting his housekeeper. Drake replaced his own leading man during tryouts, then called in veteran comedian Joe E. Brown to open the show on Broadway, where it lasted just a month. He also directed and cowrote the musical *The Liar*, based on a Goldoni play, but it, too, folded quickly.

People wanted to see him playing big, lusty leading-man roles, and they nearly got another great one when Rodgers and Hammerstein offered him the role of the King of Siam in their 1951 classic *The King and I*. But Drake had grown cocky and asked for more than the golden team (who were also producing) wanted to pay, and the role of a lifetime went instead to Yul Brynner. In the end, Drake briefly played the King while Yul Brynner was on vacation. But Drake wanted a role of his own.

Kismet

Kismet, or "fate," was the title of a costume epic that had been popular since 1911 when Edward Knoblock's nonmusical play version had first entertained audiences with its story of poet-beggar Hajj, who finagles his way from the streets to the stars—becoming emir of Baghdad for a day and winning a prince as his daughter's husband.

This sort of "How to Succeed in Baghdad Without Really Trying" story was perfectly tailored for Drake's strengths. With a book by Charles Lederer and Luther Davis and a score Robert Wright and George Forrest (based on themes from the work of classical composer Alexander Borodin), the show was crammed with songs, dances, costumes, and sets—an extravaganza in the traditional sense of the word.

To play Hajj, Drake grew a pointed beard that gave such an appealingly devilish cast to his face that he wore it most of the rest of his career, including in the 1958 TV version of *Kiss Me, Kate*. It became his trademark.

Drake got one delicious comic or dramatic solo after another. "Rhymes Have I" is a W. S. Gilbert-like patter song, in which he demonstrated his facility with impromptu verse. The rhymes get progressively worse, until "dromedary" is paired with "very hairy," and then the singer squeals out a "Very sorry!" Faced with dismemberment for stealing, Hajj uses his fast-talk skill in the song "Gesticulate" to demonstrate how he requires the use of his hand to make his living as a storyteller.

In the song "Fate," Hajj wonders what his life will bring. In "The Olive Tree," he tells a parable about a man who passes on a chance for greatness—which strengthens Hajj's own resolve to seize it.

The only drawback from Drake's point of view was that the prettiest melody in the show, and the one best remembered—for the song "Stranger in Paradise"—went to the show's juvenile future star Richard Kiley, who played the prince.

As great as Drake was, the show itself was something of an overstuffed turkey that benefited from a newspaper strike called just before the show opened. Without critics to point out its faults, audiences were attracted by the show's exterior charms, "Stranger in Paradise" heard on the radio, and the chance to see Drake. Word of mouth was excellent, and by the time the critics weighed in with their objections, the show had become critic-proof. It won the 1954 Tony Award as Best Musical, and Drake won the Tony as Best Leading Actor in a Musical. The show ran a respectable 583 performances. Too bad that Drake never had another success like it.

His hits were epic, and so, unfortunately, were some of his flops. *Kean* (1961), for which Wright and Forrest wrote their first complete score on their own, was based on the Jean-Paul Sartre play about Edmund Kean, nineteenth-century London stage star who wins adulation on the stage but is snubbed by society in real life. As time goes on, his stage life starts to become his real life.

In the book *Not Since Carrie*, Ken Mandelbaum wrote, "The idea of Alfred Drake, Broadway's grandest, wittiest musical actor, as Kean was an inspired one . . . but the show received the standard, semi-floperetta treatment in score, decor and even book. Kean's identity crisis was frequently announced but never fully dramatized." It ran ninety-two performances.

His "Prisoner of Zenda" musical, *Zenda* (1963), suffered a similar fate, though Drake got to play dual leads. The librettist got into a fight with the producer over book alterations, and the show closed in its road tryout.

There was always something dashingly Shakespearean about Drake, although he had no formal training in the Bard. Nevertheless, in the late 1950s he appeared at the American Shakespeare Festival in Stratford, Connecticut, as Iago in *Othello*, and again, opposite Katharine Hepburn, in *Much Ado About Nothing*, in which they subsequently toured.

His 1964 Broadway appearance as Claudius in Richard Burton's *Hamlet* earned a footnote in history. Directed by John Gielgud, the modern dress production of Shakespeare's play was filmed in its entirety and shown in special engagements at cinemas. The experiment was not a financial success and not repeated but did leave a record of what Drake looked like onstage during a period when he was making few other film appearances.

The year 1964 is also when Drake turned fifty. He made no more Broadway musical appearances for nearly a decade. The rock revolution had taken hold, and Drake's kind of leading man was in eclipse. Also, his face and figure had thickened somewhat, so that he was no longer suitable for such roles even if they had been written. He appeared in two non-musical plays, Michael Stewart's *Those That Play the Clowns* (1966) and Alfonso Paso's *Song of the Grasshopper* (1967). They had one thing in common besides Drake; they ran just four performances each. Drake grew increasingly bitter about the turn in his fortunes (and in his art form), but he kept on working as long as he could.

I saw Drake live onstage twice, in his last two major theatrical productions. I had seen him on the legendary 1971 Tony broadcast that reunited stars of nearly all the Tony-winning musicals of the previous quarter century, many of whom were still alive and working. Channing, Mostel, Verdon, many others in this book took part, singing their signature tunes. Drake did two: "Where Is the Life That Late I Led?" from *Kiss Me, Kate* and "The Olive Tree" from *Kismet*. He brought such brio to his segments that I made sure to seek him out the next time I read his name.

My first chance was the Broadway adaptation of the Lerner and Loewe movie musical *Gigi*. Drake played the role of Honoré, originally assayed on film by Maurice Chevalier. Easily able to command the Uris Theatre (now the Gershwin), the largest theatre on Broadway, Drake played the role as a dapper and thoroughly charming rake, with the look of injured innocence when anyone tried to call him on it. He brought great comic warmth to "I Remember It Well" and a sweet delight to "Thank Heaven for Little Girls." He was still handsome in a gray-fox sort of way, still the master of darting eyes over a Mephisthophelean beard now shot with gray.

I also saw his final Broadway role—twice, as it turned out, once in the Boston tryout and again at the Mark Hellinger Theatre. José Quintero chose Drake to play Mr. Antrobus, the Adam-like father of all humanity, in a 1975 revival of Thornton Wilder's allegorical *The Skin of Our Teeth*. There were funny moments, but mainly here was Drake using neither his singing voice nor his gifts for romance and comedy. It was just Drake the actor, face to face with an audience he knew would likely have preferred a chorus of "So in Love." He brought a kind of fallen majesty to the role of a man who remembers the Garden of Eden and on whom the stain of original sin is still fresh. One who is tempted to cheat on his wife with the eternal harlot Sabina and yet who desires to hold his family, mankind, together and move them forward toward whatever mysterious purpose God has in mind.

Drake was at his best when he gave his Act II acceptance speech as president, well, of all of creation, it seems. Walking the line between profound and ridiculous was all in a day's work for Drake, but he also embodied a sort of Charles Foster Kane quality, full of hubris and flawed grandeur. The man may have been flawed, but his vision was pure. If he didn't actually sing in the role, there were moments like this one where he almost seemed to.

In 1983 he had a small role in the movie hit *Trading Places*. In the "Prince and the Pauper"–style story, Dan Aykroyd plays a spoiled stockbroker and Eddie Murphy a street con artist who find themselves changing places thanks to a bet by two mischievous millionaires. Drake appeared in the movie mainly to serve as a kind of comic piñata in one scene, playing the president of the stock exchange. He is grossly insulted by Murphy over a restaurant dinner, and we see a series of emotions crossing his face—outrage, confusion, anger—before he surprisingly decides to take it as a joke and laughs uproariously. It's a small, very actorly moment, flawlessly executed. Theatre fans everywhere laughed—then stopped and thought, "Wait a minute, wasn't that . . . ?" It was.

Drake battled cancer through the twilight of his life. In 1990 the Tony Awards bestowed on him a special Tony Honor of Excellence in the Theatre for his body of work. He died in

1992, at age seventy-seven, of heart failure at Mount Sinai Medical Center in New York, just a few miles from the spot where he had hailed all those beautiful mornings a half century earlier.

Mary Martin in the title role of *Peter Pan* (1954). PHOTOFEST

MARY MARTIN
I'm Flying

Upon the opening of the musical *Peter Pan, New York Herald Tribune* critic Brooks Atkinson famously commented, "I don't know what all the fuss is about. I always knew Mary Martin could fly."

This pixieish five-foot-four-inch actress, a self-described hayseed from Texas, managed to reach the pinnacle of Broadway stardom through a mixture of girl-next-door sweetness and wholesomeness mixed with vivacity and a certain sexiness. There was just something delightful in the lilt of her voice and the way she moved.

Rodgers and Hammerstein wrote three of their classic musicals with her in mind for the lead. Thanks to the wonder of television, several pre-CGI generations grew up watching her sprinkle fairy dust on the three Darling children, rise off the floor, and zoom off into the night. Many of those children dreamed of running away to Neverland and living with Martin's Peter Pan forever.

Martin was neither a great singer nor a great beauty, yet the top songwriters of her age clamored to write shows for her, and when a show was written about the goddess of love coming to Earth, Martin was the choice to play Venus. She had a je ne sais quoi that made her characterizations unique.

Her performance as the original Maria in *The Sound of Music* has been obscured by the phenomenal success of the film, starring Julie Andrews. But "Do-Re-Mi," "My Favorite Things," and the title song were written for Martin, not Andrews. Martin was already in her late forties when she played the part yet was completely believable as a girlish postulant.

She was also enormously proud of her talent as a whistler. And as fans of *Peter Pan* know, when it came to crowing like a rooster, no one could top her.

In her autobiography, *My Heart Belongs*, Martin wrote that her mother had a difficult time with pregnancy, and the signal to her Weatherford, Texas, neighbors that the baby had arrived safely was to be the raising of a curtain on her bedroom window. The very first of many curtains went up on Mary Virginia Martin on December 1, 1913.

Weatherford was a tiny peach- and watermelon-farming town in northeast Texas, where her dad was a lawyer and her mom gave violin lessons. Martin was a painfully skinny tomboy. She claimed once to have tried wearing an unstrung tennis racquet as a hat, only to have it fall the length of her lanky frame and land around her ankles. That may have been a Texas tall tale, but looking at pictures of her as a girl, you can see it wasn't far from the truth.

She wasn't classically pretty, and she spent much of her early adulthood obsessed about her long neck, flat chest, and ever-so-slightly bulbed nose. But these are the sorts of things that can prey on the mind of an insecure teen. The rest of the world saw a vivacious young woman with graceful movements, large, warm eyes, and an expressive voice.

She loved to play dress up and sang every chance she got.

In his work as a lawyer, her father represented the owner of the local movie theatre—the Weatherford Palace. As a result, the Martins got a free pass, and young Mary spent many happy hours watching the stars of the first talkies. She wrote that Al Jolson's rendition of "Mammy" made her cry, and she cried whenever she heard the song for the rest of her life.

Her parents let her try all the churches in town, and she settled on the Episcopal church. The minister gave a sermon about talent and how it comes as a gift from God—but one that can be withdrawn if it isn't used properly. That sermon had a great impact on the young Mary.

Her big dream in life was opening a dance school in Weatherford, but that got put aside when she got married at age sixteen to a high school chum, Benjamin Hagman. Life took them in different directions, and the marriage ended not long thereafter but left her with one lifelong keepsake, her son, Larry Hagman, later a star in his own right on TV's *I Dream of Jeannie* and *Dallas*.

But life took a series of unexpected twists at this point that sent Martin on her trajectory to Broadway. She opened the dance school in the midst of the Great Depression, but it prospered because people wanted to dance like Fred Astaire and other film hoofers they saw at the Palace. To help bolster her teaching repertoire with the latest dances, Martin traveled to Hollywood for training. Folks who heard her sing booked her into some concert gigs, and she began to think she might have a career in show business.

Back in Texas, she auditioned with her student dancers for legendary showman Billy Rose, who was putting on one of his extravaganzas in Fort Worth. After the audition, Rose told Martin to forget about show business and go back to her family, but the rejection only redoubled her resolution. When her dance school was destroyed in a fire, Martin took it as a sign. Back she went to Hollywood—hoping this time to stay. Over the next two years, she became what she called "Audition Mary," trying to break into clubs, radio, recordings, movies—any place that would hire her. Despite her dance background, she generally got singing jobs. Her screen tests got nowhere, as she wrote in her autobiography, *My Heart Belongs*: "The consensus was always the same: neck too long, cheeks too thin, nose too round, hair the wrong color."

Her break came in a roundabout and unlikely way. She was helping some orchestrators who were arranging Arditti's light-classical piece "Il bacio" ("The Kiss") for Deanna Durbin, and Martin tried "swinging" it for fun. The reaction was so positive that she started using it as an audition piece. She was quickly booked and just as quickly moved from one club to another until she was earning a remarkable four hundred dollars a week at the Trocadero in Los Angeles with her swing "Il bacio" as the centerpiece of her act. There, she was "discovered" by Broadway producer Lawrence Schwab, who hired her for his upcoming New York musical *Ring Out the News*. She'd finally made it—or so she thought.

"My Heart Belongs to Daddy"

When she arrived in New York, an unhappy surprise awaited. Financing for *Ring Out the News* had fallen through, and so there was no show to do. She figured she'd go back to being "Audition Mary": same grind, different coast. One of her auditions was for Bella Spewack and Cole Porter, who were trying to cast a featured role in their new musical, called *Leave It to Me!* As soon as she sang her swing arrangement of "Il Bacio," she knew she had the job. Porter liked it so much he originally planned to interpolate it into the score. But, in the end, it may have been too good for the tyro performer, who was getting a bigger hand than the star during the show's tryout. The number got cut on the road.

Martin was furious, but Porter had something even better for her to do. He wrote Martin her first big song hit, "My Heart Belongs to Daddy," in which a young lady of the world cautions young men that they may dally with her but she will always remain true to the man who pays her bills. It's a sister song to "Always True to You (In My Fashion)" from *Kiss Me, Kate*.

Porter included every rhyme he could think of for "Daddy," including "dine on my fine finan haddie," a kind of fish filet popular in Scotland. It also had the advantage of sounding vaguely dirty, always a plus for Porter. She sang it to an adoring chorus of parka-clad Russian lads, including future star Gene Kelly.

Martin claimed in her autobiography that she was naively unaware the song was racy, but you couldn't tell that from her delivery, which was teasing and sultry. The staging also called for a striptease, though Martin still had a lace chemise on when she was done. In any case, the song certainly didn't sound like it was being sung by a hayseed. Martin had shed her Texas accent completely (at least when onstage) during her time in Hollywood and projected an urbanity that she didn't actually fully possess yet. But the illusion was a good one. Her social life exploded, especially after Life magazine put her on its cover. Today, not much is remembered about *Leave It to Me!* other than Martin's "My Heart Belongs to Daddy."

West Coast Interlude

Martin's triumph in *Leave It to Me!* finally earned her something she'd sought for years—a contract with a major film studio, in her case, Paramount Pictures. She later said that she hated leaving Broadway but snatched the movie offer only because she'd worked so hard and so fruitlessly to get one before. If so, her initial instinct proved to have been sound. She spent the next five years appearing with no great distinction in a series of light comedies and musicals, including *The Great Victor Herbert, Kiss the Boys Goodbye,* and *Birth of the Blues.* She was treated as a midlevel standard, perky singing ingenue, not as a unique talent. It was a sad waste of a wonderful performer in her prime. One of this period's films, *New York Town* (1941), paired her with future Music Man Robert Preston, with whom she would star in Broadway's *I Do! I Do!* a quarter century later.

Martin's second Hollywood sojourn may not have boosted her career, but it steered her to her soul mate. While there she met the love of her life, Richard Halliday, a story editor at Paramount. Once they married, he gave up his career to manage Martin full-time. He built a fearsome reputation as a demanding and tough negotiator on his wife's behalf and at times was a controlling presence in her life. Together they had a second child, Mary Heller Halliday, known as Heller.

Martin might have stayed in Hollywood and built a modest career there, but she wasn't thrilled with the parts she was getting. She also missed live audiences and hated the drudgery and endless waiting around of filmmaking. Besides, she had two offers for starring roles onstage. Vinton Freedley, who had produced *Leave It to Me!*, wanted her to star in his new musical, *Dancing in the Streets*, by Vernon Duke. And the newly forged songwriting team of Richard Rodgers and Oscar Hammerstein II wanted her to star in their new musical western, called *Away We Go!* Not sure what to do, Martin said she and Halliday literally flipped a coin and went with the Freedley project. As it happened, both shows tried out in Boston at the same time. *Dancing in the Streets* closed there, but *Away We Go!* continued on to Broadway under the new title *Oklahoma!* Martin had missed out the biggest hit of the wartime years and on one of the great musicals of the twentieth century. She would always regret the decision, and she resolved never to say no to Rodgers and Hammerstein again.

Her next project was an unusual one: producer Cheryl Crawford wanted her to play the goddess of love in *One Touch of Venus*, with music by Kurt Weill. In the story, someone slips a ring on a statue of Venus, causing her to come to life and complicate things for a mortal man before returning to her rightful place on Olympus.

Martin, always insecure about her looks, didn't think she was beautiful enough to play the part. But after a trip to a museum to see how many different ways Venus had been imagined by artists through the centuries, she agreed to take the part. She was seduced by the haunting Kurt Weill–Ogden Nash score, which included "Sing Low," "I'm a Stranger Here Myself," and "Foolish Heart," as well as by the Agnes de Mille dances and by the elegant and otherworldly costumes designed by couturier Mainbocher. For once, she truly felt beautiful.

In his review, Robert Garland, in the *Journal American*, wrote, "Miss Martin has grown into a performer of the first magnitude; that not only is she lovely, but that she can dance, act, sing, and project a serious scene—the finale of the piece is really touching—with the best of them."

Most of the critics agreed, and Martin at last had the Broadway starring role she'd prayed for. She resolved to stay and build on it. Martin rarely returned to Hollywood and never re-created any of her stage roles on the big screen.

Seeking a challenge, she next chose an unusual musical called *Lute Song*, based on the Chinese play and legend *Pi Pa-Ki*. She played a young wife whose husband disappears on a quest. When the wife goes in search of him, she discovers that he has married a princess.

John Houseman's production was sumptuous, with intricate oriental sets by Robert Edmond Jones and Martin's flowing costumes by another celebrity designer, Valentina. In the role of the husband was Yul Brynner in his first leading role. He had auditioned for Martin and the producers at her home in Connecticut, and Martin later claimed that she and her husband discovered him. Singing "Mountain High, Valley Low" by Raymond Scott and Bernie Hanigan, Martin rustled across the stage of the Plymouth (now Schoenfeld) Theatre for six months and toured.

Martin spent the next two years on a pair of adventures, one happy, one not. Noël Coward invited her to London to appear in his musical *Pacific 1860,* though they quarreled over costuming. She cast jealous eyes on Irving Berlin's *Annie Get Your Gun*, by then a great Broadway hit for Ethel Merman. After her two elegant roles in *One Touch of Venus* and *Lute Song*, producers Rodgers and Hammerstein needed to be convinced that she could play a rootin'-tootin' cowgirl like Annie Oakley. Martin auditioned and got to play the role for the national tour.

South Pacific

When Rodgers and Hammerstein approached Martin to create the lead in their next musical, *South Pacific*, she jumped. The 1949 show was based on the Pulitzer Prize-winning *Tales of the South Pacific* stories by James Michener, about the cultural clash among Polynesian natives, French colonials, and American military personnel in the Pacific theater of World War II. Hammerstein's libretto braided two of the stories together. One was the story of Lieutenant Cable, who falls in love with a Polynesian girl but finds himself unable to marry her because he knows he could never bring her home to his family. The other was the story of Nellie Forbush (Martin), an American nurse who falls in love with a handsome French planter, the widower Emile De Beque (Ezio Pinza), but finds it difficult to accept his two children, who are half Polynesian. It was a controversial show because it came out emphatically against racial prejudice and, in fact, endorsed interracial romance. In a time just before the civil rights movement of the 1950s and 1960s, *South Pacific* was a show about the need to learn tolerance.

This was a musical drama of the kind that would have been unthinkable ten years earlier, but much had changed, and performers with dramatic chops like Martin reaped the benefit. Rodgers and Hammerstein tailored the part to her, just as Mainbocher had tailored her *One Touch of Venus* costumes. In "A Wonderful Guy," the final repetition of the words "I'm in love" thirteen times is just the sort of exuberance Martin herself radiated and the writers saw in her. The first time the songwriters played it for her, she got so excited at the end that she fell off the piano bench where she was sitting.

She wrote that Rodgers looked down at her solemnly and said, "Never sing it any other way."

The song "Honey Bun," which Nellie performed in a baggy sailor suit as a show-within-a-show in Act II, reflected her self-deprecating sexiness. "I'm Gonna Wash That Man Right Out of My Hair," in which Martin actually washed her cropped hair onstage each night, was suggested by her, and Rodgers and Hammerstein leaped on the unusual staging idea. Hammerstein also crafted the upbeat-and-proud-of-it lyric of "A Cockeyed Optimist" for Martin, though he might have been describing himself just as well.

"From the very beginning *South Pacific* was pure joy," Martin wrote in her autobiography. "Everyone had a beautiful voice, great talent. We couldn't wait to get to rehearsals. No matter how many hours we worked we never wanted to stop. We couldn't wait to get back. It was the excitement of an operating room, when somebody's life is being saved by a team, or like a delivery room when a new life is coming."

One of Martin's insecurities came to the fore on *South Pacific*. Her leading man was basso Ezio Pinza, who had sung with the Metropolitan Opera and whose voice was as majestic as his charisma. Considering their differences, the two performers had extraordinary chemistry, but Martin was so insecure about her singing that she asked Rodgers and Hammerstein to write them no duets. The closest they come is "Twin Soliloquies," in which each sang in turn but they never harmonized together.

The show was the longest-running Broadway hit of Martin's career—nearly two thousand performances. It won nine Tony Awards, including Best Musical and Best Actress in a Musical (for Martin), and then it won the Pulitzer Prize for Drama, only the second musical to do so. Martin toured with the show and re-created the role of Nellie in London.

Merman/Martin

Despite her loathing of film work, Martin was coaxed to do a 1953 television special celebrating the fiftieth anniversary of the Ford Motor Company, taped at the old Center Theatre. The primary lure was the chance to work with costar Ethel Merman. The two divas got along well, though Merman seemed determined to upstage Martin in subtle ways and played to the camera more than Martin. The special consisted of a series of skits and songs featuring each of the two stars. Martin got to use her mime skills in a segment that satirized absurd extremes of women's fashions over the previous half century.

But the centerpiece of the show was a fifteen-minute medley of songs in which the two stars alternated in solos and then harmonized. Assembled by master conductor Jay Blackton, the segment, which came to be known as the "Merman-Martin Medley," showed them each singing their biggest hits, like "Wonderful Guy" and "No Business Like Show Business," plus some old chestnuts like "Shine on, Harvest Moon." Each performed flawlessly, and the special drew ratings stunning even for that pre-cable, pre-Internet time. It was seen by millions, which only increased Martin's drawing power on Broadway and on tour.

Peter Pan

Martin said she always wanted to play Peter from the first time she heard the story of the boy who wouldn't grow up and who flew through the night sky to wondrous adventures in Neverland—a place where "there's hardly any room between one adventure and the next."

Martin reported having flying dreams, even as a child, and knew somehow that she would one day fly. That's why, when she was approached by director Jerome Robbins to play Pan, she said yes as soon as he outlined his plans for a kind of flying ballet. Martin was forty years old when she created the role in the musical.

The character had been created in 1902 by Scottish novelist and playwright J. M. Barrie and first appeared on the stage in 1904. For many years the definitive Peter was Maude Adams, who established the tradition of having Peter played by a woman. She was later succeeded by Eve Le Gallienne. A 1950 Broadway version with songs by Leonard Bernstein starred Jean Arthur. Disney's 1953 animated film musical used a male voice for Peter.

So how did Martin manage to make the role her own in such ample company? Much credit should go to the two composing teams that worked on the show. First, Mark "Moose" Charlap and Carolyn Leigh, who gave Martin "I've Got to Crow," "I'm Flying," and "I Won't Grow Up." Then Jule Styne, Betty Comden, and Adolph Green, who added "Wendy," "Distant Melody," "Mysterious Lady," and one of the most beautiful ballads ever written for Broadway, "Neverland."

Martin was at the peak of her power as a performer. Hands on hips, shoulders thrown back, feet widely spaced, she was a defiant, insouciant Peter, the very picture of joyously arrogant boyhood. For once, being flat-chested was a boon. She was never saccharine. Her Peter was bossy and conceited one moment, loving and loyal the next, mysterious and supernatural the third, and ready to do fierce battle the fourth. It was exactly kind of Peter who could deliver Barrie's line "To die would be an awfully big adventure."

She threw herself into every moment of Peter Pan, including those in which, standing on a ledge twenty feet above the stage, she would leap out into thin air, fully trusting the harness and piano wire managed by Joseph Kirby and Peter Foy to hold her aloft. Flinging fistfuls of "fairy dust" as she swooped, she played Peter with such force of conviction that the mind's eye could erase the wire and see her as simply flying. This quality was crystallized in her crow. Her lusty "Er-er-er-errrrrrrrh" became one of the touchstones of the performance.

Peter Pan had only a short run on Broadway—152 performances in the two months before Christmas 1954, and the two months after. Like The Wizard of Oz, it transformed into a cultural icon only when it began to be shown at holiday time on television.

In 1955, NBC was looking for material to broadcast in color to help spur sales of TV sets using its newly perfected color television format. The "Peacock Network" invited Martin to re-create her performance as Peter Pan for its *Producers' Showcase* anthology series. The program aired March 7, 1955, just nine days after the musical closed on Broadway and became the highest-rated TV production to that time, exceeding even the ratings for the Ford anniversary show with Ethel Merman.

One of the NBC graphic artists working on the production was a man named Harvey Schmidt, who also was trying to break in as a composer. One of Schmidt's enduring memories was first arriving at the Brooklyn studio where Martin was rehearsing her "I'm Flying" ballet and having her swoop toward him and call out, "Hello!" A fellow expatriate Texan, Schmidt dreamed of someday writing a musical for her. A decade later, after composing the score to *The Fantasticks*, Schmidt would write *I Do! I Do!* for her.

Sad to say, that initial live broadcast of *Peter Pan* was not preserved in any form; nor was it taped when the whole production was reassembled for a rebroadcast the following January after young fans clamored for it. For many children across America, it was their first glimpse of a Broadway show, and the magic and delight created by Martin's and Ritchard's performances, Robbins's dramatic staging, and Foy's fabulous flying left a lasting impression.

Finally, in 1960, NBC brought everyone into the studio a third time, with Lynn Fontanne as narrator and Margalo Gillmore as Mrs. Darling, and this time preserved the performance on tape. This version was rebroadcast in 1963, 1966, and 1973 but then was apparently lost. Rediscovered and remastered in the late 1980s. This version is available today on home video.

In addition to her many lucky breaks and wise choices, Martin had a stunning track record of turning down projects that became major hits. After passing on *Oklahoma!*, she declined the lead role in *Kiss, Me Kate* when Cole Porter tarried in sending her copies of the music.

In the mid-1950s the songwriting team of Lerner and Loewe played Martin the score they were writing for a new musical based on George Bernard Shaw's *Pygmalion*. She famously remarked to her husband, sadly, "Those boys have lost their talent." The show was *My Fair Lady*, and the role went instead to Julie Andrews—who would also later snatch away the movie version of Martin's starring role in *The Sound of Music*.

Martin wore the big red dress as one of the many successors in the title role of Jerry Herman's *Hello, Dolly!* but passed on the chance to originate the title role in his *Mame*. The role instead went to Angela Lansbury.

Imagine Martin's career if, in addition to everything she *did* do, she had originated those four classics. That their creators envisioned Martin first stands as a tribute to her.

The Sound of Music

Mary Martin was the only star for whom Rodgers and Hammerstein wrote two of their musicals (three if you count the rejected offer for *Oklahoma!*). The third became one of the most popular shows in the history of Broadway, *The Sound of Music*. The project began in the 1950s when Martin saw a film about the singing von Trapp family of Austria. Maria Rainier, a postulant in an Austrian abbey, couldn't adapt to the cloistered life, so she was sent to be nanny to the large motherless family of an Austrian naval captain. She taught them to sing and fell in love, first with the kids, then with their father, just in time to escape the invading Nazis by scaling the Alps to freedom in Switzerland.

Nuns and Nazis were not the usual stuff of Broadway musicals, and after Rodgers and Hammerstein agreed to take on the project, everyone from director Vincent J. Donehue on down strove mightily to keep it from becoming either too sunny or too grim. Though the show is today considered the epitome of saccharine sweetness and light, it may be because the creators worked so hard to keep it from becoming the opposite and to give each child and each nun a distinct personality.

Lyricist Hammerstein was battling cancer during the writing of the show but nevertheless gave Martin a bouquet of upbeat songs, such as the title number (sung in a tree, not on a mountaintop as in the film), "My Favorite Things," "The Lonely Goatherd," and one of the team's most delightful creations, "Do-Re-Mi," in which Maria teaches the children the C scale, as well as harmony and counterpoint—all within a single five-and-a-half-minute song.

"Edelweiss," set to a heartbreaking Rodgers waltz, compares Austria to a flower that blooms on snowy mountainsides. It's a paean to the renewing power of life. It was the last song Hammerstein ever wrote. He lived long enough to see the show's successful opening and died a few months later. Martin's great booster and collaborator was gone.

Martin's sprightliness enabled the audience to suspend its disbelief in a fortysomething woman playing a twentysomething postulant. When the show was sold to Hollywood, Martin was already approaching her fiftieth birthday. The movie role of Maria went to Julie Andrews, and the film entered history as one of the most successful ever made. Though *The Sound of Music* was Martin's second-longest-running show, few members of the general public today associate her with the part she created. She did profit from it, however. She and Halliday were major investors and got a slice of all the money Andrews earned singing Martin's "Do-Re-Mi."

Jennie

Following *The Sound of Music*, Martin agreed to play Laurette Taylor, queen of the melodramas, in a 1963 musical biography called *Jennie*, by the songwriting team of Arthur Schwartz and Howard Dietz.

Though she didn't quite fly, she had all sorts of other acrobatic fun to perform in re-creating some of Taylor's girl-in-peril film adventures. The show is remembered, if at all, for a scene in which Martin was being "tortured" while strapped to a revolving platform that spun faster and faster as she sang. In reality, the gizmo was one she'd found at the sporting-goods store Hammacher Schlemmer to improve the circulation. She enjoyed it, but audiences found it harrowing.

The show attempted to tell too much story with too little emotional connection to the characters, and while Martin got to sing the pretty "Before I Kiss the World Goodbye," *Jennie* stalled after just eighty-two performances, giving Martin the first big Broadway musical flop of her career.

Martin visited her friend Janet Gaynor, who had discovered the unusual appeal of farm life in the jungle near Anápolis, Brazil. Today the city is an industrial center, but then it was still part of the jungle in Brazil's eastern highlands. The Hallidays ventured into the South American outback and were immediately seduced by the primal beauty of the place. They purchased an adobe house on a hilltop and called it Nossa Fazenda, or "Our Farm." Over the next decade, Martin would spend more and more time there.

I Do! I Do!

In 1966, Harvey Schmidt, Martin's old friend from the *Peter Pan* days, approached her with an idea for a musical, to be called *I Do! I Do!* In the intervening year he had written the music to *The Fantasticks*, which would become the longest-running musical in history, and *110 in the Shade*, which had run nine months on Broadway. The producer of *110*, David Merrick, was behind this new project, a musical based on Jan de Hartog's play *The Fourposter,* depicting fifty years in the life of a middle-class married couple.

I Do! I Do! offered a challenge to the fifty-three-year-old Martin: there were only two characters, and they had to carry the entire show—no chorus, no secondary romance, no comic specialties. It would be just Mary Martin as Agnes and, as her husband Michael, screen and stage veteran Robert Preston, who was still enjoying the afterglow of his performance in *The Music Man.*

Schmidt fulfilled his dream of writing a show for her. He and partner Tom Jones gave her a series of warmly funny duets, including "When the Kids Get Married," "Good Night," and "Nobody's Perfect"; beautiful ballads "What Is a Woman?" and "My Cup Runneth Over"; and a showboat bump-and-grind, "Flaming Agnes."

While there were very few sharp edges, the show proved to be a great showcase for two old pros. Martin and Preston got along very well, and audiences could feel the warmth from out front.

Critic Norman Nadel of the *World Journal Tribune* allowed, "Mary Martin will have the gift of youthfulness as along as she lives." But others weren't so sure.

Historian Steven Suskin wrote in his book *Opening Nights on Broadway*, "She brought to the role a certain dignified tone, due not only to age but also to an apparent change in personality. Mary seemed to have undergone a transformation in 1959 upon donning the habit and wimple of Maria von Trapp. The kittenish hoyden ceased to be kittenish, the cornily vivacious Nellie Forbush stopped turning cartwheels, and a demure prudity overtook the exuberant Lost Boy of only a few years earlier."

The show, which opened in December 1966, ran a year and a half.

Legends! and Later Career

After *I Do! I Do!,* Martin fulfilled a promise to her husband to spend two years at Nossa Fazenda. Two years stretched to more than four as the Hallidays settled into rural life. In 1973, Halliday passed away, and Martin gave up the farm to return to the United States.

In 1977 Martin made what turned out to be her final Broadway performance in *Do You Turn Somersaults?,* a nonmusical Russian play that ran just two weeks.

Merman and Martin reunited one last time in May 1982 for a Carnegie Hall concert that, among other things, re-created a version of the Merman–Martin medley that they had performed on TV nearly three decades earlier. The sold-out event was Martin's New York swan song.

Martin did some television work in the 1980s and survived a serious car accident in which her friend Janet Gaynor was seriously injured and Gaynor's husband killed. But as the decade moved into its second half, Martin took on two big projects designed to bring her back to Broadway. Both went on the rocks, though for very different reasons.

Playwright James Kirkwood, who had shared the Pulitzer Prize for *A Chorus Line,* wrote *Legends!,* a comedy/drama about two fading older female performers who team up for a mutual comeback and spend a long evening airing all their grudges and grievances to each other. As it turned out, life imitated art all too well. Martin was paired with another *Hello, Dolly!* star, originator Carol Channing for the bitchy play, which launched a twenty-plus city tryout tour in 1986, with the goal of opening on Broadway in spring 1987.

They never made it. In his book *Diary of a Mad Playwright,* Kirkwood chronicled the manifold backstage disasters that led to the show's closing on the road. Channing played Sylvia Glenn, the nastier of the two; and Martin played the supposedly sweet-tempered Leatrice Monsee. But Kirkwood charged both his stars with the worst kind of competition and diva behavior. The lion's share of the blame seemed to fall on Martin, who, at age seventy-three, was unable to memorize her lines fully.

She also began to engage in some odd and undignified behavior. One night she took down her drawers and mooned Channing onstage. Kirkwood dutifully recorded that her fundament was "firm and pink and pretty." Things had come to such a pass in the show that the moment was left in (!), with Martin agreeing to use a pink body stocking to cover her bottom.

Kirkwood quoted director Clifford Williams as saying, "It's like doing a school play with two elderly 12-year-olds."

Things finally hit bottom for real when Kirkwood and Williams decided to eliminate Martin's Act II speech about breast cancer, which she regarded as central to understanding the character. Martin issued a press statement saying, "This is a very rare moment in my professional career. Not only is the speech ruined for me, but also the play is ruined for me. I will go on, but I will not play London, and I will not come to New York. I'll fulfill my contract, and then you can get someone else and cut anything you want."

Attempts to find a replacement failed, and *Legends!* closed out of town.

There was one more attempt at a last hurrah. The *I Do! I Do!* songwriting team of Tom Jones and Harvey Schmidt conceived of a musical based on Thornton Wilder's classic American drama *Our Town*. Retitled *Grovers Corners*, the musical would tell the same simple story of two neighboring families in rural New Hampshire. The setting was not unlike that of *The Fantasticks*. Like *Our Town*, *Grovers Corners* found the deepest insights into human behavior in the tiniest moments of small-town life. Both the play and the musical were to be filled with presentational devices, including a narrator called the Stage Manager. In addition to welcoming the audience and sketching in details about characters, the Stage Manager also has the power to speed up time, or to jump the action forward or backward in time to illustrate a point.

The Stage Manager was usually played by a man, but in *Grovers Corners* the role was to have been played by a woman—Martin. But her stage comeback was never to be. Just as *Grovers Corners* was gearing up for its tryout in 1987, Martin announced her withdrawal. She was ill with what turned out to be colorectal cancer. She was well enough to attend the Kennedy Center Honors ceremony in 1989 but spent the next year in a losing battle with the cancer.

Martin died November 3, 1990, at age seventy-six. Peter Pan was off on his greatest adventure.

Danny Kaye in *Wonder Man* (1945). PHOTOFEST

DANNY KAYE
Geet-Got-Gittle-Oddle-Got-Go-Say

There are a lot of photos of Danny Kaye, and not one does him justice.

Oh, he looked like that, all right. But Kaye existed in a frenzied world of scats, squeaks, pops, thrums, oofs, and gargles delivered at rat-tat-tat velocity and with Olympic-class mugging no still image could hope to capture.

Sharp-featured, with an explosion of red hair and a manner that could be sweet and shy and retiring one minute and wildly bombastic the next, his specialty was high-speed verbal and physical gymnastics performed with almost supernatural energy. Cole Porter, Ira Gershwin, and Kurt Weill were intrigued enough by his special abilities that they wrote musicals to showcase him. Adorable onstage, Kaye had a tendency to temperament and temper offstage, vigorously encouraged by his wife and frequent writer, Sylvia Fine.

He was beloved by audiences for decades and was such a tireless fundraiser for UNICEF that the children's organization chose him to accept its Nobel Peace Prize. Yet in the end his restless running from one form to another left him not only with a spotty record on Broadway (just four musicals and two special concert appearances), but overall a career in film, variety, and television that was great, but not as spectacular as everyone who experienced him live in those early years would have predicted.

★

Kaye was born Daniel David Kaminsky ("Kominsky," according to some sources) on January 18, 1913, into a family of Ukrainian Jews who immigrated to Brooklyn three years earlier. His father was a tailor, not much different from Motel in *Fiddler on the Roof,* and like Motel, he made sure his family didn't starve—but couldn't do much beyond that.

The family had the immigrant's near-worship of doctors, and young Daniel harbored a lifelong dream of becoming a surgeon. But there was no hope, financially, of medical school, so he dropped out of Thomas Jefferson High School when he was fourteen and worked at a soda fountain before creating a little singing vaudeville act called Red and Blackie, with his friend Louis Elison. They sang and danced, and Kaye began displaying his facility with physical comedy, silly voices, and funny faces.

But his entry into vaudeville came just as the art form was expiring, partly due to the

Great Depression. He toured the United States, adopting the shortened name "Kaye," and even traveled to East Asia, where he developed his unique style of double-talking gibberish, which, combined with his nonverbal clowning, helped him transcend the language barrier. It would become his trademark.

Returning to the United States, and finding little employment in vaudeville, he took his skills to the 'Skills—the Catskill Mountains northwest of New York City, where middle-class "campers" with any money at all retreated to leafy resorts to escape the pre-air-conditioning summer heat. His job was to serve as "tummler," a combination emcee, social director, and street performer, who kept things lively by bringing people together for outdoor activities by day and entertaining onstage by night. It was a good training ground for Kaye.

In his quest for employment, Kaye traveled to London to perform in music halls there, beginning a lifelong love affair between Kaye and the British. Back in New York in 1938, he auditioned for *Saturday Night Vanities*, a small-time revue. There he met a dark-haired pianist and songwriter named Sylvia Fine. She penned parodies of classic songs, along with original material of her own. "I walked in and saw Danny doing a song called 'Vultures of Culture,'" she later told a magazine interviewer. "He terrified me. I was never naive and before I had left that day, he made offers of a suggestive nature."

They were married within a year. It was the turning point for both of them. She understood his abilities, and they matched her satirical instincts. For the rest of their lives she was his most reliable writer and he was her most reliable interpreter. She crafted (sometimes with help) many of his signature songs, like "Anatole of Paris," "Lullabye in Ragtime," and "Melody in 4-F." She also served as his business manager, earning a reputation for assertiveness (and sometimes brusqueness). Later, she coproduced his films *The Five Pennies* (earning an Oscar nomination for her songs) and *The Inspector General*. They also produced a daughter, Dena.

While both Kaye and Fine bristled when one commentator snidely remarked that Kaye "has a Fine head on his shoulders," the truth remains that the Danny Kaye known to the world was in a great part the creation of Sylvia Fine. He was her masterpiece. But it's not easy being someone else's masterpiece. Though they stayed married until death, there was no small amount of friction in their relationship. They even separated for four weeks in 1947. There were rumors of affairs over the years, with Kaye, at various times, being connected with Eve Arden and even the pre-Fosse Gwen Verdon.

The most sensational claim came in Donald Spoto's 1992 biography of British master actor Laurence Olivier, with whom he alleged Kaye carried on a ten-year homosexual relationship—an assertion backed by Olivier's wife, Joan Plowright. However, in a 1994 biography of Kaye, *Nobody's Fool*, Martin Gottfried rebutted the story, saying, "There is no evidence of, and there are no witnesses to, a Kaye-Olivier sexual relationship."

Whether the stories are true or not, the Kaye-Fine alliance survived the difficulties and lasted more than forty years.

"I Love Russian Composers"

With better material, Kaye was able to get work at the well-paying Camp Tamiment in the Pocono Mountains of Pennsylvania, where he began cultivating a swankier class of fans. Among them was Harry Kaufman, who worked for the producing and theatre-owning Shubert brothers. Kaufman arranged for Kaye and other Tamiment talent, including future Broadway giants Alfred Drake, Jerome Robbins, and Imogene Coca, to appear on Broadway in *The Straw Hat Revue*, a reference to its origin in the summer theatres known as the Straw Hat circuit. Fine cowrote the music and lyrics. The production opened September 29, 1939, and, considering the cast, elicited mostly critical yawns and closed the week following Thanksgiving after just seventy-five performances.

Nevertheless, Kaye's verbal gymnastics earned him his breakout role(s), a pair of plum featured parts in the Kurt Weill/Ira Gershwin/Moss Hart musical *Lady in the Dark* (1941). Gertrude Lawrence starred in the prefeminist show about a high-power female fashion editor torn between the demands of her career and her "proper" womanly urges to marry and have children. Her conflicts come to a head in Act II during a dream sequence in which she sees her life as both a circus and a courtroom trial. Kaye played an effeminate clothing designer in Act I, but in Act II he was transformed by her subconscious into an imperious ringmaster/judge who hears the "evidence" against her.

The centerpiece of Kaye's performance was a non-sequitur (this was a dream, after all) set piece. Crafted by Gershwin especially to suit Kaye's talent, "Tchaikovsky" called on him to machine-gun the names of forty-nine Russian composers in thirty-eight seconds, ending with an apology that rhymes "Rachmaninoff" with "You all have undergone enough."

The song may have been partly inspired by Fine's "Stanislavsky" (poking fun at the pooh-bah of the Moscow Art Theater) but was not written by Fine, as some sources claim; it included several Gershwin private jokes, including the original name of his friend composer Vernon Duke (né Dukelsky) and Gershwin in-law Leopold Godowsky.

The number proved to be a classic Broadway showstopper. Poleaxed early audiences would shriek and applaud until Kaye did an encore. There was concern that he would actually overshadow the billed star, Lawrence, but Lawrence was secure enough to allow Kaye his moment in the sun, knowing she would soon top him with the show's eleven-o'clock number, "Jenny."

Offers for starring roles poured in. One came from a source hard to pass up: composer Cole Porter. Kaye had struggled in showbiz for seventeen years, through the teeth of the Depression, to arrive at the moment of his first Broadway starring role. Porter and his collaborators, Dorothy and Herbert Fields, were making a musical out of the 1920s farce *The Cradle Snatchers*, about three neglected wives who try to recruit three college boys to help make their husbands jealous. In the wartime musical adaptation, retitled *Let's Face It!* (sometimes rendered without the exclamation point), the women turned to young soldiers as their would-be gigolos. The main wife was played by Eve Arden and the main GI by Danny Kaye.

Coming a decade after *Anything Goes* and three years before *Kiss Me, Kate, Let's Face It!* was not one of Porter's great scores. Kaye and Fine pressed to interpolate her specialty material, and Porter acquiesced. And here's where Broadway got one of its classics. Fine and Liebman's "Melody in 4-F" is a great artifact of World War II–era America. In it, Kaye narrates how he got his draft notice, reported for duty, underwent a physical, got trained by a bossy sergeant, and went on to distinguished military success. But it wasn't that simple. It started out like a slow spiritual, "Oh they made a law down in Washington, D.C. . . . " and described how the draft works. The song then suddenly veered into up-tempo scat singing for the entire rest of its narrative. Kaye mimed the physical, the training and combat, while babbling out an amazing stream of geet-got-gittle-oddle-got-go-say gibberish, interspersed with occasional intelligible words. It was a startling work of unique virtuosity. It gave apprehensive wartime audiences a chance to laugh at a very stressful rite of passage—and have a happy ending.

Reviewing the show, *Time* magazine wrote, "The mad gestures and faces Kaye makes are enough to win him a niche in comic pantomime; they shrink to nothing compared with his whirlwind patter, his miraculous doubletalk."

The title turns out to be ironic, since the narrator plainly is judged 1-A (a rating indicating prime draft material) instead of 4-F (unfit for service). The title is doubly ironic since Kaye had, just before that time, been summoned by the draft but was rated 4-F owing to a medical condition. Inspectors later claimed the health problem was faked, and for many years the FBI maintained a file on Kaye, seeking unsuccessfully to link him with communist groups.

When Kaye left the show "Melody in 4-F" went with him, but *Let's Face It!* managed a run of 547 performances, one of the longest in Cole Porter's career. It would be Kaye's last Broadway appearance for a decade and his last appearance in a book musical until 1970.

Headed West

Just as there are no photos that do Kaye justice, film and television appearances were not much better. Kaye was at his best only in front of a live audience. His shtick was about perfection at top speed. His appeal was the appeal of the high-wire act. You have to feel that Kaye is able to fall, to trip up or forget the words, in order to fully thrill when he doesn't. Some of Kaye's best films captured that energy by showing him doing his "bits" in front of audiences of various kinds. His 1960s TV series would be filmed in front of a live audience, as well.

When *Let's Face It!* was bought for Hollywood, Kaye was replaced by Bob Hope, minus Fine's specialty material. The Hope film flopped, but "Melody in 4-F" got its film debut, after all, in *Up in Arms* (1944), a war-themed comedy crafted around Kaye. That fragment remains the best document of Kaye's Broadway hit.

Among his other best movies were *The Secret Life of Walter Mitty* (1947), based on a James Thurber story about a mousy man who imagines himself the hero of all sorts of swashbuckling situations, and *The Court Jester* (1955), which includes a cherished routine in which he tries to memorize the life-saving phrase "The pellet with the poison's in the vessel with the pestle. The chalice from the palace has the brew that is true."

Kaye never forgot the stage, and the stage didn't forget him. Kaye won a special honor from the Tony Awards in 1953 and an honorary Oscar in 1954, though he never won regular versions of either award.

However, Kaye passed on a chance to star in a new musical being developed for Broadway in the mid-1950s. Originally titled *The Silver Triangle*, about a traveling con man who tries to bamboozle an Iowa piano teacher, the musical was rechristened *The Music Man*. The only song Fine liked was a fast-talking patter number that seemed custom-made for Kaye, "Ya Got Trouble," also known as "Trouble in River City." Instead, the role and the song and the glory went to Robert Preston.

Kaye's greatest film success came in a project that was closest in form to a traditional Broadway musical and one of the few that was written by someone other than Sylvia Fine. Frank Loesser, composer of *Guys and Dolls*, had been working on a collection of songs based on children's fairy tales. Many grew out of the fables of Danish writer Hans Christian Andersen. The collection became the basis of a 1952 musical film biography also called *Hans Christian Andersen*—a pseudobiography, really, since so many of the details were made up.

Kaye starred as Andersen, a cobbler whose business is going to pot because he keeps interrupting his work to tell stories to children. He goes to the capital, "Wonderful Copenhagen," to make ballet slippers for the greatest ballerina in Denmark and winds up falling in love with her. His romantic dreams are dashed, however, when he finds she is married, but the ballet company discovers his storytelling ability and uses his tales as the basis for great ballets, and so his fortune and name are made.

It was a radical departure for Kaye, a far gentler and sweeter sort of comedy than he'd generally done before. There was none of the fast-talking freneticism of his most familiar work. The closest thing to a patter song was "No Two People," in which the two singers step on each other's lines as they proclaim their love, somewhat in the style of Loesser's "Baby, It's Cold Outside." Instead, Kaye got to sing beautifully harmonized ballads, like "Inchworm," "Ugly Duckling," and "Anywhere I Wander," that showed Loesser at his best and revealed Kaye as a credible romantic leading man with a simultaneous enormous appeal to children. People who have seen only this film still think of Kaye as an innocent, melodious sprite, not as the antic kangaroo seen in his other works. *Hans Christian Andersen* was one of the most successful motion pictures in the history of MGM Studios, which is saying a lot for that musical-film powerhouse.

Kaye made several more films and returned to Broadway in 1963 for a sold-out concert show at the Palace Theatre that ran fourteen weeks, beating even William Gaxton's long-standing record of ten weeks for a male performer. The success of that show helped launch him onto television, where he hosted a variety hour, *The Danny Kaye Show*, on CBS from

1963 to 1967. Kids who first saw *The Wizard of Oz* on TV during its annual CBS airings from 1964 to 1967 may also remember him as the host.

But even before the cancellation of his TV show, Kaye began to feel restless. He entered a period when he was constantly busy, but in an unfocused way. He immersed himself in UN work, Jewish charities, cooking, and golf. He indulged his fascination with doctors and surgery by convincing some to let him watch over their shoulders as they worked. He similarly indulged his love of classical music by taking gigs as (comedic) guest conductor for prominent symphony orchestras. He once conducted "Flight of the Bumblebee" with a flyswatter.

He also released a popular record album of stories for kids. Many baby boomers grew up with an LP of Kaye bawling, "Mommyy! Get me a drinka water!"

Two by Two

Kaye made his final return to Broadway in a 1970 musical that spun off considerable legend.

Richard Rodgers and Martin Charnin collaborated on *Two by Two*, telling the biblical story of Noah and his ark but (based on Clifford Odets's *The Flowering Peach*) portraying the Noah clan as a squabbling middle-class Jewish family subjected to the strains of a literal catastrophe.

Kaye had a few melodic and mildly comic songs, including "When It Dries," "Hey Girlie," and the title song, but none had the punch and élan of his old Sylvia Fine material. The closest Kaye had to a real audience-pleasing workout was "Ninety Again," in which the superannuated Noah is zapped back to youth by God. Kaye got to use his wacky voices and pliable body to illustrate a song about a withered body coming back to life. It wasn't exactly another "Melody in 4-F," but it was the Danny Kaye people hoped and expected to see. Kaye became restless in the part and began inserting more and more Kaye "business" into the proceedings, over the objections of the writers but often to the delight of the audience—or those who were already his fans, at any rate.

During one of these unscripted capers, Kaye tore a ligament in his left leg. It looked like a show-closing injury, but then, two weeks after the accident, Kaye was back! The producers announced that the show had been restaged to accommodate a now wheelchair-bound star (he later graduated to crutches). Some saw it as the epitome of the show-must-go-on tradition, but others saw that it gave him license to ad-lib more and more of the show. Kaye, who had grown more difficult offstage over the years, now also acquired an onstage reputation as a ham. He never did another Broadway show.

Later Career

Kaye continued to work, virtually until his death. He could have starred in almost any stage show he chose. He just didn't choose to, alas.

Instead, he continued his unfocused, restless ways. He flew a jet; he raised money for UNICEF; he bought a one-sixth interest in the Seattle Mariners baseball team; he cooked some more. The Culinary Institute of America named its auditorium the Danny Kaye Theatre after him.

Kaye's film and stage legacy, coupled with his charity work, enabled him to spend many pleasant evenings collecting awards. There was the Screen Actors Guild Award for "outstanding achievement in fostering the finest ideals of the acting profession," the French Officier des Arts et Lettres and the French Legion of Honor award. In 1984 he accepted Kennedy Center Honors from President Ronald Reagan.

His final starring role came in a TV movie, *Skokie*, playing a Holocaust survivor who takes part in a protest when American neo-Nazis march through an Illinois town with a large Jewish population.

Kaye endured a successful quadruple bypass operation in 1983, but on March 3, 1987, while fighting off a bout of hepatitis, Kaye died of a heart attack at age seventy-four. Sylvia Fine followed him (from emphysema) on October 28, 1991.

Though he's ultimately better known as a film star, the stage has reclaimed Kaye in several ways. Nathan Lane performed a tribute concert to Kaye with the Boston Pops, re-creating some of Kaye's choice bits. Brian Childers and Perry Payne starred in *Danny & Sylvia: A Musical Love Story*, done off-off-Broadway in 2002. A New York theatre for a time carried their name: the Sylvia and Danny Kaye Playhouse.

Kaye remains a byword for limitless energy absorbed from his audiences and blazed back at them.

Carol Channing makes her entrance into the Harmonia Gardens in *Hello, Dolly!* (1964). PHOTOFEST

CAROL CHANNING
Dolly

Carol Channing is one of the most iconic Broadway stars. Her wild blond hair, anime-character eyes, and shquawking voice virtually *are* Broadway in many people's minds.

But, in fact, it can be said that her actual Broadway experience was two feet wide and a mile deep. Her immortality rests on just two major roles, Lorelei Lee in *Gentlemen Prefer Blondes* and Dolly Gallagher Levi in *Hello, Dolly!* But those, it turns out, were more than enough.

The Dolly character became so identified with Channing that it virtually became her name. She reported being introduced as "Dolly" or even as "Hellodolly" as if that were her character's name or even *her* actual name.

And she so tirelessly promoted Dolly and Broadway and herself in such a powerful and integrated way that perhaps we should add a third character to her repertoire, one we'll call Miss Broadway. It was an image that evolved over the years. In her later years she became a caricature of herself: the poufed hair, the screechy voice, the slightly Gracie Allen–esque sense of humor. There was always something a little bit mad about Channing. She always protested that she sounded perfectly normal to herself and didn't really see what legions of impressionists were doing

But even in her early years, when she was perceived as a nubile Amazon, she was sui generis. This was good and bad for her career. Being unique also made her hard to cast. She spent most of her career seeking roles that suited her persona, and when she found one, like Lorelei Lee or Dolly, she clung to it like a barnacle.

★

For a person so outgoing, who was seen as virtually the embodiment of extroversion, Channing, born January 31, 1921, in Seattle, carried a lot of secrets in that Dolly handbag, including three big ones that were revealed only when she was in her eighties.

The first was that she was partly African American. No big deal today, but in her day it would have severely limited the kinds of roles she would have been allowed to play. It was especially hard to hide this heritage since she adored her mixed-race father, George Channing, a devotee of Christian Science who was a newspaper editor, author, and worldwide lecturer on the subject.

The first time Channing set foot in a theatre was when she and her mother were distributing Christian Science literature at the Curran Theatre in San Francisco. Her mother was not easy to get along with, especially since she seems to have resented both Carol's closeness with her father and her precocious talent. She once talked a teacher out of giving Carol an oratorical award and gloated over her failures.

These were few. When Carol was in fourth grade, she was nominated as class secretary and turned her campaign speech into standup comedy, doing impressions of teachers and the principal. The speech earned Channing her first laughs, and she remembers running to the school coatroom and crying her eyes out from pleasure, vowing to get herself in front of an audience again as soon as possible. Channing chose to attend the progressive Bennington College in Vermont. She claimed it was the only college she could find that would let her major in both drama and dance. The school also expected students to get a job each summer in whatever field they were studying. Call it naïveté, call it chutzpah, Channing went directly to the William Morris talent agency in New York and asked to see the president, Abe Lastfogel.

What followed was one of Channing's favorite stories, told again and again over the years, in which she auditioned with a funeral chant for Orestes in medieval French, which "lamented the ravages of war and the shortage of men . . . in 9/5 time."

Lastfogel was not impressed, so Channing followed with a Haitian corn-grinding song, and finally a Yiddish lullaby, the last of which brought tears to the über-agent's eyes and led to her first professional assignment. Composer Marc Blitzstein cast her in his 1944 revue *No for an Answer* at the New York City Center, in which Channing helped introduce the song "I'm Simply Fraught with You."

Her rise to stardom began when she auditioned for a revue being assembled in Los Angeles by Gower Champion, a dancer in partnership with his wife, Marge, who was trying to modulate his career to that of a director and choreographer. One of his first efforts was the musical comedy revue *Lend an Ear*, for which Channing auditioned by doing impressions of Ethel Merman, Fanny Brice, and Lynn Fontanne. *Lend an Ear* featured Channing in its Act I finale, "The Gladiola Girl," a mini musical poking fun at 1920s shows. Reviews for Channing were so enthusiastic after the Los Angeles opening that Joshua Logan stepped in and agreed to move the show to Broadway in 1947. Along the way he added several new sketches for Channing, including one that called upon her to speak a jumble of faux French, then turn to the audience and translate, "Yes." It brought down the house.

Broadway audiences and critics were introduced to the voice that would be described over the years as having a "Looney Tunes accent" (Frank Rich, the *New York Times*), as having a "range from a penny whistle to Tubby-the-Tuba bass notes" (Iris M. Fanter, the *Boston Herald*), as "improbably graft[ing] Tallulah Bankhead onto Baby Snookums" (Hulbert, *Variety*), and even recalling "gargling with Drano" (Leslie Bennetts, *Vanity Fair*).

That voice would forever stamp her next show, and first starring role, *Gentlemen Prefer Blondes*.

A Little Girl from Little Rock

Author Anita Loos's greatest creation was Lorelei Lee, the ultimate gold digger with a heart (and other key parts) of gold. A success as a novel in 1925, *Gentlemen Prefer Blondes* told the story of how a girl from the wrong side of the tracks loses her virtue—but wins fame, fortune, and, yes, even true love. The cheerful vice-rewarded story was adapted as a musical by Loos, working with composer Jule Styne, lyricist Leo Robin, and co-librettist Joseph Fields. The creative team assumed that their greatest challenge would be finding someone with the right combination of innocence, sexiness, and brass to play the main role.

When Loos and Styne went to see Channing in *Lend an Ear*, Loos reportedly leaped up like Max Bialystock and said, "That's my Lorelei!" It might have seemed an odd choice, since the book describes the character as "five-foot-two and eyes of blue." Channing's hair was (at the time) light brown and she was considered of Amazonian height in the 1940s.

Playbill's Harry Haun reported that not everyone was similarly delighted with the choice. At least one of the collaborators said, "For chrissakes, she can't sing and she looks crazy. Those big eyes, that funny voice. She's weird!"

But Loos and Styne persisted, even though it meant they had a great deal of difficulty raising the money for the show. Everyone advised them against using an unknown like Channing and recommended going for star power. But eventually the money was raised, and they plunged into writing the score that eventually included such standards as "A Little Girl from Little Rock" and the gold digger's anthem "Diamonds Are a Girl's Best Friend," both of whose titles entered the American lexicon as catchphrases.

Styne and Robin fashioned the score to make best use of Channing's "weird" multi-octave voice, employing her growl on gutbucket sections about her gritty past and the real world, and saving her screechy upper register for expressions of her sweetly warped ideals. Channing also donned a blond wig for the role, and in a sense never took it off. Henceforth, Channing would be a blonde.

New York Times critic Brooks Atkinson called Channing's Lorelei Lee "the most fabulous comic creation of this generation," and caricaturist Al Hirschfeld did the first of many sketches of her on the cover of the *Times*'s theatre section.

In an era when *Time* magazine focused mainly on politics and hard news, the editors put Channing on the cover, praising her performance by saying, "On Broadway, an authentic new star is almost as rare a phenomenon as it is in the heavens, perhaps once in a decade a nova explodes above the Great White Way with enough brilliance to reillumine the whole gaudy legend of show business."

Channing settled into a two-year run of the show. But the problem of her career soon presented itself: in what else could such an extreme personality be cast?

Lawrence Langner of the esteemed Theatre Guild saw her as a Shavian heroine. He cast her in a production of *The Millionaire* and tried to coax her to play Eliza Doolittle in *Pygmalion*, five years before *My Fair Lady*. Not many critics shared Langner's enthusiasm.

Channing next replaced Rosalind Russell as Ruth, the aspiring writer from Ohio sampling the dubious joys of Greenwich Village, in Leonard Bernstein's musical *Wonderful Town*. This was over the initial objections of director George Abbott, who felt she looked nothing like dark-haired Russell, who was his image of Ruth. Nevertheless, Channing did very well in the tour, giving the rest of the country its first taste of Channing live. They liked what they saw, and she would spend much of the rest of her life in one tour or another.

Not so in New York. John La Touche and James Mundy thought they had found a perfect vehicle for her, *The Vamp*, in which she played a character modeled on pioneering silent-film sexpot Theda Bara. The film ran out after just six weeks. The disappointment came at a time when Channing was still smarting from losing the movie version of *Gentlemen Prefer Blondes* to Marilyn Monroe. Channing had known something was up when she noticed the screen goddess sitting in the third row center and pulling the audience's (and orchestra's) attention for several weeks running. When Monroe finally came backstage to visit her, Channing later wrote, "she was so sweet and childlike that I just couldn't hit her." Channing generously has said she thinks Lorelei Lee was one of Monroe's best film performances, but it was cold comfort for losing a signature role. It wouldn't be the last, as we'll see.

It didn't help any that when Channing finally got a significant film role, in *The First Traveling Saleslady* (1956), she was, frankly, terrible—an assessment she readily accepts. The low point comes when she sings "The Corset Song," in which she tries on the nether garment of the title and sings about how appealing corsets are to men.

Trying to explain Ethel Merman's lack of film success, Channing wrote in her autobiography, "On stage she was like a nuclear explosion. But on film it was like sun through glass. Not all the ultraviolet rays got through." Channing might as well have been talking about herself. The exaggerated facial and vocal tics that delighted the balcony on Broadway simply looked grotesque in camera close-up.

There was one place where Channing's voice was an asset and her looks were not a problem. She made a series of children's record albums starting in the 1950s, impersonating the likes of Winnie the Pooh (before the Disney cartoons) and memorably voicing the sultry feline Mehitabel in a popular recording of *archy and mehitabel*. In all, her work earned ten gold albums.

Years later she told Sheryl Flatow of *Playbill* that she suffered a variety of physical ailments for years, which she blamed on the chemicals she used to bleach her hair blond (before she switched to wigs), until she visited an all-organic farm in northern California in 1958. She felt so much better that she eschewed all chemically treated food for much of the rest of her life, having food from the farm shipped to her wherever she was playing. She became known for packing a special Tiffany silver serving kit to all events involving food and even brought her own meal with her when she later visited the White House.

While banging her bewigged head fruitlessly against the Hollywood door, Channing did no further Broadway work until *Show Girl*, a revue that staggered through a four-month run in 1961.

Her private life was problematic, as well. Channing had gone through two marriages, the first to a writer who turned out to be a drug addict, the second to a Canadian football player who turned out to be an alcoholic. The second provided a blessing, however: he fathered what was to be her only child, who was given Channing as his first name.

While she was working on *Svengali and the Blonde*, a mid-1950s television play in which Channing played the puppet-like Trilby, she met TV producer Chad Lowe. They married in 1956 after Channing obtained a divorce from the football player. Lowe quickly took over the Svengali role in her real life, serving not only as her manager, but as her artistic consultant—with veto power over all her projects—and as her one-man cheerleading squad. Lowe even adopted her son Channing, who grew up to be editorial cartoonist Chan Lowe at the *Sun-Sentinel* newspaper in Florida.

Channing's new husband attended all her live performances, wrote her curtain speeches, and leaped to his feet to lead standing ovations after each show. He went nearly everywhere she went and stage-managed not only her appearances, but her friendships, as well.

If anyone saw anything sinister in Lowe's relationship with Channing, no one did much about it. They just saw him as a stage mother–like "stage husband." Lowe apparently took things a step further, as was finally revealed many years later. But first there was *Hello, Dolly!*

Hello, Dolly!

Thornton Wilder won Pulitzer Prizes for *Our Town* and *The Skin of Our Teeth*, two plays that found cosmic significance in the tiniest details of small-town life. He wrote few other plays. One of the them was *The Matchmaker*, which takes the form of a classic farce about Dolly Gallagher Levi, a matchmaker in early twentieth-century suburban New York, who finds mates for three people—and, along the way, finds one for herself. An evening's worth of chases, mistaken identities, derailed schemes, and slamming doors passes before everyone winds up with the right partner. Dolly's collected wisdom about human nature constituted Wilder's career valedictory.

A young composer named Jerry Herman, who had had gotten a moderate Broadway run out of *Milk and Honey*, was working with librettist Michael Stewart to adapt *The Matchmaker* as a full-blown big-time musical for Ethel Merman as Dolly. But Merman turned it down and missed a shot at what might have been her greatest role.

Instead, it would be Channing's. When Channing heard about the project, and the fact that it was being staged by her *Lend an Ear* director Gower Champion, she contacted Herman and told him, "If I don't play this character, I'll die!"

The show went through a famously rocky out-of-town tryout, during which producer David Merrick nearly closed it and cut his losses. Champion's keen instincts won the day. The show had many lively and touching production numbers, including "Put on Your Sunday Clothes" and "It Only Takes a Moment."

But the show boasted two numbers that changed both Broadway and Channing. The first was the title song, a paroxysm of joy sung by the waiters at the Harmonia Gardens, a restaurant Dolly frequented in her youth. The song doesn't really do anything to advance the plot. In effect the waiters are just saying "welcome back." But it tells us that Dolly, for all her eccentricities, was once extremely social and wildly beloved. It was the first number Champion staged, and he used its style to define the look and feel of the entire rest of the show. Channing wore a crimson dress, topped with an impossible headdress, and sang (or rather *received*) the number as she descended a Ziegfeldian staircase. She would later write that audience approval of the song hit her like a shockwave that she could feel in her bones.

"Hello, Dolly!" became Channing's new signature tune (though she never sings the famous chorus, of course). As sung by Louis Armstrong, it became a big hit, adopted by President Lyndon Johnson as a theme song (à la "Camelot" for the Kennedys). For a time in 1965, it even pushed the Beatles out of the number-one position on the pop chart, the last show tune, so far, to do such a thing.

The *Journal American*'s John McClain said that Gower Champion "has certainly created a whole new career for Carol Channing, the star, who had been relegated for years to a fixation with diamonds as a girl's best friend. She dominates the proceedings like a hirsute Y. A. Tittle [a bald football player of the period]. . . . Last night the audience nearly tore up the seats as she led the parade of waiters in a series of encores over the semi-circular runway which extends around the orchestra pit out into the audience. It is a whale of a tribute to the personal appeal of Miss Channing and the magical inventiveness of Mr. Champion's staging."

But there was another song that was equally important for both the show and for Channing: "Before the Parade Passes By" lies closer to the heart of *Hello, Dolly!* than does the title song. It's Dolly's way of saying that we all will someday die—but that day hasn't come yet, so let's hold hands and make the most of it together. Life is too precious to squander alone behind locked doors.

The song takes the form of a prayer or a conversation to her late husband, Ephraim Levi. It is staged with Dolly standing down center in a shaft of light, addressing the ghost of her late husband, who seems to reside in the general direction of the mezzanine. She tells him she has decided to embrace life, "to rejoin the human race" by remarrying, and she wants her late husband to give her away. Her metaphor for life is a parade, just like the one coming down the street toward her. And lo, as she sings, the parade arrives, full of colorful costumes and floats. Dolly takes her place at its head. Simple as this concept may sound, it was amazingly effective.

Perhaps the most magical thing about it all was the way it transformed Channing herself. Suddenly it seemed that we could glimpse a strength and wisdom we hadn't seen before. For an instant, this crazy dame came to symbolize all life, and her nutty effort to find mates for feedstore clerks, at some level beneath the ridiculous shenanigans, is really about the perpetuation of mankind. Channing's mannerisms actually helped, for once, to humanize her. Despite her oversize hat and troweled-on makeup, for one moment Channing was defiant and human. It explained her: Channing was always in costume for the parade of life. Those who saw her do "Before the Parade Passes By" in context (not in the chopped-down excerpt shown on the Tony Awards broadcast) never thought of her in the same way again.

In the 1965 Tony Awards, she beat a field that including Barbra Streisand in her iconic Fanny Brice role in *Funny Girl* for the Best Actress in a Musical prize.

Channing was, briefly, a hot property. She was even one of the actresses offered the lead in Jerry Herman's next musical, *Mame,* but her husband/manager, Lowe, turned it down because it was "too similar" to Dolly. Instead, Channing played Muzzy, a wealthy ding-a-ling, in the original film version of *Thoroughly Modern Millie* with Julie Andrews and Mary Tyler Moore. Her performance earned her an Oscar nomination and a Golden Globe Award. She would never get a chance at such a great piece of material again.

Channing's fame in the late 1960s, weirdly concurrent with the hippie culture of the period, was such that—hard as it may be to believe for twenty-first-century readers—she was the lead entertainment at the 1970 Super Bowl halftime show. Writing about what he called "The Curse of Carol Channing," *Maxim* magazine writer Tommy Dee charted the downward spiral of the careers of all who followed her into that halftime gig in the ensuing years.

The Film and Tours

After playing Dolly for 1,273 performances on Broadway, Channing took the show on what would turn into the first of three huge tours, including one in the 1990s that returned her to Broadway. In all, she would play Dolly Gallagher Levi more than five thousand times.

She had the pleasure of seeing bigger stars—stars who would ordinarily never consider replacing someone else in a long-running show—follow her into the Broadway production as Dolly, including Betty Grable, Ginger Rogers, Pearl Bailey, and the actress for whom it was originally written, Ethel Merman.

But Channing assumed that the role would always be identified primarily with her. It came as a shock, then, one morning in a Montreal hotel, when she discovered that another of her signature roles had been snatched away for the film version. She read in a newspaper that Barbra Streisand, her rival for the 1965 Tony Award, would play Dolly in the film. She claims that she thought seriously of jumping out the hotel window.

It was some comfort that the movie of *Hello, Dolly!* was one of the great movie-musical catastrophes. The film's failure nearly bankrupted its studio, Twentieth Century Fox, and helped end the era of movie musicals dating back to the beginning of sound films.

Channing was nursing another sorrow—her second great secret that was revealed to the public only years later. Throughout the peak of her fame during *Hello, Dolly!*, and in the decade after, she was battling cervical cancer. She underwent a hysterectomy between tours in the early 1970s, and she takes it as a point of pride that she never missed a performance.

Ever the trouper, she punctuated *Dolly!* tours with nightclub shows, Las Vegas appearances (*Carol Channing and Her 10 Stouthearted Men*), Atlantic City gigs (with her pal comedian George Burns), television appearances (including on *Sesame Street* and *The Muppet Show*), and even Danny Kaye–like comedic conducting stints with symphony orchestras, including one with the Boston Pops that was broadcast on PBS's *Great Performances*.

Her camp persona also attracted the admiration of the gay community. In 1975, *After Dark* magazine called her "the darling of the impersonators, the impressionists' dream."

Although she had achieved the kind of name and face recognition that celebrities can only dream about, few actual viable new projects came her way. She suffered through several Broadway and road flops that are utterly forgotten today. A revue called *Show Girl* came and went quickly in 1961. *Four on a Garden* had a seven-week run in 1971. *The Bed Before Yesterday* expired on the road in 1976. A revised version of *Gentlemen Prefer Blondes*, retitled *Lorelei*, lasted nine months at Broadway's Palace Theatre in 1974.

In 1985 *A Chorus Line*'s co-librettist James Kirwood wrote a play about two older stars trying to make a comeback. Titled simply *Legends!*, it starred Channing and Mary Martin. The production looked like a can't-miss smash, and, indeed, on the road it grossed a reported $10 million in 1985 dollars. The only problems were that the play wasn't actually very good—it was full of pointless bitchiness and in-jokes—and the two stars very pointedly did not get along. The production collapsed without ever reaching Broadway, and Kirwood eventually wrote an entertaining (if self-serving) account of the debacle in his book *The Diary of a Mad Playwright*, which portrayed Martin as unable to learn her lines and Channing as undermining Martin at every turn. In her own autobiography, Channing claimed never to have read the book.

Channing simply returned to touring *Dolly!* It returned to Broadway in 1978 and 1995, earning her waves of fresh affection. Though now in her midseventies, she relentlessly promoted the show, agreeing to all kinds of publicity stunts, including, in one city, riding on the local traffic helicopter and reporting on jam-ups in character as Dolly. Channing played her final Broadway performance as Dolly on January 28, 1996. One magazine calculated that she had spent a total of nine thousand hours in the role, the equivalent of 375 days as Dolly.

Back in the Headlines

Channing's third great secret came out in the tabloids, unfortunately.

In 1997 Charles Lowe, then in his mideighties, suffered a stroke. The following spring, after Channing had other eyes look over her finances for the first time in four decades, she abruptly filed for divorce.

Not only did she charge the eighty-six-year-old with squandering her fortune—"spending money like a 'drunken sailor'" was the way it was termed in divorce papers filed in Los Angeles District Court and quoted in the *New York Post*—but it appeared their long marriage was something of a sham. She charged that she had been "regularly physically assaulted by him" and—here was the red meat—he hadn't had marital relations with her since their honeymoon in 1956. Lowe denied her assertions and threatened to sue her.

Even in the early Internet age, it was a seven-day wonder. "Sex-Starved Channing Demands Divorce at 77," read the headline in the *Post*.

All you could say was, "Poor Dolly."

Lowe died in 1999 before the divorce was finalized.

Channing announced not long afterward that she was planning an autobiography. When it finally came out, titled *Just Lucky I Guess*, readers were startled to discover that it made no reference at all to the tabloid divorce—but did reveal her mixed-race parentage and her battle with cancer. The racial revelation that might have cost her work in the 1940s was barely worth a raised eyebrow in 2002.

In the book she told of her high school crush on a handsome boy named Harry Kullijian. The eighty-three-year-old Kullijian, who had never seen Channing perform on a stage, heard about the story and contacted her. Like Dolly herself, Channing decided that the parade wasn't over for her yet and, at age eighty-one, accepted Kullijian's proposal of marriage. He became her fourth husband in 2002.

Channing continued to work in the twenty-first century, trying out a planned solo show, doing guest spots, and keeping her "Miss Broadway" image in the public eye. She appeared on the 2004 Tony Awards and presented an award alongside rapper LL Cool J. The comedy improv series *Whose Line Is It Anyway?* had a segment in which the actors had to impersonate Channing. The comedy/science-fiction series *Mystery Science Theatre 3000* did an episode in which the main character was transformed into Channing. The off-Broadway parody revue *Forbidden Broadway* had made fun of her so many times, she appeared in person on *Forbidden Broadway, Vol. 3: The Unoriginal Cast Recording* to give a master class on how to "do" her and to sing an original song called "Imitation Is the Sincerest Form of Flattery." Dozens of clips of her crazy TV appearances can be found on websites that delight in deconstructing pop culture.

In 2007 she was in the news because a thief had stolen one of her suitcases as she was checking into a hotel. Luckily, she told reporters, although the stolen bag contained the sparkly dress she wore to sing "Diamonds Are a Girl's Best Friend," the bag holding her Tony Award had remained untouched. The dress was eventually returned.

What does this episode teach us about Channing? That at age eighty-six she was still trouping, still carrying her sparkly "Diamonds" dress (just in case?), and, more than four decades after she won it, still bearing her Tony Award for *Dolly* everywhere she went.

Yul Brynner in *The King and I* (1951). PHOTOFEST

YUL BRYNNER
When You Are King

Few Broadway actors became so completely identified with a single character as Yul Brynner was with the King of Siam in Rodgers and Hammerstein's *The King and I*. The image is so indelible even today, more than a half-century after the show's opening, that all you have to do is put your fists on your hips and shout "Et cete*rah*, et cete*rah*, et cete*rah*!" and people will know: it's the King.

Part of this iconic power stems from Brynner's distinctive look: shaved bald, with almond-shaped eyes that suggested someplace vaguely to the east of the Istanbul. He had a resonant and fragrantly accented baritone voice, as well as the superbly muscled body of the circus acrobat he once was.

The other part was his sheer power and stage presence. He was one of those force-of-nature characters who can dominate a stage the minute he steps onto it. He was a supermacho egomaniac who suffered from a few deep insecurities, including one about his height. He was capable of enormous warmth and generosity to those he liked and also could be savagely rude and dismissive to those he didn't.

Abandoned by his father when he was a boy, he was sometimes a neglectful father himself, and he subjected his four wives to serial infidelities.

Brynner worked as an actor and director for nearly four decades, playing dozens of roles and winning an Oscar and a Tony Award in the process. But long after he's gone, the image of the King of Siam, a role he played more than 4,600 times, is the one likely to live on in the Broadway pantheon.

★

There are so many versions of Brynner's birth and childhood that all of them, including the ones claiming to be "authoritative," have to be regarded as suspect. Blame for the confusion has to be laid at Brynner's own bare feet, because in his early years he would tell interviewers entertaining but false stories about being part Japanese, being born on the island of Sakhalin, having gypsy blood, having the real name Taidje Khan, and so on. From an early age Brynner saw himself as a legendary character, and he was constantly rewriting the legend.

A 1989 biography by his son, Rock Brynner, *Yul: The Man Who Would Be King*, has become accepted as the most factual account. Yul Brynner was born Yuliy Borisovich Brynner on July 11, 1920, in the Soviet Far East port city of Vladivostock. Yul's mother, Marousia Blagovidova, was an ethnic Russian. Yul's father, Boris Bryner, was Swiss and a fraction Mongolian, which gave the boy the mysterious Asian look. The name Yuliy is a Russian variation on "Jules," which was the name of his paternal grandfather.

When Yul was still quite young his father abandoned him, his mother, and his sister Vera in Vladivostock, a traumatic and humiliating blow. Marousia moved her children first to the industrial city of Harbin, China, where Yul attended school and had his first contact with theatre folk, through a neighbor who performed in Chinese operas. Yul saw him in a Chinese staging of the folk tale *Pi Pa-Ki*, which would later coincidentally serve as the basis for Brynner's Broadway musical *Lute Song*.

With World War II gathering in the Far East, Marousia wanted to move to the United States, but after experiencing passport problems with U.S. Immigration, she opted instead to move the children to Paris. She enrolled Yul in the Lycée Moncelle, but he preferred the company of musicians and actors. After learning to play the guitar and sing folk songs from the Russian émigré community that had helped his mother get settled in Paris, he quit school and began performing at nightclubs, even doing some beefcake modeling as he grew into a young man with a trim, muscular physique.

He also worked for a time as a trapeze artist at the Cirque d'hiver, a company with its own permanent theatre in the center of Paris, before a tragic fall during curtain call left him with forty-nine fractures (as he claimed), including to his left arm, shoulder, and leg. Months in a cast effectively ended his acrobatic career at age seventeen. He tried continuing as a clown with the same troupe but decided he was destined for other things.

"What it did to my life," he said, "was that I decided that I would not contemplate any kind of acting career which had been kind of in the back of my mind, eventually to leave the circus and become and actor or have a pantomime company of my own. . . . It turned my mind toward other things. I decided to cover a lot more ground in the theater, train myself eventually to become a director . . . a director can limp and I did have a limp."

He covered up the limp well for the rest of his life, but it would become more evident was he was ill or tired. He also became addicted to opium for a time, though he eventually kicked the habit.

Several forces came to bear in his decision to relocate to the United States in 1941. First, the Nazis had overrun France, making life very difficult for a Russian native with a Chinese passport. Second, his mother was suffering from leukemia and needed treatment in the United States. Third, Yul had met Michael Chekhov, son of the playwright and director of the Moscow Art Theatre, when he passed through Paris en route to asylum in the West. Chekhov settled in Connecticut, and Brynner wished to study with him.

Life in the United States was hard for a young man who spoke French, Russian, and Chinese but no English. Chekhov brought him into the company and took him on a tour of Shakespeare's *Twelfth Night*, with Brynner playing Fabian, the servant. The production wound up on Broadway on December 2, 1941, but was panned by critics, none of whom mentioned Brynner. It closed after fifteen performances. Brynner returned to Broadway in February 1943 with *The Moon Vine*, which ran twenty performances and earned Brynner his first review—a pan—from the *New York Sun*.

Also in this period, Brynner married stage and film actress Virginia Gilmore, and they had one child together in 1946. It wasn't a happy marriage. Brynner had women throwing themselves at him constantly, and he was compulsively unfaithful, not just to Gilmore, who divorced him in 1960, but to three more wives, Doris Kleiner, Jacqueline de Croisset, and Kathy Lee. Among these three wives, Brynner had four more children, two of them Vietnamese orphans whom he adopted at the height of the war in that country. His first three marriages ended in divorce; his fourth wife became his widow. The image of Brynner in *The King and I*, with his stable of wives and concubines, was actually not too far removed from his offstage married life, though, as in the fictional role, he dearly loved all his children, even if he wasn't always there for them.

Brynner's big break came not long after *The Moon Vine*. Producer Michael Myerberg met Brynner socially and told him about a new musical he was producing, called *Lute Song* (1945). The star was to be Mary Martin, who had just made a splash playing the goddess Venus come to Earth in the musical *One Touch of Venus*. Her new project was based on the Chinese legend *Pi Pa-Ki* he had seen as a boy in Harbin, about a young man who abandons his wife and aged parents to seek something greater in the world and winds up with a princess. Brynner's exotic look and smoldering eyes were perfect for the role of the young traveler. *Lute Song* ran six months, toured, and won Brynner the Donaldson award as Most Promising Actor.

Acting was not his only love, however. As he had promised himself after the circus injury, he developed a career as a television director and kept pursuing it by day even while he was working steadily at night on Broadway.

The King and I

In 1951, songwriters Richard Rodgers and Oscar Hammerstein II, who were the golden boys of Broadway after writing classics *Oklahoma!*, *Carousel*, and *South Pacific*, agreed to do something they had never done: write a vehicle for a star. Gertrude Lawrence, longtime muse of Noël Coward, who had asked them to write a musical based on *Anna and the King of Siam*, a film with Rex Harrison and Irene Dunne, which in turn was based on the Victorian-era memoir of an English schoolteacher who had been engaged as tutor to his many children by the Thai monarch.

Lawrence was not a strong vocalist and tended to sing flat; nevertheless, she possessed such charm and stage presence that Rodgers and Hammerstein went ahead with the project, even producing it themselves. The big question was: who would play the king? Harrison was initially considered, but he'd never done a musical at this point, and the authors wanted someone with a strong voice. Alfred Drake, who had played Curly in their first hit together, *Oklahoma!*, was offered the role, but he wanted more money than the team was willing to pay. So they decided to hold auditions. First up was Brynner, whom their *South Pacific* star Mary Martin had recommended as the result of working with him on *Lute Song*. In his autobiography, *Musical Stages*, Rodgers wrote of the audition, "He scowled in our direction, sat down on the stage and crossed his legs, tailor-fashion, then plunked one whacking chord on his guitar and began to howl in a strange language that no one could understand. He looked savage, and there was no denying that he projected a feeling of controlled ferocity. When he read for us, we were again impressed by his authority and conviction, Oscar and I nodded. . . . out of nowhere, we had our king."

Never was a putative star vehicle so resoundingly stolen by a secondary character. Though the King was written as a secondary role to Anna Leonowens, or "Mrs. Anna" as she's called in the script, the power of Brynner's performance quickly elevated the King's importance.

A master's thesis could be written on Brynner's performance in *The King and I*, parsing each kingly stance, each emphatic hand gesture, each blazing arch of his eyebrows. Classes in movement teach you that the most powerful stance in acting is planting your feet apart, like the Colossus of Rhodes. Brynner seemed to play the entire role in that position, chin up, with fists on hips or with one arm wrapped around the other so his shoulders bulged. He would rock on his hips when he was feeling cocky and would make his eyes blaze when he was angry. When vexed, he could toss a sarcastic comment over his shoulder with an angry smile, punctuated with a triumphant, "Ha!"

For all this ferociousness, he could also startle the audience by hooding his eyes like a contented cat when he was happy, and in the gentle moments with his bevy of princes and princesses, his voice would become a warm burr. Unlike so many other classic Broadway star performances of this era, Brynner's was beautifully captured in the 1956 film version, with Deborah Kerr as Mrs. Anna.

In the libretto, Hammerstein created for the King a pidgin dialogue, which some people in the coming years would see as condescending. But Hammerstein was trying to convey someone who is doing very well considering he has taught himself most of what he knows of English from books, and Brynner played the lines with total confidence. Hammerstein wrote him the tic of repeating three times the phrases he most wished to emphasize. "Go on! Go on! Go on!" "Teach, teach, teach!" And the most cherished, "Et ceterah, et ceterah, et ceterah!"

All this, meanwhile, in a musical where the King has almost nothing to sing. His only solo is "A Puzzlement." He leads a chanted prayer to Buddha, asking for guidance and grumpily promising Mrs. Anna her house. He has a quick solo passage ("Man must be like honeybee . . . ") in the run-up to "Shall We Dance?" and then sings in "Shall We Dance?," which is a full-scale duet with Mrs. Anna.

But that's it for the King's songs.

For all his onstage confidence, Brynner was suffering acute embarrassment because he was quickly going prematurely bald. By the time he was cast in *The King and I*, all that was left was a fringe of hair at the sides and back and a few stray strands on top. Costumer Irene Sharaff is credited with proposing that he shave his head completely, to suggest a Buddhist monk. Brynner complied, and the bald look quickly became one of his trademarks.

During tryouts, the show did poorly, partly because there was no love story. Rodgers and Hammerstein may have written a plea against racism in *South Pacific*, but American society as a whole was still not thought to be ready for an explicit affair between a white woman and an Asian man. Besides, romance was not what happened between those two characters, at least not overtly. Brynner has taken credit for the idea of having Gertrude Lawrence and himself play the show with sexual attraction as the subtext to all their encounters. Rodgers and Hammerstein responded by writing the "Shall We Dance?" scene, so that the sexual electricity between the two crackles as she teaches him to dance the polka. After that (plus some judicious cutting), the show was a triumph. It opened on March 29, 1951, and ran more than three years.

Lawrence, who was diagnosed with cancer, was in and out of the show during the last year of her life and gave her final performance as Mrs. Anna just three weeks before she died in September 1952. One of her final requests was that Brynner's name be placed over the title.

And there it stayed for the rest of his life. Brynner took many other roles in the years to come, but the King would remain not only his signature role, but a kind of alter ego. Ted Chapin, executive director of the Rodgers and Hammerstein Organization, told an interviewer that in his later years, Brynner could no longer be distinguished from the King. In a way, "he sold his soul to that role."

The 1952 Tony Award as Best Actor in a Musical, and then the Academy Award for the 1956 film version, gave Brynner an exceptional asterisk next to his name in the history books. Brynner is one of just eight actors to have won both the Tony and the Academy awards for the same role, and one of only three actors for a role in a musical. The other two were Joel Grey for *Cabaret* and Rex Harrison for *My Fair Lady*.

Brynner played many other roles and even created one other iconic one, in his film *The Magnificent Seven*. But people identified him completely with the role of the King. People who might not know his name would see him, put their fists on their hips, and spout, "Et ceterah! Et ceterah! Et ceterah!" at him. He was the King.

Nonetheless, Brynner worked hard to keep from becoming typecast. And considering his singular appearance—the bald head, the Eurasian features—he landed a wide variety of film acting roles, in addition to his directing. His first three movies after *The King and I* in 1956 were the all-star biblical epic *The Ten Commandments* (1956, in which he played another king, Egyptian Pharaoh Rameses); *Anastasia* (also 1956); and an adaptation of Dostoyevski's *The Brothers Karamazov* (1958, as Dmitri Karamazov). He played a pirate (*The Buccaneer*), a southern patriarch (*The Sound and the Fury*), a homicidal robot (*Westworld*), another biblical king (*Solomon and Sheba*)—more than three dozen film roles in all.

One performance, already mentioned, was especially notable. John Sturges remade Akira Kurosawa's Japanese classic *The Seven Samurai* as an American western, *The Magnificent Seven* (1960), about seven gunslingers hired to defend a Mexican town against an army of bandits. The cast was a who's who of Hollywood's toughest tough-guy actors, including Charles Bronson, Steve McQueen, Eli Wallach, Robert Vaughan, and James Coburn, but Brynner played their leader. Brynner, who was sensitive about his height, and whose *King and I* character made a great point that Mrs. Anna's head should never be higher than his own, was much the same in real life. He played several scenes in this film on a small mound of earth, so he'd seem to be just as tall as costar McQueen.

Brynner tried to originate a Broadway musical role one more time. In 1974 he got involved in one of the biggest flops of the 1970s, *Home Sweet Homer*, a musical about the legendary Greek hero and wanderer Ulysses. Omitting the whole part of his story about the Trojan War and the Odyssey, the musical focused on Ulysses' return home to his patient (twenty years patient) and long-suffering wife, Penelope.

The show was directed by Albert Marre, had a score by Mitch Leigh, and starred brass-lunged Joan Diener as Penelope. All three had worked together on one monster hit, *Man of La Mancha* but had seen nothing but bombs since then. *Home Sweet Homer* added to the latter list. After a disastrous out-of-town tryout fraught with lawsuits, screaming matches, and scathing reviews, the show opened and closed on Broadway at a single matinee, January 4, 1976.

Home Sweet Homer was quickly forgotten, but demand for Brynner's performance as the King remained intense twenty years after *The King and I*'s Broadway debut. The musical was revived twice on Broadway with Brynner, on May 2, 1977, with Constance Towers as Mrs. Anna, for a nineteen-month run; and on January 7, 1985, with Mary Beth Peil, for a six-month run, and it spent years on the road in between.

Brynner, a lifelong heavy smoker, learned that he was suffering from lung cancer on September 13, 1983, a date memorable because he celebrated his four thousandth performance as the King in a tour of the show. He had been feeling weak and had noticed a lump on his neck. He immediately began treatment and took a break from the tour. Although the cancer had spread throughout his body and was diagnosed as terminal, he responded to treatment well enough to resume the tour in early 1984, rebilled as *The King and I: The Farewell Tour*.

On June 30, 1985—almost exactly fifty years after his singing debut in Paris—Brynner gave his 4,633rd and final performance as the King, an event widely covered by newspapers, magazines, and television. Brynner died October 10, 1985, but he had one more role to play. In early 1986 his fans were startled by a television public-service announcement from the American Cancer Society that began with a voiceover saying, "Ladies and gentlemen, the late Yul Brynner." What followed was the image of a weakened Brynner, almost like the Brynner of the death scene from *The King and I*, but with his eyes wide open, speaking from the lip of the grave: "I really wanted to make a commercial when I discovered that I was that sick and my time was so limited," he said, scowling. "Now that I'm gone," he said, looking directly into viewers' eyes through the camera "I tell you: Don't smoke. Whatever you do, just don't smoke. If I could take back that smoking, we wouldn't be talking about any cancer. I'm convinced of it."

He had taped it a year earlier, knowing he was dying. That characteristic "I tell you" was him delivering the wisdom he had gleaned from his life's fatal mistake–from a guy who rarely acknowledged a mistake. It was also a last gesture of defiance against death. It was a classy, bold, and dramatic exit line for one of Broadway's most macho men. And, in its own way, it was worthy of a king.

Zero Mostel records the original cast album of *Fiddler on the Roof* (1964).
PHOTOFEST

ZERO MOSTEL
Comedy Tonight

Where some stage stars find themselves diminished by television and film, Zero Mostel was simply too gargantuan for them—an outsize talent who was usually too wild, too loud, and too boisterous for the electronic media.

The only place that could comfortably fit his talent was the stage, but he earned his stage stardom in a backward way. Blacklisted during the anticommunist witch hunts of the 1950s, he found himself embraced and championed by the independent and defiant directors and producers of Broadway. As a result, we got his *Fiddler on the Roof, A Funny Thing Happened on the Way to the Forum, Rhinoceros, Ulysses in Nighttown*, and other indelible midcentury performances.

But Mostel is something of an interloper in this book. He no doubt earned his stardom many times over. But he was not a trained musical comedy performer and certainly not a trained singer. His unique talent and persona made him *seem* like a musical comedy star, and people who understood this put him in musicals, where he triumphed.

Unlike many Broadway stars who were born in poverty and came up through vaudeville, Mostel was born into a middle-class family and came up through nightclubs as a comedian.

Samuel Joel Mostel, early nickname "Sammy," was born February 28, 1915, in Brooklyn, New York, the seventh of eight children of two Eastern European immigrants. His father operated a kosher slaughterhouse for a time and became a specialist in winemaking. Mostel later claimed that he earned his nickname from his grades at school; in fact, he was a moderately successful scholar, if something of a cutup in the classroom. He attended PS 188, Seward Park High School, and City College of New York, where he majored in fine arts and minored in English. He graduated CCNY in 1935.

Mostel got his first exposure to the theatre during this time, notably the Yiddish theatres that were coming to the end of their boom along Manhattan's Second Avenue. But he was much happier going to the Metropolitan Museum of Art to examine and copy the masterpieces housed there. One of the paradoxes of Mostel's life was the fact that while he was a genius as a performer, performing didn't command his highest respect. It was something he did for money. Painting was his first love and true calling. He poured his greatest creative energies into it. Unfortunately, like Salieri in *Amadeus*, he was merely good at it. Greatness as a painter always remained beyond his grasp.

There were few jobs to be had in the mid-1930s. Mostel worked for a bakery and as a longshoreman. But it wasn't until FDR's Works Progress Administration noticed him that his career finally got under way. He was hired by the Federal Art Project, which gave him a salary as an artist but also required him to teach painting to children at Manhattan's Ninety-second Street YM-YWHA. Another part of the job was to give lectures on art at the Museum of Modern Art and other New York museums. His talks were so funny—he would impersonate the figures in the paintings or improvise dialogue among multiple figures, or make wildly absurd comments on the art world in general—that he began getting offers to perform at private parties and other events outside the museum. His eyebrows could go up and make him look as innocent as an angel, or bunch up around his eyes to present the image of burning fury. He had the ability to bulge his eyes slightly out of their sockets, giving him a madly intense look. He employed a wide repertoire of dolphin-like squeaks and squawks that he used as sound effects in his stories or to give his grotesque movements a cartoonish emphasis. All these were only tools, however, to communicate his absurdist views on art and life. Though he was still only in his twenties, Mostel also began to achieve his trademark rotundity just as he was losing his hair. His incongruous look only made him funnier. His body, face, and voice were perfectly matched to his wild imagination.

Because many of his museum talks were peppered with social commentary, he was invited to perform for labor union gatherings and other groups working for social change. Some people were attracted to communism in the 1930s simply because capitalism seemed to be breaking down. Some did it just because their friends were doing it. Most realized fairly quickly that communism was a dead end. But their curiosity would come back to haunt them in the blacklists of the 1950s. Mostel's political gigs eventually got him into some of the worst trouble of his life, but at the time they helped keep food on the table.

Mostel did the gallery talks from 1937 to late 1941, when his extracurricular performances earned him an offer to perform a professional comedy gig at the nightclub Café Society Downtown in Greenwich Village. He debuted there February 16, 1942, under his new professional name, Zero Mostel. Jared Brown, author of the superb biography *Zero Mostel*, reported that Mostel got the moniker from club publicist Ivan Black, who based it on the fact that Mostel was "starting from nothing" and leaping into big-time club work.

The first few months of 1942 were a dark time for the United States. The Japanese attacked Pearl Harbor in December 1941, and by spring 1942 the entire country was mobilizing for war. Those same months were a mini golden age for Mostel. People wanted to laugh, and within weeks he became the number-one draw at the club. He did more than go from "Zero" to sixty; his nightclub salary rose from $40 to $1,250 a week. Mostel made his official Broadway debut on April 24, 1942, in the musical comedy revue *Keep 'Em Laugh-*

ing, alongside William Gaxton, Victor Moore, and other comics. The show ran only a few weeks, but Mostel was immediately transferred by producer Clifford C. Fischer into his next show, *Top-Notchers*, which opened on May 29, giving Mostel his second Broadway opening night in less than five weeks.

By 1943, Mostel commanded more than four thousand dollars a week for nightclub work. During a golden age of film, Broadway, and nightclub comedy, *Life* magazine called Mostel "just about the funniest American now living."

After a stint in the army during World War II, he returned to lucrative nightclub work, soon branching out into Broadway musicals (he played Peachum in Duke Ellington and John La Touche's *Beggar's Holiday*, an adaption of *The Beggar's Opera*); film (*DuBarry Was a Lady, Panic in the Streets, The Enforcer*); and even television (playing Banjo, a role based on Harpo Marx, in *Ford Theatre Hour*'s 1949 adaptation of *The Man Who Came to Dinner*).

There was a sad side to all this success. Mostel's first marriage, to a girl he met at CCNY, had broken up partly because he was spending too much time painting or out of the house, but also partly because he was bringing home so little money. They separated in 1941 just before his career and income skyrocketed.

Mostel soon found his soul mate in Kathryn Harkin, a onetime Radio City Music Hall Rockette. They married on July 2, 1944, and she stuck with him for richer, for poorer, and for richer again for the rest of their lives. They had two sons, Josh (born 1946), who became an actor, and Tobias (born 1949), who became a musician.

The Blacklist

Mostel's career hit a wall in the 1950s when he was named (along with more than 150 others) by screenwriter Martin Berkeley as a communist sympathizer before the House of Representatives Committee on Un-American Activities (HUAC). Mostel was himself summoned before HUAC on August 14, 1955. He was extremely droll during his appearance, first joking with the committee members, then responding to their pointed questions by intoning the ten amendments in the Bill of Rights and finally invoking the Fifth Amendment against self-incrimination. He steadfastly refused to give the committee any other names.

His bravado and loyalty gave him self-respect but effectively torpedoed his career. Mostel's name appeared in *Counterattack* and *Red Channels*, publications that studios and advertisers used to blacklist "suspect" writers and entertainers. It's hard to overstate how traumatic the blacklist was for Mostel and his fellow blacklisted friends. Actor John Garfield suffered a fatal heart attack not long after he was summoned by HUAC, and Mostel's close friend Philip Loeb took his own life. Mostel's own low point came when he traveled to upstate New York's Concord Hotel, where he had once commanded more than $2,000 a night, but had agreed to work for $500. When he arrived, he was bluntly informed that the fee would only be $250, take it or leave it. With no other work in sight, he took it. But the whole experience was a humiliation from which he never really recovered.

Unable to get steady work as a comic, Mostel retreated to his studio, but his paintings brought in next to nothing and his finances soon became desperate. At this moment he was befriended by Toby Cole, an agent who had admired his work since the Café Society days and who was vehemently opposed to the blacklist. Mostel became her special case. She is largely responsible for finding him the many interesting theatrical projects he tackled in the late 1950s and early 1960s, rebuilding his career through the stage. Mostel later turned his back on Cole, without explanation, when he became famous and successful. It was one of the more unsavory chapters in the actor's life.

Among the greatest of the challenging roles Cole found him was Leo Bloom in *Ulysses in Nighttown*. The script was adapted from James Joyce's masterpiece of elliptical story-telling, the novel *Ulysses*, which followed Irishman Leo Bloom on a day in his ordinary Dublin life. The work lifted Bloom's mundane peregrinations to the level of an epic adventure by narrating his every thought, emotion, and urge in a complicated and fragmentary language, full of made-up words, obscure cultural references, slang, and knotted syntax. Adapting even a part of this idiosyncratic saga to the stage was a challenge, since its interior monologues needed to be turned into exterior action as much as possible. But finding an actor who (a) understood every line and (b) was able to communicate them to an audience was a tremendous challenge.

The well-read Mostel was delighted to accept that challenge. Here was an actor who indeed understood every line of *Ulysses* (or was bold enough to offer his personal interpretation of each), and here was a project almost as interesting as painting.

Now the gallery guide in him came to the fore. He used his full repertoire of voices, noises, faces, and emotions to embroider and illuminate the dense text. He managed to make his own sense of passages like this one, from the original book:

(Shaking hands with a blind stripling.) My more than Brother! (Placing his arms round the shoulders of an old couple.) Dear old friends! (He plays pussy fourcorners with ragged boys and girls.) Peep! Bopeep! (He wheels twins in a perambulator.) Ticktacktwo wouldyousetashoe? (He performs juggler's tricks, draws red, orange, yellow, green, blue, indigo and violet silk handkerchiefs from his mouth.) Roygbiv. 32 feet per second. (He consoles a widow.) Absence makes the heart grow younger. (He dances the Highland fling with grotesque antics.) Leg it, ye devils! (He kisses the bedsores of a palsied veteran.) Honourable wounds! (He trips up a fat policeman.) U.p.: up. U.p.: up. (He whispers in the ear of a blushing waitress and laughs kindly.) Ah, naughty, naughty! (He eats a raw turnip offered him by Maurice Buterly, farmer.) Fine! Splendid! (He refuses to accept three shillings offered him by Joseph Hynes, journalist.) My dear fellow, not at all! (He gives his coat to a beggar.) Please accept. (He takes part in a stomach race with elderly male and female cripples.) Come on, boys! Wriggle it, girls!

Many who came to see the 1958 production at the tiny Rooftop Theatre in Greenwich Village still feel it was the greatest work of Mostel's life, outshining even his later Broadway and film triumphs. Those who treasure *Fiddler, Forum,* and *The Producers* need to add *Ulysses in Nighttown* to the list.

Harold Clurman wrote that Mostel "is theatrically right as can be to the very 'boiled eyes,' which Joyce gives Bloom. I do not want to see Bloom in the flesh—he is such a character as dreams are made on—but Mostel's 'flesh,' expanding and contracting like some heartbreaking ogre of human anguish and absurdity, is equivalent to, though essentially different from, the author's more covert and spectral creature."

Mostel won an Obie Award for outstanding off-Broadway performance. (A 1970s revival at Broadway's huge Winter Garden failed to capture the spirit of the original.)

Blacklist or not, Mostel's talent simply couldn't be ignored any longer. Offers began to arrive from producers interested in seeing him do the classics. Mostel did dream of playing some of the great Shakespearean roles like Falstaff, for which he would have been ideal.

The most interesting offer came from England, where he was asked to appear opposite Laurence Olivier in a fascinating new play by absurdist playwright Eugene Ionesco, *Rhinoceros.* An allegory about what Ionesco perceived as the growing coarseness and inhumanity of mankind, the play tells the story of a man named Berrenger, who finds himself in a world where human beings are gradually turning into rhinoceroses. He tries to barricade himself with his civilized friend John (Mostel), but a substantial part of the action involves the friend's gradual and terrifying transformation into the animal of the title.

Mostel ultimately did not perform the role in the West End but was engaged for the 1961 Broadway production, which costarred Eli Wallach as Berrenger. Where the original London production used offstage quick-changes of makeup to indicate the transformation, Mostel proposed to undergo the transformation onstage, just by using his body and voice—the sort of challenge for which he was perfectly suited.

The result was startling and often actually frightening for those in the forward rows. Mostel began to stamp his foot, shake his head, and twist his body, but the most remarkable change was his voice, a strangled bellow so unhuman that he once, during this time, employed it on the street to frighten away a mugger.

When it came time for the Tony Awards that spring, Mostel won as Best Actor in a Play. Here was mainstream recognition that he had achieved on his own terms.

Comedy Tonight

Mostel's agent, Cole, fielded all sorts of interesting proposals. One of them came from young producer Harold Prince, who had on his schedule a musical based on two of the plays of third century B.C. Roman playwright Titus Macchius Plautus, *Pseudolus* and the fortuitously named *Mostellaria* (from the name of a type of house ghost). Prince's musical would be called *A Funny Thing Happened on the Way to the Forum*, a pell-mell musical farce with a score by a young guy named Stephen Sondheim, who had written lyrics to respected hits *West Side Story* and *Gypsy* but who was writing his own music for the new project.

Mostel would be the first leading man in a show with an all-Sondheim score, and he would play Pseudolus, a sly Roman slave willing to go to any lengths to win his freedom. Mostel had proven he was the go-to guy as far as going to any lengths was concerned. But Mostel initially turned down the role, claiming the script was just a lot of old jokes (2,200-year-old jokes, in some cases) and he was looking for projects with more substance. Mostel's wife, Kate, however, loved the script and threatened violence if he didn't take it, not least because the paycheck would finally put them back where they'd been a decade earlier. He'd also get to work with comedian Jack Gilford, a friend since the Café Society days.

There were questions. Mostel hadn't done a musical in two decades and had never starred in one. Also, could he dance? His leg had been injured in a bus accident in January 1960 and he had trouble walking, let alone dancing. But after reluctantly taking the gig, Mostel proved to be hilarious, and his aggressive clowning proved so perfect for the part that his deficits in other areas were barely noticed. Audiences got to see Mostel mugging and shouting and scheming and growling and googling his eyes as the cast paraded with majestic ridiculousness behind him, and on opening night, May 8, 1962, they collectively fell in love with the actor. The show ran nearly a thousand performances.

John McClain of the *Journal American* called Mostel "a very animated blimp."

Mostel had become hardened by his years in the blacklist wilderness and was insecure. But once in command of the stage, he acknowledged no superior, including the producer and director. His ad-libbing became notorious and sometimes made things difficult for the other actors, who were waiting for specific cues. But while he could be scolded, he couldn't be forced to stop. Having earned the right to perquisites, he seized them.

Co-librettist Larry Gelbart later told Sondheim biographer Craig Zadan, "Zero was a giant. He was a giant talent . . . and a giant pain in the ass."

He also established himself firmly in the public's mind as a Broadway musical star, and whatever his colleagues thought of him, they knew he could deliver the goods. Robbins, who as artistic director of the New York City Ballet had ruthlessly insisted on the highest level of terpsichorean and physical perfection from his dancers, now sought out the limping, overweight Mostel as the unlikely star of his unlikely next musical. Based on the story "Tevye and His Daughters" by Yiddish author Sholom Aleichim, it would take place in a run-down Russian-Jewish shtetl, with no traditional chorus line, women who always kept their legs and heads covered, and only limited opportunities for Mostel's broad clowning. As *Fiddler on the Roof*, it would also prove to be the greatest success either of Robbins or Mostel would ever experience.

The Robbins issue was touchy. Robbins had been called before HUAC and had given them the names of others he believed to be sympathizers. As a result, Robbins avoided blacklisting. This action earned Mostel's loathing, but he had agreed to work professionally with Robbins, saying, "We of the Left do not blacklist."

Now they headed into their second major project together. Mostel was no stranger to Aleichim's material, having appeared in a local television broadcast of the off-Broadway play *The World of Sholom Aleichim* around the time of *Ulysses in Nighttown*. More importantly, he was familiar with the people Aleichim was writing about, Russian Jews who lived with not quite enough food and always in fear of a pogrom or organized attack by the government. He was the son of just such people.

He knew that there was one area where such people were very rich: in their spiritual life and their relationship with God. Behind the painting and the literature and the crazy clowning, Mostel himself was a pious Jew. *Fiddler on the Roof* allowed him to bring out all these colors that had largely remained hidden in his career hitherto. When Tevye quibbled and cajoled in his speeches to God, you got the sense that Mostel himself may have done the same more than once. When he sang Tevye's aria "If I Were a Rich Man," you felt the poverty he had gone through and the comfort religion brought him, especially in the final verse, when he fantasizes that being a wealthy man would allow him the greatest freedom of all—the time to "to sit in the synagogue and pray."

Sheldon Harnick's lyric calls upon Tevye to punctuate his fantasies with a "Diga-diga-dum," that's supposed to suggest a gurgle of pleasure. Mostel took it and, while sticking to Jerry Bock's music, turned it into a cantor's scat.

Walter Kerr in the *Herald Tribune* described the song's performance thus: "For every other line of the lyric he simply substitutes gratified gargles and cascading coos until he has arrived, mystically, at a kind of cabalistic coloratura."

There were other, uncharacteristically tender moments. "Sabbath Prayer" was just that, no fooling around. "Sunrise, Sunset" was his moment of sorrow and wonder at watching his daughters grow up and marry. "Do You Love Me?" was technically a comedy song in which Tevye asks his wife, Golde (Maria Karnilova), after twenty-five years of an arranged marriage, if she ever actually loved him.

For those who had seen only *Forum* and his nightclub work, *Fiddler* was a revelation: his first commercial success in which he showed he also had soul and heart. *Fiddler* ran for eight years, eventually becoming (for a time) the longest-running show in Broadway history. Mostel once again won the Tony Award, this time for Best Actor in a Musical.

In recognition of his achievement, he was invited by President Lyndon B. Johnson to appear at the White House. Now, for Mostel, the blacklist was truly broken. Following his success in *Fiddler*, Mostel found that not only had the stigma of the blacklist disappeared, but that he was very much in demand.

Later Career

It would be satisfying to say that he used his sudden mass stardom to pursue the classics and other great literary projects he had always dreamed of doing. It would also be nice to say that success made him more gracious to those around him.

Alas, neither proved to be the case. If anything, poverty and desperation had inspired his best work and prompted his innate kindness and generosity. Wealth and fame caused him to become imperious and sometimes nasty (though many from this period report great acts of benevolence, as well). The success also led him to take a lot of second-rate films like *Great Catherine* (as General Potemkin), *Marco* (as Kublai Khan!), and others. Even a 1974 film adaptation of *Rhinoceros*, with young comedian Gene Wilder replacing Eli Wallach, proved to be a disappointment.

On the happier side, he hosted an episode of *The Muppet Show*, in which he (attired as King Henry VIII) sang "What Do the Simple Folk Do?" from *Camelot*. He also endeared himself to a generation of children by appearing in *The Sesame Street Book of Opposites*, which simply showed him on facing pages embodying concepts like "happy" and "sad" clad in white long johns, a red kerchief, and a battered top hat.

The Wilder teaming on *Rhinoceros* came about as a result of the one golden exception from this period, and one of the great classics of Mostel's career: Mel Brooks' 1968 comedy *The Producers*. Mostel played Max Bialystock, a once-great Broadway producer whose career is in a tailspin. A chance remark from his mousy accountant, Leo Bloom (Wilder), prompts Bialystock to carry out a crazy scheme: to sell thousands of percent interest in a new Broadway show, then keep the extra money when the show flops, knowing no one will expect profits from a flop. The only catch, of course, is that they must guarantee the show will flop. So they set about hiring Broadway's worst director, worst actors, and worst designers to mount the worst show they can find: *Springtime for Hitler*, billed as "a gay romp with Adolf and Eva at Berchtesgaden."

This black farce, which Brooks in 2001 rewrote as an actual Broadway musical (with Nathan Lane in the Mostel role), was the perfect vehicle for Mostel's broad talents, allowing him to use his expressive voice, his plastic face and eyes, and his overall physical comedy in a first-rate script that earned Brooks a 1969 Oscar. The moment when Wilder gambols around the fountain at Lincoln Center is focused on Wilder, but Mostel expresses just as much joy by arching his back and waving his hand in a way only he would do.

In the mid-1970s, Mostel did a triumphant tour of *Fiddler on the Roof* (just at the time when the film version, starring Israeli actor Topol, had been released). He also took part in a fascinating film project, *The Front*, about the blacklist. Woody Allen, in the unusual position of playing a role he did not write himself, played a nonblacklisted film writer who agrees to put his name on screenplays written by blacklisted writers in return for a percentage of the fee. He sees nothing morally wrong with this—until he's confronted with the fate of a secondary character, played by Mostel. Mostel took the role of blacklisted comedian Hecky Brown, whose wrecked career and repeated humiliations lead him to commit suicide. Mostel was one of a mob of once-banned artists who took part in *The Front*.

Though not perfect, the film was a respectable contrast to many of the potboiler projects Mostel had been taking since his triumphs in *Fiddler* and *The Producers*. It perhaps signaled a new self-respect for his talent, which led in turn to his final project, the ambitious stage play *The Merchant*, in which he finally fulfilled his dream of playing a Shakespearean role.

Arnold Wesker's drama retold the story of Shakespeare's *The Merchant of Venice* but reinterpreted the character of Shylock the moneylender. Shylock has been derided for centuries as an anti-Semitic caricature (Shylock demands a pound of flesh as collateral for a loan to a Christian)—and simultaneously praised as a plea for the humanity of all "outsider" groups ("Hath not a Jew eyes . . . ?"). Wesker's drama depicts Shylock as a complicated and misunderstood character whose motivations are nobler than he's given credit for. Those who saw rehearsals and Mostel's single out-of-town tryout preview in Philadelphia said it was one of his most moving and effective performances.

On the day of the second preview, Mostel was getting into makeup when he began to feel ill. Rushed to the hospital, he seemed to rally for several days as doctors treated him for what they believed to be exhaustion. But he then collapsed and died on September 8, 1977, at age sixty-two. The cause was subsequently determined to be an aortic aneurysm—the same ailment (similarly misdiagnosed) that would kill *Rent* composer Jonathan Larson in 1996.

Would *Merchant* have been a hit? Would Mostel finally have taken on other classical roles (like Falstaff), as everyone had been urging him for years? Would he have had the breakthrough and recognition as a painter that he craved?

Why not? He survived career "death" and came back bigger than before. Who's to say the man who gave us consummate survivors Tevye, Pseudolus, and Max Bialystok wouldn't have done whatever he set his mind on?

John Raitt as Billy Bigelow in *Carousel* (1945). PHOTOFEST

JOHN RAITT
You with the Stars in Your Eyes

John Raitt's life is the story of a rugged baritone who stood at the innermost circle of Broadway stardom for just a brief moment when he created the role of Billy Bigelow in *Carousel*. And then, like Adam, spent the rest of his life trying to find his way back into Eden.

Raitt actually made it back in an amazing second time, as Sid Sorokin in *The Pajama Game*, but then found himself on the outside once again. He was a hero trapped in an age of antiheroes. He fought for decades to assert his stardom in endless tours back and forth across North America, where he was seen as the embodiment of Broadway long after Broadway itself could no longer find a place for him. As he accused himself in his signature tune, "Hey There," Raitt truly had the stars in his eyes.

The lion-faced actor had a trademark slightly muscle-bound look, derived from his early years as track star and shot-putter. He had an aquiline nose and bright, darting eyes set in a head that a Roman emperor would have been proud of. Called "Mr. Virile" by the New *York Sunday News*, he had a strongly masculine approach to acting and singing.

Trained in operetta, he acted with a slightly elevated style that looks artificial to twenty-first-century eyes but that was much prized in his own age. When singing, he rarely threw in trills or grace notes or other stylistic embellishments; his style consisted of hitting his notes foursquare with power and personality.

Born John Emmett Raitt on January 19, 1917, in Santa Ana, California, he began singing at shows put on by the local YMCA, where his father worked. When he became a teenager his interests turned to sports, though he also appeared in school productions. He played on the Fullerton High School track and football teams, where he won the California state high school track championship and then a scholarship to the University of Southern California. When he found that they wouldn't let him pursue both football and shot-put, he transferred to the more amenable Redlands University.

He was considered a prime candidate for the U.S. Olympic Team in Helsinki for the 1940 games. But World War II intervened and the Olympics were canceled. Tough. He stayed at Redlands, working toward a degree in physical education, planning to be a gym teacher.

He also fell in love. He had known Rosemary Yorba since high school. She was descended from one of the aristocratic Spanish families that had first settled the area in colonial days. They announced their engagement, but one or both of the families disapproved of the match. Under pressure, Raitt broke it off, to his lifelong regret. Yorba married well and became a socialite; Raitt launched toward his legendary show business career. But he never forgot her.

As a devout Quaker, Raitt was granted rare conscientious-objector status during World War II. Instead he worked a year repairing pipes in oil fields, which helped him to preserve his shot-putter physique. But he had other aspirations. In the summer of 1944 he tried out for the Los Angeles Civic Light Opera, a company run by showman Edwin Lester, who had a taste for the big-shouldered operettas of the 1870s–1920s. He cast Raitt in the chorus of Gilbert and Sullivan's *H.M.S. Pinafore* for $35 a week but soon promoted him to bigger roles in shows like *The Merry Widow* and *Carmen*. The gym teacher/pipefitter suddenly found himself a matinee idol. MGM, then at its peak, gave him bit parts in a handful of minor musicals. He also returned to Redlands University as a guest artist to play the lead in its production of *The Vagabond King*. The leading lady was Marjorie Haydock, and shortly afterward they married.

But now something arrived on the horizon that made the light-opera world turn its attention to the present. A musical called *Oklahoma!* was turning the conventions of operetta on their heads. Raitt sized up the lead role of singing cowboy Curly and decided it was for him. When the songwriting team of Richard Rodgers and Oscar Hammerstein II announced they were auditioning actors for the national tour of *Oklahoma!*, Raitt headed east preceded by enthusiastic scouting notices.

For his audition, Raitt sang Figaro's aria from *The Barber of Seville* and did so not only with remarkable power, but with exquisite expressiveness. Raitt showed he could be both funny and serious while hitting every single note perfectly and in a way that was audible to the back of the balcony. By several accounts, it was one of the great auditions of all time. Rodgers and Hammerstein signed Raitt immediately and bundled him off on the tour. But they had even bigger plans.

Carousel

Raitt's audition had thrown Hammerstein into a frenzy of creation. Here was a rugged guy who had a huge legit voice and energy to spare. He might have been okay for Curly in *Oklahoma!*, but he'd be *perfect* for the lead in their new musical, which was based on the Hungarian play *Liliom*. Retitled *Carousel*, it was the story of Billy Bigelow, a ne'er-do-well carnival barker, little more than an overgrown street tough, who finally becomes a man—but only after he's dead. Half the story is played with Bigelow as a spirit, working directly with the godlike Starkeeper to undo some of the damage he did in life to his wife, Julie Jordan, and their child.

For this unusual story, Hammerstein was inspired by Raitt to write a six-and-a-half-minute solo. Raitt himself came to think of it as a mini opera. Titled "Soliloquy," it was an interior monologue from a guy who has just found out that he was going to be a father for the first time. Many people think the title of "Soliloquy" is "My Boy Bill," because that's how it starts out: Billy imagines all the fun he'll have with his son. About halfway through this fantasy, just when he's in the midst of giving the conjectured Bill pointers on ways to get around girls, it suddenly dawns on Billy that the child his wife is carrying might also turn out to be a . . . girl.

A girl! Well, now, that's a different matter. Suddenly Billy is jolted into considering that he may need to transform his entire life and take responsibility as a grownup. "You can have fun with a son, but you've got to be a father to a girl." He realizes that he'll need to get some steady source of money so he can feed, shelter, and protect her. Billy suddenly matures a bit.

It's one of the great audience fake-outs in lyric history. Hammerstein had gauged his listeners' expectations and knew they'd go right along with Billy into this fantasy, and then experience the same shock and bursting sense of responsibility that Billy does. The moment tells so much about audience attitudes toward male children and female children of the time.

At the same time, the song contains a seed of Billy's eventual destruction. When listing how he will try to get money, he indicates he *would* do anything for it, including steal, even die.

Coming into rehearsals, Raitt slipped into this song like an ace driver into a turbo racer. He swaggered in the first part, mourned in the second, and seemed to physically expand in the final section. Clad in a pectorals-tight striped shirt with a handkerchief knotted around his neck, and sporting his shock of curly hair, he was a gimlet-eyed punk with an inflated bad attitude. The attraction/repulsion felt by every woman in the audience was embodied by his Julie Jordan, played by the demure-seeming Jan Clayton, who appears totally in control until you realize that her steadfastness also leads her to disaster.

He and Clayton then created one of the greatest single moments in all musical theatre: "If I Loved You." Another mini opera within *Carousel*, the extended scene shows Billy and Julie in a wooded park in late spring, petals fluttering down from the branches. The tough-guy Billy is feeling something other than the usual for this sweet girl. What is it? He's in a bit of a panic because he thinks she's trying to make him fall in love with her. It isn't love, no way. He enumerates all the things he'd be doing differently if he were actually in love. She tells him not to worry. If she were in love here are all the things *she'd* be doing differently.

But all of this is just jabber. The audience knows the truth: they're in love, all right. And as the petals fall, they gradually move into each other's arms. The falling petals tell the story: They are the symbols of both sexual desire in its beautiful form—and of inexorable death. Billy wonders why the petals are all falling at once. She observes that the blossoms are just coming down by themselves.

They draw closer.

"Just their time to, I reckon."

They kiss.

What a gift that scene was for an actor like Raitt. And for audiences. Upon *Carousel*'s opening, Jon Chapman of the *New York Daily News* wrote that it was "one of the finest musical plays I have ever seen and I shall remember it always. It has everything the professional theatre can give it—and something more besides: heart, integrity, an inner glow—I don't know what to call it."

It helped shape the attitudes of a generation. Raitt later told an interviewer that the song "Soliloquy" "meant a great deal to a great many people. When I went backstage to see Dick Gregory at the hungry i club in San Francisco he told me, 'You are the reason I'm in show business. I was in a hotel room in the Midwest, really down, I had made my girlfriend pregnant and I was out of work, then I heard this song in the radio, I called the station to find out who the singer was and I went out and bought your record. It absolutely inspired me, I married the girl and we had our baby."

A lot of other men returning from World War II who were preparing to settle in the suburbs and give birth to the baby boomers went into parenthood carrying this sober reminder of where their real responsibilities lay.

Raitt's performance was seen across America in 1954 when he and Clayton re-created "If I Loved You" on a salute to Rodgers and Hammerstein, sponsored by General Foods, that was broadcast on all existing American television networks simultaneously. Imagine such a thing today.

After two years in *Carousel*, Raitt felt it was time to make a grab at movie stardom. He was red-hot, and it was still the golden age of movie musicals. Again he signed with MGM . . . and again they never offered him leading roles. Hollywood singing was becoming more influenced by swing and big band styles, and Raitt's blocky baritone just didn't fit. Back to Broadway he went. Raitt tried three times for success in musicals over the course of five years and failed all three times.

First, Raitt returned to his operetta roots with *Magdalena* (September 20, 1948), billed as "a costume operetta." Produced by his old mentor Edwin Lester of the California Civic Light Opera companies, *Magdalena* had a score by highbrow Brazilian composer Heitor Villa-Lobos, plus lyrics and something billed as "patter" by Robert Wright and George Forrest, who had enjoyed a hit with *Song of Norway* and would do so again later with *Kismet*. Unfortunately, *Magdalena* was saddled with a dour plot about a Colombian woman (Dorothy Sarnoff) trying to draw Pedro, her fiery betrothed, back to the arms of the church.

Brooks Atkinson of the *New York Times* gave the show a blunt thumbs-down, calling *Magdalena* "one of the most overpoweringly dull musical dramas of all time. . . . like being hit over the head with a sledge hammer repeatedly all evening."

Raitt, costar Irra Pettina, and "a company of 100" were all out of work after just eighty-eight performances.

Lester and Raitt next engaged composer Ralph Blane and librettist Abe Burrows (recently of *Guys and Dolls* fame) to create a score for the Charles O'Neal novel *The Three Wishes of Jamie McRuin*, about an Irishman (Raitt) who wins three wishes from the Fairy Queen Una: to travel, to marry a beautiful woman, and to have a son. In the course of the musical, titled *Three Wishes for Jamie* (March 21, 1952), the musical tells how Jamie fulfills the first two wishes quickly, traveling to Georgia and meeting the comely Maeve (Ann Sothern). But Jamie's rival curses her with barrenness, so they must adopt a child to achieve the third wish. The child, who turns out to be mute, is eventually the subject of a miraculous transformation and begins to speak—in Gaelic.

The show opened on Broadway March 21, 1952, to critical shrugs. It all seemed done before and old hat, with its heavy operetta trappings and its too-familiar brogued characters. Some found the infertility plotline in questionable taste, as well. It ran just ninety-four performances.

Raitt now jumped out of the frying pan and into *Carnival in Flanders* (September 8, 1953), which turned out to be one of the legendary flops of Broadway history. He played the romantic Spanish duke who, at the head of an army invading Flanders, descends upon a small town where the mayor pretends to be dead in order to elude capture. Unfortunately, the duke takes an immediate shine to the mayor's supposed widow, played by Dolores Gray, and begins to romance her right under the outraged but impotent husband's nose. Though adapted from the lighthearted French film *La kermesse héroique*, the show substituted leering and uncomfortable humor for lighthearted farce. Writing in the *New York Post*, Richard Watts Jr. said Raitt "has a fine voice but is perhaps inclined to throw masculinity and the flash of teeth about a trifle self-consciously."

The three flops were a great trial to Raitt, but something good came in threes during this dark period: He and his wife Marjory had three children Stephen, David, and, in 1949, future singing star Bonnie.

The Pajama Game

Raitt the track-and-field man was used to long races, and he finally came up a winner once again. Two young composers, Richard Adler and Jerry Ross, had written a sparky little musical called *The Pajama Game*, based on the novel *7½ Cents*, about a romance between a union leader and a shop superintendent at a pajama factory just as a strike is being called. Raitt played the superintendent Sid Sorokin, opposite Janis Paige as the union official. Directed by Broadway legend George Abbott, the silly little show snapped from one brightly conceived number to the next, with only its labor-strike scenario to provide ballast—that and the central characters, whose sizzling personal chemistry upped the ante in each scene. Their duet "There Once Was a Man" provided a good red-blooded lust song complete with Raitt's rat-a-tat delivery and Paige's fervent "Tell me!"

Raitt shone in a ballad called "Hey There," a song full of rueful advice about how to avoid making a fool of himself over his budding love. But "Hey There" had something extra: it was a solo that qualifies as a duet because Raitt, alone in his office, sings the first verse into his desk recorder. Then, when he plays back his own voice full of good advice for himself, he joins in with the harmony for a second verse. The witty songwriters had coopted a new piece of technology and made it serve storytelling ends.

Raitt finally got to star in a big Hollywood musical, re-creating the role of Sid in the 1957 movie version of *The Pajama Game*, opposite Doris Day as Babe. It turned out to be his only starring role in film and the final film credit of his career.

The same year as the *Pajama Game* film, he launched a first-class national tour of *Annie Get Your Gun* playing Frank Butler opposite Mary Martin as sharpshooter Annie Oakley. It sold out everywhere and was taped as an NBC-TV special. Raitt worked extensively on TV in the early 1960s, appearing on some of the variety shows of the period, but he made it known that he was ready to try another Broadway musical. In August 1965 he re-created his performance as Billy Bigelow once more in a Lincoln Center's Music Theatre revival of *Carousel*.

In December 1966 Raitt returned to Broadway in a mishmash of a musical titled *A Joyful Noise*. It had a lot going for it: Michael Bennett as choreographer, a cast that included Susan Watson, and, in the chorus, Baayork Lee and a young Tommy Tune. Based on the Borden Deal novel *The Insolent Breed*, it told the story of a backwoods folksinger (Raitt, as Shade Motley) who becomes a country music star but pines for his sweetheart (Watson) back in the hills of Tennessee. The musical proved to be neither fish nor fowl. Martin Gottfried in *Women's Wear Daily* put his finger on the problem, saying, "still another chance for a fresh musical went down the drain, dragged most of the way by an interfering, irrelevant injection of brassy nonsense, put together cheaply and ignorantly." He pronouced Raitt miscast because "he is a romantic leading man and a mature one. This part called for an electric performer—a young Elvis Presley." It ran just twelve performances.

In November 1975 Raitt performed his last regular role on Broadway, in a revue called *A Musical Jubilee*, assembled by the once-august Theatre Guild. Tammy Grimes, Larry Kert, Lillian Gish, Dick Shawn, and Patrice Munsel joined to tell the story of the development of musical theatre from operettas to what was then the present. However, despite Max Wilk writing the script and Morton Da Costa directing, the show seemed to embalm the songs rather than celebrate them, and the drawing power of its stars was all that kept it running three months.

Raitt claimed to have been offered the role of Daddy Warbucks in *Annie*, a role that eventually went to Reid Shelton. Raitt has been quoted variously as saying he didn't want to shave his head and that he didn't consider the role up to his standards.

Raitt took his final bow in *A Musical Jubilee* from the stage of the St. James Theatre on February 1, 1976. It was his last moment in a Broadway show.

The Road

Changing styles in American music and American theatre meant Raitt's type of leading man was no longer in demand on Broadway. However, the great middle of America, the so-called flyover states, didn't necessarily get this news. Audiences there still loved the old-style musicals and were thrilled to see Raitt in the flesh. For the next twenty years, Raitt toured the country and played summer stock doing the classics. To sift through the records of his life is to run fingers through piles of programs and playbills. Here he is doing *Man of La Mancha* in Connecticut. Here he is starring in *Kiss Me, Kate* in San Francisco. *Shenandoah* in San Diego. *I Do! I Do!* in *Ogunquit*, Maine. *The Pajama Game* in Arizona. *The Music Man, Shenandoah, 1776, Camelot, Kismet* . . . He did bus and truck tours of municipal halls and high school auditoriums, including the one at Fullerton High School in California where he made his stage debut. These appearances were a long way from Broadway, but they enabled him to cling to his dream of stardom as tightly as *Gypsy*'s Mama Rose—one of the few big musical roles he never played.

For many Americans who had never and would never see a show on Broadway, it was Raitt, not the people on the original cast albums, who embodied these roles. In one newspaper, Raitt claimed to have driven 50,000 miles in ten months playing in 110 cities. When he finally performed a gig in South Dakota, he made an announcement declaring that he had now sung show tunes in all fifty states.

Family Life

But all the travel took its toll. His first marriage broke up in 1970. His second wife, Kathy Landry, was a former Miss Nevada and runner-up for Miss Universe. Landry went on the road with Raitt and served as his business manager. Her marriage to the self-described "workaholic" lasted seven years.

But he wasn't quite alone. His daughter Bonnie had resented his neglect of the family during her childhood and had earned Grammy-winning stardom of her own with the blue-eyed versions of old-time blues, a style completely at odds with her father's. But, slowly, the two began to rebuild their relationship as adults. In the 1970s, Raitt would get ruffled when people started referring to him as "Bonnie Raitt's father" instead of her as "John Raitt's daughter." But by the 1990s, he accepted it and was proud of it. Father stood by daughter during her battle with alcohol in the 1980s and her divorce from actor Michael O'Keefe.

Living as a touring performer herself, she began to understand and respect her dad more.

The first time they performed in public together was in a 1992 Boston Pops concert. They must have enjoyed themselves, because at Bonnie's 1994 concert at Radio City Music Hall, she introduced him from the stage and they sang together again. Though he still insisted that show music was "the *real* music," they had found common ground. "We're both storytellers," he told one reporter. John and Bonnie even got arrested together at a 1996 protest to save California redwoods.

In 1981 the elder Raitt was introduced to an attractive widow named Rosemary Yorba Lokey. It was Raitt's high school girlfriend, the one to whom he had been engaged four decades earlier. It was love all over again. They married in 1981, adding her two daughters to the Raitt brood, and stayed married for the rest of his life.

As Raitt passed his seventieth birthday, he found the big musical roles getting harder to come by, even on tour. So he organized his own show, a revue of his favorite show tunes, sung concert-style, as Bonnie might. Simply titled *An Evening with John Raitt*, the show consisted of Raitt performing twenty-three songs from sixteen Broadway musicals, including Raitt's *Carousel* and *The Pajama Game*. In 1995 some of these songs were featured on a CD release, *John Raitt: The Broadway Legend*, which included three duets with Bonnie: "They Say It's Wonderful," "Anything You Can Do," and even "Hey There."

In November 1993, fifty years to the day since the opening night of *Oklahoma!*, Raitt was invited to mark the occasion by singing the title song of that musical on the stage of Broadway's St. James Theatre, where it had been introduced. "And then," wrote the *New York Times* in its terse summary of the event, "the curtain rose on a preview of *Tommy*." Operetta met rock opera, and rock opera won. The story of his life.

I met Raitt twice. The first time was in the early 1990s at the Shubert Theatre in New Haven before a fund-raising event. The Shubert stage was special to him, because it was the place he first sang "Soliloquy" in front of an audience. He sang it again on the stage that night with amazing power. Even in his midseventies he had great posture, his shoulders thrown back and his weight on his heels. He must have had a diaphragm like a radial tire, because he would take stupendous breaths for long passages and big notes.

I sat next to him at dinner and he still looked rugged, with the big shock of graying hair and tiny, sharp eyes. What did he want to talk about? Did I know of any roles being written for men his age? Real singing roles. He knew he was too old to play Jean Valjean in the recent *Les Misérables*. But he asserted that he would be perfect for the part.

I met him again a decade later when I was cohosting the Webcast of the 2004 Tony Awards with Paige Price. The back was not quite as straight as it had been a decade earlier. But something else looked wrong, too. His makeup looked very heavy. On closer inspection, it appeared that he had small bandages on parts of his face, which were spackled over with makeup. It turns out that during rehearsal he had fallen and hurt himself, but he had insisted that *he was going to go on*, and doctors literally patched him up. He put on his tux and, at age eighty-seven, placed himself before the Broadway audience. P.S., he blew the joint down with "Soliloquy" once again.

Raitt was not necessarily so tall—but "tough as a tree," truly.

The tough guy made it to age eighty-eight, finally felled by a nasty bout of pneumonia on February 20, 2005. When he got to heaven, I wouldn't be surprised if the angels greeted him with "You'll Never Walk Alone."

Gwen Verdon performs "Whatever Lola Wants, Lola Gets" in *Damn Yankees* (1955). PHOTOFEST

GWEN VERDON
Two Lost Souls

If there is a spirit on these pages of the pure joy of virtuoso dancing, it would have to be Gwen Verdon. The emerald-eyed, sunrise-haired muse of choreographer Bob Fosse defined the image of the female Broadway dancer in a two-decade-plus career lasting from her first big splash, when she stole the spotlight from the star of *Can-Can* in 1953, to her triumphant swan song, creating the role of Roxie Hart in the original production of *Chicago*, in 1976.

The stories told about Verdon have ripened over the years into legends, lovingly narrated by elder gypsies to the "kids."

There's the story about how Lilo, star of *Can-Can*, demanded that Verdon's first featured dancing role be cut to almost nothing—but that almost nothing was enough to stop the show on opening night and led to a standing ovation at the end with audiences shouting, "Verdon!" "Verdon!" and Verdon being compelled to return from her dressing room and take bow after bow clad only in a bathrobe (or a towel, depending on the account).

Of how she did not get cast in the film of *Sweet Charity* but consented to teach Shirley MacLaine the dances.

Or the story of how she cradled a dying Bob Fosse in her arms as he lay dying of a heart attack on a Washington, D.C., street corner on the opening night of a *Sweet Charity* revival.

This bright cartoon, the idol of young dancers everywhere, was instantly recognizable from her quivering flute of a voice, her athleticism, her vulnerability, her rolling hips, and her ability to play a sexy vamp while at the same time poking fun at the whole idea of sexy vamps.

Verdon was born January 13, 1925, in Culver City, California, to showbiz parents who had come to the United States from Great Britain. Her dad was an electrician at MGM during its heyday as the home of colorful musicals. Her mother had been a member of the Denishawn modern dance troupe and a vaudeville performer.

Young Gwyneth was sickly and her legs deformed by a childhood bout with rickets. She was forced for a time to wear knee-high orthopedic boots to help straighten her outward-turned toes. One of her nicknames, "Boots," referred to this. But she loved to dance and seems literally to have danced her legs back to health after her mom put her in classes at age three. By age six she was performing as "the fastest little tapper in the world."

Her precocious talent and her parents' professional connections helped her to get her film debut at age eleven as a ballerina in *The King Steps Out* (1936). She went to a public high school but took private ballet lessons with Ernest Belcher. She seemed on her way to a classical dance career when she made the impetuous decision, at age seventeen, to elope with a smitten writer for the *Hollywood Reporter*, James Henaghan, with whom she had a son, Jimmy. The marriage lasted only a short time, after which she hit the pavement doing rounds of auditions as a professional dancer, a prototypical "gypsy." Her fellow gypsies have never forgotten that she started as one of them—she was known to ride home with them on the bus even after she became a star—and made it all the way to the top in a career path that nearly every one of them still dreams of emulating.

Her first great artistic alliance was with eccentric choreographer Jack Cole, who put her in his dance company and employed her as his assistant. The Jack Cole Dancers were sought after both on Broadway and in Hollywood, and during the early 1950s she appeared in several films, like *On the Riviera* and *David and Bathsheba*, in brief dance sequences. She even assisted (sans credit) Stanley Donen and Gene Kelly on the classic *Singin' in the Rain*. She also helped nondancers Jane Russell and Marilyn Monroe move convincingly through Cole's choreography for the film *Gentlemen Prefer Blondes*.

Her first stage show, *Bonanza*, folded in Philadelphia. But Cole, who directed, could see she was destined for greater things. She made her Broadway debut in Cole's 1950 flop *Alive and Kicking*. Verdon devoted herself to Cole's demanding style but ultimately became weary of his temper tantrums. His misconduct must have been really something, because her patience with the bad behavior of her collaborators became one of her hallmarks.

She got her big break in 1953 (at age twenty-eight—late for a dancer) when she was cast by choreographer Michael Kidd as the second female lead in Cole Porter's musical *Can-Can*, which had been written for French chanteuse Lilo. Verdon was only a featured dancer, and her big moment came in the risqué Garden of Eden Ballet, in which Verdon capered in a costume designed to make her look nude, with a few strategic fig leaves. During the tryouts, the critics only had eyes (and praise) for Verdon, and some said she outshone the star. Lilo stamped her foot and Verdon's role was reduced, but it was no use trying to keep this particular light under a bushel.

As previously described, on the Broadway opening night, the Garden of Eden stopped the show, and at curtain calls the audience was chanting her name. Verdon, who was already getting out of makeup, had to make her legendary return to the stage for one more bow, still gamine and scantily clad.

"Last night," wrote William Hawkins in the *World-Telegraph & Sun*, "the audience did some elevation on the billing. The little French import, Lilo, went into the show a star. And Gwen Verdon came out of it a star. The crowd's increasing delight with Miss Verdon was exciting to feel. She spellbound the house with the quadrille and the can-can, and after the 'Apache' uproar they had to send her out for a last bow with her costume already off and clutched in front of her."

This triumph set the tone for the rest of her career.

Meeting Bob Fosse

It wasn't long before other producers cooked up a starring role for Verdon. The project was titled *Damn Yankees*, a musical Faustian tale set in the world of baseball. Joe Hardy, a rabid fan of perpetual underdogs the Washington Senators, is approached by the Devil (working under the name Applegate) with a damnable offer. Applegate will transform Hardy into the greatest player in game history—able to beat even the unbeatable New York Yankees—in return for his home-run-loving soul. Where would Verdon fit in all this? As insurance against backsliding, Applegate employs a sexy demon named Lola to make certain Hardy doesn't think of calling off the deal and making a home run of his own, back to his loving wife.

The choreographer of the piece was a red-hot young talent named Bob Fosse, who had earned raves for his spirited steps in the youthful musical *The Pajama Game* the year before.

Fosse, who had thought he'd be working with Mitzi Gaynor or Zizi Jeanmaire on the project (both turned it down), was not sure about Verdon at first. Verdon was not sure about him, either. Cole had a very emphatic style; Fosse's was just as well defined but completely different. The producers brought them together at a rehearsal studio on Manhattan's West Side near the site of what would become Lincoln Center. Verdon and Fosse tried a few steps together, and he found she understood his style perfectly. It felt comfortable and natural to her. Fosse biographer Martin Gottfried speculates that the corrective shoes she had to wear as a child made it easier for her to do the knock-kneed, pigeon-toed moves Fosse was experimenting with at the time.

From the start, it was one of those "perfect blendships" that Cole Porter wrote about. The craftsman had found his tool, and vice versa. He would be her boss, then her mentor, then her lover, and then her husband.

Verdon later told the *New York Times*, "I was a great dancer when he got hold of me, but he developed me, he created me."

Fosse, who had come up in the world of strip joints, loved the dark sleaziness of it all, and his dances always emphasized rolling hips and flexing buttocks. Though Verdon said on one occasion that she looked to herself like "a rabbit," men, and not a few women, who watched her dance felt she was the one of the sexiest human beings they'd ever seen.

First there were her flirty eyes and red hair. Then there was her distinctively quavery voice, which only got huskier and more quavery as she got older. Third, not only was her lithe body curvier than the standard dancer's, she moved it in provocative ways with ease. Usually she would do it in an exaggerated, self-parodying way. But, to most audiences, it looked an awful lot like the real thing. All her roles with Fosse would have a strong element of sexuality.

Which brings us to another Verdon legend, the one involving the poster for *Damn Yankees*. Originally showing a girl in a baggy baseball shirt (which generated yawns among ticket buyers) it was replaced by a photo of Verdon standing defiantly in a teddy, hands on hips, her amazing legs stretched apart. Ticket sales suddenly boomed.

Producers never made that mistake again. Posters for *Redhead, New Girl in Town,* and *Sweet Charity* all featured Verdon's character in one provocative pose or another. For her part, Verdon just laughed at it all. The sexuality was real, of course, but Fosse's provocative dances gave her permission to display it.

Though she would have many great roles, Lola was her greatest. "Whatever Lola Wants (Lola Gets)," a locker-room striptease designed to fascinate poor dumb Joe, was a showcase for both Verdon and Fosse. It went over so well in the Boston tryout (it became her signature number) that composers Richard Adler and Jerry Ross quickly wrote her a new introductory number, "A Little Brains, a Little Talent," that proclaimed her irresistibility.

Fortunately, both numbers were preserved more or less in their original form in the 1958 film of *Damn Yankees*, and they got the lion's share of attention from critics. Historians tend to focus on the "Who's Got the Pain?" number, in which Verdon and Fosse perform an amazing pas de deux making fun of the grunt that was part of the then-popular mambo. It's the only time on film that the two dance together. A lot of the number is done in unison, and it's easy to see how perfectly their styles matched.

But the essence of Verdon is most completely captured in the "Two Lost Souls" number late in the film. Dancing in the middle of a wild pack of bodies, Verdon sports a huge grin as she throws her head and arms down to the floor and then up to the ceiling in bursts of pure dancerly joy. For a moment she transcends sex and just dances like a flame.

Damn Yankees was put together rather quickly after the success of *The Pajama Game,* and Lola is, in the end, a ridiculous character, a cartoonish bimbo. But Verdon turned it into something more. The pure abandon of Verdon's dancing always had something supernatural about it. Here was a part that made that literally true: She is a demon from hell, and both her looks and, presumably, her dancing are created through black magic.

For the rest of her life the roles might have changed, but there would always be something magical about her.

Golden Age

Verdon's golden age was comparatively brief, from *Can-Can* in 1953 to *Redhead* in 1959. During that time she enjoyed nearly a hit show a year, usually at the Imperial Theatre, and each role invariably led to a Tony Award. She won the 1954 Best Supporting Actress Tony for *Can-Can*; the 1956 Best Actress in a Musical for *Damn Yankees*; the 1958 Best Actress in a Musical for *New Girl in Town*; and the 1959 Best Actress in a Musical for *Redhead*. That's four for four on consecutive Broadway roles, a remarkable and special record never equaled for a musical actress.

She was already in her thirties when she did *Damn Yankees* and tended to play characters who clearly had been around the block once or twice (or thrice) and were looking for salvation of one kind or another, often in the wrong places.

Lola in *Damn Yankees* is supposed to be hundreds of years old, just transferred into a youthful body but clearly having the outlook of someone who's seen more than her share of sinners. Anna in *New Girl in Town* (based, somewhat incongruously, on Eugene O'Neill's *Anna Christie*) is a reformed streetwalker who is trying to start a second life. The aptly named Charity Hope Valentine in *Sweet Charity* has plainly had a lot of "boyfriends" and, like Anna, is looking for a fresh start. Roxie in *Chicago* is a housewife who is taking her first sip of celebrity after years of obscurity and likes the taste.

The closest thing to an ingenue Verdon played in the prime of her career was Essie Wimple in *Redhead*. She played a sculptor at a turn-of-the-century waxworks, who re-creates famous murders, relying partly on her extrasensory visions of the murders. She uses this ability to help solve a new murder, winning a handsome swain in the process. Verdon's girlish exuberance on numbers like "'Erbie Fitch's Twitch," "I Feel Merely Marvelous," and "Look Who's in Love," and in the big Act II ballet "Essie's Vision," carried her through, though she turned thirty-four the same year.

Perhaps significantly, both shows were so closely tailored for Verdon that neither *New Girl in Town* nor even the Tony-winning Best Musical *Redhead* has ever been revived on Broadway.

After four shows in five years, plus tours, plus the movie of *Damn Yankees*, Verdon felt it was time to make some important life decisions. In 1960 she and Fosse tied the knot officially (though secretly at first). While Fosse went off to choreograph *How to Succeed in Business Without Really Trying* and other shows, Verdon took things relatively easy for the first time in more than a decade. She gave birth to their first and only child, Nicole Fosse, in 1963. She told *Dance* magazine at this time that she toyed with the idea of doing a revival of *Pal Joey* with her husband but also of giving up dancing altogether. Luckily, the latter was not to be.

Sweet Charity

She was enticed back to the stage in 1966 by a role in a musical custom written and choreographed for her by her husband: *Sweet Charity*. Verdon had been considering several literary properties for stage adaption, and the one that came through first was Italian auteur Federico Fellini's *Nights of Cabiria*, the story of a hooker with an ever-hopeful heart of gold. Softened somewhat to a taxi dancer in a Times Square dance hall, Charity Hope Valentine suffers through one romantic disappointment after another but never completely loses her optimism that someday her prince will surely come. Charity isn't the brightest bulb on the marquee—she's mainly a victim of her own soft heart—but there's a kind of nobility in her unwillingness to give up on her emotional charity, her hope, and her faith that her valentine was just around the corner.

Fosse reveled in the sordid atmosphere of the dance hall, and the show's iconic number, Cy Coleman and Dorothy Fields's "Big Spender," shows the girls (but not Charity) calling out to customers with cooing voices but dead eyes.

Charity is a ray of sunshine in this dark place, and composer Cy Coleman and lyricist Dorothy Fields gave Verdon half a dozen juicy numbers in which to let her gleam: the slinky "You Should See Yourself," the optimistic "There's Gotta Be Something Better Than This," the triumphant "I'm a Brass Band," the heartbreaking "Where Am I Going?," and the comic "The Bravest Individual." Her tour de force, however was "If My Friends Could See Me Now," sung when a handsome Italian movie star invites her up to his swanky apartment and she gets a glimpse of the high life she's only read about in fan magazines. Never mind that he's only trying to make his real girlfriend jealous: Charity will take what she can get. He happens to give her a cane and collapsible top hat as souvenirs, which were all the props Verdon needed for a stop-the-show dance solo. Along with "Whatever Lola Wants," it became her second signature song.

Verdon had the bad luck to open *Sweet Charity* the same year as *Mame,* which put her up against Angela Lansbury (along with Barbara Harris and Julie Harris) for Best Leading Actress in a Musical at the Tony Awards. Lansbury won, marking Verdon's first loss for a major role.

It was during the run of *Charity* that she injured her vocal cords when she accidentally inhaled a feather from the boa she used in one scene. By the time she recovered, her tremolo was even more distinct and her voice had acquired a huskiness that was actually rather appealing.

Verdon was in her forties when she made *Sweet Charity,* and she was known to omit some of her solos if she was having a particularly hard day. Coleman tells the story of an audience member who wrote angrily to complain that she had dropped "Where Am I Going?" the day he attended. Verdon reportedly prorated the cost of the song as a percentage of his ticket price and sent him a check for that amount.

The strain of performing the vehicle began to affect her more and more, until finally Verdon decided to hand Charity over to Helen Gallagher. When producer Robert Arthur hired Fosse to direct and choreograph the film version of *Charity,* he decided he wanted Shirley MacLaine for the title role. As Fosse's assistant, Verdon dutifully helped teach her signature role to the other actress. Others might find such an assignment demeaning and her acceptance of it masochistic. But Verdon had always enjoyed the role of backstage supporter; stardom had pursued her, not the other way around. She had her time in the sun, and there were few on whom the sun shone as brightly. When it came time for the light to grace others, she was secure and humble enough to let them have their turn with grace.

And here's where Verdon's story modulates into an interesting minor key. All artistic collaborators have their own interior clockwork. That clockwork becomes even more complex when an artistic collaboration turns into a personal relationship. But despite their close personal and professional collaboration, Fosse was faithful to Verdon only sporadically, if at all. The sex goddess had competition almost from the start. Fosse always acknowledged his unique connection with Verdon, but he also had a series of relationships with other women, and by the late 1960s, his blatant infidelities began to disrupt their marriage.

There's nothing unusual about showbiz marriages coming to grief. But while Verdon and Fosse obtained a legal separation in 1971, they continued to work together the rest of their lives. Moreover, while they never formally divorced, Verdon not only tolerated Fosse's girlfriends, but often befriended them, worked with them, and even sometimes mediated their conflicts; Fosse was no more faithful to them than to Verdon. She accepted him for what he was and consented to live on his terms. They were true bohemians, and they made their own rules—though Fosse biographer Gottfried reports that Verdon continued to sign her name "Mrs. Bob Fosse" on occasion.

Verdon enjoyed just one more Broadway hit from the stage. Fosse got the rights to adapt Maurine Dallas Watkins's 1926 nonmusical play *Chicago* as a vaudeville-style musical with a grimy and cynical edge. It tells the story of a corrupt young woman manipulating a corrupt media and a corrupt court system to get away with murder, literally. It was just the sort of tawdry story Fosse relished, and the 1920s setting gave him lots of period music and dance steps to draw upon. For this show, he turned to his *Cabaret* collaborators John Kander and Fred Ebb. They created a score that glittered, however evilly, and was so filled with razzle-dazzle that they even wrote a song of that title about valuing appearances over reality.

Verdon and costar Chita Rivera were both in their late forties when the show went into production. It was delayed more than a year when Fosse suffered the first of his heart attacks, brought on by overwork and various other addictions. When *Chicago* finally opened in 1975, Verdon had turned fifty, and going out on stage was an act of bravery. Fosse and costume designer Tony Walton sent the ladies out in form-fitting short-shorts. Any flaw would be instantly visible, especially for someone sitting in the fifth row, as I did on one of my visits. Their faces may have shown some of the effect of the passing years, but their legs, amazingly supple and strong, looked like they belonged on dancers in their twenties.

Perhaps it was just the part; perhaps Fosse's respect for Verdon had grown. But Roxie was no soft-hearted (and -headed) victim like Charity. When her boyfriend is untrue to her in the opening scene, she shoots him dead—and is perfectly content to frame her cuckolded husband for the crime.

As in *Sweet Charity*, Fosse gave her one show-off dance number after another: "Roxie," "Funny Honey," "We Both Reached for the Gun," "Me and My Baby," "My Own Best

Friend." Each was a gem, but none provided a breakout like "Lola" or "If My Friends Could See Me Now." Despite the darkness of the subject matter, the show was one of Fosse and Verdon's longest-running successes, second only to *Damn Yankees*. For all Fosse's obsessive fear of failure, in the end he never had a flop when Verdon was onstage.

Broadway was just happy to have her back. Even one of Verdon's competitors paid her homage. Verdon is mentioned by name in the Pulitzer Prize–winning script to *A Chorus Line*. "I want to be the next Gwen Verdon!" says the character Judy Turner. "Don't you just love her?" It was a pretty ballsy tribute, considering that *A Chorus Line* was in direct competition with *Chicago* for that season's Tony Awards, and its star, Donna McKechnie, would eventually compete with Verdon for the Best Actress in a Musical Tony—and win. In fact, despite eleven Tony nominations, *Chicago* found itself completely shut out of that year's awards by *A Chorus Line* and *Pacific Overtures*.

Verdon had some satisfaction, however. She lived to see the 1996 Broadway revival of *Chicago* become one of the great successes of its season and go on to be kind of monster hit she and Fosse dreamed it could be. The Oscar-winning 2002 film of *Chicago* would be dedicated to Verdon's memory.

Later Career

Verdon worked with Fosse again on *All That Jazz* (1979), his thinly veiled autobiographical film about a Broadway choreographer who smokes too much, eats too little, cheats on his wife and girlfriend, adores his daughter, and eventually overworks himself into a fatal heart attack.

Verdon, who had helped tend Fosse through real-life heart attacks, served as his assistant on this brilliant, chilling (and prescient) roman à clef, collaborating with his new favorite dancer Ann Reinking, who played more or less herself on screen. Leland Palmer played the role based on Verdon. Perhaps Fosse was inspired by Michael Bennett, who turned his unhappy relationship with leading lady Donna McKechnie into a story line in *A Chorus Line*. In any case, *All That Jazz* offers an enduring account, from Fosse's fractured and often self-serving point of view, of his marriage to Verdon and their experience together on *Chicago*. And the title of the film, of course, comes from that musical's opening number.

Verdon, Reinking, and Fosse collaborated again on the hit Broadway revue *Dancin'*. Among her other late-career projects was a major success, *Cocoon*, a science-fiction movie about aliens who come to Earth and, among other things, grant renewed youth to a group of senior citizens, including Don Ameche and Verdon, who plays a dance teacher and former star dancer. Verdon can also be glimpsed in Francis Ford Coppola's *The Cotton Club*. She earned three Emmy Award nominations for appearances on *Magnum, P.I.* (1988) and *Dream On* and *Homicide* (1993).

In 1987, Verdon agreed to help Fosse mount a major revival of *Sweet Charity*. In Verdon's signature role Fosse cast the same Donna McKechnie who had beaten Verdon for the Tony in 1976. On the afternoon of September 23, after wrapping up a final rehearsal for the Washington, D.C., opening, Verdon and Fosse set off on foot back to their hotel (where they had separate rooms). At the corner of Pennsylvania Avenue and Thirteenth Street, Fosse collapsed on the sidewalk. Verdon at first thought he was having an epileptic seizure and tried to shoo away onlookers, but a passing doctor correctly read the symptoms as exactly the sort of heart attack Fosse had imagined for himself in *All That Jazz*. He died shortly afterward in the emergency room of George Washington University Hospital, leaving Verdon, technically, widow Fosse.

Though Fosse himself was now gone, Verdon found a way to continue their partnership. In the years following his death, Verdon became his chief exponent, spokesperson, archivist, and interpreter. She served as artistic director for the Emmy-winning 1990 PBS documentary *Bob Fosse: Steam Heat*. In 1998–99 she collaborated (as "artistic advisor") with Reinking on a full-scale Broadway revue of his choreography, titled simply *Fosse*, in which she helped re-create some of his (and her) greatest dances. The show went on to win that year's Tony Award as Best Musical, and it ran 1,093 performances—longer even than *Damn Yankees*. Fosse couldn't have asked for better in a keeper of his flame.

Verdon, still adorable, still loving, remained a fixture around Manhattan's Upper West Side for years. Fellow gypsies and other fans would wave at her on the street, and she always took compliments with a smile. In 1998 she accepted a National Medal of Arts from President Bill Clinton.

Her mission of living for others was tested in fall 2000 when Verdon traveled to Woodstock, Vermont, to console her daughter Nicole after Nicole's husband, Andrew Grenier, was killed in an automobile accident. As it turned out, there was more grief to come for Nicole. On the morning of October 18, she discovered that her mom had died in her sleep of a heart attack.

The marquees of Broadway were dimmed in Verdon's memory.

The *New York Times* obituary said she was "widely regarded as the best dancer ever to brighten the Broadway stage."

In the *Village Voice*, Michael Feingold wrote, "Hers was a greatness of spirit, not just of technical facility and leg muscles. Verdon's voice was piquant and unique, a throaty, fuzz-coated warble with unexpected flavors in it, indomitably cheery but never cloying. . . . When Verdon was on stage, the world seemed full of wonders, and she its irrepressible Alice. . . . Half Puck and half Ariel, she was the embodiment of joy, a creature all flesh and blood and feeling, yet at the same time all graceful motion, and surely lighter than air."

Barbara Cook in *Candide* (1956). PHOTOFEST

BARBARA COOK
Glitter and Be Gay

There were two Barbara Cooks in Broadway history.

One was the slender ingenue who starred in 1950s musicals like *Flahooley* and *Candide*—not to mention her signature performance, originating the role of Marian the librarian in *The Music Man*.

The second Barbara Cook emerged in the 1970s, a full-figured cabaret performer who became queen of her profession, easily selling out venues from nightclubs to Carnegie Hall.

Both were the same woman, of course, and to understand why she was adored for decades by a succession of generations, you have to understand several things.

First, her connection with history. She is a golden piece of the golden days, still walking and singing among us (as of 2009).

Then there's her suffering and transcendence of suffering—often a key to a special kind of stardom. She endured a difficult childhood but moved past it. She endured the loss of her ingenue beauty, something anyone past the age of twenty-two could identify with. At midlife she underwent a weight gain, though she turned that into a point of pride. She fought a battle with alcoholism, though she became clean. It was as if the younger Barbara Cook had died and a new one emerged like a phoenix.

Next, there is her superb musical taste, particularly her loyalty to show music. And she doesn't just sing oldies; she keeps up on the new composers and new shows, though her heart runs from the 1930s to the late 1970s. She makes carefully chosen current songs sound like classics and persuades you that perhaps they are new classics.

But the most important thing you need to understand about Cook is The Voice. Cook had, arguably, the best voice of any female performer in Broadway history. Smooth, sweet, like polished silver or moonlight on gently undulating water. It wasn't an operatic voice, not completely a jazz voice, yet not truly a belt, either. She had her own approach to being a soprano.

The purity of her tone and angelic timbre didn't vary with dynamics. She had as much control on *fortissimo* notes as she had on *pianissimo*, and as much intensity on *pianissimo* as on *fortissimo*. There was a chest voice that could roar through gutsy blues, and a sweet and pearly head voice that could break your heart on either ballads or operatic arias. She would press certain carefully chosen notes until they quivered and burst like little bubbles of honey.

She always had a special power and certainty in her upper register that songwriters prized. In the prime of her stage career, composers such as Leonard Bernstein and Jerry Bock wrote specialty numbers expressly to showcase her prowess, which set impressive challenges for the actresses who tried to follow her into those roles.

Aside from her technical ability, she is a singing actress who moves into every song like a new home and fills it with emotion. The songs become little chapters from her life, and she sings them to you like a medieval troubadour.

Cook discovered The Voice as a child growing up in Atlanta, Georgia. Her father was a traveling salesman, and she recalls singing to him over the telephone in hopes of luring him home. But her folks divorced when she was six, after her only sibling, a sister, died of whooping cough (pneumonia in another account). Her relationship with her mother was close but not especially healthy. Cook later said that her mother openly blamed her for giving the fatal disease to her sister and told her that if her sister had lived, the father would not have left them. Still, the two were all each other had left, so Cook continued to live under her roof. At five-foot-three, she also began a three-decade battle with weight. She would later describe herself as "a neurotic girl from Atlanta. I did not have a lot of self-esteem."

Her voice always seems to have a little sob in it, even on the most upbeat numbers. When asked by an interviewer if she was drawn to sad songs, she replied "I prefer the word 'triste': sad but not tragic. It's always been a part of my personality, I guess. When I was 12, growing up in Atlanta, I wanted to sing torch songs like 'When Your Lover Has Gone.'"

As a teen Cook sometimes gave recitals at local fraternal organizations but got little other encouragement. After high school she helped support herself and her mother by working as a typist. This was, however, the golden age of Hollywood musicals, many of which glamorized Broadway. She later said these movies made Broadway seem fascinating to her.

She was already nearly twenty-one in 1948 when she and her mom made a fateful two-week visit to New York City. The city worked its magic and, at the end of the trip, Cook worked up the gumption to send her mother back to Georgia alone. She had decided to stay and try to break in as an actress, just like a million other girls. She had no connections and no "pull." Though very pretty, she was no lovelier than ten dozen other young women seeking the same roles. She persisted despite some humiliating setbacks. She still remembers walking on the street and hearing a stranger yell out, "Hello there, chubbo!"

She had one ace, however: The Voice. Word got out that there was a pretty new singer on the scene with amazing pipes. She got work singing in Manhattan nightclubs, including the Gold Key Club, where in 1950 composer Sammy Fain heard her and invited her to audition for a new musical he was writing, *Flahooley*, with lyrics by E. Y. "Yip" Harburg of *The Wizard of Oz* and *Finian's Rainbow*. Like the latter, *Flahooley* was a social satire, but its targets in big business and politics were more diffuse than the straight-ahead racial prejudice parodied by *Finian*.

Cook remembers being embraced by Harburg at the conclusion of her audition, and she was soon cast as the female lead, Sandy. She's the girlfriend and motivator of Sylvester, an inventor who works for the B. G. Bigelow Toy Company. The story takes off when Sylvester designs a new doll named Flahooley, the first doll to be able to blow bubblegum bubbles and laugh. There ensues a series of improbable complications—including a genie from a lamp who sees to it that a Flahooley doll winds up in every home in America—before things are happily resolved and Sandy and Sylvester tie the knot.

Cook got two numbers, the inspirational solo "Here's to Your Illusions," which showed that—with the first song of her first show—the Cook style was already nearly fully formed. She made even a third-rate song like "He's Only Wonderful" sound like a million bucks.

Along the way, Flahooley took some absurdist shots at American capitalism, which offended many in the Korean War–era audience. The rest were just confused. The show closed after just forty performances, but the cast album lived on as a cult favorite. For many years, the LP was a coveted symbol that its owner was a true musical-theatre aficionado.

Richard Rodgers now stepped in and cast her as Carrie in his 1954 revival of *Carousel*, singing "When I Marry Mr. Snow" and "You're a Queer One, Julie Jordan" at the New York City Center, which led to her being cast as Hilda Miller, the sheltered Amish girl who falls in love with a visitor from the city in *Plain and Fancy* (1955). The latter show was very popular at the time and became a staple of summer-stock theatres for the next decade. Cook stopped the show nightly with the score's best song, "This Is All Very New to Me," a lively scherzo in which she marvels at how good first love makes her feel.

Cook had by now flowered into a delicate beauty whose virginal prettiness, added to The Voice, sent her personal stock through the roof. None of the songs she'd been given to sing so far really tested the limits of The Voice. Composer Leonard Bernstein, who moved back and forth between the Broadway and classical worlds all his life, now decided to see how far she could push it. *Candide* was Bernstein's third full-scale musical, following *On the Town* (1944) and *Wonderful Town* (1953). He collaborated with Lillian Hellman, Dorothy Parker, and John La Touche on a musicalization of Voltaire's epic satirical novel poking fun at self-satisfied philosophies and philosophers—an ambitious subject for a musical comedy.

Cook would play Cunégonde, the noble young lady who steadfastly adheres to her teacher's belief that "all is for the best in this best of all possible worlds"—but who nevertheless finds herself abandoned, impoverished, and compelled to work as a courtesan. As her centerpiece number, Bernstein tailored the song "Glitter and Be Gay" specifically to fit Cook's voice. The song is a spectacular show-off piece, one of the great virtuosa songs ever written for a Broadway coloratura, and only a soprano with a throat of silver and ovaries of steel can sing it. In it, Cunégonde sings a dirgelike verse about the "dreadful shame" she feels at her life as a whore . . . while admitting in the somewhat sprightlier chorus that she does enjoy all the jewels and fancy clothes that go along with it. She finally decides to rise above her shame and "show my noble stuff" by reveling in her bling. In the song's climax she illustrates her delight with raucous laughter that comes in the form of twenty-four bars of trills, hitting (as written) no fewer than fifteen high C's, six D-flats, and five E-flats.

It was the perfect showcase piece for a comic ingenue with amazing pipes. Years later it would become a staple of her nightclub act, and she'd stick with it until the upper end of her register began to mellow in late life. Along with "Till There Was You" and "Ice Cream," it remained her signature piece.

Marian the Librarian

The stage was now set for her to create her greatest stage role. Cook seems today like such a natural to play Marian the librarian in *The Music Man*, but she wasn't the first choice, and she debated with herself whether it was the right career move. After all, she had already enjoyed major roles being customized by famous songwriters. What was she doing taking a role in a musical by tyro composer Meredith Willson, a show that had been in rewrites for a decade and had no real show-off songs (at least not until she made them such)?

As it turned out, the show about a traveling con man who gets his "foot stuck in the door" was to become an American classic. Her costar Robert Preston gave an iconic performance as Professor Harold Hill, who goes to River City, Iowa, to sell the supposedly gullible country folks a "boys' band," complete with (paid in advance) music lessons in the professor's patented "Think System"—then to abscond with the money. The only person standing in his way is the skeptical local librarian and piano teacher Marian Paroo, played by Cook. She is like a locked-up secret garden. But Professor Hill soon finds the key.

The show is full of unusual musical ideas, including two numbers subsequently described as "white rap": "Trouble in River City" and "The Piano Lesson," both of which used rhythmic unrhymed talking in place of traditional singing. Cook had no trouble spinning gold with this innovation, but she really shone on the show's big ballad, the slow waltz, "Till There Was You," in which she explains the show's magic: that whatever Harold Hill's nefarious intentions, he managed to spread some real enchantment and vitality around their dull, sleepy town. He may have been trying to steal their money with a fake boys' band, but along the way he woke them up to the beauty of music and life. He gave them something to get excited about and look forward to.

Who couldn't fall in love with such a girl? Hill does, and he confesses his scam. As a reward, the show ends with one more bit of white magic. The Think System works! The boys' band plays (more or less)! Hill is exonerated and is free to marry the lovely Marian.

How big a hit was *The Music Man*? It swamped its main competition, *West Side Story*, for Tony Awards that year. Cook was nominated for Best Supporting Actress in a Musical and won. It was to be her first and only Tony.

When Warner Brothers bought the film rights, they retained Robert Preston as Harold Hill (at the insistence of composer Meredith Willson), but instead of Cook they cast girl-of-the-moment Shirley Jones as Marian. Jones had also been allowed to cherry-pick female-lead roles in *Oklahoma!* and *Carousel*. The 1962 *Music Man* film uses nearly the entire Broadway score but replaces "My White Knight" with "Being in Love."

Cook never made a movie. "I never really fought to get into films," she wrote in answer to a fan's question on her website. "All I ever really wanted to do was musical theatre."

Cook never had another hit like *The Music Man*, but she did create two more important stage roles.

Composer Arthur Schwartz provided her with a nice shivering high note in the song "Magic Moment" from the 1961 musical *The Gay Life*, based on Arthur Schnitzler's *Anatol*, about a compulsive womanizer (played by Walter Chiari) who eventually realizes Cook is the girl for him. The book by Fay and Michael Kanin didn't do justice to the score or to the performers, and the show folded after just 113 performances.

Songwriters Jerry Bock and Sheldon Harnick (later to write *Fiddler on the Roof*) adapted Miklos Laszlo's romantic comedy *Parfumerie* as the 1963 musical *She Loves Me*. Cook played a worker in a perfume shop who loathes her coworker, played by Daniel Massey, but spends the day mooning with love over her anonymous pen pal, who, you can figure out, will turn out to be Massey. The story was silly, but music historian Steven Suskin calls Bock and Harnick's work "the best score of the sixties," which is saying a lot. The show had a disappointing six-month run but supplied Cook with the third of her signature songs, "Ice Cream," in which she describes her surprise, horror, and eventual delight at finally meeting her pen pal and discovering his true identity. A wonderful piece of acting, the song also ended on a very satisfying stratospheric high note, which Cook would ace for years to come.

During the late 1950s and early 1960s, Cook was also back in demand at the New York City Center, which continued its series of revivals of classic musicals. Among other roles, Cook played Magnolia in *Show Boat*, Julie Jordan in *Carousel,* and an especially radiant Mrs. Anna in *The King and I*. But as she approached her fortieth birthday in 1967, the "Broadway's favorite ingenue" act became more and more of a strain.

Her whole intensive work pattern, in fact, had begun to oppress her. Terming this period "middlescence," she began to drink and gain weight, ballooning from 106 pounds in *The Music Man* period to 250 pounds—effectively dynamiting a career that had been built on precision, clarity, and a wasp-waisted profile. Her marriage to David LeGrant ended in divorce in 1965, and, as an indication of how much she was letting things slide, her beloved only son, Adam, went to live with her ex-husband.

She told one interviewer, "I remember thinking that I didn't know where to aim myself. I think I needed to stop working for a while, sit back and take stock of things, . . . I don't know how to explain it, but I didn't know how to get it together somehow."

She continued to work here and there. She appeared in the brief Broadway run of the Jules Feiffer's nihilistic nonmusical *Little Murders* and then didn't return to the Broadway stage for four years. When she did return—in 1971's *The Grass Harp*—no one would have predicted that it would be her final Broadway musical. *The Grass Harp* closed after just seven performances; "folksy and fey" the *New York Times* called it, though it became yet another flop that attracted a cult following owing to the cast album.

It's worth pausing for a moment over this show, the last book musical Cook did on Broadway. Truman Capote's whimsical pastoral story tells of a band of friends, led by Cook, who gather to whip up a batch of Dolly Heart's Secret Gypsy Dropsy Cure and who nearly come to grief when an unscrupulous salesman plays on Cook's emotions to get her to hand over the recipe. The score is a secret recipe all its own, with handfuls of country, folk, and gospel thrown into a show-music broth. Cook gets only a few solos, but they're just lovely, including "Chain of Life" and "Reach Out," and also leads a chorus on the show's anthem, "Yellow Drum." It's hard to find a copy of the recording today, but well worth it for Cook fans who want to hear how her voice sounded just as she was pupating from Barbara Cook I to Barbara Cook II.

Though she would subsequently tell interviewers that she always felt there was a fat girl inside her longing to get out, she hid the transformation from the world for several years in the early 1970s while she sorted out her demons.

She burst out of her cocoon in 1975 in spectacular fashion. Wally Harper, a Broadway conductor, arranger, music director, and sometime composer who was also a friend of Cook's, persuaded Cook that she should focus on the part of the business she liked the best: pure singing. He organized a concert at Carnegie Hall that would focus attention on the amazing flexibility and range of her vocal instrument and free her from the need to play a particular character of any specific age or size.

This first solo concert on January 26, 1975, came after, as the *New York Times* put it, she had "struggled for some ten years with depression and alcoholism."

Michael Feingold of the *Village Voice* later analyzed her career transformation, saying, "she was trapped early on in a recognizable category: the ingénue, blonde, soprano, and eternally virginal. The career slump came when she was getting too mature for this role. Instead of becoming either a recovery case or a personality, she went deeper into her singing, and found acting there."

Harper remained her arranger, conductor, and accompanist until his death in 2004. They toured together again and again during that time, traveling across the United States, to Europe, and back again to Broadway, to Lincoln Center, to the Café Carlyle, to Michael's Pub, and to Carnegie Hall. She played command performances at the White House for four different presidents. In time, Cook became the unchallenged queen of the nightclub world. Her act set the standard for artistry, creativity, technical perfection—and heart.

In 1985, Stephen Sondheim asked her to costar in a concert version of his musical *Follies* at New York's Lincoln Center, in which she would play Sally Durant Plummer, the brokenhearted wife of Buddy Plummer (Mandy Patinkin), whom she married on the rebound after her real love chose another girl.

It's hell, of course, to realize that the girl you married doesn't really love you, and that's Buddy's story. But it's a separate kind of hell to spend your life in a relationship where you see the love in your partner's eyes but know you can't return it. That's Sally's story, and it's crystallized in the song "In Buddy's Eyes." For the concert version, Cook delivered possibly the most bittersweet and lovely rendition of a song that's been extensively covered by female singers. Luckily, it's preserved on the two-CD concert album. When she goes for that final bittersweet high note on the word "eyes," you can hear her control, you can hear her inhabiting the note with the character's despair, and you can hear just how powerful *pianissimo* can be.

Cook maintained a close relationship with Sondheim and his music. He would later inspire one of her most successful concert shows, the Tony-nominated *Mostly Sondheim*, and they would even appear together in a *New York Times* forum on singers and songwriters.

Cook came very close to making one final appearance in the lead role of a big musical comedy on Broadway. Emboldened by her success in *Follies*, Cook accepted an invitation from the Royal Shakespeare Company in London to take the role of the steely, religious-fanatic mother in a musical based on the Stephen King horror novel *Carrie*, about a sensitive girl who possesses the power of telekinesis and uses it to get back at her fellow high school students who humiliated her. This supernatural Columbine story would seem a dicey subject for a musical, but Cook gave it a chance.

After a poorly reviewed tryout at Stratford-upon-Avon and four weeks in London, Cook decided to withdraw. Betty Buckley took over, riding the show like a barrel over the falls and into history books as one of the greatest disasters ever.

Cook had dodged a considerable bullet.

She went back to touring in her concerts, earning near universal praise. In preparing this chapter I looked at dozens of reviews from across the country over a thirty-year period. Not one was less than positive, and most were waves of raves, a remarkable record.

In 2000, Stephen Sondheim sat down with *New York Times* columnist Frank Rich for a magazine story marking Sondheim's seventieth birthday. In it, Sondheim listed not his favorite of his own songs, but songs by others that he wished he'd written. These included a wide range of twentieth-century composers and a tasty list of songs, both well-known and obscure.

A light went on over Wally Harper's head: How great would it be to have Barbara Cook sing a selection of those genius-kissed songs, as a counterpoint to a concert devoted to Sondheim's own work (including "Anyone Can Whistle," sung a capella)? The result was *Mostly Sondheim*, which she performed in January 2002 at the Vivian Beaumont Theatre at Lincoln Center. It was nominated for the first-ever Tony Award in a new category, Best Special Theatrical Event, but lost to another musical solo show, *Elaine Stritch: At Liberty*. Cook earned another Tony nomination for her follow-up concert, *Barbara Cook's Broadway*, in 2004.

In 2006 Cook had the honor of being the first female pop singer in its 123-year history to appear with the New York Metropolitan Opera Company. Even after so many years, she was still being creative, taking chances, and happily playing the instrument, "a living refutation," as *The Stage and Television Today* put it, "of [F.] Scott Fitzgerald's dictum that there are no second acts in American lives."

As she passed her eightieth birthday in 2007, Cook continued to release albums, continued to plan concerts, continued her master classes at the Juilliard School in how to sell a song. Like the end of a recording, she has picked a favorite musical phrase to repeat if not fade.

Robert Preston as Professor Harold Hill in *The Music Man* (1957). PHOTOFEST

ROBERT PRESTON
The Music Man

"Folks, may I have your attention, please! Attention, please!"

With these words, Robert Preston launched into "Seventy-Six Trombones," one of the sparkling songs in *The Music Man* and one of the most widely recognized and loved show tunes ever written.

Its bright vision of an all-American dream marching band is irresistibly stirring—which is exactly what makes the fact that it's a skillful con by a master con man so effective. The character who can balance such an inspiration that's also a betrayal is Professor Harold Hill, phony bandleader of nonexistent boys' bands, and the actor who so perfectly brought him to life was Robert Preston.

The fact that such a great role came to Preston only after many others had passed on it is the story of his career. Bitten early by the acting bug, Preston earned a contract with Paramount Pictures at age nineteen and embarked on a twelve-year movie career that started brightly but faded from romantic heroes in "A" films to villains and sidekicks in "B" films. Then, suddenly, when he was forty, he landed the role of a lifetime in *The Music Man*, which he defined and which ultimately defined him. Preston appeared in several more musicals, even winning a second Tony Award, for *I Do! I Do!* And he even enjoyed a successful second film career, earning an Oscar nomination for *Victor/Victoria*.

But, as the role of Harold Hill so perfectly illustrated, people were never quite sure whether he was a good guy or a bad guy. Or, at any rate, which side of him was dominant.

He was handsome and tall, with curly hair and a growling baritone. But there was something sly around his narrow eyes and long nose, something satyr-like, frustrated, and predatory.

At the same time there could be a sweetness about him, a sense that, deep down, he was an okay guy. When the boy Winthrop in *The Music Man* confronts him with his lies, he immediately moves to reassure him that he's a great kid, and that's why he wanted him in the band. Winthrop replies bitterly, "*What* band?" Hill finally cops to his con—and also to his realization that he sometimes even cons himself: "I always think there's a band, kid."

That took a lot of different colors to play, and Preston had them. On top of everything else he had a great star name, one with a crisp presto-like sparkle to it.

Naturally, it wasn't his real name.

★

Robert Preston Meservey was born June 8, 1917, in Newton Highlands, Massachusetts, the son of a garment worker. When he was two, the family moved to Los Angeles, where his dad worked as head of the shipping department at a garment factory and his mom worked at a music company. She was a regular theatergoer and took young Robert to see acting legends Alfred Lunt and Lynn Fontanne.

The boy attended Lincoln High School, where his teacher Edward J. Wenig instilled in him a love of Shakespeare. He played Hamlet at age fifteen and Julius Caesar at age sixteen. When still in his teens, Robert joined a repertory company run by Patia Power, the mother of actor Tyrone Power, and eventually took part in forty-two productions of all kinds, which toured small theatres in the Los Angeles area.

Robert was drawn to the nearby Pasadena Community Playhouse, where the director, Gilmor Brown, offered him a fellowship at the theatre's training school. The prize student was soon playing every sort of part in the theatre's mainstage productions, both dramas and musicals. In 1936, when Robert was playing the Alfred Lunt role as a singing, joking, straw-hatted vaudevillian caught up in an impending war in Robert Sherwood's drama *Idiot's Delight*, he was spotted by a lawyer in the Paramount Studios legal department, who arranged for the studio to give the tall (six-foot-one) and ruggedly handsome young man a screen test. At age nineteen, with a newly shortened name, Robert Preston became a movie actor.

During his time at Pasadena Playhouse he met actress Kay Feltus, who worked under the stage name Catherine Craig. The night of his first success there, she gave him a gift with an enameled tin four-leaf clover for luck. He carried it with him the rest of his life and would jiggle it in his pocket before a particularly tough scene. Preston and Craig married in 1940. Apart from a separation in the mid-1960s, they stayed together the rest of their lives. They had no children.

Preston made his film debut in *King of Alcatraz* (1938) and did two more "B" movies before starring with Barbara Stanwyck in *Union Pacific* (1939) when he was twenty. He also starred opposite Gary Cooper and Susan Hayward in *Beau Geste* and had featured roles in *Reap the Wild Wind, This Gun for Hire*, and other films.

But Preston's movie career, like so many others, was interrupted by World War II, in which he served as an intelligence officer with the U.S. Ninth Air Force, rising to the rank of second lieutenant. Preston was still under contract to Paramount when he returned from service, but he found that something had changed. Instead of romantic leads, he started to get sidekick and villain roles.

"Back in 1938," he later complained, "I was playing Harry Van in *Idiot's Delight* at the Pasadena Playhouse, singing, dancing and telling jokes. That's what Paramount signed me up for—a twelve-year contract no less—but I never got to do any of that stuff in films. I spent four years in the army and by the time I got back they forgot what they hired me for."

He complained to the *New York Post*, "All the scripts I got went first to Fred MacMurray. If he didn't want them they went to Ray Milland—and then to me at the end of the line."

That was an exaggeration, but it didn't feel like one to Preston. Soon, all the westerns started to look the same; "only the horses changed," he lamented. In all, Preston made a dozen so-so films between 1947 and the end of his Paramount contract in 1951, a time he would refer to as "those lost years." *Music Man* composer Meredith Willson told an interviewer that during this period, "Preston was like a man in a prison cell, shaking the bars."

During his final year at Paramount (1950–51), Preston took a location-shooting trip to London that changed his life. He observed that "all the British actors in the film we were working on went from bit parts during the day to starring roles in the West End. It renewed my taste for the theatre. I couldn't get back to New York fast enough."

Preston made his Broadway debut May 15, 1952, in a revival of James Thurber's comedy *The Male Animal*, about a college professor suspected of being a communist. He appeared in six more Broadway plays, with nothing more than a modicum of financial success but with a greater sense of satisfaction with his craft.

In a Philadelphia production of *The Front Page*, Preston was playing Hildy Johnson, the ultimate hard-boiled tabloid reporter—a man who will lie, playact, and bamboozle if need be to get a scoop—when he was seen by director Morton Da Costa, who was having trouble casting the lead in his new show and decided that perhaps they had finally found the man they were looking for.

The Music Man

Composer Meredith Willson spent the early 1950s working on a pet project, a semiautobiographical Broadway musical he called *The Silver Triangle*. Willson, a flute and piccolo player with "March King" John Philip Sousa's orchestra early in his career, had grown up in Mason City, Iowa, and seen his mother courted by a fast-talking salesman. He conceived the idea of a show about that courtship, and the effect it had on the boy, whom he envisioned as suffering from cerebral palsy.

Willson had become one of the most sought-after musicians in Hollywood, but he never entirely put aside his project. Over the years, at the urging of his composing mentor Frank Loesser (*Guys and Dolls*) and playwriting mentor N. Richard Nash (*The Rainmaker*), Willson and co-librettist Franklin Lacey developed the character of the salesman into the lead, turned the mother into the boy's older sister, softened the boy's affliction from CP to a lisp, made the story into one about how the salesman affected the entire town, and changed the title to *The Music Man*.

Ready at last for Broadway, the project was a dark horse. Willson was an unknown quantity on Broadway, and many of the big stars offered the main role, Professor Harold Hill, felt it was too unappealing. Among those who turned it down were Danny Kaye,

Milton Berle, and Art Carney. Preston was far down the list, a has-been movie star with virtually no professional singing experience. But Da Costa liked him in *The Front Page*, and Willson agreed that he had the right personal quality for Hill. Besides, as Rex Harrison demonstrated in the 1956 hit *My Fair Lady*, one didn't necessarily have to be a trained singer to play the lead in a musical.

As it turned out, Preston's singing voice wasn't bad at all. He had a resonant, gravely baritone that sounded just fine next to costar Barbara Cook's chiming soprano on their Act II duet "Till There Was You." But he also stood alone on atmospheric solos like "Marian the Librarian," "The Sadder-but-Wiser Girl," and "Gary, Indiana."

However, on one of his biggest solos he didn't need to sing at all. Originally designed for the fast-talking Danny Kaye, "Ya Got Trouble" was the setup for his big con of the people of River City. He warns of the danger to their children's morals from the presence of the local pool hall. Like a preacher at a revival meeting, Preston doesn't sing so much as rap his way through his sermon, conjuring up his visions of kids smoking, drinking, dancing, and acting wild all around, while "Telling jokes from *Captain Billy's Whiz Bang*."

But even that song stands in the shadow of Preston and Willson's crowning achievement, the classic march "Seventy-Six Trombones," in which Hill gets River City fired up to start a boys' band by painting a vivid picture of the greatest marching band ever assembled.

During this number, Preston himself almost seems to disappear, and as the kids leap up to enact his vision, he almost seems to become the parade himself. It was a real feat of stage magic, unforgettable to anyone who witnessed it.

The song did another job, too. It linked Hill with the leading lady, the local piano teacher who at first is cold and suspicious about his motives, then gradually melts as she sees the electric effect his con is having on the formerly dull folk of River City, who suddenly have something in their lives to be excited about. One of her two tunes is "Goodnight, My Someone," which has the same melody as the up-tempo march of "Seventy-Six Trombones" but is sung more slowly and in waltz time.

When *The Music Man* opened on December 19, 1957, audiences saw a daguerreotype of small-town American life in the year 1912—a life before radio and television and world wars, when the prospect of an "ice cream sociable" could rouse a whole town.

They also saw a lovable con man who bamboozles a city council into forming a barbershop quartet, who bamboozles the local ladies' guild into forming a dance company, who teaches a little boy with a thick lisp a song "with hardly any esses in it," who promises that his revolutionary "Think System" will somehow enable tone-deaf boys to play their shiny new instruments, and who captures the heart of a cynical young woman.

Hill fools even the audience into thinking he's a great guy—and gets the audience to root for his gold-plated con. It was a beautifully wrought performance, the work of a real craftsman. Each moment was elegantly conceived and masterfully executed.

Ah, but *The Music Man* has another twist. Just as Hill is casting a spell over River City, the eccentric little town casts its spell on him, too. It's a terrible fate for a con man: he actually starts to personally like his marks. Though he has a girlfriend in every county in Illinois, he falls in love with the pretty Iowa piano teacher. "For the first time in my life," he explains when the law is finally about to catch up with him, "I got my foot stuck in the door."

And then, in the final moments of the story, there is a wonderful moment of white magic. Forced to see what happens when the kids use his bogus "Think System," he is stunned to see that . . . it works! They don't play the "Minuet in G" very well, but they play it! He didn't con them, after all. Hill discovers, to his astonishment, that he accomplished what he promised.

Finally Preston had found a role that enabled him to do all the things that had impressed the Paramount lawyer back in 1936 in *Idiot's Delight*. He even got to wear a straw hat, as he had in that production. It also enabled him finally to find the perfect balance between his outward shiftiness and his inward sincerity. Rarely has a role so perfectly matched a performer, and vice versa.

Robert Coleman in the *Daily Mirror* wrote that producer Kermit Bloomgarden "made a 10-strike in landing Robert Preston for the title role. We don't have to tell you that we've been beating the drums for Bob over the years. But it took his current vehicle to bring home to us just how versatile our boy really is. He paces the piece dynamically, acts ingratiatingly, sings as if he'd been doing it all his life, and offers steps that would score on the card of dance judges. A triumphant performance in a triumphant musical!"

In the race for the 1958 Tony Award, *The Music Man* tidal-waved its main rival, *West Side Story*, in the estimation of the voters, taking nine awards, including Best Musical, Best Score, and Best Book. Preston won the Tony as Best Leading Man in a Musical and stayed with the show for much of its 1,375-performance Broadway run.

After such a triumph, you'd imagine that Preston was a shoo-in to re-create the role on film, but that's not the way Hollywood thinks. Luckily, Hollywood already knew Preston, but that didn't mean other actors weren't considered. Several bigger stars were hungry for the part, and Warner Brothers wanted a top draw for the expensive property. Syndicated columnist Cindy Adams reported, "Jack Warner wanted Cary Grant to play Hill, but Grant refused. 'Press is so magnificent in this that not only wouldn't I take the part away from him, but if he doesn't play it—I won't even see it.'"

Warner also considered Frank Sinatra for the role, but this time it was Meredith Willson who vetoed the actor, threatening to pull the plug on the film if Preston didn't get the part.

Ultimately, theatre lovers cherish the film, overlong as it is, in no small part because Professor Harold Hill stands as one of the few great 1950s Broadway roles (Gwen Verdon's Lola in *Damn Yankees* was another) actually re-created on film and not handed over to a "movie star."

"If you're going to do the film version of *The Music Man*, you get the best Harold Hill," Preston said in a 1961 interview as he was gearing up to shoot the movie. "At this late date, there's nobody who can do it better that I can. The role is part of me and I'm part of the role."

Released in 1962 with Shirley Jones replacing Barbara Cook as Marian, *The Music Man* was a major hit for the studio, earning an Academy Award nomination for Best Picture and earning Preston a Golden Globe nomination as Best Actor. It was the high-water mark of his film career, as it had been of his stage career.

Second Career

How to follow up such a career-defining hit as *The Music Man*? Preston made a number of odd career choices around this time, including the decision to play Mexican revolutionary Pancho Villa in the musical *We Take the Town*. There exist production photos of Preston sporting a huge sombrero and long moustache, leering arrogantly at the camera. But the misguided show closed out of town.

He also appeared in several distinguished stage dramas and films, notably playing an amoral advertising executive in Broadway's *Nobody Loves an Albatross*, a doomed father in the movie of *All the Way Home*, and a sexually frustrated husband in the film of *The Dark at the Top of the Stairs*.

But just as he'd once been typecast as a heel, he was now haunted by Professor Harold Hill. At an especially dark moment in *Nobody Loves an Albatross,* an audience member shouted out to him, "Mr. Preston, would you please sing 'Seventy-six Trombones'?"

The forty-seven-year-old Preston next agreed to appear in the musical *Ben Franklin in Paris* (1964), playing the seventyish founding father. It was a traditional musical comedy based loosely on a lesser-known but key chapter of American history. It's about Franklin, that brainy, cultured scalawag, trying to arrange recognition of American Independence by romancing King Louis XVI's mistress (a composite of several women Franklin knew). Preston even shaved his head for the role. Though the show is not likely to appear on any-one's top-ten list, it did offer Preston several eyebrow-wiggling moments, notably the mischievously egotistical "I Invented Myself" and "God Bless the Human Elbow," largely a paean to that joint's ability to hoist drinks.

Preston's leading lady was Swedish musical comedy star Ulla Sallert, a traffic-stopping blond bombshell who was also a real-life Scandinavian baroness. Preston had managed to avoid backstage romances, but Sallert proved irresistible. Listening to the cast album of *Ben Franklin in Paris*, you can hear their warmth in "To Be Alone with You" (one of the best-remembered numbers in the show, performed supposedly aloft in a balloon). Tabloids rejoiced as Preston separated from, and reunited with, his wife three times over the course of the show's run. Preston even announced at one point that he was planning to marry Sallert. Ultimately the Prestons reconciled, and Sallert flew back to Sweden.

Preston told *Playbill* years later that he and his wife had a tradition: whenever they would to go to the theatre, just as the lights would go down, Preston would roll up the program and whisper through it, "I love you" in his wife's ear. That tradition resumed after the Sallert episode and continued until his death.

Later Stage Work

Having played a man who bamboozled a king, Preston next played a king himself—England's Henry II in James Goldman's political drama of twelfth-century palace intrigue, *The Lion in Winter* (March 1966). The setting was Christmas at the castle, but this was no warm family idyll. Henry, Queen Eleanor of Aquitaine, their three grown sons, and Henry's mistress all try to use the occasion to backstab each other.

Though Preston went out on a limb for the role, his reviews were not ecstatic, in one case complaining that his performance lacked subtlety. Peter O'Toole took Preston's role in the 1968 film version. Preston was so demoralized by the experience he nearly reneged on a promise to appear in his next musical, *I Do! I Do!* (December 1966), coincidentally about a long marriage that survives a midlife crisis.

Based on Jan de Hartog's two-character play *The Fourposter,* the musical follows middle-class newlyweds Agnes and Michael going through all the usual troubles and strife over the course of their fifty-year marriage. It was written by Tom Jones and Harvey Schmidt, the team that had earned immortality with *The Fantasticks* but who had followed it with only the modest success of *110 in the Shade.* Preston played Michael as a little bit vain, a little querulous, but ultimately deeply in love with Agnes. Preston's costar was Mary Martin, still deeply beloved by the audience for her roles in *Peter Pan, South Pacific,* and *The Sound of Music,* who played Agnes as a bit of a naïf but adorable all the same.

Jones and Schmidt wrote them an impressive variety of solos and duets, fast and slow songs, comedy songs, ballads, and production numbers—even though it was always just the two of them doing it all. Preston and Martin had appeared together in the 1941 film *New York Town* and now rediscovered a marvelous chemistry.

It began with the title song, one of several Jones and Schmidt concocted for the show, in which they ticked off all the great things about marriage. The scene of their first night together ("Good Night") was touching rather than smutty, followed by Preston's afterglow song "I Love My Wife."

The idyll doesn't last. In "Nobody's Perfect" he got to unroll a list of her faults, including wearing cold cream to bed. She responded with a far longer roll of his faults, including chewing in his sleep. Inevitable strains led to Preston's midlife-crisis song, "It's a Well-Known Fact," which probably cut pretty close to the bone. Crisis past, they looked forward to getting older in "When the Kids Get Married," and Preston got to complain about his daughter's choice of husband in "My Daughter Is Marrying an Idiot." And so it went, through the beautiful duets "My Cup Runneth Over" and "This Has Been a Very Good House."

While the show didn't break much new ground, other than in the size of its cast, it showcased the two stars doing what they did best. In 1967, Preston won his second Tony

Award as Best Actor in a Musical. The show, which ran a year and a half, proved to be Preston's last Broadway success.

Preston had a thankless role as suave southern gentleman Beauregard Jackson Pickett Burnside in the awful film version of the Jerry Herman musical *Mame*. His job was mainly to sing the title song and then die. But Herman liked his work well enough to engage Preston for his next Broadway musical, *Mack & Mabel*.

To tell the story of silent film pioneers Mack Sennett and Mabel Normand, producers assembled much of the same creative team that had created *Hello, Dolly!* a decade earlier, including Herman, librettist Michael Stewart, and director Gower Champion. In Mack Sennett they found a robust and charismatic male character. However, as it turned out, that didn't make things any easier—even with the much-younger Bernadette Peters, then in the first flush of her stardom, playing comedienne Mabel Normand.

Sennett was a visionary artist and helped to define film comedy in ways that were still being employed close to a century later. He discovered Normand when she was working as a delivery girl and put her on the screen, where her incandescent comic gifts made her one of the world's first movie stars. Soon, director and star were in each other's arms.

It seemed like a heavenly idea for a musical, but Sennett was a workaholic who had little time or energy left over for building personal relationships, which made him funny, but not warm. Normand needed far more than he was able to give. In real life they broke up and went their separate ways. Boy got girl, boy lost girl—and that was that, which was hell on the second act.

The writers tried to "write the problem" by giving Preston the song "I Won't Send Roses." And they tried to reassure the audience with his song "I Promise You a Happy Ending." But despite all efforts by Preston and the creative team, Sennett remained a cold man who never managed to get his foot stuck in the door. Despite big stars and high hopes, *Mack & Mabel* ran less than two months in fall 1974.

After a brief return the stage in 1977, replacing George C. Scott in the comedy *Sly Fox*, based on *Volpone*, Preston made one last try at Broadway stardom—again, as in *We Take the Town*, taking an extreme ethnic role for which he was perhaps not best-suited. In Bob Merrill's 1978 musical *The Prince of Grand Street*, Preston played Nathan Rashumsky, a variation on Yiddish theatre superstar Boris Thomashefsky. At his Grand Street theatre Thomashefsky was a larger-than-life figure, serving simultaneously as impresario, playwright, director, and star of melodramas and musicals, often adapted from classical works with his own distinct spin—and all performed in Yiddish. Preston had the right lust for life to embody this latke luminary, but not necessarily the right accent. With little in the way of a plot, *The Prince of Grand Street* closed in Boston and canceled its planned opening at Broadway's Palace Theatre.

Preston's last major role was Carroll "Toddy" Todd, a gay cabaret performer in the Julie Andrews/Blake Edwards film musical *Victor/Victoria* (1982), for which he received an Academy Award nomination as Best Featured Actor.

Seeing his poor, talented opera-singing friend (Andrews) starving and unable to find work in Depression-era Paris, Toddy gets the bright idea of passing her off as a (male) female impersonator as one of the city's gay nightclubs. She/he/she is an instant sensation, but the deception complicates Andrews's love life and threatens them both when she falls for a visiting American gangster. Sparklingly witty, but always with a great warmth toward his triple-dealing friend, Preston anchored the picture and displayed a remarkable chemistry with his costar. There was talk of adapting the show for Broadway, but by the time that happened in the mid-1990s, Preston was no longer around.

Always adept at playing rogues, he next took a role as a kind of alien military recruiter in the 1984 film *The Last Starfighter*, which took advantage of the nascent video game craze by imagining that one such game was actually a recruiting tool for young paladins in an age-old galactic war.

Among Preston's last projects were the TV movies *Finnegan Begin Again,* in which he played a newspaperman enjoying a December romance (with Mary Tyler Moore), and *Rehearsal for Murder*, in which he played an Agatha Christie–like playwright.

Preston worked up until just a few months before his death on March 21, 1987, of lung cancer. He died in Santa Barbara, California, not far from his home in Montecito. He was just sixty-eight years old.

Richard Kiley as Don Quixote de la Mancha in *Man of La Mancha* (1965).
PHOTOFEST

RICHARD KILEY
Out of the Commonplace into the Rare

Richard Kiley slid onto Broadway just under the wire. A sturdy and flexible baritone, he arrived just in time to rise from juvenile to leading man and create three or four big roles and one iconic role—Don Quixote in *Man of La Mancha*—before changing theatrical tastes eliminated the kind of roles at which he excelled. He spent the rest of his long and distinguished career in TV and movies but never rose to his Broadway heights again.

Kiley was, in many ways, a typical leading man of the period: masculine, with a high forehead and a pointy nose, but sensitive—or eventually sensitive after the leading lady sets him straight. Critic Peter Filichia has pointed out that most shows of this period were about how women eventually get the leading man to do what they want (usually to get married). Kiley excelled at this sort of role. He was a pretty man who dressed up well, and it would have been easy to applaud and then quickly forget him. But Kiley had two things that set him apart. First was his voice, which had a sturdy foundation of baritone but also displayed a keening, yearning quality that made him especially good at love songs. He could take a florid line like *Kismet*'s "Don't send me in dark despair from all that I hunger for" and make you forget the words and feel the hunger.

The second thing Kiley had going for him, from a historical perspective, was his one immortal performance. He played the triplet roles of Miguel Cervantes/Don Quijana/Don Quixote de la Mancha in *Man of La Mancha* with such an amazing range from grandeur to madness to disillusion that it made you go back and take a look at his earlier roles to see where there was evidence of this splendid actor inside the matinee idol.

★

Kiley was born on the South Side of Chicago on March 31, 1922. His father was an Irish-Catholic railroad statistician, but young Richard picked up a love for theatre from his grandfather, who was known to quote Shakespeare and sing opera around the house.

Richard attended Mount Carmel High School, an all-boys' Catholic high school in the Woodlawn neighborhood, where he took part in the school plays. Acting, he discovered, was " a wonderful way to communicate without a one-to-one relationship." He continued his studies at Loyola University until World War II intervened. He served in the navy and put his public speaking experience to work as a gunnery instructor.

After the war he headed for New York, where he was cast in a 1947 production of *The Trojan Women* at Equity Library Theatre, part of the nascent off-Broadway movement. He also got some work in radio but had so little overall success in acting that he nearly gave up and for a while considered a career in forestry management.

Kiley got his break in 1948 when he was cast in the first national touring company of Tennessee Williams's *A Streetcar Named Desire,* as understudy to Anthony Quinn, who played Stanley Kowalski. When Quinn left, Kiley found himself in the coveted role that had been created by Marlon Brando. Across America, in the two years before the film version came out, the robust twenty-six-year-old Kiley was everyone's image of Stanley. He performed the famous "Stella!" scene hundreds of times between 1948 and 1950.

After that, he went through a period in which most of his work was in serial radio and the budding medium of TV. Over the next few years, Kiley made dozens of appearances in dramas for anthology series like *Studio One, Playhouse 90, Kraft Television Theatre, Alfred Hitchcock Presents,* and *You Are There*—prime examples of what would later be called the Golden Age of Television. "It was shocking," Kiley later said of his sudden fame." People stopped me on the streets of New York. The medium was so new [it was] almost magical to them."

Kiley literally crashed through the ceiling onto Broadway. His debut came at the end of Act I in the 1953 New York City Center revival of George Bernard Shaw's *Misalliance,* another of the author's examinations of the "life force." After an hour of listless flirting and debating by Victorian-era aristocrats in an English country home, fresh blood arrives in the form of virile young aviator John Percival, whose airplane plows through the roof of the conservatory. Directed by Cyril Ritchard, the production also featured Tamara Geva, Roddy McDowall, and Jerome Kilty.

His dashing performance won Kiley a Theatre World Award for promising newcomers. Other recipients that busy year included Gwen Verdon, Paul Newman, Geraldine Page, and Edie Adams. *Misalliance* was produced by the New York City Drama Company, whose artistic director was Albert Marre. Marre recalled how Kiley and McDowall would spend part of their time backstage competing to sing operatic arias—something he remembered later that same year when he had to replace the "juvenile" in a new musical he was staging, called *Kismet.*

Arranger-lyricists Robert Wright and George Forrest had made a career of taking the (usually public domain) oeuvres of classical composers and using them as raw material for Broadway operettas. The most successful of these was *Song of Norway* (1944), which arranged themes from the music of Edvard Grieg to tell a dramatized version of his own life. In the early 1950s, working with Charles Lederer and Luther Davis, Wright and Forrest decided to musicalize the popular 1911 play *Kismet,* about a Hajj, a poet-thief in medieval Baghdad, who aspires to make his daughter the wife of the prince and to win the heart of the queen for himself. This he accomplishes in the space of a single day through cunning, his wits, and an amazing ability to fast-talk everybody. For music, Wright and Forrest delved into the works of Russian composer Alexander Borodin, known for the "Asiatic" sound of his music.

The part of Hajj was already earmarked for Alfred Drake, and that of the female lead to a West Coast actress named Joan Diener. But Marre (Deiner's husband) needed a sturdy young man with good voice to sing the role of the eligible prince. It wasn't the lead part, but it had two of the score's showcase songs, "Night of My Nights" and "Stranger in Paradise."

The latter was drawn from the opening theme of the Polovetsian Dances in Borodin's opera *Prince Igor*. Given a luxuriantly romantic lyric likening the presence of Hajj's daughter to paradise, and bidding her to guide him through it, "Stranger in Paradise" was sure to be the "take-out" song from the score—the one pop singers everywhere would want to cover.

Marre knew just the guy to introduce the song—the one he'd heard singing backstage at *Misalliance*. Kiley was resistant at first. He had no formal training as a singer and saw himself as a dramatic actor. But he took the job, donned the caliph's robes, and walked into Broadway history. "Stranger in Paradise" turned out to be one of the great hits of 1953–54 and one of the most successful classical-to-pop crossovers ever. The tune was recorded by the likes of Tony Bennett and The Four Aces right away, but it also had a curiously long life as a standard. It was still being covered as late as 2003 when Sarah Brightman included it on her album *Harem*, and it was even licensed as a theme for the PlayStation video game *Parodius*.

For all its popularity, it's a hard song to sing well. A lot of singers who attempt "Stranger in Paradise" come off sounding ridiculously bombastic. But audiences thrilled to the scene in which Kiley embraced actress Doretta Morrow and joyously boomed the harmony on the song's triumphant final chords. People now saw Kiley in a new light: musical comedy star. Kiley had a surprisingly supple voice with a unique timbre. He was the Gene Kelly of singers: masculine but not muscle-bound. He balanced emotion with strength and humor. To keep from damaging his newly discovered instrument, Kiley was hustled off to a vocal coach.

And then the phone started to ring.

Redhead

Kiley was naturally gregarious, and among the many friendships he struck up in this period was one with choreographer Bob Fosse, who the next year would fully come into his own with *The Pajama Game*, featuring the dancer who became his wife, Gwen Verdon. They all achieved stardom within the same two or three seasons and trusted one another. In the late 1950s, after Verdon had established herself with one hit after another—*Can-Can* in 1954, *Damn Yankees* in 1956, and *New Girl in Town* in 1957, Fosse sought Kiley out to be his leading man in the next of the series, *Redhead*.

As the title indicates, the show was tailored to Verdon in every way, down to her hair color. It told the story of Essie Whimple (Verdon), a sculptress at an English waxworks that specializes in the horrific and the macabre. Essie has the supernatural power to envision real-life murders as they actually took place, and then she renders them in wax. Kiley played Tom Baxter, who is upset at first when she makes a wax statue of his murdered brother. Their romance develops as the murder mystery unfolds.

Working with Fosse, composer Albert Hague and lyricist Dorothy Fields gave Verdon one big dance number after another and plenty of juicy solo turns, like "'Erbie Fitch's Twitch" and "The Right Finger of My Left Hand." However, Kiley dominated the show's best number, "Look Who's in Love," an old-fashioned little foxtrot with dippy lyrics about how surprised they are to find they're in love. It was no "Stranger in Paradise." Nevertheless, when the song turns into a duet, the warmth and charm of the two stars shines through. Once again, Kiley showed a surprising ability to bring a human touch to a somewhat stiff song.

New York Times critic Brooks Atkinson praised Verdon at comparative length; his comments on Kiley were terse but laudatory: "Mr. Kiley is an excellent leading man. He has humor; he has force of personality; he can sing."

The Tony Awards went that one better and gave him, in 1959, its award as Best Leading Actor in a Musical for his first leading role.

Kiley found another prize, as well, in the chorus of *Redhead*: a pretty dancer named Patricia Ferrier. Kiley had been married since 1948 to Mary Bell Wood, but that marriage ended in divorce. Kiley stayed in touch with Ferrier and married her in 1968. In all, Kiley would eventually have six children. He once told a magazine, "As turbulent as things can get, home and family are what we build on."

No Strings

Kiley's ability to serve the music brought him to the attention of perfectionist composer Richard Rodgers, who had embarked on an unusual project.

Rodgers had been composing on Broadway since the 1910s, first with the legendary Lorenz Hart, which would have been enough of a career right there. But he then moved on to collaborate with Oscar Hammerstein II on some of the greatest musicals of the twentieth century, including *Oklahoma!, South Pacific*, and *Carousel*. Hammerstein died of cancer in 1960, and Rodgers would go on to team with Stephen Sondheim and Martin Charnin. But in 1961 he started collaborating for the first time with . . . himself. Rodgers wrote both music and lyrics for *No Strings*, a musical about a novelist with writer's block—a self-described "Europe bum"—who comes to France looking for inspiration and has an affair with a pretty fashion model.

Rodgers pretty much had his pick of New York leading men to showcase his work. He chose Kiley. For leading lady he picked black actress Diahann Carroll. It was not the first interracial romance shown on the musical stage. This issue had been raised in 1927's *Show Boat*, though the actress playing the biracial part had been white. Rodgers and Hammerstein had explored it themselves in *South Pacific*, where it was the central conflict. *No Strings* presented the interracial romance but didn't make a big deal about it. It was barely mentioned; in fact, the parts were so generic they could have been played by actors of almost any race. Given the racial tensions of the time, with the civil rights movement about to explode across America, this casting choice was seen as extremely bold, though, considering the light touch, actually was fairly mild.

Nevertheless, during 1962 tryouts in Detroit, about a hundred audience members walked out during the first Kiley–Carroll kiss. Rodgers got letters calling him a "nigger lover," which he shrugged off.

The show got warm, though not rave, reviews and had a mildly successful run of more than a year. The lion's share of the acclaim for *No Strings* went to Carroll and, of course, Rodgers.

Despite his good work, Kiley had allowed himself to become homogenized in these two starring roles. He had become the guy you went to when you needed nice, unobtrusive dark-wood male frame for the main attraction, the leading lady or star comedian. He even found himself playing straight man to potty-mouthed standup comedian Buddy Hackett in the latter's short-lived musical *I Had a Ball*, about life among the shabby-but-colorful denizens of Brooklyn's Coney Island amusement-park district. Kiley played more or less the romantic lead (recently out-of-the-pokey crook "Stan the Shpieler"). But, as with *Redhead* and *No Strings*, the focus of attention lay elsewhere.

Kiley might have spent the rest of his career in such stolid and colorless roles.

Man of La Mancha

But it was during *I Had a Ball*'s brief Broadway tenure that fate arrived in the form of his old pal, Albert Marre, director of *Misalliance* and *Kismet*. It was kismet, all right. Marre was coming with the role of a lifetime.

Asked when he knew the role of Don Quixote was his, Kiley told *Equity News*, "I remember the moment well, it was before I had committed a line to memory or heard a note of the music. I was sitting in my dressing room at the Martin Beck Theatre, waiting to go on. . . . There was knock at the door and Albert Marre, a director I'd known for years, came in and asked if I had a few minutes before curtain. He had an idea for a musical repertory theatre. He proposed three shows and one was [*Man of*] *La Mancha*. At that instant a hundred-watt bulb went on and I said yes, it was that simple."

Located on the Connecticut River about a three hours' drive from New York, the restored 1877-vintage Goodspeed Opera House had begun offering high-end summer stock just a few years earlier. Instead of just recent hits or revivals of 1940s warhorses, Goodspeed had two specialties in those early years: revivals of 1910s or 1920s antiques (appreciated by an audience that sometimes still wore straw hats to the theatre as late as the 1980s) and brand-new shows they developed themselves.

For a stretch of summer 1965 they allowed Marre to stage three original musicals, *Chu Chem*, described as a "Buddhist Hebrew musical" about a colony of Jews in China; *Purple Dust*, a musical based on a Sean O'Casey farce; and a musical based on the sixteenth-century classic Spanish novel *Don Quixote*. The latter musical was retitled *Man of La Mancha*, and it had tyro composer Mitch Leigh working with lyricist Joe Darion and librettist Dale Wasserman. None of the shows sounded especially promising, though *La Mancha* turned out to be one of the those *Springtime for Hitler* projects where the parts go wrong but then finally add up to a hit.

In his often cranky memoir, *The Impossible Musical*, librettist Dale Wasserman had a take on Kiley substantially different from Marre's. Wasserman wanted Rex Harrison, but that marginal singer threw up his hands when they played him the show's big anthem, something called "The Quest." The project intimidated more than Harrison. "Kiley . . . was perhaps sixth or eighth on our list," Wasserman wrote. "Kiley, arguably was not a star, he was known as a reliable singer/actor but usually was cast as a second banana [*sic*]. We were running out of time, however, and agreed that under the circumstances he was the best we were able to get." Wasserman would warm up to Kiley later.

All three shows were performed in a sort of repertory, with the stars of one show playing the spear-carriers in the next. Kiley was chosen for the lead of *Man of La Mancha*, alongside one of his *Kismet* costars, Joan Diener as Aldonza, the slut in whom Quixote sees an angel.

Kiley saw immediately that not only was the role of the wise madman Quixote incredibly meaty, but it presented a unique acting challenge: It was really three separate performances. First, Kiley had to play the author Miguel Cervantes in the framing scenes. Then he had to play the aged nobleman Alonso Quijana, who has read too many romances about knights and ladies fair and has gradually gone mad. Finally, and most significantly, Kiley had to play Don Quixote, Quijana's imaginary alternate identity, a crusading knight in the grand style who sets out into the very ordinary and workaday Spain to battle imagined dragons, wizards, and other such. Quixote is the original gamer who gets lost in his game. But, as it turns out, there is beauty and magnificence to his principles and his goals. This last part is what lifts the story "out of the commonplace into the rare," as Kiley had sung in *Kismet*.

As the play begins, Cervantes has been arrested by the Spanish Inquisition and placed on trial for heresy because he had been cheeky in his dealings with church officials. The penalty for a guilty verdict is burning at the stake. The show opens with a huge staircase lowering like a drawbridge into a black dungeon filled with dangerous criminals. Cervantes and his manservant are marched down these stairs by armed guards.

The criminals strip Cervantes of all his belongings, including a ragged bundle. What's in it? A manuscript. The prisoners are about to destroy it when Cervantes makes an impassioned appeal for its preservation. Amused, they decide to put him on mock trial themselves. As his defense, Cervantes acts out his story of gently mad Don Quijana and the noble, foolish product of his fevered imagination, Don Quixote. He enlists the other prisoners to play the rest of the characters in the story.

Whatever else it may have been, the show was immensely theatrical and filled with lovely songs like "Dulcinea," "To Each His Dulcinea," and "Little Bird."

And then there was that song Rex Harrison had found so off-putting, "The Quest." Sung as part of Quixote's all-night vigil before his official dubbing as knight, "The Quest" laid out his master plan for his coming knighthood. He would adopt only hopeless causes, causes that other knights would flinch from. He plans "to dream the impossible dream," the line that gave the song the title by which most people know it.

The song was perfectly suited for that majestic overtone to Kiley's singing that sounded so odd in musicals about everyday people. It was a voice for an epic character, and, in Quixote, Kiley had at last found the glove to fit his hand. Still, Kiley said, "Nobody gave [the show] much of a chance—friends said I'd made a terrible decision, it was bound to flop. But there was something in that driving idiot, the dreamer Quixote, that really grabbed me, inspired me. Can you imagine singing 'The Impossible Dream' to an audience for the very first time? It was utterly exhilarating."

Still, he struggled. The role was an immense physical challenge. Kiley's assertion to *Playbill* that he lost five pounds for each performance was obvious hyperbole—but it felt that way to him.

Once performances got under way, Wasserman started to appreciate Kiley more. He wrote that marrying good acting to good singing in a single performer is a "peculiarly American quality" and added that "Richard Kiley was a performer par excellence in that area."

In the midst of it all, Kiley found himself with a personal crisis on his hands. His oldest son, David, was seriously injured in a car accident, losing an eye. Kiley stayed at the hospital holding his son for hours, praying for his recovery. He later reported, "When I went back [to the show] the next day it was as if some plugged-up spaces in my head—or heart—had been blown clean by a tremendous pressure. After that it was very light. . . . Light was very good for Quixote, because he was so light at times he floated right off the ground."

Goodspeed audience reaction was powerful and immediate. Forget about the other two shows, *Man of La Mancha* was a hit and needed to go to Broadway. Theatre pros were less certain. Even Kiley's agent tried to talk him out of continuing with the show after Goodspeed. But it moved to Broadway that fall and proved to be the biggest hit of Kiley's career and one of the great hits of the 1960s.

Maybe Kiley was great all along, merely waiting for a truly great role. Maybe he had just passed the age of forty in 1962 and was worried about his legacy as actor, which inspired him to a superhuman effort. Maybe he had just one truly great role in him and he was lucky enough to have found it.

In any case, none of the critics, who had been reviewing him for years, said, "Oh, yes, we expected this all along." Most of the reviews were along the lines of Howard Taubman's review in *Time* magazine: "Mr. Kiley . . . has never given a finer performance. . . . As Cervantes he is a man of spirit with a quizzical humor and keen flexible intelligence. Shading into Quixote, he became the amiable visionary, childlike in his pretensions and oddly, touchingly gallant. His eyes take on a wild, proud other-wordly look. His posture is preternaturally erect, His folly becomes a kind of humbling wisdom."

In addition to providing the kind of career landmark that most actors dream of having, the show obviously represented an annuity for Kiley, who would eventually play the gentle knight more than 2,300 times, including national tours and two Broadway revivals. Sadly, he shared a fate with Ethel Merman, Carol Channing, and Angela Lansbury in seeing his signature Broadway role being given to somebody else in the movie version—in this case to the nonsinging Peter O'Toole.

Hopes were stratospheric for Kiley's next starring role, playing Julius Caesar in the 1968 musical *Her First Roman*. Based on Shaw's *Caesar and Cleopatra*, it was the story of the attraction between the future emperor and the current child-queen, to be played by Leslie Uggams (fresh off her Tony-winning performance in *Hallelujah, Baby!*). How could it miss? Here's how: The critics sang in rare unison that Ervin Drake's book, music, and lyrics made hash of Shaw's play, including the startling addition of a happy ending in which Cleo didn't clasp the asp to her bosom but went merrily home to Rome with her new boyfriend! Despite some last-minute doctoring by the *Fiddler on the Roof* team of Bock and Harnick, the show sank after just seventeen performances, though Clive Barnes in the *Times* offered condolences to the stars, noting, "Kiley's singing always has a certain heroic tone to it that gives an almost moral dimension. It is an extraordinary voice, inimitable and attractive."

The show was unquestionably a devastating flop, but few could have predicted at the time that, except for two revivals of *Man of La Mancha* in 1972 and 1977, Kiley would never sing in another Broadway musical.

Instead, he tried his hand at drama, bringing in *The Incomparable Max* (1971), a portrait of late nineteenth-century writer Max Beerbohm as told through two of his stories. Then, in 1974's American premiere of Alan Ayckbourn's *Absurd Person Singular*, Kiley played half of one of three couples whose progress on a series of Christmas Eves charts their changing social status.

In 1974 Kiley was cast as the leading man in an unusual film musical, an adaptation of Antoine de Saint-Exupéry's beloved allegory *The Little Prince*. He played a World War I flier who crashes in the north African desert and is nearly delirious with thirst when he comes across the odd figure of a child dressed as a prince. The boy claims that he once ruled a tiny asteroid in space, with room for little more than a Rose (who speaks to him) and several small extinct volcanoes that he must keep clean. The Aviator and the Little Prince have some philosophical fun interacting with a number of interesting strangers before the bittersweet ending. "It's only with the heart that one can see clearly," goes one line translated directly from Saint-Exupéry. "What's essential is invisible to the eye."

Kiley seemed perfect for the part of a man torn between dreams and harsh reality (though it had originally been offered to Richard Burton), and stars lined up to play the rest of the tiny cast, including Donna McKechnie as the Rose, Gene Wilder as the Fox, and even Bob Fosse, in his first dancing role in more than a decade, as the Snake. To write the score, lyricist Alan Jay Lerner coaxed his partner Frederick Loewe out of semiretirement.

The parts were all there but never quite added up. On the giant screen, the intimate and idiosyncratic story lost a lot of its magic. All the big stars tended to overshadow the not-very-charismatic child actor Steven Warner as the Prince.

Possibly the best thing in the film was Kiley's singing of the lush title ballad. It's one of the few moments when *The Little Prince* rises to Lerner and Loewe's *My Fair Lady* and *Camelot* quality.

It was Kiley's last original musical performance.

In between stage assignments, Kiley had always maintained a career in television. After the failure of *Her First Roman*, he focused on it more and more. He never had the same smashing success as he did onstage, but he worked steadily and lent his presence to dozens of series, specials, and made-for-TV movies. He almost never sang.

There was scarcely a cop, western, or science-fiction series during this period that did not make use of his gravitas and his mellifluous voice. He made guest appearances on *Gunsmoke*, *Hawaii Five-O*, *Cannon*, *Columbo*, *The New Twilight Zone*, *Rod Serling's Night Gallery*, *The Rockford Files*, *Star Trek: Deep Space Nine*, *Picket Fences*, and *Ally McBeal*, to name just the best known. He won an Emmy Award for playing Paddy Cleary in the 1983 miniseries *The Thorn Birds*.

Kiley made a few other film appearances, as well, including in *Looking for Mr. Goodbar* (1977), *Endless Love* (1981), and *Patch Adams* (1998). He played the voice of the tour guide in Steven Spielberg's dinosaur epic *Jurassic Park* (1993), identifying himself as Richard Kiley and observing wryly that the adventure park of the title had spared no expense to get him.

Later Years

After the 1977 revival of *La Mancha*, Kiley played Ebenezer Scrooge in a touring version of *A Christmas Carol*, by Michel Legrand and Sheldon Harnick, which producers Fran and Barry Weissler talked about bringing to Broadway. But the project never made it across the Hudson.

In the end, Kiley returned to Broadway just one more time, though not in a musical. He appeared in a lauded production of Arthur Miller's *All My Sons*, playing the munitions-maker Joe Keller, whose long-buried secret rises from the grave. Costarring Joyce Ebert and Jamey Sheridan, the production opened on Broadway in April 1987. Despite a brief run, it won the Tony Award for Best Revival. Kiley also found himself with some late-career accolades, including his fourth (and last) Tony Award nomination, as Best Actor in a Play.

Kiley's final musical-theatre project was a long-delayed studio cast recording of his 1968 flop *Her First Roman*, for which he reunited with leading lady Leslie Uggams, helped by Ron Raines and Priscilla Lopez. Kiley's voice was still strong, and he still filled every note with emotion and grandeur.

Kiley died of cancer March 5, 1999, in his adopted hometown of Warwick, New York.

His tragedy—if that's the right term for someone who enjoyed steady success all his professional life—was that they just stopped writing his kind of show. He was an Apollonian presence in an increasingly Dionysian world. By the time big baritones came back into style, Kiley was just too old, and the roles (including eventually *La Mancha* itself) all went to the Brian Stokes Mitchells of the world. Broadway had stopped creating roles for Kiley's unique voice for too many years, and it was the poorer for it.

Chita Rivera shows off the moneymakers (circa 1991). PHOTOFEST

CHITA RIVERA
All That Jazz

Chita Rivera is the queen of the dancing stars. Her crown was earned partly through her ferocious dance style, partly through her equal facility as an actress, and partly through her simple and amazing longevity. She has had one of the single longest careers at the top of the Broadway star list of anyone in this book.

She created major Broadway musical roles in each of five decades. First was Anita in *West Side Story* (1957), then Rosie in *Bye Bye Birdie* (1960), Velma Kelly in *Chicago* (1975), Anna in *The Rink* (1984—Tony Award), and the title character in *Kiss of the Spider Woman* (1991—Tony Award). She added Claire Zachanassian in the out-of-town tryout of *The Visit* (2008) at the age of seventy-five, an amazing legacy for a performer whose primary instrument is a body, something that usually starts to wear out after less than thirty years.

The record is doubly remarkable because she overcame efforts to pigeonhole her in spitfire Latina roles, and triply so because she sustained and prevailed over a major injury to her legs in the 1980s that would have ended almost any other dancer's career.

A recipient of the prestigious Kennedy Center honor for lifetime achievement, Rivera has won two Tony Awards as Best Leading Actress in a Musical and received six additional Tony Award nominations. She's one of the few stars who created major dancing roles for the cream of her era's choreographers, including Jerome Robbins, Bob Fosse, Michael Bennett, Peter Gennaro, Jack Cole, and Michael Kidd. She created them in musicals with songs written for her by Leonard Bernstein, Stephen Sondheim, Kander and Ebb, and Charles Strouse. And she did so while sharing the stage with other Greatest Stars of four generations, including Gwen Verdon, Jerry Orbach, Liza Minnelli, and Brian Stokes Mitchell.

She was born Dolores Conchita Figueroa del Rivero in Washington, D.C., on January 23, 1933, the third of five children. Her father, a Puerto Rican named Pedro Julio Figueroa, played clarinet and saxophone. His claims to fame include stints with the United States Navy Band and the Harry James Orchestra, plus, significantly, the pit orchestra of the Gershwins' 1924 Broadway hit *Lady, Be Good*. He was playing with Washington-area big bands when he passed away, leaving his seven-year-old daughter Chita with memories of a handsome man in a white suit.

Her mother Katherine née Anderson (of Scots-Irish/Puerto Rican background) took a job as a government clerk to support her brood, and Chita grew up as a self-described hyperenergetic tomboy who could run faster than the boys. One of her favorite games was performing on a makeshift stage set up by her older brother Julio in the basement of their home.

Seeing this, her mother channeled her energy into various kinds of music lessons—voice, piano, and dancing. Chita immediately conceived a passion for dancing. When she was eleven, her mother enrolled her in the Jones-Hayward School of Ballet. Her teacher, Doris Jones, found herself with a student who had many of the insecurities of an ethnic person in the primarily Eurocentric world of dance, but also a unique electricity to the way she threw herself into the dance. The five-foot-three-and-a-half-inch Miss del Rivero had a long face, tightly curled black hair, and almond-shaped eyes that she could use to make herself seem frightening or seductive, depending on how she looked over and around a long, wide nose. But her joints, particularly her back and hips, were loose in a catlike way, and her legs were long and powerful.

Taking note of her talent and her "look at me" quality, Jones arranged for the fifteen-year-old Miss del Rivero to audition for an associate of ballet master George Balanchine, and Chita found herself the recipient of a scholarship to Balanchine's School of American Ballet in New York City.

Realizing the seriousness of her daughter's ability, Katherine placed her daughter with an uncle in the Bronx, where Chita attended Taft High School (graduating in 1951) while commuting to Manhattan to study ballet. She made a lot of friends in the ballet school and, one fateful day in 1952, agreed to accompany one who was nervous about venturing out of the world of classical dance to attend an open-call audition for the national tour of a Broadway musical titled *Call Me Madam*. The friend didn't get the role, but del Rivero, on a whim, decided to audition, as well, and got her first professional job as a dancer. She was billed as Conchita del Rivero.

The show starred Ethel Merman and boasted one of the last original scores by Irving Berlin. It gave del Rivero a chance to watch Merman up close and to learn how a leading lady should (and shouldn't) conduct herself. Later, Elaine Stritch replaced Merman and del Rivero kept watching and learning. She was being watched, too. The choreographer of *Call Me Madam* was Jerome Robbins, who would figure so prominently in her later career. Her lean, catlike body was ideal for the kind of dance he was designing.

Word soon got around, and things moved quickly for her after that. She was featured briefly as a principal dancer in the late original run of *Guys and Dolls*, from which she was hired by choreographer Michael Kidd for the chorus of Cole Porter's *Can-Can*. There she met her lifelong friend and frequent collaborator Gwen Verdon.

On *Can-Can* she also met dancer Dania Krupska, who was building a career of her own as a choreographer. Krupska was working on an off-Broadway revue for songfest impresario Ben Bageley, to be called *The Shoestring Revue*, and they needed someone who could not only dance, but act. Rivera took this plunge and was featured in several skits, including one where she did an impression of Marilyn Monroe. As the title indicated, there weren't a lot of production values to *The Shoestring Revue.* With a cast that also included Beatrice Arthur and Arte Johnson, all it had was talent.

It was Bageley who took Conchita del Rivero aside and suggested that she should change her name. And so she did. For three days she went around telling people her new name was Chita O'Hara. Cooler heads prevailed, and she decided to keep her ethnicity, but just to slim it down and feminize the final vowel. Chita Rivera it would be, henceforth.

From *Shoestring* she was hired to play the role of Fifi, one of three comic French prostitutes in *Seventh Heaven,* which provided her with one-third of the showboat song "Camille, Colette, Fifi." The show lasted just six weeks but led to the role of Rita Romano in the musical *Mr. Wonderful.* It was a vehicle for star Sammy Davis Jr. but proved a great showcase for Rivera, as well.

The next role came from director Jerome Robbins, who had been watching her blossom. He wanted her to appear in a new musical he was directing and choreographing, *West Side Story.* Playwright Arthur Laurents and composer Leonard Bernstein were working with the twenty-seven-year-old first-time Broadway lyricist named Stephen Sondheim on a musical adaptation of Shakespeare's *Romeo and Juliet,* but with the action shifted to Manhattan's Upper West Side, where recent arrivals from Puerto Rico were coming into conflict with the established Anglo community. Instead of "two houses, both alike in dignity" there were two teen gangs, the Sharks and the Jets. Their fights, called "rumbles," get increasingly violent when Tony, a member of the Jets, falls in love with Maria, a sister of one of the Sharks. In Shakespeare, Juliet's nurse both disapproves of the romance and grudgingly helps facilitate it. In *West Side Story,* the character is Anita, girlfriend of the Sharks' leader, Bernardo. This was the role Robbins had in mind for Rivera. Instead of being a matron, Anita is a hot-blooded young woman who suffers terrible indignities at the hands of the Anglo boys.

In expanding the role for Rivera, Robbins and the writers gave Anita four shining moments, and Rivera was ripe to make full use of them.

She first gets to show off in "The Dance at the Gym," where the two gangs bust out their best dance moves.

In "America," she is the cold voice of reason when the other women start to get nostalgic about San Juan. She may not love everything about her adopted land, but she came to New York for a purpose. Nevertheless, all the talk of Puerto Rico—which she wryly points out is in fact part of the United States—turns into a joyous explosion of dance, punctuated by distinctive puppy-like yips of Rivera's invention.

The Act I finale, "Quintet," shows the inner thoughts of the two gangs, the two lovers, and Anita, who practically rubs her hands at the idea of how virile Bernardo will be when he returns from the rumble.

Finally, Anita shares the eleven-o'clock number with Maria. Her bitter solo "A Boy Like That" is braided with Maria's steadfast "I Have a Love," in which Maria pleads that she still loves Tony even though he has killed Bernardo, and the grieving Anita accepts that when love is that strong, there's just nothing you can do to stop it. It's very easy for the number to edge over into camp, but Rivera's total conviction, her anger, her sorrow, and her wisdom all converged to keep it powerfully on target.

Despite Robbins's efforts to keep actors playing members of the two gangs apart (they still gathered in separate groups fifty years later at a reunion at the New Amsterdam Theatre), Rivera developed her own Romeo and Juliet romance with Tony Mordente, who created the role of Jet gang member A-Rab. They married during the run of the show. Producers famously postponed the London production of *West Side Story* until after Rivera gave birth to their daughter, Lisa Mordente, on July 30, 1958.

Tony Mordente and Rivera had a stormy relationship. Mordente would serve as assistant choreographer on several Broadway shows, including *Bye Bye Birdie*, before moving into TV directing. They divorced in 1966, and Rivera never remarried.

In addition to the complexities of the role, Anita was, of course, a classic Latin spitfire. And here lay danger. Rivera took the role knowing there was a chance that she would be typecast. Rivera lent the role legitimacy and a unique personality that was never captured in quite the same way again. But she had made it out of the chorus because she could act as well as dance, and she was determined to break out of the ethnic cage and show she could play many roles. Was she ever cast as Laurey in *Oklahoma!*? No. But over the next several decades, Rivera created believable roles in more than a dozen different ethnicities— Greek, Italian, French, Gypsy, Brazilian—to the point that it practically became her trademark. She played one major role of indeterminate ethnicity, Velma Kelly in *Chicago*, who certainly didn't seem Irish. She even created one more major Spanish character, Rosie in *Bye Bye Birdie*. The joke is, Rosie is a completely Americanized girl from "Allentown, PA," but her incipient mother-in-law thinks she's practically Carmen Miranda. The *Birdie* songwriting team of Strouse and Adams wrote her "Spanish Rose," a song that expressed her whole exasperated attitude on the issue by wallowing in every cliché of the Latina. "I'll be so Spanish, it will make you sick," she promises.

Rivera battled the stereotype all her life and, on a personal level, won. Her struggle was one of the many qualities that made her a true star.

She spent a short stint in the musical *Shinbone Alley* (subbing for and eventually replacing Eartha Kitt, before the moment came that she'd been waiting for: a starring role in a new musical. *Bye Bye Birdie* was that rare bird, a completely original story not adapted from any preexisting source. It told the story of Albert Petersen (Dick Van Dyke), who had trained to be an English teacher but instead became a pop songwriter and head of a broken-down music company. His fiancé, Rosie (Rivera), is unhappy both with his career and with the fact that Albert is completely under the thumb of his mother, whom she believes will do anything to sabotage their relationship. This serves as the frame for the main action of the play, which parodies Elvis Presley (rechristened Conrad Birdie), whose singing career is about to go up in smoke because he's being drafted into the army. Albert conceives an elaborate scheme to get Conrad on the Sunday variety show *The Ed Sullivan Show*, to sing Albert's hit "One Last Kiss" and make a fortune for all of them and solve all their problems. As Rosie tries simultaneously to aid him and crowbar him out of his mama's clutches, complications ensue.

In addition to "Spanish Rose," Rivera had two other plum comedy numbers—"An English Teacher," "What Did I Ever See in Him?"—and a sensational dance number, "Shriners' Ballet," in which she assuages her hurt pride by attempting to seduce an entire convention of fez-wearing Shriners. The performance earned her a Tony nomination as Best Supporting Actress in a Musical.

Rivera and Van Dyke remained friends. In the 1970s Rivera had a recurring role in *The New Dick Van Dyke Show* as Connie Richardson, his next-door neighbor. When Rivera's autobiographical show *Chita Rivera: The Dancer's Life* was struggling in 2006, Van Dyke agreed to step in for a few performances to provide a bump of publicity.

Movies

Sometimes, being a star means hanging tough when things don't go your way. That's what happened in 1961 when the film version of *West Side Story* was made and Rivera was passed over for the part of Anita in favor of studio favorite Rita Moreno. As it would happen, Rivera would never get the chance to re-create any of her great stage roles on film. Janet Leigh got *Birdie*, and Catherine Zeta-Jones got *Chicago*.

One of Rivera's few champions in the film industry was director-choreographer Bob Fosse, now husband of her old pal Gwen Verdon, for whom she had starred in the 1967–68 national touring company of *Sweet Charity*. Though Universal pushed Moreno for the role of Nickie in the 1969 movie of *Sweet Charity*, Fosse insisted on Rivera. Rivera's high point in the 1969 film version of *Sweet Charity* is the exuberant trio "There's Gotta Be Something Better Than This," in which Rivera, Shirley MacLaine, and Paula Kelly practically fly over the rooftops of New York as they imagine themselves escaping from their grim lives as Times Square taxi dancers. It's one of the very best records of how powerfully Rivera was dancing at the time.

In 1964 Rivera starred not just as a gypsy dancer, but as a dancing Gypsy—an actual Romana—in the musical *Bajour*.

Based on two *New Yorker* stories by Joseph Mitchell, *Bajour* told the story of a young anthropology student who is studying the Gypsy culture in New York. This brings her into contact with Johnny Dembo (Herschel Bernardi), the local Gypsy king, who hatches a scam—a "bajour" in Gypsy terminology—to get money for a dowry so he can purchase Anyanka (Rivera), the beautiful princess of the New Jersey Gypsies, as a bride for his son.

The show gave Rivera a chance to work with rising young choreographer Michael Bennett (later of *Follies* and *A Chorus Line*) on a number of wild Gypsy dances. The show ran only six months but helped remind the theatre world just how good a dancer she was.

In the late 1960s and early 1970s, Rivera appeared in several national tours and in a number of tryouts of new shows that closed out of town. She starred opposite John Raitt in *Zorba*, with Alfred Drake in *Zenda,* and with John Cullum in Frank Loesser's last completed musical, *1491.*

But one person who needed no reminding of her talent was choreographer Bob Fosse, for whom she had starred in the road company of *Sweet Charity* and whom he had featured in the film.

Fosse was working on a major new project, based on Maurine Dallas Watkins's 1926 play *Chicago*, a profoundly cynical jazz-age tale about a young woman who kills her husband in a jealous rage, then rises to become a seven-day wonder by manipulating the thoroughly corrupt media and court system. Fosse's concept was to have the story told as if it were a vaudeville show, with each number done in the style of a different type of act, from dance specialty to baggy-pants comedian to ventriloquist show. Verdon played Roxie Hart, and Rivera played another murderess she meets in jail, Velma Kelly. The two become allies—for a while.

Here was everything Fosse loved best, in one glittering package: a tawdry, underworld story, a self-referential showbiz setting, and two of his favorite dancers, who understood his unique technique in their bones. And *Chicago* was a special tribute to Verdon and Rivera, both of whom were now in their forties. Neither of them was as sinewy or flexible as they'd been in their 1950s heyday, but both were still muscular (as Patricia Zipprodt's abbreviated costumes showed) and great-looking. And Fosse worked them hard.

Rivera got to sing the opening number, the iconic scene-setter "All That Jazz." Songwriters John Kander and Fred Ebb, who had first seen her do their work in a mid 1960s national tour of their *Zorba*, wrote several more showstoppers for her, including the comic duet "Class," but the best is "But I Can't Do It Alone." In it, Velma is trying to ride Roxie's coattails by inviting her to share her dance act. The lyric trick on this number is that in trying to describe the act to Roxie, Velma sings a series of cut-off phrases, with dance moves substituting for the missing words. Each stanza ends with the plea "But I can't do it alone!" Dance became Velma's lyric and provided a tour de force for Rivera.

Rivera and Verdon both were nominated for Tony Awards as Best Leading Actress in a Musical, and both lost to Donna McKechnie of *A Chorus Line*. Afterward, fans began to take note of the fact that Rivera had been nominated for the Tony five times by this point and had been passed over each time. Was it bad luck? Was it racism? Rivera took it in stride. Kander and Ebb, who had fallen in love with her, wrote special material for her nightclub act (directed by Ebb), including a song, "Losing," about her quandary. "I'd rather not get Tony Awards and get this good material," she told the *New York Times*. "It lasts longer."

Kander and Ebb went on to write three more musicals for her: *The Rink, Kiss of the Spider Woman*, and *The Visit*. They made sure she had a cameo in the Oscar-winning film version of *Chicago*, a role named "Nicky," similar to her *Sweet Charity* character.

In the decade following *Chicago*, Rivera appeared in three musicals, none of them distinguished and none of them a hit.

The first was a 1981 sequel to *Bye Bye Birdie* titled *Bring Back Birdie*, with film legend Donald O'Connor taking the role of the older Albert and trying to put across a flaccid story about Conrad Birdie trying for a comeback. Few sequels to stage musicals have ever been successful, except revues like the *Ziegfeld Follies* or revue-like shows like the *Nunsense* musicals. *Bring Back Birdie* had some good songs by Strouse and Adams and offered Rivera a chance to dance, but otherwise it was an appalling bomb that closed after four performances.

Next up (and down) was the 1983 *Merlin*, a vehicle for magician Doug Henning, who had enjoyed a stunning success with the 1974 extravaganza *The Magic Show*. *Merlin* was derived from the King Arthur legend, with Arthur himself reduced to a walk-on (played by a young Christian Slater) and the battle between Arthur's wizard ally Merlin (Henning) and a Morgan Le Fay–type character called just the Queen (Rivera) brought to the fore. Rivera, who had flirted with the dark side in a few of her roles, here got to plunge in as an über-campy wicked witch, battling Henning's illusions with apparently magical dancing. Barely visible amid the battle was young Nathan Lane, as Rivera's quivering worm of a son, whom she seeks to place upon the throne of Britain. It was only his second Broadway role, and he was destined for bigger things.

Rivera's fans loved the way she munched the scenery, but the show was a mess and ran just six months, adding heft to almost no one's résumé.

The most interesting and respectable of Rivera's 1980s flops was Kander and Ebb's *The Rink*, a little domestic drama pumped up by Rivera's pals John Kander and Fred Ebb into a tawdry musical set at a roller rink. Rivera played Anna, the foulmouthed Italian-American owner of the rink, who has endured little but heartbreak from the men in her life and from her daughter, played by Liza Minnelli, who comes back into her life after a seven-year estrangement. The not-exactly-maternal Anna, who has been forced to serve as "Chief Cook and Bottle Washer," as she explains in a great character song, excoriates her prodigal daughter in a tour-de-force patter song called "Don't Ah Ma Me," but eventually accepts her back and learns how to be a mom again.

People weren't used to seeing Rivera this coarse or vulgar, because even when she was playing a murderess or a con woman, she always maintained a kind of grand Hispanic dignity that was absent here. But the role had one important distinction—it earned Rivera her first Tony Award as Best Leading Actress in a Musical. A lot of voters may have felt the honor was overdue, but the consensus today is that she won the award for one of her least technical performances. For Rivera and Minnelli, however, who worked together briefly on *Chicago* when Verdon fell ill, it was a blast.

The Accident

In late 1985, Rivera appeared in *Jerry's Girls*, a Broadway revue of songs by *Hello, Dolly!* composer Jerry Herman, alongside Dorothy Loudon, Leslie Uggams, and others. About midnight on April 7, 1986, during the run, Rivera was driving on West Eighty-sixth Street en route to her home in upstate New York when a taxicab smashed into her, wrecking her car and shattering one of her magical legs. It was a compound fracture, meaning it was so severe that the bone had torn through the flesh. Doctors at Lenox Hill Hospital determined that the tibia and fibula of the left leg weren't just snapped, but were broken in twelve places. A hardware rack of eighteen screws and two braces was required to piece the legendary limb back together.

Herman announced that *Jerry's Girls* would go on—but with no fewer than seven chorus dances needed to handle all of Rivera's assignments.

Years later, Rivera dismissed the episode, saying, "Just like the movies, they told me I would never dance again. And just like the movies, here I am, I don't know how many performances later."

But she was just being flip. She faced years of grueling rehab. But even though she was fifty-three years old, an age when most dancers have long since retired, Rivera was determined not just to walk but to get her dancing career literally back on its feet.

Kiss of the Spider Woman

Her old *Chicago* and *The Rink* pals Kander and Ebb hadn't lost their admiration for her, so in 1993 they brought her a project they had initiated at Harold Prince's SUNY Purchase workshop, and which now had Broadway financing from the up-and-coming Livent Inc. of Canada. Titled *Kiss of the Spider Woman*, the musical had a libretto by playwright Terrence McNally, based on Manuel Puig's play and popular international film. Moreover, although Rivera would emphatically be the leading lady, the story was structured so she didn't have to carry the weight of one scene after another. In fact, her character existed only in the imaginations of the two leading men.

Kiss of the Spider Woman may have one of the least likely settings ever for a musical: a Brazilian prison. Valentin, a hard-boiled would-be revolutionary, has been pitched into a dank cell with Molina, a gay department-store window dresser. Antipathy between the two is immediate. As time goes on they do at least talk, and Molina reveals that he survives by immersing himself in wildly colorful fantasies built on scenes and production numbers from old movie musicals he saw long ago. As Molina describes these scenes, they come alive before our eyes. A recurring character in these scenes is the sultry Spider Woman, played by Rivera. At first she seems like a figure of glamour and freedom, but as time goes along and the prisoners are tortured and threatened with execution, she gradually comes to be understood as Death, stalking and seducing the two men into her web for a final, lethal kiss.

There was always a dark side to Rivera's stage persona, which is one of the things that had always made her a little extra interesting as a dancer. This quality is in evidence at least as far back as Anita, when she played the character who should have been supportive of Maria's love but instead warned her to "forget that boy and find another." Anna bitterly rejected her own daughter; Anyanka was a thief; Velma was a murderess. But Kander and Ebb and McNally were the first to create a whole canvas from this color in Rivera's palette. Every dance in *Kiss of the Spider Woman* was a dance of death. Rivera, who had gone so long without a Tony Award, now won her second for the role.

Nine

In 2003, Rivera got to add yet another ethnic role to her résumé, playing lushly accented French film producer Liliane La Fleur Roundabout Theatre Company's Broadway revival of the musical *Nine*, based on the Fellini film *8½*, about movie director Guido Contini (Antonio Banderas) who is completely stuck for an idea for his next movie.

One of the conceits of the musical is that all the adult roles but Contini are played by women. Even in a cast that included Jane Krakowski, Laura Benanti, Nell Campbell, and Mary Stuart Masterson, Rivera stood out. She brought a sexy brio to composer Maury Yeston's showstopper, "Folies Bergère," in which the producer upbraids Contini for making depressing art-house films and demonstrates the sort of colorful musical she wants him to make. It plays like a *Folies* floorshow. Costumer Vicki Mortimer put Rivera in a no-nonsense business suit for the top of the song, then allowed Rivera to pin it back daringly for the climactic tango with Banderas, showing off her superbly toned legs and still-curvy hips. At age sixty-eight, sixteen years after the car accident, she was able to kick up her rehabilitated left leg to Banderas's shoulder. The performance earned her a Tony nomination as Best Featured Actress in a Musical.

Also in 2003 I had the opportunity to work with Rivera on my book *The Alchemy of Theatre*, a volume of essays on the art of collaboration, as told by people I chose for being the top of their respective professions. Harold Prince was my director, Edward Albee my playwright, William Ivey Long my costume designer, et cetera. I chose Rivera to write the essay on how one collaborates as a leading lady.

Her essay is fascinating. For one thing, she starts with the premise that the word *collaboration* does not accurately describe what she does. The essay, which grew out of a conversation we had on the topic, consists of Rivera feeling for precisely the right word. Citing her experience starting in the chorus and working her way up to star, she considers "learning," "living something together," "sharing," "creating together," and finally, recalling an epiphany she had while spending time with her daughter settles on "playing." She wrote, "In the theatre we play. That's why we call them 'plays,' right? We're playing together. That's a sweet and gentle way of saying it. Except it's very real. It's grown-up play. And that's how we stay in touch with the child within us."

It was her formula for success as a performer, whether as a chorus dancer or the star of the show. Brian Stokes Mitchell, who worked with her on *Kiss of the Spider Woman*, recalled how Rivera would strive to know everyone on the production, including tech people and the people who worked the "front" of the house in the box office. It was her way of "playing."

The Dancer's Life

At this stage of their career, most stars would have been content to sit down with a ghost-writer and dictate their memoirs. (Most did, luckily for me.) But that wasn't enough for Rivera. She decided to retell, or more accurately, re*dance* her life—as a Broadway musical.

Directed and choreographed by Graciela Daniele, *Chita Rivera: The Dancer's Life* (2005) was a highly structured autobiographical musical revue, narrated and largely performed by Rivera herself with help from a carefully selected corps of Broadway's top dancers, who were beyond delighted to be working with the legend.

A child dancer named Liana Ortiz played Rivera as a girl and got to perform a pas de deux with the real thing. Most of the music came from Rivera's many great hits, though the songwriting team of Lynn Ahrens and Stephen Flaherty supplied several original songs, notably "Dancing on the Kitchen Table" about Rivera's hectic childhood.

Unfortunately, *The Dancer's Life* may have been produced a decade or two too late for Rivera. Her fan pool was still very deep and devoted but no longer sufficiently wide to support a full-scale long-run musical about nothing but her. Despite nightly entreaties from the stage for people to dragoon their friends to see the show, it closed after just seventy-two performances. Rivera soldiered on, touring *The Dancer's Life* around North America.

She was still showing off her gams in 2006 when she took part in a tenth-anniversary reunion performance of the cast of the long-running revival of *Chicago*. As conceived by director Walter Bobbie, three dozen stars from throughout the long run alternated in scenes and songs from the show. As guest of honor, Rivera, who had never appeared in the revival, was invited to sing the opening number, "All That Jazz."

The Kander and Ebb musical had become a much bigger hit the second time around, partly owing to shrewd replacement casting by producers Fran and Barry Weissler, and partly owing to the fact that the playgoing public's cynicism had caught up with Ebb's and Fosse's. The show that had been ahead of its time had finally found its proper era.

And Kander and Ebb were at work on another project, one that was even darker than *Chicago. The Visit*, based on the drama by Swiss author Friedrich Dürrenmatt, is the story of half-Gypsy, half-Jew Claire Zachanassian, the richest woman in the world, who returns to the economically depressed town of her birth to wreak revenge on the man who seduced her, then abandoned and disgraced her, when she was a girl. In truth, she wants revenge on the entire town, which had ostracized her in her youth and now grovels at her feet, hoping she can get them out of their economic straits. She can and will—but at a price. The townspeople must kill the man who done her wrong.

The show was originally conceived as a vehicle for Angela Lansbury, and a tryout was even planned in the late 1990s. But Lansbury withdrew at the last moment to tend to her ailing husband.

Kander and Ebb, working with librettist Terrence McNally, turned to Rivera, with whom they'd enjoyed such success on *Kiss of the Spider Woman*. The writers had obviously liked the light touch Lansbury had used to leaven the darkness of *Sweeney Todd*. But, in truth, Rivera was a better fit for *The Visit*. There is little that is comic in Claire Zachanassian, but much that is blistering. The production tried out at the Goodman Theatre in Chicago in fall 2001, just weeks after the terrorist attacks of September 11, and perhaps that recent event colored the audience reaction. People were not in the mood for tragedy, even with Rivera performing Ann Reinking's choreography. The show got a second mounting at Signature Theatre in Virginia in 2008.

As of this writing, Rivera looked like she was headed into her second half-century of stardom still near the top of her game.

Julie Andrews as Eliza Doolittle in *My Fair Lady* (1956). PHOTOFEST

JULIE ANDREWS
I Could Have Danced All Night

All children who saw Julie Andrews in the film version of *Mary Poppins* or *The Sound of Music* dreamed of having her as their own personal magical nanny.

And yet this vision of a pure-voiced, virginal, ever-patient, firm, but benevolent perfected mother was not all there was to Andrews, and she spent much of her long career trying to escape these two monumental performances created within a two-year period in the early 1960s.

Her stage career gives a much fuller accounting of her skill set, but, remarkably, none of her greatest stage performances were filmed, leaving theatergoers with an image of Andrews slightly at variance with, and certainly more three-dimensional than, those of the rest of the world.

The one thing everyone gets properly is a voice of almost unearthly purity and laser-like pitch control. Until she encountered vocal difficulties late in life, exacerbated by what was alleged to be an especially tragic incidence of medical malpractice, her voice was one of the great treasures of the legitimate stage.

★

Julie Andrews lived a quiet early childhood until age four, when the breakup of her parents' marriage had the effect of thrusting her into show business. Julia Elizabeth Wells was born October 1, 1935, in Walton-on-Thames, England, to Edward C. Wells, a shop teacher, and Barbara Morris Wells, a piano teacher who also accompanied students at a local dance school.

That school was the place where Julia—called "Julie" by all—made her stage debut at age two playing a fairy in a school pageant. At age three she had a speaking role in a dance based on the nursery rhyme "Wynken, Blynken, and Nod" and sang the title song. Things weren't happy in the Wells home, and when her mother met a singer named Ted Andrews ("the Canadian Troubador") in a traveling show for the USO-like Entertainments National Services Organization in 1939, Barbara left her husband behind. She joined the show to travel and perform with Andrews, bringing the four-year-old Julie along. Her folks discovered that she had not just perfect pitch, but a four-octave range. After the war they began sending her for formal singing lessons and gradually worked her into their act. On December 5, 1946, she joined them in a Royal Command Performance in London. She was presented to Queen Elizabeth, wife of King George, who complimented her, nearly causing her to faint.

Julie, who adopted her stepfather's last name, soon became the center of the act. The child prodigy got her first booking outside the family when she was twelve, singing abbreviated versions of opera arias for the *Starlight Roof* revue at the legendary London Palladium. When still only thirteen, she played a second Royal Command Performance, appearing on a bill with Danny Kaye and the Nicholas Brothers at the Palladium. She was billed as "a 13-year-old coloratura soprano with the voice of an adult."

After taking dance lessons she appeared in a regional production of a third-rate musical called *Mountain Fire* in the northern city of Leeds. It was there that she was "discovered" by the director of a hit London musical, *The Boy Friend*, which was assembling a cast to take to Broadway. Despite playing a pregnant Tennessee girl with a ghastly faux-Southern accent, the eighteen-year-old Andrews impressed Vida Hope, who had seen her in a panto at the London Palladium, and invited her to London for an audition.

Depending how you looked at it, Sandy Wilson's *The Boy Friend* was either a loving homage or a spot-on parody of ditzy 1920s musicals like *No, No, Nanette,* in which romantic misunderstandings and secret identities lead inexorably from the boy meeting the girl to the boy losing the girl to the boy getting the girl as wedding bells ring. This stylized little bonbon proved to be a great success and a reminder of happier days in postwar Britain. Producers Cy Feuer and Ernest Martin wanted to export it to Broadway as soon as possible, so Wilson and Hope put the call out for English maidens to play their "perfect young ladies" at a finishing school in the French Riviera.

Producer Feuer sketched this portrait of Andrews at seventeen: "The first thing I noticed was that she had perfect pitch. There was no piano lead-in, no instrument to guide her to the right note, but she hit the note dead center every time. The music followed her. That was pretty amazing. But even more impressive was her voice. She had a glorious soprano voice that filled the theater. On top of that, she was cute."

Once they heard Andrews sing and saw that she could handle the dances, she was cast in the lead role of Polly Browne and whisked off to New York, where she opened to rave reviews. Andrews's first original cast album offers a glimpse of the actress at age eighteen. Her amazing vocal range is on good display throughout. She shoots up a startling octave at the end of "I Could Be Happy," and some of her arpeggios in the third verse of "Poor Little Pierrette" sound nearly ultrasonic.

Audiences were delighted with her innocent demeanor and the unearthly purity of her voice. Word got around Broadway that something very special was happening at the Royale Theatre.

First out of the gate was the team of lyricist/librettist Alan Jay Lerner, composer Frederick Loewe, and director Moss Hart, who invited her to audition for a musical they were writing, based on George Bernard Shaw's *Pygmalion*. It was to be called *My Lady Liza*. While the demanding role traditionally was played by an older and more seasoned actress, Hart biographer Jared Brown wrote that Lerner thought the eighteen-year-old Andrews would be a good choice considering "how refreshing it might be if, for the first time since the play was written, a girl of precisely that age [specified by Shaw] played the role."

Shortly after accepting the part, she heard from Richard Rodgers of Rodgers and Hammerstein, who were then at the peak of their power and fame. Rodgers wanted her to star in his next musical, *Pipe Dream*. When he learned that she was already set to do *My Lady Liza*, Rodgers famously urged her to stick with the Lerner and Loewe project, predicting that it would be the greater star-making part. He was correct; *Pipe Dream* had the shortest run of any Rogers and Hammerstein musical and today is remembered only by theatre cognoscenti. *My Lady Liza*, on the other hand, became *My Fair Lady*, one of the most successful and well-regarded musicals in Broadway history. It was the beginning of a warm relationship between Rogers and Andrews.

My Fair Lady is based on Shaw's 1913 drama about accent and class in Great Britain. Poor cockney flower girl Eliza Doolittle, a young woman of tremendous spirit, wants to learn to talk like a "proper" lady in order to better her lot in life. Dialectician Henry Higgins takes her case on a bet with his friend Colonel Pickering, promising that he will be able to improve her accent enough to pass her off as a duchess at an embassy ball. The original play is a model of social criticism; the musical used its score to explore the emotional richness of the situation.

Andrews was only twenty when *My Fair Lady* went into rehearsal, and she was paired with the talented but temperamental British actor Rex Harrison as Higgins. It quickly became apparent that Andrews's inexperience was presenting a problem. Director Moss Hart canceled rehearsals and, over a long weekend, went through the script line by line to help bring out Andrews's inner Eliza. This legendary master class resulted in one of the great musical comedy performances not only of the decade, but of Broadway history. It also mirrored the Higgins/Eliza story.

Lerner and Loewe took a scene that did not exist in Shaw's play and turned it into the centerpiece of the musical. In the play, Eliza sheds her cockney accent offstage. In the musical, we see Higgins struggling with her, poking marbles into her mouth, running her through nonsense phrases to help with problem areas, like dropped "aitches": "In Hartford, Hereford and Hampshire, hurricanes hardly happen."

The drill continues to the point where Pickering begins to pick up her stubborn cockney accent and all of them are exhausted. At this point, Higgins delivers a speech about the beauty and majesty of the English language. The speech has a magical effect. Eliza repeats a phrase she's said a million times, except instead of pronouncing it "The ryne in spyne stays mynly on the plyne," she suddenly opens up with "The rain in Spain stays mainly in the plain."

This simple utterance turns into a little flamenco of joy in a scene beautifully choreographed by Hanya Holm, with the two elder men dancing with the beautiful and graceful Eliza, happy at last.

That song was followed by "I Could Have Danced All Night," whose final triumphant note told all of Broadway that there was a new queen in its midst.

"Miss Andrews does a magnificent job, " wrote Brooks Atkinson in the *New York Times*. "The transformation from street-corner drab to lady is both touching and beautiful. Out of the muck of Covent Garden something glorious blossoms, and Miss Andrews acts her part triumphantly."

The entire show had a sparkle and a class to it that was especially satisfying to Anglophile New York. But the appeal extended far beyond its borders. The cast album stayed on the charts for months and remains one of the best-selling ever.

Cinderella and Marriages

You would have thought that somewhere in here Rodgers and Hammerstein would have written an original musical for Andrews, and they sort of did.

Cinderella was one of the first musicals written expressly for television. Rodgers and Hammerstein wanted to explore the new medium, but in the end they created what was basically a short (yet padded) stage-style musical that follows the broad outlines of the timeless fairy tale. Andrews starred in the title role, with Jon Cypher as the Prince and a host of stage regulars in supporting roles. In its first broadcast on CBS, March 31, 1957, the show attracted more than 100 million viewers. It was remade in 1965 with Lesley Ann Warren and in 1997 with Brandy Norwood.

Perhaps inspired by the fairy-tale setting and traditional storytelling, Rodgers and Hammerstein produced several melodic highlights, like the duet "Do I Love You Because You're Beautiful," a cute character number for Andrews in "My Own Little Corner," and a classic Rodgers waltz in "Ten Minutes Ago."

After *Cinderella*, Andrews wed set designer Tony Walton, whom she had known since 1948 when she was working in London. They married on May 5, 1959, and had a daughter, Emma Walton. The Waltons divorced in 1967. Andrews's second marriage, to film director Blake Edwards in 1969, was an enduring success. They had four children together, Geoffrey, Jennifer, Amy, and Joanna.

Camelot

The team that created *My Fair Lady*—Lerner, Loewe, and Hart—organized a reunion with Andrews for their next project, a musical based on the King Arthur legend, to be called simply *Camelot*. The success of *My Fair Lady* ensured that the creators would have their pick of stars, and indeed, King Arthur was played by Richard Burton, then a rising star of the English dramatic stage. For Lancelot there was the newcomer Robert Goulet—someone who was considered quite the stud and not the self-parody he later became.

The centerpiece of the production was Andrews as a glowing Queen Guenevere. They gave her plenty of material to show off her range, including a comically bloodthirsty "I-want" song, called "Where Are the Simple Joys?"; a bawdy character song, "The Lusty Month of May"; a comic duet with Burton, "What Would the Simple Folk Do?"; a sorrowful love duet, "I Loved You Once in Silence."

At this point in her career she hadn't yet become the lacquered doll later critics judged her to be. There were still considered to be two sides to her, and she could play both equally, which is why she handled the part so well. In *My Fair Lady* the earthy, bawling flower girl became a transcendent vision. In *Camelot*, the vision was shown to have feet of clay. She was playing a queen, all right, but an abundantly adulterous one.

It was perhaps overly ambitious of Lerner to try compressing the sprawling epic into a single evening. Reviews were mixed, and it was only after Andrews and her costars appeared on the popular Sunday-night television variety program *The Ed Sullivan Show* that the musical began to sell out.

There was another helping hand, and a big one. President John F. Kennedy and First Lady Jacqueline Kennedy were signally moved by the show's final scene, in which the dream of Camelot is crashing down around King Arthur and he is facing his own death on the battlefield. He takes a moment to knight a young boy and commands him to live and pass on the story of the ideals of Camelot—of using great power for great good. Of making sure the power of law transcends the weakness of man.

These notions, expressed so rarely in popular entertainment, so moved the president that he and his wife tried to adopt these ideals for his administration, which came to be identified with Camelot.

But, for all that, if there were such a thing as a Phyrric hit, *Camelot* was it. Both Loewe and Hart retired, Hart died soon after, and Loewe didn't work again for more than ten years. Lerner never had another hit on Broadway. Burton continued his film career but never did another musical. And Kennedy, who identified himself so closely with the idealistic image of Camelot, paid the price that Arthur paid.

For her part, Andrews, despite being a Brit, had been embraced as a Broadway star. Her iconic status persisted despite the fact that after the *Camelot* experience, she didn't return to the legitimate stage to do anything more than host the Tony Awards or shoot a movie scene, for nearly three decades. Like Barbra Streisand, Meryl Streep, and other great young Broadway stars of the period, Andrews went to Hollywood, and it looked like she'd never come back.

Mary Poppins and *The Sound of Music*

Though this book is concerned mainly with stage work, Andrews's performances in her first two films, *Mary Poppins* and *The Sound of Music*, are so theatrical in their roots and execution, and provided such touchstones for a generation of theatre artists and theatre audiences, that they deserve the status of honorary stage performances in a way her succeeding films do not.

Despite the international acclaim for her stage and TV work, Andrews was an unproven quantity in Hollywood in 1964. When *My Fair Lady* was purchased for Warner Brothers, Harrison and Holloway were asked to re-create their Broadway roles, but Andrews was not. That the role went to nonsinger Audrey Hepburn added insult to injury.

Perhaps if the moviegoing world had gotten to see Andrews's earthier Eliza Doolittle as her first movie role, the rest of her career might have gone quite differently. Though many love Hepburn's film performance, the decision to pass over Andrew remains one of the studios' grosser casting crimes.

Instead, Walt Disney snapped up Andrews for his upcoming film musical, based on the P. L. Travers stories about a magical nanny, *Mary Poppins*. Andrews was more than a smash in the role; she became an icon for children who grew up in that era. She was the first "star" many of us knew. And in the 1965 Academy Awards, Andrews had the satisfaction of trouncing Hepburn for the Best Actress Oscar, a remarkable feat for any film debut, let alone one with so much emotional baggage.

At age twenty-nine, Andrews had matured into a slim, bright-eyed beauty who danced gracefully, sang like an angel, and had an amazingly warm loveliness in close-ups. She had learned to play two sides of a character in *My Fair Lady*, and she brought that skill to *Mary Poppins*. There was always a trace of sadness around the edges of her large blue eyes, but when she was really happy those eyes would light up and make you feel great, too, notably on songs like "A Spoonful of Sugar" and "Supercalifragilisticexpialidocious."

When those same eyes flashed with anger you wanted to run—or, better yet, to do all you could to make her smile again. The perfect combination for a nanny.

Accompanying songs like "Jolly Holiday" with costar Dick Van Dyke, the lullabys "Stay Awake" and "Feed the Birds," and the dance number "Step in Time" were perfectly tailored to her strengths. And the camera just loved her.

For many children, it was the introduction to Broadway-style musicals and set a standard for melody and magic that would shape tastes for the next five decades.

There was another legacy, as well. For the rest of her life, whenever Andrews would appear anywhere or take part in any event, there was a special delight in her mere presence. Forty-three years later Disney needed a warm, magical voice to set the scene for its half-cartoon *Enchanted*. The first voice you hear is that of seventy-two-year-old Julie Andrews.

Mary Poppins convinced Hollywood that Andrews could indeed carry a picture, and there was intense anticipation about what she would do next. But that was already decided.

Director Robert Wise reportedly cast her as Maria in *The Sound of Music* based on the daily rushes of *Mary Poppins* alone.

It was a good match. Rodgers had enjoyed working with her on *Cinderella* (Hammerstein had passed away in 1960 shortly after *The Sound of Music*'s opening on Broadway), and he even wrote her music and lyrics for two extra songs, "Something Good" (a duet with costar Christopher Plummer) and the solo "I Have Confidence." And if Andrews now plucked away a Broadway star's stage role, she was, at age twenty-nine, perhaps better suited for the role of young Austrian postulant Maria than Broadway's original Maria, Mary Martin, who would have been fifty-one at the time of shooting.

Andrews played Maria, a young nun in training who can't keep her mind on her devotions but is forever wandering in the hills, singing. The opening scene of Andrews whirling through the grass on an Alpine hilltop as she sings the title song became one of the iconic moments of twentieth-century cinema (even if the helicopter used to film the scene repeatedly blew her over during shooting).

Sent to care for a family of seven unruly children (a nanny again), she teaches the children the fundamentals of music and how to sing in the beloved "Do-Re-Mi" sequence, followed by a hit parade of memorable tunes like "Climb Ev'ry Mountain," "Sixteen Going on Seventeen," "Edelweiss," "My Favorite Things," and "So Long, Farewell."

The film grossed a whopping $163 million, a respectable number even today. In its time it became the highest-grossing movie released up to that point. Its appeal has endured. Fans even organized sing-along screenings of the film. In 2007, the American Film Institute ranked it number forty on its list of the Greatest Movies of All Time.

In less than a decade, Andrews had gone just about as far as an actress of her day could go. And, aged only thirty, she now faced the fact that she would always have that perfect former self to compete with.

Andrews continued to make films into the twenty-first century, though never again with the success of her first two. She starred in *Hawaii* (1966) and *The Torn Curtain* (1966), before returning to her *Boy Friend* flapper roots for the 1967 film *Thoroughly Modern Millie*, in which she played a "modern" young 1920s woman who comes to New York looking to have some fun and land a wealthy husband. The film costarred Mary Tyler Moore, Beatrice Lillie, and Carol Channing, but Andrews got the title character and the title song.

The movie did well, but in 1968 Andrews starred in *Star!*, a biopic about *King and I* star Gertrude Lawrence, which gave Andrews the chance to perform some of Lawrence's best songs. Despite a huge publicity buildup, the film was a flop, one of three in the period (along with *Doctor Dolittle* and *Hello, Dolly!*) that almost bankrupted 20th Century-Fox and helped bring the golden age of film musicals to a crashing end.

Part of the problem seemed to be that audiences had a hard time accepting Andrews as anything but a virginal magical nanny. She had gotten typecast. Looking back on Andrews's great roles, we see a clear progression in the archetypes she played, deliberate or not.

In *The Boy Friend* she played a silly girl. In *My Fair Lady*, she played a silly girl who transforms into a kind of princess. In *Cinderella* Andrews played a girl who becomes an actual princess. Finally, in *Camelot*, she played a princess who becomes a queen.

In the movie phase of her career she started playing a magical nanny who becomes a mother figure in *Mary Poppins*, then a real nanny who becomes a real stepmother in *The Sound of Music*. But here the progression stalled for twenty years. Though she played actual mothers in several films and a dowager queen in *The Princess Diaries*, movie audiences had trouble accepting her as having any sexual dimension.

It wasn't until she played a woman who becomes a man in *Victor/Victoria* (1982) that audiences again embraced one of her personas. Her only other notable film appearances in the next decade were *The Tamarind Seed* in 1974, *10* in 1979, and *S.O.B.*, directed by her second husband, Blake Edwards, in 1981. *S.O.B.* is worth mentioning for one notorious scene. As a gesture of defiance against Andrews's goody-two-shoes typecasting, Edwards and Andrews embarked on this uncomfortably autobiographical project about a failing film producer who reedits one of his flop movies to include a topless scene of his wife, a famous singing actress. Andrews was called to actually bare her breasts on camera for the scene.

It worked. People's perception of Andrews did change somewhat, which helped lead to perhaps Andrews's best post–*Sound of Music* movie: *Victor/Victoria* (1995), in which gender issues were front and center. Andrews played a starving singer who gets work the only place she can find it: in a gay cabaret, "passing" as a gay man who is unusually skilled at playing a female impersonator. In other words: a woman pretending to be a man pretending to be a woman. Henry Mancini and Leslie Bricusse provided a score, which won an Oscar. Oscar nominations also went to Andrews and Edwards (as screenwriter), as well as her costars Robert Preston and Lesley Ann Warren.

Late Stage Appearances

More than thirty years would pass before Andrews returned to the New York stage. She was lured back by the opportunity to appear in a revue of songs by Stephen Sondheim.

Andrews and Sondheim had never worked together directly, though her first husband, Walton, had designed sets for Sondheim's *A Funny Thing Happened on the Way to the Forum*. In the meantime, Sondheim and British actress Julia McKenzie assembled a loosely constructed revue of his songs called *Putting It Together*. Andrews was on the short list of dream actresses to play the lead, and Sondheim approached her personally to take the role. She had "always said privately . . . that if Sondheim ever asked me to do a show it might be the one time that I would have to say, simply, yes." And so she did.

The show's limited seven-week off-Broadway run quickly sold out, but reviews did not contain the expected hosannas. "*Putting It Together*," wrote Frank Rich in the *New York Times,* "too often displays [Andrews] gingerly, as a fragile porcelain figurine that might be shattered if handled too much." The production did not move to a Broadway run, as fans had hoped. When a revival of the show finally came to Broadway several years later, the Andrews role was played by her friend Carol Burnett.

In the meantime, though, reviews notwithstanding, the taste of the legitimate stage had whetted Andrews's appetite for more. Andrews worked with husband Blake Edwards to adapt *Victor/Victoria* for Broadway. From the start, *Victor/Victoria* (1995) was a project of the heart for Edwards, who had always wanted to do a big Broadway musical and who was credited as librettist, director, and lead producer on the stage production. A lot of Andrews's emotional investment in the project was a product of her loyalty to her husband. Critics and audiences were simply delighted to have Andrews back after thirty-five years, and she gave a marvelous performance that added depth to her film characterization, even if she no longer fully participated in the dance numbers. The show as a whole, however, was derided as clunky, which infuriated her.

Her anger came to a boil in May 1996 when that year's Tony nominations were announced. Although it had been a lean year for musicals in general, *Victor/Victoria* earned just a single nomination, for Andrews herself, as Best Leading Actress in a Musical. Reporters including me were invited to a hastily organized press conference two days later to hear her response—not in a studio or rehearsal room, but, dramatically, inside the Marquis Theatre itself at the conclusion of a matinee performance.

Andrews took her bows, and then, stepping forward in costume, hushed the audience and explained what had happened. It was clear, she implied, that the Tony nominators had set out deliberately to snub her husband in his many roles on the production, claiming the rest of the show had been, in her memorable phrase, "egregiously overlooked." In solidarity with her husband and fellow cast, crew, and creators, she therefore renounced her Tony nomination.

It was a bold step, considering that many felt she herself had been "egregiously overlooked" by Tony voters for her roles as Eliza Doolittle and Guenevere, as well. Instead, she chose to stand by her show—and her husband.

During the run of *Victor/Victoria*, Andrews began to experience vocal discomfort and difficulty with tone control. She frequently missed performance owing to illness and in 1997 submitted her golden larynx for surgery to remove callus-like growths. Andrew subsequently discovered that the crystalline purity of her singing voice was gone. She sued the surgeon, Stuart Kessler, and settled for $20 million, but her instrument had suffered permanent damage. She lamented at the time that she would never be able to sing again, and she has stuck to that—with a few exceptions, like the tune "Your Crowning Glory" for the 2004 film *The Princess Diaries 2: Royal Engagement*.

Dame Julie

In her later years, Andrews has taken a somewhat lower professional profile, especially after 2000, when she was made a Dame Commander of the British Empire (DBE). Among other laurels she has collected: the Kennedy Center Honors in 2001 and the Screen Actors Guild's

Lifetime Achievement Awards in 2007. Kennedy Center Chairman James A. Johnson described Andrews as "a beloved actress whose performances in films and the musical theater are treasured by millions of Americans."

Dame Julie Andrews had two modest hits in supporting roles as queens in both the *Princess Diaries* films and in the *Shrek* animated films, and as the warm-voiced storyteller who opens and closes the aforementioned *Enchanted*.

In 2005 she made her debut as a stage director with a revival of *The Boy Friend* at Bay Street Theatre, a playhouse in Sag Harbor on New York's Long Island where her daughter, Emma Walton Hamilton, is artistic director. Andrews and her daughter collaborated on several books for children, including *Dumpy's Extra Busy Day* and *The Great American Musical*, the latter about a mouse theatre troupe trying to put on a Broadway musical when their leading lady gets stuck in a mousetrap on opening night.

Andrews's career was expected to come full circle with the production of a musical based on one of their stories, *Simeon's Gift,* about a medieval minstrel who sets out to find the music in his soul. It debuted in a reading at Bay Street Theatre and was planning a more ambitious production as this book went to press.

Jerry Orbach as Chuck Baxter in *Promises, Promises* (1968). PHOTOFEST

JERRY ORBACH
The Lullaby of Broadway

There was always something mysterious about Jerry Orbach. When he played bad guys, you always felt that there was a decent person inside, perhaps stuffed into a trunk somewhere. When he placed nice guys, there always seemed to be a shadow behind the smile.

Which is ironic, because he tried very hard throughout his career to keep things real and to build his characters on a foundation of truth. This approach enabled him to play both fantastical characters and workaday ones with grit in their souls and both feet on the ground.

He brought a sinuous dark intensity to his work in musicals from 1958 through 1981. His commitment to naturalistic acting might have marked him as more of a dramatic actor, but his surprisingly forceful and resonant voice kept winning him musical roles like El Gallo in the original *The Fantasticks*. Fans of his stage work have a hard time imagining him in nonsinging roles. Fans of his later TV work, especially the dramatic *Law & Order*, have a hard time imagining that he won Tony Awards as a singer and dancer.

Orbach had an unusual look for a leading man. His face was long and tapered, with deep-set eyes, heavy brows, an aquiline nose, and a jutting chin. Tall and lanky, he had broad shoulders but narrow hips. The combination could be gawky at times, but he deployed it all with a Heathcliff-like brooding intensity that earned him, in his early years, a matinee idol's following. A strongly masculine leading man, he also had just the right touch of self-parody to keep it from becoming overbearing. He never got too full of himself.

He had little formal dance instruction, but he possessed a quality that caused director/choreographers Bob Fosse (*Chicago*) and Gower Champion (*Carnival!*) to choose him to serve as leading man in their shows.

And as much as he loved the lights of Broadway, he was fascinated with the underclass, especially the small-time crooks, billiard players, and other Runyonesque characters he encountered in the Hell's Kitchen neighborhood between Times Square and the Hudson piers where he eventually made his home. A child of New York, he loved the city and loved creating characters based on its denizens.

★

Orbach had showbiz in his blood. He was born Jerome Bernard Orbach on October 20, 1935, in the Bronx. His father, former vaudeville performer Leon Orbach, was from Hamburg, Germany, of Sephardic Jewish ancestry, which gave Jerry his dark features. His mother, Emily (neé Olexy), a singer on the radio, was a Polish-American who raised Jerry in her religion, Roman Catholicism. The family relocated frequently to small towns in Pennsylvania, New York, and Massachusetts, with all the rootlessness and perpetual adjusting that implies. They finally settled in Waukegan, Illinois, where Jerry attended high school.

He attended college at Northwestern University and headed straight for New York, where he was accepted into the Actors' Studio by Lee Strasberg and also took classes at HB Studio and the Mira-Rostova studio. These connections, plus the fact that he'd exhibited an expansive baritone, led to his first professional job, understudying in the long-running off-Broadway production of *The Threepenny Opera* at the Theatre de Lys. He advanced to playing Smith, the police constable, late in the run. He also understudied and occasionally went on as the lead role of the charismatic, amoral killer Macheath.

During those years, Orbach had his first chance to put down roots in a community, and he liked it. He lived with his first wife, Marta Curro, on Perry Street in Greenwich Village, an easy walk through the Beatnik-era bohemia to the theatre on Christopher Street. He became something of a beatnik himself, according to those who knew him during those years. He loved billiards and spent hours in area pool halls and coffeehouses, getting to know the blue-collar denizens of the city's demimonde, which was not much different from the fictional one he was helping create each night in *Threepenny*. He put this knowledge to work in the low-budget exploitation film *Cop Killer*, filmed around Manhattan in 1958. He remained fascinated with scruffy characters all his life.

Realism

Through his work at the various acting studios, Orbach became friendly with a director named Word Baker, who at the time served as associate producer of Jules Monk's Upstairs at the Downstairs revues. Orbach was visiting him backstage one night and was complaining that he'd lost out on his chance to make his Broadway debut when the musical *Lock Up Your Daughters*, in which he'd been cast, closed out of town. Baker invited him to audition for a new show he was working on. It was a tiny musical about two fathers who scheme to trick their children into falling in love and marrying. Presiding over the proceedings is a mysterious and scoundrelly narrator. Baker thought Orbach might be right for that role.

Originally conceived as an *Oklahoma!*-style western musical titled *Joy Comes to Dead Horse*, the show had been stripped of virtually all scenery and elaborate costumes for economy's sake and renamed *The Fantasticks*. The narrator retained his bandito name, however: "El Gallo." Authors Tom Jones and Harvey Schmidt had seen Orbach in *Threepenny*, and Schmidt admiringly thought he resembled "a Navajo prince."

Though they were considering another actor for the role, they switched their allegiance to Orbach immediately following his audition. El Gallo is more than just the narrator of *The Fantasticks*. He is a demi-supernatural character who has powers to alter the lives of the people in the play. He appears in their lives to help teach them a lesson, a sort of Mary Poppins being who augments his worldly wisdom with a touch of white magic.

In the late 1980s I worked with Donald C. Farber on the book *The Amazing Story of* The Fantasticks, and I sought to get firsthand accounts from everyone involved in the original production who was still living.

Schmidt, who helped audition and rehearse *Fantasticks* performers for decades, said they picked Orbach not only because of his awe-inspiring stage presence and majestic voice, but because he had a perfect balance of machismo and humor about his machismo. Schmidt said they've had many excellent El Gallos down through the years but never again found exactly that same perfect combination.

Much of the show is written in verse, which was a challenge for tough-guy Orbach. "My big thing was realism," he told me when describing how he assembled his performance as El Gallo. "I hated anything false or phony. My goal was naturalistic, realistic acting. I was working in musicals because I could sing. And because I could sing I was getting jobs while other friends of mine who didn't sing were stuck. Still, I wanted no hokeyness, except where it's really called for, like in the 'Rape Ballet.' But as far as everything else—talking to the audience and the poetry—I wanted truth. That was very, very important to me, much more important to me, I think, than even the writers or the director. I think that was my particular contribution to the structure of that play: you have to have the reality when you're doing the little poetic speeches, leading to 'Soon It's Gonna Rain' or whatever, otherwise the high-flying poetry and comedy have nothing to bounce off of."

Orbach also got the chance to introduce a song that would become an American standard, the nostalgic little waltz "Try to Remember," which transports the audience into the world of the play and introduces the themes of nature and passing seasons. In the years to come, he'd be called upon to sing it on TV specials, at memorial services, and for retrospectives of all kinds. At age twenty-five, Orbach had a signature song.

Orbach was ambitious to succeed as an actor but to do so on his own terms through good and worthwhile work. He took the $45-a-week job on *The Fantasticks* not because he thought it would make him rich or even get him noticed, but because he thought it was an interesting project. In the end, his least commercial choice turned out to be the cornerstone of his career and, eventually, the longest-running musical in world history—17,162 performances by its closing in January 2002.

Legendary producer David Merrick perceived that a new star had arisen and offered Orbach the chance to make his Broadway debut in the lead role of the brooding puppeteer his next show, *Carnival!* (sometimes also listed without the exclamation point). It was based on the hit film *Lili*, about a sweet, simpleminded young woman who runs away and joins the traveling carnival of the title. Surrounded by frightening grotesques, she befriends the affable puppets in the puppet show. She confesses to them how terrified she is of the dark, angry puppeteer—not fully able to understand that it is he who is operating them, and the only way he can speak to her gently and lovingly is through them.

The role gave him a wide range to play and a broad arc to traverse. The experience of taking care of Lili (who has "the mind of a child," according to one lyric) takes him from bitter, withdrawn, and selfish—he's partially disabled from a war injury—to tender and generous. His warm aria of self-realization, "Her Face," was effective enough to earn him a booking to re-create it on the nationally broadcast *The Ed Sullivan Show*.

Carnival! was directed by Gower Champion, who placed the story in a fantasyland of balloons and streamers and constant movement to balance Orbach's black hole of a character at its center. Champion would direct both Orbach's first Broadway musical, and his last, *42nd Street*.

In the mid-1960s after *Carnival!,* he worked twice on shows at the New York City Center. In 1965 he played Sky Masterson in *Guys and Dolls* in a cast that included Anita Gillette as Sarah Brown, Alan King as Nathan Detroit, and Sheila MacRae as Miss Adelaide. The role represented a considerable promotion for Orbach, who had played an unbilled role as a barbershop patron in the 1955 film version of *Guys and Dolls*, backing Frank Sinatra on "The Oldest Established."

In 1966 he played Charlie Davenport opposite Ethel Merman in a revival of *Annie Get Your Gun*. A highlight from the cast album of the latter show is Orbach singing "No Business Like Show Business" with "La Merman."

In 1968 David Merrick, who had produced *Carnival!*, now sought to bring Orbach back to Broadway in an innovative new musical, *Promises, Promises.*

Based on the Oscar-winning 1960 Billy Wilder/I. A. L. Diamond film *The Apartment*, the show told a contemporary morality tale about a sweet little guy, an office worker named Chuck Baxter who is in love with a pretty secretary named Fran, though she barely notices him. He figures that a quick promotion might impress her. So, he suppresses his conscience and yields to his superiors' pressure to let them use his apartment for their extramarital affairs. What he doesn't know is that one of these apartment jockeys is having an affair with Fran. Baxter undergoes heartbreak, epiphany, and reformation before collecting his heart's reward.

To give the story a contemporary feel, Merrick brought in the songwriting team of Burt Bacharach and Hal David, who had enjoyed numerous pop hits with "Close to You," "What the World Needs Now Is Love," and "I Say a Little Prayer." But Orbach, as leading man, was not going to have an easy ride. Bacharach supplied a score that was surprisingly sophisticated, full of restlessly shifting time signatures, keys, and rhythms. The orchestra pit was organized like a recording studio with sound baffles and microphones, and Bacharach used scat singers in the pit like musical instruments. The result was a musical that sounds like no other, except possibly *Company*, which was written shortly afterward and clearly shows traces of the *Promises, Promises* influence.

Bacharach might have taken musicals in a different direction if he hadn't hated the pressure and loss of control that came with collaborating on a musical. He never wrote another. The subject matter has dated badly, and *Promises* has never been revived, except by the off-Broadway Encores! series. (A revue of his songs, *The Look of Love*, folded quickly in 2003.)

Orbach may have seemed an odd choice for Baxter. He'd always played glowering authority figures; here he played a schlemiel. He bore a slight resemblance to Jack Lemmon, who had played Baxter in *The Apartment*, but where Lemmon was bumbling and wormy, Orbach allowed his gawky side to come out. Orbach was always the kind of guy you'd see scowling in the corner, but when you approached him and said hello you'd get a big sincere smile and discover he was really a great guy. *Promises, Promises* was his big sincere smile.

He got to introduce two songs that became huge Top 40 hits for Bacharach and David, "I'll Never Fall in Love Again" and the title song, though the hit versions were recorded by the team's favorite singer, Dionne Warwick.

However, Orbach's crowning moment came in his Act I solo, "She Likes Basketball," one of the most underrated show tunes of the period. The song is simply a burst of happiness on Baxter's part when he discovers that he and Fran have one tiny thing in common. Orbach played it on a bare stage, and Baxter's only prop is his raincoat, which he converts into an imaginary basketball as he awkwardly dribbles and leaps around the stage in Michael Bennett's joyous choreography. Significantly, it was "She Likes Basketball" that Orbach was asked to perform on the 1969 Tony Awards broadcast. It remains one of the sweetest, brightest moments in a generally dour career. For his performance as Baxter, Orbach won the Tony Award as Best Actor in a Musical.

During this period he appeared in two nonmusical plays on Broadway: Leonora Thuna's 1967 *The Natural Look*, which closed on opening night despite a cast that also included Gene Hackman, Doris Roberts, Brenda Vaccaro, and Dolph Sweet; and Bob Randall's 1973 comedy *6 Rms Rv Vu* with Jane Alexander, which ran six months. As far as Broadway was concerned, Orbach was exclusively a musical star.

Nevertheless, Orbach didn't fall for the trappings of stardom. When he finally moved out of his Greenwich Village apartment, it wasn't to Greenwich, Connecticut, or to Malibu, but to Manhattan's Hell's Kitchen, the working-class neighborhood between Times Square and the Hudson River piers that has undergone repeated transformations. Once the locale for many of Damon Runyon's *Guys and Dolls* stories about gamblers and small-time criminals, it is substantially gentrified today and rechristened "Clinton." In the 1970s, when Orbach moved there, it was grimy and run-down but not quite a slum. There were still bars and pool halls where he could relax, and grimy movie houses (some of which still showed mainstream films) on Forty-second Street where he could watch pictures until the wee hours, smoking cigarettes and debating the pictures' merits.

He rarely sought—or attracted—publicity. He went through a divorce from Curro in 1958 and took a second wife, Broadway dancer Elaine Cancilla, and remained married to her for the rest of his life. They lived in an apartment near the corner of Fifty-third Street and Eighth Avenue. After Orbach's death, New York Mayor Michael Bloomberg renamed a section of Fifty-third Street at Eighth Avenue "Jerry Orbach Way."

Orbach did have one tabloid moment—he was seen partying with mafia chieftain "Crazy Joe" Gallo on April 7, 1972, just hours before Gallo was shot to death in an infamous mob-war incident at Umberto's Clam House in Little Italy. Orbach and Gallo had been friends since Orbach played "Kid Sally" Palumbo, a role based on Gallo, in the movie *The Gang That Couldn't Shoot Straight*. But Orbach generally kept his personal life out of the headlines.

Royalty

Orbach's next musical, *Chicago*, was a morality tale, too. But in this version, Orbach's character was clearly allied with the forces of wrong. Yet in a show whose morals were completely topsy-turvy, that made him the hero. The inverted moral of the story is that in 1920s Chicago, where the courts, the media, even the institution of marriage itself were so pervasively corrupted, everything had become a kind of tawdry showbiz. "Razzle-dazzle 'em," said Fred Ebb's lyric, "and they'll never catch wise."

The original production is today overshadowed by the hugely successful 1996 revival, which was still running when this book went to press, not to mention the Oscar-winning film version. When the public thinks of crooked, manipulative lawyer Billy Flynn, they tend to think of suave James Naughton from Broadway or even more suave Richard Gere from the movie.

As conceived by Bob Fosse and performed by Orbach in the 1976 original, Flynn was abrasive, mustached, cigared, and homburged. If he looked like an aggressive vaudeville clown, that's because Fosse had imagined the show as "A Musical Vaudeville," as per its subtitle (later dropped), in which each number by Ebb and John Kander would be played like a different species of variety act.

Even in a show whose virtually every character song is a full-throated lie, Orbach's big introductory solo, "All I Care About Is Love" stands out. He proclaims the sanctity and purity of his motives even as he's doing a striptease behind huge feathered fans like Sally Rand.

His client Roxie Hart (Gwen Verdon) is on trial for murdering her husband, and Flynn ruthlessly uses every dirty bomb in his legal arsenal to get her off. He's particularly adept at manipulating the press, and in the press conference number "We Both Reached for the Gun," he had Gwen Verdon sitting on his lap twisting, turning, and lip-synching her answers to reporters' questions in a falsetto as if she were his puppet—which, of course, she was.

The glittering cynicism of the show may have been a little too much for 1970s audiences. The show was nominated for eleven Tony Awards but lost in all categories, mainly to *A Chorus Line*. Still, it was a peak experience for Orbach. There were few enough shows that featured two of this book's Greatest Stars. *Chicago* had three: Orbach, Verdon, and Chita Rivera. They were all getting older—Orbach turned forty while working on the show—but Orbach was now standing alongside Broadway royalty.

In 1980 David Merrick was assembling what would be his biggest and final hit, a stage adaptation of the classic 1933 backstage film *42nd Street*. As director he engaged Gower Champion, and to complete the *Carnival!* reunion he hired Orbach to play the superhuman director Julian Marsh, the role originated onscreen by Warner Baxter. The showbiz legend tells the story of Peggy Sawyer, a chorus girl from Allentown, Pennsylvania, who finds herself called upon to step in for the injured leading lady on the opening night of a big Broadway musical, on whose success everyone is depending for their very livelihoods. "You're going out there a chorus kid," Marsh tells Sawyer in the film's iconic line, "but you've got to come back a star!"

Champion and Merrick agreed that there were few Broadway leading men at the time with the stature and presence to deliver the line straight and without camp so that it landed the way it was supposed to. And yet, at the same time, the actor had to be able to kick his way through the classic "Lullaby of Broadway." Orbach could (and he would do on commercials in the New York area for years to come).

Orbach was discreet enough to look the other way when Champion, still married to his longtime dance partner Marge, engaged in an affair with *42nd Street*'s pert leading lady, Wanda Richert, during the show's Washington, D.C., tryout and Broadway previews. Champion had another secret, too. He was suffering from a condition described as a rare form of blood cancer. In exactly the kind of showbiz coincidence that would not have seemed out of place in *42nd Street* itself, Champion died the morning of the opening, August 25, 1980, and Merrick decided not to tell anyone in the cast so they could have a triumphant opening night, which they did. As the applause was dying, Merrick came forward to center stage, hushed the crowd, and, standing in front of the cast, flanked by Richert and Orbach, announced that Champion was dead.

In the stunned moments following, it was Orbach who had the presence of mind to call for the Winter Garden stagehands to ring down the curtain on the sobbing actors.

Orbach's Annuity

During the 1980s Orbach began working more and more in TV and films. He just wasn't right for the big pop operas that were popular at the time. Instead, he settled for character roles—often as detectives, doctors, or other authority figures—in films including *Dirty Dancing* (as Jennifer Grey's father), *Brewster's Millions*, and *Prince of the City*. Woody Allen cast him as Jack Rosenthal, a criminal hired to kill his brother's mistress, in his 1989 film *Crimes and Misdemeanors*.

As the years went on, it became apparent that *42nd Street* would be his last Broadway show. However, theatre fans were thrown a bone when he supplied the suave French accent for Lumiere, the amorous enchanted candlestick, in the Oscar-nominated animated film musical *Beauty and the Beast*. He was the lead singer on the animated film's Broadwayesque hit song "Be Our Guest."

Orbach had been working increasingly on TV during the 1980s, and had already made numerous guest appearances on shows like *Murder, She Wrote*, *Simon & Simon*, and *Tales from the Darkside*. But shortly afterward he read for the role of Detective Leonard "Lennie" Briscoe on a new crime show, to be called *Law & Order*. Shot in New York, the show (and most of its numerous spinoffs) eventually became known as a virtual employment office for Broadway actors over the better part of the next two decades, and it was especially congenial to Orbach, who became one of the leads and appeared in hundreds of episodes.

Orbach had played a lawyer during the show's second season but introduced the Briscoe character in its third (1992). Briscoe's hangdog looks and world-weary attitude as senior detective of the New York City Police Department's Twenty-seventh Precinct contrasted with his constant wisecracks. Writers Walon Green and Rene Balcer gave him a history of two divorces, a struggle with booze, and complicated relationships with his two daughters, one of whom was killed by crooks during the run of the show. His persistence and humor in the face of these very dark demons made him one of the series' most popular characters. Bravo TV voted Detective Briscoe the thirtieth greatest character of TV history. The New York Landmark Conservancy named Orbach himself a "living landmark" of New York City in 2002.

He finally achieved most of what he wanted: acclaim on his own terms, playing a meaty role set in a tough, masculine world. And the show went on and on, providing him with the annuity he'd craved. He didn't even have to tour. Briscoe is how Orbach is known to most of the world.

Orbach didn't get to enjoy his annuity as long as he should have. He was diagnosed with prostate cancer in the late 1990s. On March 26, 2004, during his twelfth season with the *Law & Order* franchise (as an original cast member on *Law & Order: Trial by Jury*), he made a brief announcement that he was withdrawing from the show due to illness. He died of the disease on December 28, 2004.

He had outlived the original production of *The Fantasticks* by nearly three years. But *The Fantasticks* never forgot him. The musical was revived in 2006 at a new two-theatre complex called the Snapple Center at the corner of Broadway and Fiftieth Street, within view of the Winter Garden, where he'd starred in *42nd Street*. In spring 2007, the space where *The Fantasticks* was playing was rechristened the Jerry Orbach Theatre.

Angela Lansbury in the title role of *Mame* (1966). PHOTOFEST

ANGELA LANSBURY
Open a New Window

Broadway offered a bright second career to Angela Lansbury, and she took it.

A wartime refugee from her native England, she was an immediate hit in films, earning Oscar nominations for her first two movie performances and then settling into a Hollywood career that lasted the better part of two decades. She was already in her late thirties when she made her Broadway debut and in her forties when she had her first Broadway smash, in *Mame*.

Having spent her ingenue years on the West Coast, she never went through a sexy-young-thing era on Broadway and thus never had to live up to it. In the eyes of most theatergoers, she had always been a classy older dame. She quickly snapped up fab older women roles in the 1960s and 1970s: Mame, Mama Rose, Mrs. Lovett, Cora T. Hooper.

Lansbury made good use of her wide, bright, deep-set eyes; pinchable cheeks; sparkling native English accent (though she mastered enough regional accents to earn a nod from Henry Higgins); and her highly defined, animated physical style. In her nineteen-year career in musical comedy, 1964–83, she made a memorable impact and won four Tony Awards, all as Best Actress in a Musical. A formidable competitor, she won every single time she was nominated during those years.

When the work began coming less frequently, she pulled up stakes once again and headed Left to California, where she established yet a *third* career, on TV in the long-running series *Murder, She Wrote*.

She proved herself a master of all media, creating major roles and winning major awards in television and movies, as well. She also proved herself immune from the curse of many stage performers: being diminished on the screen.

But because she picked such tough, big stage roles and assayed them with such power, glamour, and unerring command, she was embraced by Broadway as one of its own. She played the role of theatrical grande dame magnificently and fully earned her place in this book. But she was never true to the stage.

★

Lansbury was born October 16, 1925, into a theatrical family on her mother's side. Her grandfather was a director of the Belfast Opera; her mother, Moyna Lansbury, was an actress of minor repute who inculcated in her children a love of musical theatre. She became a widow with four children in the depths of the Depression when Angela was just nine years old. The family got on with help from the grandparents, and in 1939 Angela was accepted into the Webber-Douglas School of Singing and Dramatic Art, where she blossomed, playing her first Shakespearean role, Audrey, in *As You Like It*.

Her education was interrupted by the outbreak of World War II and the Blitz. Moyna fled with Angela to New York, where the girl began taking classes at Feagin School for Drama and Radio. Legendary agent Audrey Wood spotted the now lovely sixteen-year-old Angela playing the title role in the 1941 school production of Oscar Wilde's *Lady Winde-mere's Fan* and began sending her out on professional auditions. Angela and her mother had only modest luck in New York, so, after earning her green card, Moyna again uprooted her family and moved them to Hollywood.

Angela made three films during her first two years in Hollywood, two of which earned her Oscar nominations: *Gaslight* and *The Picture of Dorian Gray*. For those who think of Lansbury only as matronly, a few minutes with *The Harvey Girls* (1946) will demonstrate what a dish she was during her ingenue period. The camera seemed to love her round face, high cheekbones, and expressive eyes with their drooping lids.

But plum roles rarely came her way after that. For most of the next two decades she worked fairly steadily in Hollywood's middle ground. Almost never the star, she was usually the girlfriend or sister (and later, mother) of the main character. Among some of the highlights: *Till the Clouds Roll By, Samson and Delilah, The Dark at the Top of the Stairs* and *The Court Jester*. In Jester she played opposite Danny Kaye in the hilarious "The pellet with the poison's in the vessel with the pestle" scene. She even earned one more Oscar nomination, as the coldblooded mother who uses her own son in a plot to suborn the U.S. government in *The Manchurian Candidate*.

It was a film career successful by almost any standard, but it wasn't a star career. As she passed her thirtieth birthday and glimpsed the fortieth on the horizon without leading-role credits, Lansbury began to look afield from Los Angeles.

Her new career came literally out of the blue in 1963—in the form of a small blue envelope that she treasured for many years afterward. It was a letter from Broadway librettist Arthur Laurents, asking if she'd like to star in a new musical called *Anyone Can Whistle*, which he was writing with Stephen Sondheim. Lansbury had appeared twice on Broadway in the years leading up to the offer: with master clown Bert Lahr in George Feydeau's sex farce *Hotel Paradiso*, and as a lusty mom in Shelagh Delaney's drama *A Taste of Honey*.

But *Anyone Can Whistle* represented a major new challenge, requiring her to sing and dance. Laurents and Sondheim had worked together as librettist and lyricist, respectively, on two of the great hits of the 1950s, *West Side Story* and *Gypsy*. Sondheim, who was on his way to the most distinguished theatre composing career of the late twentieth century, had just enjoyed a hit writing both music and lyrics to *A Funny Thing Happened on the Way to the Forum. Anyone Can Whistle* was the disquieting tale of a broken-down little town whose only solvent business is its insane asylum but that seeks to change its fortunes by staging a phony miracle—a rock that spouts water—and cashing in on the resulting flocks of suckers. The story featured a viciously corrupt "mayoress" (Lansbury), a sexually repressed asylum nurse (Lee Remick), and a fearless doctor (Harry Guardino) who tries to confront the mayoress and win the heart of the nurse—until it is discovered that he is a mental patient who has been mistaken for a doctor.

"In an attempt to be meaningful it forgets to offer much entertainment," wrote Howard Taubman in the *New York Times*. Many also saw brilliance in Sondheim's writing, and in Lansbury's performance as Mayoress Cora Hoover Hooper. Walter Kerr in the *Herald Tribune* called her "a creature who can toss her head, her arms, and her shapely legs until the sparkle from her bracelets and the sparkle from her earrings seems one and the same sparkle."

The show might not have been the clear-cut starring role she sought, but she found that she managed to have some fun despite the grueling Philadelphia tryout and heartbreakingly brief nine-performance run. She *liked* working on the stage. The project also marked the beginning of a long and fruitful collaboration with Sondheim. As his star rose, so would hers.

It's Today

There were a dozen reasons why making a musical based on Patrick Dennis's book *Auntie Mame* in the mid-1960s seemed to be a bad idea. Number one was the fact that the ticket-buying public was already familiar with the story from the 1956 stage adaptation and the 1958 film, both also called *Auntie Mame*. Number two was the fact that both of those versions had starred Rosalind Russell, who had become identified with the role of the devil-may-care 1920s flapper who finds herself suddenly having to care for her orphaned nephew and incorporates the wide-eyed boy into her flamboyant lifestyle.

Russell herself turned down the part in the musical, saying she had wrung everything out of it there was to wring.

Enter composer Jerry Herman, who was riding the wave of success that followed *Hello, Dolly!* Carol Channing had been the star of that show, but she turned down the chance to play Mame, saying (through her husband) that the role was too similar to Dolly.

Lansbury flew back to New York from her home in Malibu to audition. She shared the limelight with Lee Remick in *Anyone Can Whistle*, but she knew she would be the unquestioned comedic and romantic star of *Mame*. And while there were some initial questions about the strength of her singing voice and her box office drawing power, she landed the role and snapped her fingers in the face of her doubters by handling the toughest vocal challenges Herman could throw at her.

Lansbury became closely identified with the strutting title song—even though she didn't sing it. It was sung to her by the adoring male chorus, just as the title song in *Dolly!* had been sung to Channing. Lansbury delighted audiences with the holiday song "We Need a

Little Christmas," which became a standard; inspired audiences with the anthem "Open a New Window"; and broke hearts with the torchy "If He Walked into My Life."

Costumer Robert Mackintosh wrapped her in the most fashionable clothes, makeup artists suddenly discovered the classic features of her face, her fluting voice suddenly seemed quirky and lively and perfect. She not only embodied Mame, she made audiences forget Russell, who now seemed like merely a first draft for the *real* Mame.

"Angela Lansbury is the match of any previous Mame," wrote Norman Nadel in the *World Journal*. Stanley Kauffmann in the *New York Times* wrote, "No one can be surprised to learn that Angela Lansbury is an accomplished actress, but not all of us may know that she has an adequate singing voice, can dance trimly, and can combine all these matters into a musical *performance*. . . . In this marathon role she has wit, poise, warmth, and a very taking coolth [*sic*]."

At age forty-one, Lansbury finally had the big starring role and the big hit she had dreamed of. Lansbury would play many roles in the years to come, but Mame was her Lola, her King of Siam, her Man of La Mancha. In 1966, *Mame* won the Tony Award as Best Musical and Lansbury won the Tony as Best Actress in a Musical. Hollywood had always dangled, then snatched away its highest accolade. Broadway welcomed her with open arms and placed its diadem upon her brow.

When Jerry Herman offered Lansbury his next musical, she jumped on it. *Dear World* was based on Jean Giradoux's whimsical play *The Madwoman of Chaillot*, written in Paris during its occupation by the Nazis. A group of Left Bank street people and eccentrics, led by the title character, decide to destroy all the evil people of the world—including politicians, generals, and industrialists—by luring them into her cellar and sending them down a bottomless pit she keeps down there.

Perhaps inspired by the political activism of the 1960s, Herman and *Mame* librettists Jerome Lawrence and Robert E. Lee also saw the story as a parable about the need to protect the environment. Lansbury got to sing another anthem of hope, "Tomorrow Morning," and a beautiful ballad, "Kiss Her Now," urging a young man not to let the love of his life get away. But the theme was similar to that of *Anyone Can Whistle*—the Madwoman was the sanest person in Paris—and the environmental theme seemed grafted on uneasily. Whether the material wasn't suitable or tastes were just changing, *Dear World* was a flop. Lansbury won her second Tony Award for the show, but it ran a disappointing few months and closed at a loss.

Nevertheless, Lansbury had established an identity as a musical comedy *star*, which led to her starring in a semianimated feature film fantasy, *Bedknobs and Broomsticks*, written for her by the *Mary Poppins* composing team of Richard M. and Robert B. Sherman.

In 1974 Lansbury appeared in a London revival of *Gypsy*, the first major production of the show since Ethel Merman's original. With Merman still alive, would audience accept this daring assault on her signature role?

Absolutely, as it turned out. Despite the financial failure of *Anyone Can Whistle*, Lansbury had remained friends with librettist Laurents and lyricist Sondheim. Now they were delighted to help her find her own way through the role considered the *Hamlet* of musical theatre roles for women. This was the first production where, at the conclusion of the devastating eleven-o'clock number "Rose's Turn," Rose bowed at the end, as if stepping out of character to accept the audience's applause—but then continued to bow and bow, even as the applause died away, until it became apparent that she wasn't responding to the audience's applause, but to the applause in her own mind. With that gesture, she rendered the audience imaginary. It was a coup de theatre and became a permanent part of the productions Laurents would direct.

The production moved to Broadway, where it won Lansbury her third Tony Award as Best Actress in a Musical.

Lansbury had by now scaled the heights and could easily have rested on her laurels, accepting one glamorous, stylish leading role after another. Instead, in 1979 she accepted the most difficult role of her career: Nellie Lovett, the antiglamorous cannibalistic baker of meat pies in Sondheim's Grand Guignol masterpiece, *Sweeney Todd: The Demon Barber of Fleet Street*. Len Cariou (and later George Hearn) played the revenge-seeking nineteenth-century London barber who, deprived of his chance to kill the evil judge who ruined his life, turns his razor on the rest of mankind. The quandary of what to do with the bodies is solved by Mrs. Lovett, who turns the bodies into luscious, juicy meat pies.

There are so many ways Lansbury could have done the part wrong, making the role tasteless (so to speak) or purely disgusting. Instead, she assembled her single greatest achievement as an actress—a characterization that was at once desperate and innocent, nauseating and adorable. With her hair twisted up into two little braids that looked a bit like horns, and wearing heavy makeup that made her look a bit like a clown and a bit like a cadaver, she used a piping cockney accent that made everything she said, even the most horrifying things, sound sort of sweet. Always a physical actress, she danced around the set like a little girl, full of excitement at her mischievous plan and how well it works at first.

Fully cognizant of all her strongest suits, Sondheim wrote her a score full of wonderful songs that start with her triumphant entrance, when she sang "The Worst Pies in London," which used the percussive sounds of her hands slapping dough and swatting cockroaches to punctuate a song about how bad her business has become. In Act II, her lullaby "Not While I'm Around" showed her trying to calm a dimwitted young man who suspects the worst. She's warmhearted and motherly toward him, even knitting him a scarf, but she makes it clear to Sweeney that she'd just as soon cold-bloodedly send him to join all the other former customers.

One of her greatest moments in the role comes in the Act I finale, a duet with her co-conspirator, in which they try to imagine how people from different walks of life will taste. Actors, it is noted, always arrive "overdone." But in such an extreme role, Lansbury was never overdone. She walked a tightrope over a shark pit and succeeded. Audiences found themselves in the uncomfortable quandary of liking her and rooting for her to succeed . . . but then coming up against the damned work she was trying to succeed at. Which is precisely the balance Sondheim, librettist Hugh Wheeler, and director Hal Prince had hoped to achieve. Mrs. Lovett eventually got her comeuppance—but Lansbury got her fourth Tony Award as Best Actress in a Musical.

Looking back on her performance from 2002, Ben Brantley of the *New York Times* wrote that Lansbury's "creation of Mrs. Lovett was the high point in a career filled with pinnacles."

The embarrassing flop of a 1983 *Mame* revival helped push her into the third *and (so far) final* phase of her career, television. As far as money and recognition by the general public go, it was also the most successful phase.

Murder, She Wrote was an anthology show about a mystery writer named Jessica Fletcher who finds herself solving real-life murder mysteries. The show turned out to be one of the most successful of its era, running from 1984 to 1996 in more than 260 episodes. Lansbury was nominated for Emmy Awards as Outstanding Lead Actress in a Drama Series twelve times, once for every year the series was eligible. She won Golden Globe Awards for the role in 1985, 1987, 1990, and 1992.

In the 1990s Lansbury was in an enviable position. When she was on the West Coast, she was the beloved star of a hit TV series. When she was on the East Coast, she was, if not queen of Broadway, certainly one of its revered duchesses. Being accepted in both worlds led to assignments like hosting the Tony Awards, guest appearances, starring in Jerry Herman's TV musical *Mrs. Santa Claus*, and providing the voice for Mrs. Potts, the enchanted teapot in Disney's animated feature film *Beauty and the Beast*. She sang the lovely title ballad, which earned the Oscar as Best Original Song.

In the late 1990s, with *Murder, She Wrote* having finally run its course, Lansbury set her cap set for Broadway once again. The project was a dark, *Sweeney Todd*–like musical called *The Visit*, based on the drama by Friedrich Dürrenmatt, about a rich but embittered courtesan who returns to the small French village of her youth determined at last to get revenge on the man who set her on the path of sin.

The score, written by John Kander and Fred Ebb, songwriters of *Cabaret* and *Chicago*, was full of the glittering menace that had made those shows such hits. A tryout tour was in the planning when Peter Shaw, Lansbury's husband of nearly fifty years, fell ill. Lansbury postponed, and withdrew from, *The Visit*, saying she could not leave her husband's side. He died January 29, 2003, by which time Chita Rivera had replaced her in the Chicago tryout.

In October 2006, Broadway was startled by the announcement that Lansbury would be making stage encore the following spring in a new play by Terrence McNally. Titled *Deuce*, it was a portrait of two retired tennis pros, doubles partners and pioneers of the women's tennis circuit, who look back on their lives and careers from the stands of a tournament where they are being honored for their contribution to the sport. Lansbury played the slightly more aggressive of the two, who blames herself for losing them a key tournament. She and Marian Seldes received mainly glowing reviews, but the play itself was dismissed as thin soup. Lansbury earned a Tony nomination as Best Actress in a Play, her first in that category. It was also the first time she lost a Tony Award.

Lansbury was surprised at the play's dismissal, and soon after the opening she gave an interview in which she said of her stage career, "This is it for me. . . . People have no idea what eight shows a week are. It's OK when you're young—but at 81. . . ."

Ah, but the lure of Broadway still exerted a strange power. Two years later she was back in rehearsal to play Madame Arcati, the dotty medium in a revival of Noël Coward's *Blithe Spirit* at the Shubert Theatre.

She was home.

Bernadette Peters as Emma in *Song and Dance* (1985).

BERNADETTE PETERS
Look What Happened to Mabel

Forever youthful, Bernadette Peters was Broadway's sweetheart for nearly four decades, bringing her curvy figure, rosebud mouth, mane of curly hair, and velveted-steel voice to roles as diverse as movie star, artist's model, British immigrant, sharpshooter, and dragon stage mother.

She wasn't an intellectual but could play one. She was always heartfelt. She was one of the most professional performers on Broadway. She learned new material very fast and made it sound great. As a result, everyone wanted to work with her. Jerry Herman wrote for her the part of Mabel in *Mack & Mabel*. Andrew Lloyd Webber picked her to play Emma in the Broadway premiere of *Song and Dance*. Marvin Hamlisch and Neil Simon wrote for her Paula in *The Goodbye Girl*. Stephen Sondheim wrote her two roles, more than any of his other female stars: Dot in *Sunday in the Park with George* and the Witch in *Into the Woods*.

Peters was not a great ad-libber or extemporizer. There are few interviews in which she sounds brilliant or introspective. But she could bring a tremendous amount of complexity to any role and was an enormously resourceful and flexible actress.

Peters kept her baby-doll looks for decades. Could there be a portrait in the attic somewhere doing all the aging for her? Still sexy in her sixties, she looked decades younger, which enabled her to play ingenue and leading-lady roles long past when most other actresses had gone over to character parts.

★

Bernadette Lazzara was born February 28, 1948, to an Italian-American family in Ozone Park, part of the borough of Queens in New York City. She was the baby of the family, the youngest of three, and her mother, Marguerite, recognized her talent early. How early? When she was just three, her mom secured her a spot on *Juvenile Jury*, an NBC-TV panel show featuring precocious kids trying to help solve other kids' problems, like whether an eleven-year-old girl should wear makeup.

Mrs. Lazzara got little Bernadette some dance lessons while securing her work on early 1950s New York–based TV shows like *The Horn and Hardart Children's Hour* and even *Name That Tune*. At age nine, Bernadette earned membership in Actors Equity, taking a version of her father's first name (Peter) as her new last name. She made her Broadway debut just short of her eleventh birthday in a revival of *The Most Happy Fella*, playing Tessie. When she was a teenager, Peters was enrolled in the Quintano School for Young Professionals, where she got more formal training.

When she was thirteen, she appeared in a national touring company of *Gypsy*, understudying the role of Dainty June. She says the experience working on that show (in which she would eventually star more than forty years later) helped convinced her that her future lay on the stage. After high school, she began the usual rounds of auditions, earning roles in the off-Broadway musicals *The Penny Friend* (1966) and *Curley McDimple* (1967). In the latter, a parody of excessively optimistic Shirley Temple movie musicals, the nineteen-year-old Peters played the supporting role of a vaudevillian that Curley wants to adopt as her mother. She had a couple of nice featured numbers, including the duets "I Try" and "The Meanest Man in Town," plus the solo "Love Is the Loveliest Song." The show ran more than two years—Peters's first hit.

She returned to Broadway as a standby in the four-performance Broadway comedy *The Girl in the Freudian Slip* and played Bettina in the drama *Johnny No-Trump*, which closed on opening night. At age twenty, she was the veteran of three Broadway flops and one off-Broadway hit. Her energy and Kewpie-doll prettiness helped land her first featured Broadway role, that of Josie Cohan, sister of George M. Cohan in the tribute musical *George M!*, which ran a year and showed Broadway that she could hold her own with the likes of Joel Grey. She earned a Theatre World Award for her promising performance.

She followed that with a personal triumph, playing Ruby in the 1968 off-Broadway musical *Dames at Sea*. Like *The Boy Friend* and *Little Mary Sunshine*, it offered a parody of an older musical style, in this case early 1930s *Gold Diggers* films. With makeup and costuming to emphasize her baby face, she stopped the show with the lament "It's Raining in My Heart," causing audiences simultaneously to laugh along with the parody and cry along with the sentiment. The performance made people realize that there was something special and classic about Peters as a stage performer. Like certain others of her generation (e.g., Nathan Lane), her combination of talent and personality seemed to tap into the showbiz spirit of an earlier time on Broadway.

But it would take several years and several tries before Peters finally had her Broadway hit. She had the leading role of Gelsomina in Lionel Bart's musical adaptation of the Fellini film *La strada*, which closed on opening night in 1969. She then moved on to play Hildy the randy cabdriver in director Ron Field's listless 1971 revival of *On the Town*, which ran two months.

Mack & Mabel

In 1974 it looked like she'd finally hit the jackpot. Jerry Herman, whose *Hello, Dolly!* had starred Carol Channing and whose *Mame* and *Dear World* had starred Angela Lansbury, chose Peters for the lead in his next show, *Mack & Mabel*, a musical biography of silent film director Mack Sennett and his star female clown, Mabel Normand, who also became his lover. Peters (age twenty-six) would have as her leading man the Music Man himself, Robert Preston (age fifty-six). The show opened in the early 1970s period when Broadway was in a deep recession, with audiences afraid to approach a Times Square that had gone from seedy to outright dangerous. But hungry fans licked their chops at the thought of getting to see a musical comedy with so much old-fashioned star power.

Peters did bear a resemblance to Normand, with her mop of curls, pouty lips, and strong chin. But director Gower Champion made the mistake of opening the show with a clip of an actual Mack Sennett silent film comedy, to accompany the song "Movies Were Movies." Nothing in the rest of the show was able to top that. Among other things, it was hard to fully re-create the stunts and pratfalls of silent film onstage.

Peters did her best. When Mabel makes her entrance as a delivery girl, you could see both her gawkiness and her potential. You saw what Sennett saw. And you saw her mature into a star during the song "Look What Happened to Mabel." Peters also got to rage through "Wherever He Ain't," sparkle through "When Mabel Comes in the Room," and put a sob into the throbbing torch song "Time Heals Everything."

Herman has said that *Mack & Mabel* was his favorite score, but the book remained a problem. Normand and Sennett may have been the loves of each others lives, but their affair was comparatively brief and they went their separate ways, never to reunite. That made for a dodgy Act II, and the problem has never been completely solved through many years of rewrites and new editions.

In the end, *Mack & Mabel* disappointed nearly everyone and ran a scant two months.

Sunday in the Park with George

Peters's next Broadway project was *Sunday in the Park with George*, a musical based not on a book or a story or a film, but on a painting. After a long association with director Harold Prince, composer Stephen Sondheim had formed a collaboration with playwright and director James Lapine. They shared a fascination with the painting *A Sunday Afternoon on the Island of La Grand Jatte*, by French artist Georges Seurat (known simply as George in the show). Seurat, who had a brief life and career in late nineteenth-century Paris, was a proponent of Pointillism, a style in which the painter renders images in thousands of tiny dots, not much different from pixels in a digital photograph, but all done by hand. The colors are basic; the eye mixes them in the brain into tints and images.

Peters was engaged to play the large figure with the parasol on the right side of the painting, whom Lapine and Sondheim imagined was Seurat's model and muse. They whimsically christened her "Dot." As was the case with Mabel Normand, Peters bore a sisterly resemblance to the woman in Seurat's *Young Woman Powdering Herself*, and that painting is quoted in the staging for Peters's part of the song "Color and Light."

Sunday in the Park presented Peters with several challenges. Part of being a star is the ability to attract and hold the eye, to be *looked* at without becoming self-conscious. Peters used that ability to great effect in *Sunday in the Park with George* when she was playing an artist's model. She needed to be the kind of person you could simply gaze at. Peters's face was like a porcelain mask, constantly catching the light. She could look cold and withdrawn when she was angry in the Act I studio scenes, but appeared radiant when she smiled at the end of Act II.

The show is as much about Dot's journey of self-discovery as it is about Seurat's coming to terms with his obsession with painting. It also turns out to be a show about reincarnation and ghosts, both concepts taking for granted the indestructibility of individual human spirits. George in Act I turns out to be reborn as his own great-grandson, also named George, in Act II, set a century later. Young George has a close relationship with his grandmother, Dot and George's daughter, also played by Peters in age makeup.

PBS taped one of the final performances of *Sunday in the Park with George* for its "Great Performances" series, thereby preserving one of her best roles in almost exactly the form she gave it. Creatively directed for TV by Terry Hughes, the film captures tiny but masterful brushstrokes in Peters' performance, such as when Dot locks gazes with Seurat in the song "Sunday" just before he freezes her into the painting, or during "Color and Light" when she's gazing into her mirror as the lyric talks about "the wide eyes staring at the round face and the tiny pout," lines that were written by Sondheim especially for the painting and her. It's a marvelous artifact of 1980s Broadway at its best.

Song and Dance

Having worked for Herman and Sondheim, Peters was next approached by the most popular composer of his era, Andrew Lloyd Webber, to play the central character in his diptych musical *Song and Dance*, which combined his two short pieces *Tell Me on a Sunday* (1979), a one-act musical about an English gel's adventures in America, and "Variations" for cello and rock band, a dance piece. *Tell Me on a Sunday* was written for English actress Marti Webb, who debuted it in London, but it was felt that the show needed an American talent for Broadway, and the show was substantially rewritten around Peters.

As it turned out, the show itself was widely panned as superficial. Emma is sort of a British Sweet Charity: she meanders from man to man, always exploited and abandoned but forever optimistic about the future and about her changes of finding love. Peters brought the role all the sexiness and vulnerability it required. The character wasn't terribly bright and therefore needed to be adorable to be sympathetic. And being adorable was always Peters's strong suit.

John Simon of *New York Magazine* wrote, "She not only sings and acts and (in the bottom half) dances to perfection she also, superlatively, *is*."

After more than two decades on Broadway, Peters finally brought home her first Tony Award as Best Actress in a Musical for the role.

Into the Woods

In 1987 Sondheim and Lapine approached her again about taking a major role in their next musical, *Into the Woods*, which set out to show that many well-known fairy tales, like "Jack and the Beanstalk," "Cinderella," "Little Red Riding Hood," and "Rapunzel," were all just episodes of a larger story. All the stories involve a witch in some way, so Sondheim and Lapine decided it was all the same witch, named the Witch, and this role they envisioned for Peters. But the witches were almost all ugly, too. And if you wanted ugly, you usually didn't go to Peters. Ah, but they had that all thought out. She was an ugly crone in Act I and full of powerful magic. In Act II she was transformed into a glittering beauty (that is, she took off her hag makeup)—but only at the cost of losing her powers.

Peters was an unusual witch in many ways. For one thing, she rapped. Rap music had emerged in the late 1970s, and a decade later it was taking over pop music. Sondheim thought the 'tude perfect for his witch character, who raps about her garden. She can be petulant, impatient, and condescending, but she also is the one who always tells the truth.

The Goodbye Girl

In 1993 Peters took the lead in the Broadway musical *The Goodbye Girl*, based on comedy master Neil Simon's film of the same title about a single-mom Broadway dancer with a young daughter who is forced by economic circumstances to share an apartment with a self-centered actor, played onstage by comedian Martin Short. Although it was another of Simon's *Odd Couple* plots, like *The Sunshine Boys* having a theatrical setting, it proved resistant to musicalization. *A Chorus Line* composer Marvin Hamlisch and budding *City of Angels* lyricist David Zippel should have been able to put together a blockbuster, especially with those stars. But the whole proceeding seemed creaky and old-fashioned, despite some juicy moments for both the stars, including "A Beat Behind," in which Peters is shown huffing and puffing her way through a strenuous dance class.

The show had to work through its troubles in a fishbowl, because one of the New York television stations had decided to follow every step of this can't-miss hit from behind the scenes and wound up only chronicling its slow-motion crash and burn. It was Peters's last original Broadway musical role to date.

Other Media

In addition to her stage work, Peters worked extensively in movies and did many concert tours, voiceovers, and recordings, performing several times at Carnegie Hall and other large venues.

She had a close relationship with comedian Steve Martin, and they appeared as lovers in two of his best films, *The Jerk* and *Pennies from Heaven*. In the first they share a romantic moment chirping an adorable little love song to each other—then puncture the sweetness when Peters hauls out a trumpet and takes a blaring solo right in the middle of it.

Peters starred opposite Andy Kaufman in the oddball *Heartbeeps*, about two robots (in bizarrely off-putting makeup) who fall in love. She also played a Lola-like femme fatale in Mel Brooks's *Silent Movie*, which included one of Brooks's greatest crude sight gags. A group of bad guys are sitting around a heavy wooden conference table plotting Brooks's destruction. The movie's villain announces that he has a secret weapon that will bring about Brooks's downfall. He unveils a full-length picture of the voluptuous Peters in extremely abbreviated dress. As the men contemplate this vision, the huge table levitates about six inches.

Producer Steven Spielberg arranged for Peters to lend her voice to his 1993 animation project *Animaniacs*, which sought to revive the fun, action, and intelligent writing of the classic Bugs Bunny–era Hollywood cartoons. Peters voiced Rita, a homeless singing kitty who has adventures with Runt, a not-excessively-bright dog who never harms Rita because he thinks she's a pup like him.

Keeping Peters grounded in all this was her marriage to investment adviser Michael Wittenberg. They exchanged vows in 1996 at the home of her friend Mary Tyler Moore, with whom she would start the pet-adoption charity Broadway Barks. In 1999 Peters told *Playbill* that her marriage was "great. It's been like this secure, rooted place, so it allows my tree to branch out. I've never worked as much since I've been married, taking risks and doing things."

The Merman Roles

Over the next few years, Peters took on two of the biggest female roles in the Broadway canon, both of them originated by Ethel Merman.

In 1999 it was a revival of *Annie Get Your Gun*, using a revised version of the Herbert and Dorothy Fields libretto by Peter Stone that took some of the non-PC edge off the ending of the story, when Annie realizes she must lose the shooting contest to win her man. Peters's Annie Oakley was much younger and sexier than Broadway had seen. She was fully up to the brashness of the sharpshooting role, but she also made the character more endearing by playing her vulnerable side. Her soulful rendition of "They Say It's Wonderful" was one of the best of that number ever recorded. The performance won her the 1999 Tony Award as Best Actress in a Musical, even though some critics found her country accent a little on the shaky side. When Peters relinquished the role to Reba McEntire, praise for the country singer seemed to come at Peters's expense. But the cast album is exhibit A in defense of Peters's extraordinary work on the revival, which ran 1,045 performances, nearly matching the 1,147-performance original run.

Peters scaled the Mt. Everest of female musical comedy roles—Mama Rose in *Gypsy*, in a 2003 revival directed by Great Britain's Sam Mendes. She did so with the blessing of original librettist Arthur Laurents, who involved himself personally in all such revivals and later began directing them himself. She immediately found herself at odds with *New York Post* columnist Michael Riedel, who thought she was wrong for the part and began clocking the frequency of her absences for illness.

Peters's Rose was the least physically imposing of the five actresses who have played her on Broadway (Merman, Angela Lansbury, Tyne Daly, and Patti LuPone) but was the most flirtatious. There was much more of a cajoling aura to her pushiness than had been seen before. But her "Everything's Coming Up Roses" was more desperate and heartbreaking, and her "Rose's Turn," which she eventually performed on the Tony Awards, was grandly tragic. In addition to the Lear-like madness, she lets you glimpse how potent Rose herself might have been as a performer.

On September 26, 2005, Peters's husband was killed on a business trip in Montenegro when the helicopter in which he was riding crashed. They'd had no children. Peters had worked incessantly and hard until Wittenberg's death, after which she scaled back considerably, but she kept up participation in Broadway charity events and even appeared alongside Angela Lansbury and the stars of a dozen then-current Broadway shows to kick-start Broadway at the end of the 2007 stagehands strike. This is the final paragraph of her chapter, but I suspect we're in the midst of an intermission in her career, not at the final curtain.

Donna McKechnie rehearses as the Rose for the film *The Little Prince* (1974).
PHOTOFEST

DONNA McKECHNIE
The Music and the Mirror

Donna McKechnie has been a reluctant star. She was always ambitious about her dancing. Her drive and daring made her the darling (and, later, wife) of master choreographer Michael Bennett. She eventually became a kind of Gwen Verdon to his Bob Fosse (only not quite as amicable).

But the role of Cassie, based on her in the Pulitzer Prize–winning musical *A Chorus Line*, captured her conflict with eerie accuracy. Others saw her as a star and pushed her into lead roles. And as she's gotten older, she has been forced into more nondancing work, which has meant lead roles. But as the Ed Kleban/Marvin Hamlisch song "The Music and the Mirror" so eloquently put it, all she really wanted to do was dance.

She was born Donna Ruth McKechnie in Pontiac, Michigan, on November 16, 1942, and had a quiet unexceptional childhood until, she said, "I saw *The Red Shoes* [on TV] when I was seven and it changed my life drastically that night." The 1948 film, about an imperious dance master and a pair of magic shoes, proved to be a touchstone for many professional dancers of her generation. For McKechnie, however, it proved to be a subtext to her life. Coming full circle, her life would eventually become part of the *A Chorus Line* show and film, to inspire and instruct the next generation of dancers.

The young McKechnie begged her mother for classes and soon was installed at the side of a local ballet teacher who used a line of folding chairs as a barre. McKechnie showed a natural aptitude and quickly outgrew that school. Over the wishes of her father, who disapproved of her wasting her time on dance, her mother moved the girl to Roth and Berdon, an academy in Detroit that boasted as an alumna Joan Leslie, a hometown girl who had starred in Hollywood films. The school offered classes in ballet, tap, baton twirling, and elocution, and McKechnie took them all.

"Going to ballet class made me feel like I was living," she said.

McKechnie's father was self-employed and suffered chronic business problems, moving his family frequently in the Detroit area throughout her childhood. To help make the family's ends meet, the thirteen-year-old Donna began teaching dance to the younger students and soon had a roster of seventy-five pupils. "I tried to help out financially, really to earn his approval, but only got his resentment," she said. "I didn't realize how it made him feel: like he couldn't support his family."

While still in high school, McKechnie was offered a spot in a dance troupe that was planning to rehearse in New York, then go on a tour of one-night stands, mainly colleges, throughout the South. Seeing this as her ticket out of Detroit, McKechnie assumed her parents would allow her to drop out of school and go. When they instead resisted, she ran away from home with her boyfriend and headed for a friend's apartment in Manhattan. But her dad caught up with her and took her home. To throw a scare into the teenager, they took her before a family judge, who threatened to have her locked up if she ran away again. McKechnie defiantly called his bluff and told him she'd find a way to escape and run away again.

Seeing her determination, her parents finally relented and allowed her to go (sans boyfriend), expecting she'd soon get homesick and return. It didn't work out that way. Despite traveling with a station wagon and a U-Haul, the troupe was her first full professional experience away from home, and she loved it. When the tour concluded, McKechnie took a room at the YWCA at Eighth Avenue and Fiftieth Street, in the Broadway theatre district, and tried to figure out how she could support herself while trying to break into the world of classical ballet.

Still a kid, she made a few mistakes. One of her teachers arranged for her to have an audition for Lucia Chase, who managed the American Ballet Theatre's international touring company. Chase complimented McKechnie but told her she was too young for the company. Instead she invited her to study with ABT for a year, a rare opportunity. Naively, McKechnie failed to see it as a compliment and turned Chase down. McKechnie had a similar encounter with Radio City Music Hall, where she auditioned for the corps de ballet (now defunct) and was accepted. However, because there was so little actual dancing involved, McKechnie withdrew the day of dress rehearsal to take a job in summer stock at Carousel Theatre in Framingham, Massachusetts.

The job was not classical dance, as McKechnie aspired to, but instead it immersed her in Broadway-style musicals, including *South Pacific, Annie Get Your Gun,* and *Carousel,* working with stars like John Raitt, Howard Keel, and Ginger Rogers. The experience helped her to appreciate the technique involved in Broadway dancing and was followed by a national tour of *West Side Story,* choreographed by one of the modern masters, Jerome Robbins.

After the tour concluded, McKechnie was auditioning for an industrial show—a fully staged Broadway style extravaganza that functioned like a live infomercial in these days before cable TV—when she was spotted by Cy Feuer, producers of classics like *Guys and Dolls* and *Can-Can,* who offered her a job in his next show, *How to Succeed in Business Without Really Trying.* It would serve as her Broadway debut.

Both the industrial and *How to Succeed* were directed and choreographed by Bob Fosse, assisted by his wife and multiple Tony-winning Broadway star Gwen Verdon, who immersed McKechnie further in the discipline and artistry of Broadway dance. The production was staged by legendary director/writer/actor George Abbott, who had worked on dozens of shows over the years and was then at his peak.

In the chorus, McKechnie got to perform in the rhythmic "A Secretary Is Not a Toy" (which used tapping typewriters as percussion) and in "Coffee Break," a comic wail of anguish that results when the coffee runs out. She so distinguished herself on this project and fell so deeply in love with show music and Broadway dance that she abandoned her goal of becoming a classical ballerina.

And while she later became identified as a "Michael Bennett dancer" through her association with that choreography, she began as a Fosse dancer and continued to work frequently and closely with Fosse literally until the last day of his life.

Television

McKechnie first came to the attention of the mass public in the NBC-TV series *Hullabaloo*, a distant precursor to music videos and a 1960s update of *American Bandstand*. The show would play Top 40 tunes of the day, and an attractive corps of dancers would dance to them. It was the kind of program parodied in *Hairspray*'s *Corny Collins Show*. McKechnie found herself often featured in dance numbers and soon was getting piles of personal fan mail.

The original *Hullabaloo* chorus was staffed just like the unnamed show in *A Chorus Line* would be: four girls and four boys. One of the boys was an athletic kid from Buffalo, half Italian and half Jewish, whose given name was Michael DiFiglia but who had adopted the professional name Michael Bennett.

He and McKechnie were often paired together for the show and hit it off right away, becoming close friends. Their relationship was not at first romantic. Bennett was bisexual, but most of his intimate relationships were with men. But they spoke the same dance language and understood each other's passion for dancing on a deep level. Bennett shared with her his dream of someday becoming a Broadway director and choreographer.

On *Hullabaloo* the choreographer was Jaime Rogers, and the connection turned out to be an important one.

After *Hullabaloo* went off the air and McKechnie struggled through a brief and unhappy marriage to record promoter (and gambler) Al Schwartz, she called Rogers in 1968 desperate for work. This plea was later recounted in the recording sessions that were the basis of *A Chorus Line* and emerged as Cassie's plea to Zach, "I need a job." Both in *A Chorus Line* and in McKechnie's real life, the plea resulted in work.

McKechnie was hired for a new Broadway musical, *The Education of H*Y*M*A*N K*A*P*L*A*N*, starring Tom Bosley and Hal Linden. The musical was based on Leo "The

Joys of Yiddish" Rosten's stories about a night school for immigrants trying to become U.S. citizens. It was also the 110th production for George Abbott, and McKechnie was given a small role as the only Irish immigrant in a class filled mainly with Eastern European Jewish immigrants. She even got to sing and dance in a trio on "Ain't It a Pretty Night?," but her showcase didn't last long. Criticized as a too-mild trespass on *Fiddler on the Roof* territory, it lasted just one month. It was the first of a trio of musicals in which McKechnie sang in a trio.

Bennett cast her in his next musical, *Promises, Promises*, along with many of his favorite dancers, including future choreographer Margo Sappington and future *A Chorus Line* castmate and director/choreographer Baayork Lee. The three were featured dancers in the number "Turkey Lurkey Time," at the Christmas party of the insurance company where the show is set.

In a setup reminiscent of Fosse's "Who's Got the Pain?" in *Damn Yankees*, it was announced that the "Christmas Party Committee" asked the "Idea Committee" to come up with an idea for the Christmas party, and "without further ado" are introduced Sappington, Lee, and McKechnie ("Miss Della Hoya of Petty Cash") The trio then sashayed stage center and, to the delight of the colleagues, launched into a 1960s-style number reminiscent of *Hullabaloo*. Dressed in the bright colors of the period, they were a swirl of sexy movement. The rest of the chorus caught their excitement, some people jumping onto desks like go-go dancers, and the number dissolved into a flashing-light bacchanal of popping hips and shaking heads. The number was only peripheral to the plot, but it pumped a lot of energy into the story and gave McKechnie a real chance to shine, stage center (and, by the way, in front), on Broadway. She repeated the role in London.

It was McKechnie's breakthrough, not only as a Broadway dancer, but specifically as a Michael Bennett dancer. She had gone from his dancing partner on *Hullabaloo*, to one of his favored dancers, to his favorite dancer. In short order Bennett would be comparing their collaboration to that of other great choreographer/dancer pairings. In her autobiography, McKechnie recalls him saying, "Jerry [Robbins] had Chita [Rivera], Bob [Fosse] had Gwen [Verdon], and I can't tell you how happy I am that Donna is mine."

Company

Bennett brought her onto his next project, the groundbreaking 1970 musical *Company*, created by composer Stephen Sondheim and librettist George Furth, working with Harold Prince as director and Bennett as choreographer.

A razor-edged examination of modern urban marriage, *Company* told the story of a single man name Robert, who is pressured to get married by his married friends—even though their own relationships are far from perfect. The humor tended to be intellectual, the attitude brittle, the emotions controlled—sometimes released suddenly by a word or a drink. There was no chorus line. McKechnie was part of a trio of Robert's frustrated girlfriends (with Susan Browning and Pamela Myers) who comment on his lack of emotional connection. They're introduced as a group in the song "You Could Drive a Person Crazy," Andrews Sisters–style, lamenting his elusiveness and threatening to give him up. McKechnie can be seen in D. A. Pennebaker's documentary film *Original Cast Album: "Company,"* heavy late 1960s makeup and all, singing her heart out about the perfidy of men.

Her highlight in the show came in the Act II number "Tick-Tock." Robert (Dean Jones) and April (Browning), one of his girlfriends, wound up in bed. As they disappeared beneath the covers and the audience heard their thoughts as they made love, McKechnie expressed their physical encounter with a sexy dance. Dressed in a dark dance skirt with sparkles around the pelvis area, she kicked up her heels and shot out her arms in what looks today like an exciting first draft of the "Music and the Mirror" dance she would later do in *A Chorus Line*. "Tick-Tock," too, has a fast start, slows abruptly in the middle, and builds to an orgasmic climax. The brilliant number and the show helped land her on the cover of *Dance* magazine for the first time.

It almost didn't happen. Director Hal Prince had wanted to cut the dance, feeling that it didn't quite fit with the rest of the show. Bennett was prepared to acquiesce, but McKechnie, for the first time, put her foot down and insisted the number be kept in the show. She tried to dance it in such a way that Prince could see how important it was, not just to her personally, but as an abstraction of what the characters were experiencing. It worked. And it serves as an illustration of the kind of—not just storytelling in dance, but the *investment of emotional content* in dance that became McKechnie's trademark. She made audiences feel what her character was feeling, which made her a true (and rare) dancing actress.

The next step after such a success was normally the chance to move into featured roles and then starring roles. McKechnie enjoyed two featured roles in the early 1970s, one on stage and one on film, but both projects flopped: a 1971 revival of *On the Town*, in which she played "Miss Turnstiles" Ivey Smith, and a film musical adaptation of Antoine de Saint-Exupéry's classic *The Little Prince*, in which she played the demanding and petulant Rose.

The experience of rejection she felt in Hollywood would go into the mix that created her next, and greatest, Broadway show.

A Chorus Line

In January 1974, Bennett called McKechnie with an unusual request. He had been invited by dancers Tony Stevens and Michon Peacock to take part in a late-night planning session for a dance company they had envisioned to help provide work for New York's professional dancers. They asked Bennett to lend his considerable name to the project, knowing it would be a drawing card for the best in the business. Bennett personally invited several of his closest dancer friends to come, including, of course, McKechnie.

Bennett brought along a reel-to-reel tape recorder so he'd have a record of all the ideas that might come out. They gathered at a rented studio on the night of January 26, 1974. He took charge of the meeting and sat everyone in a circle. He began, as so many such meetings do, by going around the circle and asking everyone to tell their stage name, their real name if it was different, and how they got into dancing.

The meeting never got beyond that simple introduction. As people's life stories in show business began to pour out, everyone began to sense that something special and even magical was happening. For the next six hours the two dozen or so dancers shared their joys, sorrows, embarrassments, fears, and dreams for the future. McKechnie told the story of her conflicts with her dad, her early run-ins with the Rockettes and ABT, and her desperate call to the director of *The Education of H*Y*M*A*N K*A*P*L*A*N*, begging for a job.

All of this, Bennett quickly saw, could serve not as the basis for a dance company, but as the basis for a musical—specifically a big Broadway musical about dancers that he had been carrying in the back of his mind as a general concept. Bennett would serve as director and co-choreographer (with Bob Avian).

Over the next year, through weeks of workshops and months of anxious waiting, that taping session, and a second one a few weeks later, was hammered by librettists Nicholas Dante and James Kirkwood and by songwriters Ed Kleban and Marvin Hamlisch into the musical *A Chorus Line*. Some of McKechnie's stories were grafted onto other characters, but the core of her experiences, including her long relationship with Bennett, formed the heart of the character Cassie Ferguson.

All the characters sing about how they need a job, but Cassie's particular story is of a former Broadway dancer who had gotten a few breaks and went out to Los Angeles hoping to become a movie and TV star, only to find she "couldn't act" and bounced around fruitlessly before limping back to New York and trying to start again where her heart had always belonged—in the chorus.

The writers embellished this story with a secondary story of Cassie's relationship with the director Zach. They had lived together until his obsession with work and his coldness to her finally drove her away. This section of the story was fictional, but, in light of subsequent events, remarkably prescient. Cassie begs Zach for a job as McKechnie had once begged Jaime Rogers.

Bennett eventually asked the dancers involved in the tape sessions to audition for the show—essentially auditioning to play themselves. Not everyone was chosen, but McKechnie unsurprisingly was cast as Cassie. Although everyone in the show was supposed to be treated equally, it quickly became apparent that Cassie was the most fully developed character in the story.

The bisexual aspect of the relationship was glossed over, though Zach appeared far more sympathetic to the character of former Jewel Box transvestite dancer Paul San Marco than to Cassie, and, in Bennett's own staging, Zach put an arm around Paul to give physical comfort, something that does not occur with Cassie—though he does finally agree to hire her.

One of the emotional climaxes of *A Chorus Line* is McKechnie's tour de force dance solo in the song "The Music and the Mirror." Her plea for work builds to a frenzy of whirls and leaps in her distinctive red dance skirt. It's a pure expression of virtuosity in a show about veteran dancers who are competing for "the chance to dance for you," and it was Bennett's ultimate gift to the dancer he loved best.

That love began taking other forms, as well. While they were working so closely on their simultaneous mutual masterwork, McKechnie and Bennett began an offstage relationship that moved beyond the professional to the romantic.

Now McKechnie found herself in the barbershop mirror situation in which she was trying to live a personal and professional real life while playing a semifictionalized version of herself. She had to be Cassie having a relationship with Zach onstage, while being Donna having a relationship with Michael in their brief after-hours lives. It was as dramatic a situation as anything they were putting on the stage.

Beyond telling the basic outlines of her story, *A Chorus Line* captures a personal aspect of McKechnie in a very effective way. McKechnie has a unique quality that has helped her throughout her career and personal life and that has never been described fully in reviews but is beautifully captured in *A Chorus Line*.

Consciously or not, McKechnie makes people want to protect, help, and take care of her. Let's call it her "S.O.S. magic." She exudes a sweet vulnerability—a little-girl-lost quality—that, added to her talent, compels both men and women to cut her extra slack, go the extra mile for her, give her the shirt off their back, all the traditional things. McKechnie has a way of asking for things without seeming pushy. Sometimes she will just stand there looking forlorn and you will figure out what she needs and give it to her, even if she hasn't verbally requested it.

Many people have this quality in varying degrees. That's especially true of stars. Marilyn Miller had it, and even Carol Channing had it, which accounts for her success in winning the audience despite her crazy voice and looks. In McKechnie, the volume is turned up to eleven. She became a personal crusade for friend after friend, most notably Bennett, although some also grew tired of the crusade, also most notably Bennett.

In her autobiography she tells the story of arriving at a London airport with an expired passport and with no reservations to stay at any hotel and just standing there crying until someone she knew came off another plane and invited her to stay at his house, and airport personnel finally waved her through. Only McKechnie could have gotten away with that, and only McKechnie could have counted on that tactic to work so miraculously.

Part of the reason so few other actresses have been able to make the role of Cassie work is that they simply lack this quality.

In 1976, Tony Award voters chose *A Chorus Line* as Best Musical; Bennett as Best Director and Best Choreographer (with Avian); and McKechnie as Best Leading Actress in a Musical, beating the two other great choreographers' muses, Gwen Verdon and Chita Rivera of *Chicago*.

Marriage to Michael Bennett

After New York, McKechnie re-created the role of Cassie on the West Coast. In the midst of the acclaim for that reprise, it was announced that the show, which included so much of her personal life story, had won the 1976 Pulitzer Prize for Drama.

One of the high points in the period was an invitation to the home of dance legend Fred Astaire, where he reminisced about dancing with his sister Adele and other partners. McKechnie found herself tongue-tied. As she was leaving with Bennett, however, Astaire struck a pose from one of his classic films, which she interpreted as being "his way of telling me that he understood how intimidating his image could be. It was a gift of affirmation that only he could give."

Caught up in their mutual success, and ignoring the very example of their fictional selves in their own show, Bennett and McKechnie decided to take their relationship to a new level. They married December 4, 1976, in Paris and moved in together in a penthouse apartment overlooking New York's Central Park.

The marriage startled many in the theatre community who knew Bennett as exclusively gay. McKechnie felt that their love could overcome all obstacles, but within just a few months the tension and estrangement began to grow. Bennett took her to London in spring 1977 to help launch the West End production of *A Chorus Line* when the original London Cassie, Elizabeth Seale, was fired and her replacement was not yet ready. But the local press and British Equity were unhappy with the situation, and that pressure only added to their offstage unhappiness. The situation resolved itself, to a degree, when McKechnie injured her back and withdrew.

McKechnie never worked with Bennett again.

She returned to New York without him, "feeling defeated in every way." During their separation after London, she played in *Misalliance* at the Williamstown Theatre Festival in Massachusetts, while Bennett went into rehearsals for his next Broadway musical, *Ballroom*.

Their spells of physical separation and even the times between when they'd speak to each other grew longer and longer. It got to the point where Bennett would instruct his assistants not to put her calls through to him and not to tell her where he was.

Their relationship had grown into something even more closely resembling that of their *Chorus Line* counterparts, Zach and Cassie—Cassie accusing Zach of workaholism, and Zach rebuffing her. At last McKechnie realized that her marriage to Bennett was over. They separated after less than a year of marriage, through the divorce wasn't finalized until 1979.

The loss of his friendship was as upsetting to her as the dissolution of their marriage. For our book *On the Line: The Creation of "A Chorus Line,"* she told me, "I felt very abandoned. I didn't understand it. It was not about his being homosexual. That was not the issue. He was a very faithful husband. But he was very frightened to be loved by someone who was not being paid. I took it as rejection, his fear of intimacy.

"When I filed for divorce I said, 'Why did you marry me?' He said, 'At the time it was a whim, it seemed like the right thing to do.' I was in such a victim state and so hurt. I believed that's what he meant—that he never really loved me. But I realize now that he couldn't tell me the truth. How do you say to someone, 'I can't stand to be in this relationship because I can't stand the feelings that come up'? When I'd accuse him of never loving me, he'd say, 'I never married anybody else.' He meant that as a compliment."

Further complicating her life was the fact that she was soon overwhelmed by illness. Aches and pains that had seemed routine suddenly incapacitated her. The diagnosis was rheumatoid arthritis, which became so severe by 1979 that McKechnie prepared to face life as an invalid. She credits her recovery to two years of vitamins, therapy, holistic treatments, and psychotherapy.

She returned to the stage in 1981 with a Chicago production of the Nancy Ford/Gretchen Cryer musical *I'm Getting My Act Together and Taking It on the Road*. She appeared in James Lapine's *Table Settings* and made guest appearances on TV's *Fame, Cheers, Family Ties,* and several variety shows.

She produced and choreographed *Let Me Sing and I'm Happy*, a revue of Berlin, Kern, and Gershwin music in Burbank, California, and starred in *Get Happy* at the Westwood Theater in Los Angeles, choreographed by Tony Stevens.

McKechnie made a Broadway comeback in 1986 when she returned to playing Cassie for several months in *A Chorus Line*. The return, which attracted a great deal of press attention, replenished her visibility.

Fosse saw her and asked her to take the title role of *Sweet Charity* on tour, and things quickly took two tragic turns.

She was getting ready to do the first rehearsal on July 2, 1987, in Toronto when she heard of Bennett's death of AIDS on the radio. "I lost all sense of the world around me," she wrote in her autobiography, "and I felt so alone." She had known for some time that he was ill, but he had told her he had "a stress-related heart condition." The stigma attached to AIDS had kept him from revealing the truth to her, which also hurt.

McKechnie wrote that she had not been intimate with Bennett in a decade, and that Bennett had contracted AIDS in the meantime from an "unnamed man in San Francisco." Dealing with people's misplaced concerns for her health, the feeling of betrayal at having not been told, and, more than anything else, the loss of the person who had been her dance partner, her mentor, her primary collaborator, and then her husband, put tremendous stress on the sensitive dancer. She coped by pouring all her attention into working with Fosse on *Sweet Charity*.

Then, barely twelve weeks later, after a final rehearsal before opening night in Washington, D.C., on September 23, 1987, Fosse left to go back to his hotel to change for the opening, and never returned. He suffered a fatal heart attack while walking with wife Gwen

Verdon and collapsed on the street. McKechnie was one of the last people to see him alive.

Within the space of less than three months, McKechnie had lost the two men who had befriended her, guided her, and made great art with her. She faced a much colder world after that. She would stay closely allied with her fellow *A Chorus Line* members, and she still had a cadre of devoted fans.

In the years to come, McKechnie stayed in demand as a leading lady and sometime choreographer throughout North America and England. Her returns to Broadway were rare, but she was constantly working.

In 1987 she opened in *Annie Get Your Gun* at the Geary Theater in San Francisco. She created the role of Sheila Kelly, the villainess in *Annie Warbucks*, Charles Strouse and Martin Charnin's sequel to *Annie*, off-Broadway. She also starred in the English production of *No Way to Treat a Lady*, which she choreographed, as well.

McKechnie returned to Broadway in 1996 in the Theatre Guild/David Merrick production of Rodgers and Hammerstein's *State Fair*, for which she was nominated for a Drama Desk Award and received the Fred Astaire Award for Best Female Dancer. She played singer Emily Arden opposite John Davidson, Andrea McArdle, and Scott Wise.

She received an Ovation Award nomination for her role in *Mack & Mabel* for the Reprise! series in Los Angeles. Regionally, she played many memorable musical leading ladies, including starring in *A Little Night Music, Gypsy, Annie Get Your Gun*, and *I Do! I Do!*

McKechnie has the distinction of playing the three major female characters in Stephen Sondheim's *Follies*: she played Phyllis at the Drury Lane in London, Sally in the landmark Paper Mill Playhouse production, and Carlotta for the Reprise! series, in which she stopped the show with her rendition of "I'm Still Here."

She also put her life onstage once again in an ongoing project variously called *Inside the Music* and *My Musical Comedy Life*, directed by fellow *Chorus Line* alumnus Thommie Walsh, who was one of the great white knights of her later career. An autobiographical one-woman show, it recounts many of the highlights mentioned in this chapter, punctuated by performances of her famous songs and dances.

McKechnie was an honored guest at the opening night of the 2006 Broadway revival of *A Chorus Line*, attending on the arm of Walsh, who passed away just a few months later of lymphoma—another director and muse lost.

When she published her memoir *Timesteps* in 2007, her sweet vulnerable smile and voice were on every page.

Tommy Tune as Albert Peterson in the Long Beach Civic Light Opera
production of *Bye Bye Birdie*. (1991). PHOTOFEST

TOMMY TUNE
Famous Feet

Tommy Tune's name is so perfect for a Broadway dancer that it became a running joke, and something of a headache for him.

Long on legs, long on talent, Thomas James Tune spent his career beginning every interview with the words, "Yes, it's my real name." The answer to the second question was also always pretty much the same: "Five-feet, eighteen inches" (sometimes it was eighteen and a half)—his height.

In his early years in the chorus they always put him in the back, but he always could be seen. But he wasn't in the chorus long. His virtuosity was quickly noticed, and he was plucked from the chorus for movie roles, then featured dancer roles, then as choreographer and director on Broadway. When he finally made it to the leading role in a Broadway musical, it was in a vehicle of his own devising.

One of the first male stars to emerge on Broadway after the Stonewall Riots, he was also the first "out" gay male Broadway star and became an icon for it. For a period from the mid-1970s to the late 1980s, he was considered the Fred Astaire of his generation. Long-limbed, deft-footed, always outwardly cheerful, gay in all senses of the word, he was a recognizable Broadway image in a time when Broadway was in serious decline and when Broadway's place in American national culture was at its nadir. He helped fix an image for Broadway in the mind of the public that still has currency: singing, dancing, glamorous, talented, more than a little over the top, and gay.

Working with his partner Thommie Walsh, Tune helped keep alive this fleeting wisp of dance glory: Broadway glamour and grace, a 1930s way of dancing and choreography that's thankfully back in style in the 2000s—but now is just considered Broadway style. Tune's Jack-be-nimble figure helped keep that flame burning brightly in a dark time.

★

Tune was born February 28, 1939, in Wichita Falls, Texas, and moved with his family to Houston when he was three. His mother was a homemaker; his dad helped run a family machine works business that served the booming Texas oil industry. They were amateur ballroom dancers, and family legend has it that they met, auspiciously, on the dance floor. Father Tune's avocation was Tennessee walking horses, and young Tommy spent many hours helping his father teach the horses to move just the right way—perfect training for the dancer and choreographer to come.

His folks enrolled him at age five in dance school, where he studied tap, tumbling, ballet, modern, and jazz. In Houston he got his first brush with professional legitimate theatre when his folks took him to a national tour of *The King and I*. "Suddenly there was dancing, music, songs, story, sets and costumes all telling me something that made me cry. That was it. It was musical comedy for me from then on."

Kids teased him in school, calling him "Ichabod Crane" and "toothpick," both of which names, it must be said, were fairly accurate. Tune was extremely tall and slender. But his interest in both dancing and directing was undeniable. He would listen by the hour to cast albums, reading the credits and dreaming of being one of the dancers. He would make these dreams come to life by staging amateur shows at his house, billed as "Tune's Backyard Patio Revue." For his high school graduation present, his parents took him on a trip to New York, where he got to see his first Broadway shows.

Tune went to the University of Texas as Austin, majoring in acting and studying under the legendary B. Iden Payne. During the warm months, he danced in Dallas Summer Musicals shows, earning his Equity card in the process. Tune earned a bachelor's degree from the University of Texas in fine arts, then graduated with a masters degree in directing.

Tune came to New York with his friend (and future producer) Phillip Oesterman. They arrived the morning of March 17, 1962, and stopped at the corner of Fiftieth Street and Fifth Avenue, where Oesterman directed Tune to buy copies of *Back Stage* and *Show Business*, the two actors' newspapers that list auditions. Tune saw there was an audition that very day for the national tour of *Irma La Douce*. The audition was at two p.m., and by the end of the day, Tune had aced the audition and gotten the job.

Tune spent the 1960s in the chorus lines of various shows, both on Broadway and on tour. His Broadway debut was in the Sherlock Holmes musical *Baker Street*, playing one of Three Killers (billed as Tom Tune). After a chance meeting in an elevator, Michael Bennett chose him for the chorus in the first show he choreographed on Broadway, *A Joyful Noise*, which was also the final Broadway musical for one of his idols, John Raitt. The show also featured Susan Watson of *Bye Bye Birdie* and, in the chorus, future collaborator Baayork Lee.

Tune later said, "Being in the chorus is the thing I'm most proud of. I had to work so hard to compensate for my height."

Among other things, he asked the costume designer to put him in horizontal stripes so he wouldn't look so tall. But, as it turned out, his hypertrophied form with its size-thirteen tap shoes proved to be his ticket to the next phase of his career.

Tune was working as a dancing waiter in the chorus of the David Merrick musical *How Now, Dow Jones* when a casting director spotted him and invited him to audition for dance legend Gene Kelly. Kelly was directing the 1969 film adaptation of the smash musical *Hello, Dolly!* and needed a specialty dancer for the role of Ambrose Kemper. Tune found himself in great company: in addition to Kelly, there was master comedian Walter Matthau as Horace Vandergelder, future *Phantom of the Opera* star Michael Crawford as Cornelius Hackl, jazz legend Louis Armstrong as the bandleader, and of course Barbra Streisand as Dolly.

Tune's biggest moment came in the song "Put On Your Sunday Clothes," prancing down the steps of Vandergelder's shop, then twirling his hat through the streets of Yonkers to the train station, where all the main characters are headed for adventure in New York. Tune presented an otherworldly figure, with attenuated limbs like fireplace matches, but those long legs showed off every step, and his flawless, spirited dancing technique drew the eye even amid the big chorus. Tune can be glimpsed in a brief clip used in the 2008 Pixar film *Wall E*, about a robot in the distant future. One of the last remaining images of humanity on Earth is that clip of Tune and the chorus of *Dolly!*

While working on the film, director Kelly took Tune under his wing and suggested that he change his name, because no one would believe it was real and it would only prevent him from getting serious roles. Among the suggestions were "Clay Rollins" and "David Logan." But in the end, Tune decided to stick with his birth name, wherever it would lead him.

Dolly! turned out to be a major disappointment for the studio. But Tune had done well enough to be offered a much bigger role in Ken Russell's British-made 1971 film version of *The Boy Friend*. In Russell's hands it turned into a grotesque cartoon of life in an amateur theatre company in the 1920s, with moments of great beauty.

Tune played the little troupe's leading juvenile, who got to dance with Polly, the leading lady, played by 1960s supermodel Twiggy (née Leslie Hornby). As her stage name indicates, she made her career as a super-slender catwalker, who had been teased in her youth as "sticks" and "Olive Oyl." Tune said he liked dancing with her partly because she made him look normally proportioned. They struck up a friendship that would last decades.

It's Not Where You Start

Tune didn't become a dance icon himself until the 1973 stage musical *Seesaw*. Based on the two-character stage play *Two for the Seesaw*, about a buttoned-down midwestern businessman, Jerry Ryan, who has an affair with free spirit Gittel Mosca, the musical opened up their story and made Jerry's affair into an affair with the gorgeous mosaic of New York. Composer Cy Coleman and lyricist Dorothy Fields used *Seesaw* as an opportunity to visit the Latino community and the gay community and to revisit the Times Square demimonde they had previously explored in *Sweet Charity*.

Tune came aboard the show when it was struggling through a problematic out-of-town birth. Michael Bennett took the helm from director Ed Sherin and called on several of his showbiz stalwarts to come help. Among them was Tune, who was given the role of Gittel's friend David, a dancer and aspiring choreographer who would do almost anything to break into Broadway. It was groundbreaking in that it was one of the first overtly and specifically gay roles in a musical.

The choreographer angle gave Tune several great opportunities for specialty dances, which he says Bennett let him choreograph himself. Tune is listed as "assistant choreographer" on the show. Tune got two such opportunities to showcase himself. The first was "Chapter 54, Number 1909," a song in which David helps Jerry memorize a dull stretch of New York law about duties on salt by setting it to rhythmic dance that turns into a giant production number. In addition to helping establish character, the song told the audience that Tune could make a dance out of *anything*.

The second was an Act II showstopper called "It's Not Where You Start (It's Where You Finish)," in which he expresses his rapture at being asked to serve as assistant on a new show—an inside joke, perhaps, since that was precisely Tune's credit on the show. His character is on the way up, so Tune put everything lofty he could think of into the song, including a staircase, platform shoes, balloons—and, of course, the loftiest thing in the show, himself. He finally had a number in which his height was a plus. He wore his hair long, almost to his shoulders, then dressed himself in high-waisted white pants to make his legs look even longer. A tiny bow tie and short jacket helped the illusion. Then this beanpole vision performed a pas de deux with the famously four-foot-ten Baayork Lee (whose story would serve as the basis of the Connie Wong character she later created in *A Chorus Line*), dancing *en pointe* in a costume consisting mainly of balloons.

Just as the final chord is about to resolve, Tune stops the action and shouts, "Wait! We need a *bigger finish!*" The orchestra backtracks and starts a new build and, sure enough, the whole chorus convenes to provide him with a triumphant finale. It's a moment of pure presentational showbiz fun, and it proved to be the best moment in a generally weak show. It made Tune a star in the way that having a major role in a movie musical hadn't.

When Tune returned from a vacation, he found his name had been added to the marquee. The show won him his first Tony Award, as Best Supporting Actor in a Musical—the first of nine career Tonys in a total of four different categories as of 2009.

The overwhelming acceptance accorded him by Broadway cemented his belief, as articulated in 1992 to Patrick Pacheco in *Newsday*, that film, TV, and even recordings are "false mediums." He said his film career was "agony. It was so boring. It demands a certain coolness, a certain detachment. It can't come from here [pounds heart]. And every time you perform onstage live, it comes from here. It can't come from anyplace else."

With minor exceptions, Tune never created roles or productions for other media again.

At this moment in his career, Tune also met another artist who would prove to be one of his key collaborators in the years to come, dancer Thommie Walsh, another friend-of-Bennett who joined *Seesaw* during its tryout. Walsh, a dancer from upstate New York who would create the role of Bobbie in *A Chorus Line*, shared a vision of Broadway dance in the elegant 1930s style. They formed a close creative and personal relationship that would blossom in the late 1970s.

Following *Seesaw*, Tune found himself powerfully in demand as a dancer and even performed a nightclub show that flopped painfully. But he received one offer that intrigued him more than any other. Like many performers, Tune wanted to direct; he'd been doing so informally since childhood and held, remember, a degree in directing.

In 1976 he staged a groundbreaking off-Broadway revue called *The Club*. Often described as feminist, it made its point more in the way it was presented than in its actual content. A group of Victorian gentlemen in evening clothes spend an evening at their favorite men's club, telling stories and singing songs that reflect their condescending attitudes toward women. The gimmick was that all the "men" were played by women.

The show established Tune's directing bona fides and enabled him to take the next step—directing a full-scale Broadway musical.

In 1979 he staged another gender-bending off-Broadway show, Caryl Churchill's fascinating British drama *Cloud 9*, in which characters were played by actors of different genders from Act I to Act II, as a way of shaking up the audience's expectations of stereotyped male and female behavior. Both of these unorthodox productions were hits and also shook up audiences' expectations about what a six-foot-six-and-a-half-inch former chorus boy could be expected to produce.

The Best Little Whorehouse in Texas

Everyone finds his destiny in a different place. Tune found his on a New York bus, where he ran into an old high school chum named Carlin Glynn. She told him about this wonderful new musical her husband, Peter Masterson, had written and was directing at the Actors' Studio.

The musical was based on a real house of prostitution, known as the Chicken Ranch, because, when times were tough, the girls could be persuaded to take poultry in payment for their services. It was, as the song went, "A Lil' Ole Bitty Pissant Country Place," comfortably integrated into its community—until the age of television dawned and a crusading TV investigative reporter turned his sights upon its temptations.

Tune was engaged to help move the show to the next level, as choreographer and codirector with Masterson. It was his first project that allowed him to draw on his Texas background. It was one of the rare shows to succeed in New York with a score of primarily country-western music (by Carol Hall), and while Tune provided plenty of "Broadway" moments, such as a "The Sidestep" and "Texas Has a Whorehouse in It," he never condescended to the Lone Star Staters. Tune was one of their own, and when he did a number with country-western dancing, it was the real thing. And if the "Aggie Song" scene (a winning college football team gets rewarded with a trip to the Chicken Ranch) seemed especially vivid, remember that the Aggies were the rivals of his alma mater, the University of Texas.

The show opened June 19, 1978, and ran nearly four years. In his maiden effort as director and choreographer Tune was nominated for Tony Awards is both those categories. It was filmed in 1982 with Dolly Parton and Burt Reynolds. It even spun off a sequel, *The Best Little Whorehouse Goes Public* (1994), which wasn't staged by Tune and collapsed after just sixteen performances.

To help with the considerable choreographic responsibilities (Tune was both director and choreographer), Tune turned to his *Seesaw* friend Thommie Walsh, who worked on the show without official credit.

Walsh contributed even more to their next show, the oddly titled *A Day in Hollywood/A Night in the Ukraine*, a diptych of one-act musicals paying tribute to the golden age of Hollywood musicals. It had original songs (where needed) by Frank Lazarus and Dick Vosburgh, who also did the book. Jerry Herman eventually added some songs, as well.

Fully at the helm for the first time (Walsh assisting on the choreography, with full billing), Tune got to revel in his beloved 1930s and 1940s style of dance. Tune and Walsh's most memorable number was "Famous Feet," which solved the problem of how to present direct homage to the great dancers of Hollywood films without trying to do impersonations of the originals. They created something they called the Ankle Theatre, a narrow strip of stage that showed the dancers only from the knee down. In this way they imitated only the feet of Fred Astaire and Ginger Rogers, Mickey Rooney and Judy Garland, even Mickey Mouse and Minnie Mouse. It wasn't the last time his career would cross paths with Astaire's.

"Famous Feet" was original and eye-catching and helped earn Tune Tony nominations again as Best Director and Best Choreographer (the latter with Walsh), and this time he won both awards.

Gay Icon

With his elongated limbs, his grace, and his 1930s-influenced dancing style, Tune was often compared to Astaire.

Astaire came to see him when be was appearing in California during a tour of *My One and Only* (loosely based on Astaire's *Funny Face*), and his first comment was, "You're a tall son of a bitch!" Astaire followed it with a generous note of praise.

There was one area where Tune was crucially different from Astaire: Tune always came across as effeminate, both in the roles he chose and in public appearances. He played straight characters with straight romances in *Hello, Dolly!*, *The Boyfriend*, and in his own *My One and Only*, but he never tried to butch himself up for those roles.

Tune came to prominence during the happy years between the Stonewall riots and the advent of AIDS, a period when public acceptance of gays in public life was on an upswing. Tune's special brilliance came to embody all that was good and admirable about that change.

Tuners

In the 1970s, Tune had taken on one complex, nontraditional project after another. Tune was feeling his oats. During the 1980s, he helped assert the tradition of American musical theatre at a time when Broadway was increasingly dominated by European pop operas, primarily from Andrew Lloyd Webber and the team of Alain Boublil and Claude-Michel Schönberg. Tune, often working with Walsh, created a series of stylish musicals that drew from a half century of dance styles, while pursuing a cutting-edge integration of dance with storytelling.

The jewels in Tune's crown are *Nine* (1982), based on Federico Fellini's film *8½*, about a film director at a creative dead end (five Tony Awards, including Best Director for Tune); *Grand Hotel* (1988), based on the same material as the 1930s Greta Garbo film about strangers whose lives intersect in a luxury hotel in Weimar Berlin (Tune won Tony Awards for both direction and choreography); and *The Will Rogers Follies* (1991), based on the life of the wisecracking, lariat-twirling *Ziegfeld Follies* star (again Tune won Tonys for direction and choreography). All three of these shows glowed with warmth, style, and often brilliant storytelling.

As Tune moved deeper into directing and choreographing, he increasingly left the actual dancing to others. He had proven that he was not just a dancer, but perhaps even a potential successor for the great director/choreographers in the Jerome Robbins/Bob Fosse/Michael Bennett mode.

My One and Only

But the public wanted to see those long limbs in action. They got their chance in Tune's 1983 show *My One and Only,* an homage not only to the Gershwin brothers, from whose songbook the score was derived, but also to Fred Astaire and his elegant dancing partners.

Using the score of the 1927 Gershwin/Astaire musical *Funny Face* as a base, librettists Timothy S. Mayer and Peter Stone built up a whole new libretto riffing on the 1920s aviation craze, telling the story of daredevil aviator Captain Billy Buck Chandler (Tune), who is trying to beat Charles Lindbergh to become the first to fly across the Atlantic Ocean solo, while trying to pursue a romance with champion swimmer Edith Herbert.

Tune wore three hats on the production (four, if you count the Astaire-like black top hat he wore in the finale scene and in most of the advertising). Tune was not only codirector and co-choreographer with Walsh, he was also the leading man. So many people had compared Tune to Astaire, it was a natural for Tune to follow in his elegant footsteps.

For a costar, Tune reteamed with his *The Boyfriend* costar, Twiggy. They trusted each other and had similar dancing styles.

The show ran into trouble while trying out in Boston (always a trouble town for Tune musicals), and Mike Nichols came in to help. Baayork Lee earned an associate choreographer credit on the production.

The high point of the show came after Billy suffers a plane crash with his beloved on a seemingly deserted island. It's not so bad, they conclude; in fact "'S Wonderful." The set was designed with a shallow basin of water nearly the width of the proscenium sunk into the downstage side, to suggest the edge of the beach. Tune and Twiggy gamboled barefooted through the water, creating sparkling swirls and splashes that sometimes dampened the first few rows but created a beautiful illusion of a seaside romp.

There apparently was some romping offstage, as well. A romance blossomed between Tune and Twiggy, and they soon were living together. Tune wrote in his autobiography that while he identified as gay, an unnamed woman who was later identified as Twiggy was the true "great romance" of his life. But at the time it didn't last, and Tune went back to men.

But not to Walsh. Though they again shared a Tony Award for Best Choreography, Tune never again shared creative billing with Walsh, though he called him for uncredited help on several of his subsequent projects.

Tune himself also won the Tony Award as Best Actor in a Musical, meaning he'd now won in three different categories: Supporting Actor in a Musical, Choreography, and Directing.

Bad Break

In 1991 Tune was inducted into the Theatre Hall of Fame, taking his place alongside the Rodgers and Hammersteins and Agnes de Milles of history and legend. It was a great moment. Many felt he had reached a new peak, with only greater things ahead.

But 1991 proved to be a watershed for Tune. A combination of bad luck, bad timing, and one very bad break conspired to make *The Will Rogers Follies* Tune's last big Broadway show to date.

Later that year Tune got back on the stage and took to the road in a successful national tour of *Bye Bye Birdie* opposite Ann Reinking that fans were hoping would come to Broadway . . . but never did.

Increasingly throughout the 1980s, Tune had been asked to appear at AIDS benefits, not just to speak, but to perform. The performances became more elaborate, and he started calling upon the country string band the Red Clay Ramblers to help. These performances grew into *Tommy Tune Tonite!*, a revue that toured North America in 1992 and opened a limited run on Broadway just after Christmas of that year.

The ninety-minute show, performed with the Ramblers and a twenty-seven-piece orchestra, showcased Tune singing and dancing standards like "Dancing in the Dark," "Puttin' on the Ritz," "Blue Skies"— many of them associated with Astaire, and one, "The Old Soft Shoe," a Ray Bolger specialty. It was a vaudeville act expanded to the dimensions of a full evening, offering up Tune the musical comedy star, minus the trappings and expense of an actual musical comedy.

Fans were still hoping to see him in a full-fledged musical, and in 1994 Tune seemed to have found the right project: a new show by Robert M. and Richard B. Sherman, onetime house composers for Disney, who had written the beloved score to the film version of *Mary Poppins*. They had also written the score to a modest Broadway success, *Over Here!*, in the 1970s.

Their new Broadway project was *Busker Alley*, based on a British film about a husband-and-wife team of street musicians whose relationship is strained when the wife becomes a star.

The production was delayed while Tune tended his lover, David Wolfe, who was dying of AIDS. After his death, Tune launched into an eleven-city tryout tour opposite Darcy

Roberts, garnering mixed to negative reviews at almost every stop. On October 16, 1995, at the Tampa Bay Performing Arts Center, which was the last stop before Broadway, Tune slipped as he was turning on a lamppost during one of the dance numbers and reportedly broke a bone in his foot. Producers tried to continue without Tune; then the show canceled its opening and went on hiatus. The official word on *Busker Alley* was that it would recapitalize and reopen after Tune recovered, but that never happened. Rumors spread that Tune was faking the injury to avoid his first true critical drubbing since his 1975 club act. For his part, Tune insisted the break took years to heal fully and that he had to "reteach" himself to dance.

However much he may have healed, physically and emotionally, the one-two punch of Wolfe's death and the foot injury seemed to take the creative wind out of Tune's sails.

Tune worked for a time with a new partner, Jeff Calhoun, who assisted Tune on several projects, then broke out on his own staging a 1994 revival of *Grease* for producers Fran and Barry Weissler. Credits said, "production supervised by Tommy Tune."

Tune put a lot of his energy into a production of yet another Astaire-inspired project, *Easter Parade*, based on the film of the same title, with Twiggy playing the role originated by Judy Garland. It closed during tryouts in Australia.

After that he returned to Las Vegas, where he was earning a reported $100,000 a week in the show *EFX*. Asked by the *New York Post* in 1999 when he was planning to return to Broadway, he snapped, "If someone would write a show worth doing, I'd do it in a minute."

Tune appeared briefly in a December 2002 off-Broadway concert show titled *Tommy Tune: White Tie and Tails* with the Manhattan Rhythm Kings to inaugurate a new playhouse, the Little Shubert Theatre, on West Forty-second Street's Theatre Row.

By the early twenty-first century, however, the Broadway he helped keep alive through the 1970s and 1980s was booming without him, turning out *The Producers, Hairspray, Wicked, Monty Python's Spamalot, Jersey Boys, Spring Awakening*—one blockbuster after another. In his 1997 autobiography, Tune blamed the long fallow period, in part, on the death of his longtime agent Eric Schepard. "He was always there, supporting steadily from beneath and urging me higher up the mountain. With his guidance I won nine Tony Awards. Since AIDS claimed his life I've won nothing. My career has foundered."

Tune didn't abandon the stage entirely. He starred in the title role of *Doctor Dolittle*, a stage adaptation of the Leslie Bricusse film musical, which toured North America in 2006 but, once again, defied calls to go into New York.

To date, Tune has never again created a dancing role on Broadway, though at press time he was directing (but not choreographing) the tryout of *Turn of the Century*, a fantasy musical by *Jersey Boys* authors Rick Ellice and Marshall Brickman about a time-traveling singer and pianist who try to take credit for all the great songs of the twentieth century.

The unfulfilled promise of one more great Tune performance makes it seem like he's still out there somewhere, touring forever, the Flying Dutchman of Broadway.

Patti LuPone in *Matters of the Heart* (2000). PHOTOFEST

PATTI LuPONE
Just a Little Bit of Star Quality

The first time Patti LuPone sang "Buenos Aires" in *Evita*, proclaiming that the Argentinean capital was about to experience a real taste of "star quality," any lingering doubts about whether she had the *cojones* to play Eva Peron, the world-snubbing dictator's consort, must have vanished. LuPone fixed the audience with her hungry raptor's smile, and it was all over. The audience never had a chance.

It was similar to the effect of Barbra Streisand's singing "I'm the Greatest Star" in *Funny Girl*: It made a daring proclamation of stardom that was actually backed up with the genuine goods.

LuPone projected a brash toughness and sexiness that made her perfect for some of the strong-woman roles being written just as she came to full flower in the 1970s and 1980s. She was a ripe tomato with a razor blade inside. She could stand on her own two feet and be just as ambitious and scheming and sexually assertive as any man.

Not everyone could deal with that, however. Detractors called her arrogant—the very model of a demanding diva. Did her uncompromising nature stop her from getting all the roles she wanted or deserved? Fans would shout yes, but LuPone's personal and professional setbacks only wound up adding to her legend. Fans saw her as a kind of Samson chained to walls of the temple and loved her all the more for it.

When in 2007–8 she finally scaled Mama Rose in *Gypsy*, and came down from the mountaintop with the Tony Award, supporters were in ecstasy and detractors were scathing. But no one said, "Eh." Whatever else LuPone was, she was never fated to inspire "Eh."

★

Born in 1949, LuPone grew up in the New York suburb of Northport, Long Island, with her college-professor father, her college-librarian mother, and her twin brothers, William and Robert. Robert LuPone would later win his own Tony as the imperious director Zack in *A Chorus Line*.

They came by their show-business blood honestly. The name "Patti" isn't a nickname; she was named for her great-great-aunt, Adelina Patti, a legendary opera singer, described by the *New York Daily News* as being noted for never coming to rehearsals and "always giving farewell performances. . . . She always sent her maid or husband to see that the letters in her name on the marquee were high enough."

For young Patti, the bug bit early and hard. She later told the *New York Times* that her moment of truth came while tap dancing on the stage of the Ocean Avenue Elementary School auditorium in her first recital at age four. She said she looked out at the audience and saw that everyone was smiling at her. And she knew she was home. "Without sounding flip," she said, "I always knew I'd be a star."

When she was barely into her teens, she and her brothers formed a dance team called the LuPone Trio, doing ballroom and popular dances. They went on the *The Ted Mack Amateur Hour*, a kind of low-rent precursor to *American Idol*—and lost. Robert kept up with his dancing to award-winning effect, but Patti decided to focus on music and acting instead. She played the cello in the Northport High School orchestra and, in a characteristically attention-getting move, chose to play the tuba in the school's marching band. She also played Nellie Forbush in the school's 1966 production of *South Pacific* and did so with such élan that she became known throughout the town as its homegrown star. The 1967 senior yearbook listed her as Most Musical, Most Dramatic, Class Clown, and Most Well-Known Person in School, along with the note "Will long be remembered."

At this point, fate and timing stepped in. Legendary director John Houseman announced that he was setting up an acting program at the Juilliard School abutting the recently completed Lincoln Center for the Performing Arts in Manhattan, and it would be open only to the most conspicuously talented and hard-working students. At age seventeen, LuPone was chosen by Houseman as one of only thirty-six in that first class. He rewarded them by working them up to twelve hours a day, training them rigorously in all areas of performance.

LuPone established a reputation as a brilliant but sometimes disruptive presence. Houseman put her on probation at one point for being too "rambunctious." It may just have been a reaction to the stress. That first class suffered from eliminations, dropouts, nervous breakdowns, and at least one attempted suicide. Only fourteen of the original thirty-six remained when graduation rolled around in 1971, but Houseman was so convinced that they were extraordinary—among the classmates were Kevin Kline and David Ogden Stiers—that he decided to keep them together and use them as the cornerstone of a touring repertory group that he proudly christened the Acting Company.

For the next two years of touring, during which LuPone and Kline carried on a tempestuous love affair, that legendary group got the kind of intensive training in front of paying audiences that the American stage affords to very few actors. They got to play dramas, comedies, classics, and original plays, often on successive nights. In fall 1973, Houseman made the bold choice to showcase his prized Acting Company on Broadway with a limited run of classics in repertory, including Chekhov's *The Three Sisters*. LuPone made her Broadway debut playing Irina, the pushy sister-in-law who takes over the family estate as the three sisters of the title dream away their lives.

After a further year of touring, the Acting Company returned to Broadway with, among other things, *The Robber Bridegroom*, an original musical western based on Eudora Welty's novel, with a book and lyrics by future Pulitzer Prize winner Alfred Uhry.

LuPone and Kline starred, and they got the kind of reviews that most young actors only dream about. LuPone earned her first Tony Award nomination in the role of Rosamund. Again the Acting Company was booked only for a limited engagement, but producers felt the reviews were strong enough that *Robber Bridegroom*, which had been scheduled for only fourteen performances, could be brought back for a commercial Broadway run.

Here, LuPone suffered one of the insults that would enrage and fascinate her fans. Despite her acclaim and Tony nomination, producers led by Houseman asked LuPone to audition for the new production. LuPone refused, leading to her break with The Acting Company. With another actress as Rosamund, *The Robber Bridegroom* returned to Broadway the following year, but the momentum had been lost and it closed after a disappointing four-month run.

LuPone, however, was on her own and already on to something bigger. Two other rising stars had taken notice and concluded that something in LuPone's sensibility matched their own. One was another future Pulitzer winner David Mamet, who cast her in his drama *The Water Engine*, which eventually made it to Broadway. LuPone played the custom-written role of Lily La Pon. Mamet and LuPone would work together again and again over the years.

The other rising star was composer-lyricist Stephen Schwartz, the young King Midas of Broadway, who had struck gold with his first three musicals, *Godspell*, *Pippin*, and *The Magic Show*, all of which ran four years or more.

When he ran into out-of-town trouble with his fourth musical, *The Baker's Wife*, he replaced the talented but comparatively bland leading lady with the fiery LuPone. Though the show eventually closed out of town, the heart of the score was preserved in a cast album that would form the cornerstone of the LuPone legend. LuPone played Genevieve, a young woman who marries a much older baker for security but finds herself torn when she meets a handsome young man and falls in love for the first time.

Her quandary is expressed in a six-minute musical parable, "Meadowlark," about a caged bird that dies of a broken heart after it gets a brief taste of freedom. At the end of the song Genevieve resolves not to be like that bird and decides to run off with the young man. Despite the song's length, and the despite the fact that its vehicle never got to Broadway, "Meadowlark" quickly became LuPone's (first) signature piece. Everyone wanted to hear her sing it, and over the years at least a dozen other singers have recorded it, though none with the same passion and sorrow as LuPone. The Patti cult was born.

LuPone appeared in Schwartz's next musical, *Working*, as well, although it had only a brief Broadway run. But "Meadowlark" was being played on both sides of the Atlantic, and it helped bring her to the attention of yet another up-and-coming writer, British composer Andrew Lloyd Webber. Lloyd Webber and lyricist Tim Rice had enjoyed international success with their rock opera *Jesus Christ Superstar*. The team had next ambitiously taken on the story of Argentina's Eva Perón, wife and virtual co-dictator with Juan Perón in the years during and after World War II until she was cut down by cancer. They called the show *Evita* after the common man's sobriquet for their bedizened demigoddess.

Despite its dicey subject matter—it seemed to make fascism look awfully glamorous—the episodic mixture of rock, Latin, and show music had been a smash in London with first-time star Elaine Paige as Eva. But the American actors' union decided Paige wasn't (yet) a big enough star to import. If director Harold Prince wanted to bring the show to Broadway, he'd have to choose an American actress for the role.

Considering her subsequent lightning-bolt performance, it's hard to imagine any other actress but LuPone as Eva. But at the time, LuPone was on a long line of American actresses vying for the role—and not near the front of the line, either. Among others mentioned: Meryl Streep, Ann-Margret, and Raquel Welch. In the end, Prince and the creators decided they didn't want a famous star overshadowing their heroine, and they went for an "unknown" who auditioned with the right combination of allure and drive.

What they got from their "unknown" was LuPone at full wattage, at full command of her powers, ferociously ambitious (like Eva herself) and determined to make the absolute most of the powerhouse role of a lifetime. Rarely has there been so splendid a matching of actress and role. Eva wasn't so much a character for LuPone as an alter ego. And in Mandy Patinkin and Bob Gunton she found two strong male stars to play against.

LuPone was an immediate sensation with audiences, although many critics were cool. In their reviews, most wanted to focus on the show's unorthodox format, politics, and musical style, which was fair. But Clive Barnes of the *New York Post* took a few lines to focus on the actress inside the chignon: "All the performances are far better than in the London version, but never more so than in the casting of Miss LuPone as the whore whose heart has a Swiss bank account number. This Evita of urchin grandeur spits aspiration, she dissolves in her own glory, she keeps her head, her style, her pocketbook and voice that can belt like Merman and melt like Piaf."

It wasn't the last time LuPone would be compared with Merman. She had the Merm's projection and self-confidence but added her own distinctive touches: the cocked hip, the flaring nostrils, the fierce glare over her aquiline nose, the appraising up-and-down glance, the silky seductive coo that could swerve into a harsh, angry caw.

When the Tony Awards rolled around the next spring, LuPone was named Best Actress in a Musical. With LuPone raising her arms to sellout crowds at the Broadway theatre night after night, and singing about her "little bit of star quality" on ubiquitous TV commercials in the tristate area, the LuPone cult was able to go mainstream. To meet the demand for her presence, LuPone followed her grueling two-performance Saturdays with a legendary series of late-night nightclub shows at Les Mouches. She was especially embraced by the gay crowd, who packed the club Saturday after Saturday. LuPone's highly individualistic style attracted the admiration of female impersonators, who were delighted to find a new face to add to their repertoire of Judy Garlands and Marlene Dietrichs. In 2006, actress Leslie Kritzer impersonated LuPone and re-created her entire act, *Leslie Kritzer as Patti LuPone at Les Mouches.*

With a characteristic mix of humility and ego, LuPone decided that despite her Tony Award she wanted more training and missed the challenges of working in a repertory company. She enrolled in London's Royal Shakespeare Company and became the first American working the RSC to land a principal part when she was cast in a revival of Blitzstein's *The Cradle Will Rock.* That led to her creating the role of Fantine in the RSC production of a new pop opera in the *Evita* style, *Les Misérables,* a role she subsequently played in the West End.

Based on the epic Victor Hugo novel, *Les Misérables* was created by two Frenchmen, Alain Boublil and Claude-Michel Schönberg. LuPone was cast as a young woman whose indiscretion leads her down the path to single parenthood, poverty, and prostitution. On her deathbed (not quite halfway through Act I) Fantine entrusts her daughter, Cosette, to the story's main character, Jean Valjean, and her story is over, except for a ghostly reappearance in Act II. It wasn't a star part like Eva Perón, but LuPone used bold strokes to sketch in Fantine's downward spiral and nightly stopped the show with her lament, "I Dreamed a Dream." For that performance, as well as the reprise of her performance in the London production of *The Cradle Will Rock,* she won London's Olivier Award for Best Actress in a Musical.

Neither *Evita* nor *Les Misérables* offered many chances for humor, nor did a revival of the musical *Oliver!,* in which LuPone played the doomed Nancy. Constant comparisons with Merman led to her being cast as the jaunty Reno Sweeney in the Lincoln Center Theater's revival of Cole Porter's *Anything Goes.* Not everyone was convinced that she could play traditional musical comedy, considering that she had, as she observed at the time, come off three major roles in a row in which she "cried and died."

She laughed and lived in *Anything Goes,* wearing a curly red wig and a cocked white captain's cap and winking and shaking her hips in the title song that stopped the show every night. Her "Blow, Gabriel, Blow" seemed to blow the roof off the Vivian Beaumont Theatre and earned her another Tony Award nomination, as Best Actress in a Musical.

Like most actresses of her era, LuPone made several attempts to break into TV and the movies, and she had a great measure of success. Early on she played Lady Bird Johnson opposite Randy Quaid's Lyndon Johnson in the TV movie *L.B.J.* She later earned an Emmy nomination for an appearance on *Frasier* and enjoyed a multiseason run as the mother of a child with Down syndrome in the series *Life Goes On.* She appeared in two David Mamet films, *Heist* and *State and Main,* and had a small role in the Oscar-winning film of Alfred Uhry's *Driving Miss Daisy.*

But these experiences only reinforced the fact that LuPone is a creature of the stage—a quality she shares with Channing and, yes, Merman. LuPone doesn't command a screen the way she commands a stage. Her stature seems to diminish on the screen. On television or film the voice is still strong, but she tends to fade into the background. Her star burns fully only under a proscenium, face to face with live people.

She proved that again in 1993 when Andrew Lloyd Webber chose her to originate the star role in the London world premiere of *Sunset Boulevard*, based on the 1950 Billy Wilder film about creepily majestic 1920s silent film star Norma Desmond, who attempts a comeback in a 1940s Hollywood that has been utterly transformed. When she is invited to return to the studio where she once reigned, she assumes they want her back as a star. What they really want it permission to use her vintage car as a prop.

Lloyd Webber wrote LuPone two stupendous solos, "With One Look," in which Norma describes (and demonstrates) her power over movie audiences, and "As If We Never Said Goodbye," which she sings as she takes her first step into the dream factory of her youth after an absence of decades.

Though now in her forties, LuPone struck some as still a little young to play the over-the-hill screen goddess. But here again she gave the role a stature and a command, and at the same time a whiff of decadence and decay. She was very convincing as an old-time movie star. There were complaints that her Norma was too abrasive, but LuPone by and large delighted her British fans.

With one important exception: Lloyd Webber. Just at her moment of triumph, he administered two slaps of nearly Norma Desmond proportions to LuPone's ego. First, Lloyd Webber allowed singer Barbra Streisand to make the first recording of Norma's two big solos on her album *Back to Broadway*. It may have been intended to help marketing, but it seemed to show a lack of respect toward or confidence in the show's actual leading lady.

The second slap gave credence to that notion. After allegedly promising that LuPone would take the show to Broadway, Lloyd Webber reneged and instead tapped Glenn Close, who had given the show's U.S. premiere in a Los Angeles production, as the New York Norma. LuPone, who has repeatedly acknowledged having thin skin, sued. The eventual $1 million-plus monetary settlement paid for, among other things, a "Lloyd Webber pool" at her home in rural Connecticut she shared with her husband, Matthew Johnston, whom she married in 1988, and son, Joshua, born 1990.

During the late 1990s and early 2000s, LuPone took no long-commitment shows. She embarked on a series of Broadway concerts (*Patti LuPone* on Broadway, *Matters of the Heart, Woulda Coulda Shoulda*) and limited engagements, including a concert version of Sondheim's *Sweeney Todd* with the New York Philharmonic and *Pal Joey* in the New York City Center "Encores! Great American Musicals in Concert" series. She also released several solo albums, including two patriotic albums inspired by the events of 9/11/01.

She made three regular Broadway appearances, taking over the role of opera diva Maria Callas in the Tony-winning Terrence McNally drama *Master Class* (1996), playing a figure from David Mamet's past in *The Old Neighborhood* (1997), and playing Dotty Otley, the buffeted leading lady in the British farce *Noises Off* (2001).

She also took on projects that were just too interesting to ignore. Welz Kauffman, who had been artistic administrator of the New York Philharmonic when she did the 2000 concert of *Sweeney Todd*, had been named president and CEO of the Ravinia Festival in Chicago. Planning a series of revivals of Sondheim musicals under the "Sondheim 75" banner (Sondheim turned seventy-five in March 2005), he brought her back summer after summer to play roles like Mayoress Cora Hoover Hooper in *Anyone Can Whistle*, Desiree in *A Little Night Music*, Fosca in *Passion*, and Mrs. Lovett in *Sweeney Todd*.

LuPone's second performance as Mrs. Lovett also led to her third one, but one very different from what she'd done before. British director John Doyle envisioned a *Sweeney Todd* not only stripped of its massive set (the stage would be nearly bare), not only stripped of its chorus (all the principals doubled as chorus), but stripped of its pit full of musicians. The principals also served as the onstage orchestra.

Shades of Northport High—LuPone suddenly found that her old marching-band experience would help land her a job. In addition to having her play Mrs. Lovett as a sort of punk trollop (opposite Michael Cerveris as Todd), Doyle had her double on both the triangle and the tuba, sometimes punctuating her own scenes with a "ting" on the former. The performance earned her yet another Tony nomination.

In summer 2006, Lupone got her chance to play the Hamlet of leading lady musical theatre roles, Rose in *Gypsy*. Again, the venue was the Ravinia Festival, and the Chicago fans had her all to themselves. People had awaited LuPone's Mama Rose as some people had waited for the Beatles to reunite. Except LuPone's fans got their wish.

Greater than Merman, some were predicting.

The result had the Chi LuPonians singing hosannas. Back in New York, producers were trying to figure out how they could bring it over economically. Yes, the LuPone fans would come. But her fan base was reckoned to be a mile deep but only two inches wide on the outside. There had already been a revival of *Gypsy* just three years earlier, with Bernadette Peters, no less, and it hadn't done all that well. It ran less than a year. Could LuPone do what Peters couldn't?

Most producers decided she couldn't. But one innovative producer rode to the rescue of her honor. The good old "Encores!" series at the New York City Center, which had always played three weekends over the course of the late winter and spring, had decided to add a special summer bonus performance, and they wanted the LuPone's *Gypsy* to serve as the inaugural production. And that's just the way the posters read:

LUPONE

GYPSY

What else needed to be said?

The three-week stand was nearly sold out, and as the curtain went up, the usual onstage orchestra played the overture. But of course, this was not just any overture, but one of the greatest overtures ever. It got a huge hand. And then, just as people were sitting there thinking, *That was amazing, boom,* suddenly there was the Uncle Jocko scene, and here comes LuPone up the aisle piping "Sing Out, Louise!"

What did fans get? A sterling production with a gentle Herbie in Boyd Gaines, a sensitive Gypsy in Laura Benanti, a hilarious Tessie Tura in Alison Fraser, and, to top it off, a determined LuPone who could go from mother hen to seductress to tyrant and back with ease, and make them all seem like they were facets of the same complicated person. Both acts end with a huge Rose solo; LuPone nailed "Everything's Coming Up Roses," but she actually managed to made "Rose's Turn" seem like a smaller song. Her musical breakdown was more a portrait of a woman finally understanding her whole life, rather than a complete implosion. It was a chancy choice, and people expecting a King Lear mad scene were disappointed, though the performance did broaden out a bit over the course of the subsequent ten-month Broadway run.

Among critics, several hailed the arrival of a great *Gypsy.* The *New York Times* critic was clearly disappointed, however. He felt she had failed to rise fully to the occasion. An instant flame war burst across the web as delighted fans and disappointed fans slugged it out. The battle continued after *Gypsy* moved to the St. James Theatre in 2008.

Both LuPone's fans and detractors had a field day at one of the final performances of *Gypsy* when LuPone broke character during the climactic moment of "Rose's Turn" to tear into a fan who insisted on taking flash photos in defiance of the announced ban on picture taking. A separate fan recorded the resulting tirade, delivered by LuPone in her highest dudgeon. She shrieked, "Who do you think you are?" and refused to complete the show until the house staff obeyed her command to "Get 'em out!"

Even without a visual component, the recording became an instant sensation on the Internet clip-sharing site YouTube. It wasn't long before impersonators were re-creating the diatribe and choice phrases from the rant were reassembled into a rap remix called "LuPWNed!"

All in a day's work for Broadway's stormiest diva.

At this writing, LuPone was not yet sixty, with Mama Rose behind her. But she had few worries about having no new worlds to conquer. She was one of the few recognized stage stars who came to prominence in the 1970s and were able to maintain stage careers throughout the lean years of the 1980s and early 1990s. In the first decade of the twenty-first century, when Broadway shows needed a powerhouse older leading lady, the call would go out for LuPone. She had the chops, she had the devoted fan base, and she had that very rare thing in modern legitimate theatre: a non-Hollywood, non-TV name that can sell tickets.

Christine Ebersole as Guenevere in *Camelot* (1980). PHOTOFEST

CHRISTINE EBERSOLE
I Only Have Eyes for You

With her regal bearing, long neck, pale blue eyes, cotton-candy skin, and crowning pouf of strawberry blonde hair, Christine Ebersole was Broadway's go-to gal at the turn of the twenty-first century when it needed an aristocratic leading lady.

After initial success on Broadway in the early 1980s, and a debut as leading lady that entered Broadway legend, she became the first stage star to join the Not-Ready-for-Prime-Time Players on TV phenomenon *Saturday Night Live*. She then entered a West Coast exile that dissipated her talent and success in a series of unexceptional television and film projects, before returning to New York in the 1990s to take up her mantle as Broadway leading lady and earn two Tony Awards—so far.

Seeing her onstage you might imagine an upbringing in an East Coast prep school or a European academy. In truth, she grew up in the Chicago suburb of Winnetka, Illinois (born February 21, 1953). Her father, Robert, was an engineer who listened to Shakespeare plays on tape. Her mother, Marian, was a psychiatric social worker whose taste ran more to gospel and soul but who bought cast albums of classic musicals like *Camelot* for Christine and sent her to New Trier Township High School, where she played in the band and got to perform in musicals for the first time.

Christine moved on to MacMurray College, then to the American Academy of Dramatic Arts in New York City. She made her Broadway debut in January 1976, replacing Christine Andreas in the role of Nancy in a revival of *Angel Street*. The job lasted just a few weeks, but Ebersole earned her Actors' Equity card. She studied hard and worked hard, supporting herself in the time-honored way, waiting tables. While working at the Lion's Rock restaurant she met another actor, Peter Bergman, who was tending bar. He went into soap operas, where he created roles in *All My Children* and *The Young and the Restless* and appeared in a memorable ad campaign for cough syrup ("I'm not a doctor, but I play one on TV"). They married in 1977.

Ebersole's break came in 1979 when she was cast as Ado Annie in a touring company of *Oklahoma!*, directed by William Hammerstein, son of lyricist Oscar Hammerstein II. The production wound up at the Palace Theatre on Broadway. So far, so good. She was making her way on Broadway as a midlevel blond ingenue with expectations of a fair career. Nothing remarkable yet. But powerful people had noticed her, and her life was about to explode.

She awoke on a Saturday in May 1980 little knowing that she was about to enter the wonder week of her life. At midmorning her agent phoned. A major revival of the classic musical *Camelot* was in trouble. It was about to open its pre-Broadway tryout tour in Toronto, but the producers were unhappy with their leading lady and needed a new Guenevere (the role originated by Julie Andrews). They were considering Ebersole. On the upside, the leading man was Richard Burton, re-creating his original Broadway role as King Arthur. On the downside, the show was to begin previews in just six days, and the actress who got the part would have to learn the whole thing in that time.

Was she interested in auditioning?

Ebersole took a deep breath. Just a year earlier she had barely been in the chorus, and now she was getting a chance to work with the top people in the industry in a starring part. But would it be worth the stress of the six-day ramp-up?

"People dream about things like this," she later told the *New York Times*. "I had absolutely nothing to lose."

Here's how the timeline went, according to various reports, notably one in the *Times*:

Saturday afternoon between the matinee and evening performances of *Oklahoma!*, Ebersole did her audition.

Sunday she was called back for a second intimidating audition with Burton himself. Everyone liked her. Lyricist Alan Jay Lerner called Hammerstein and asked him to release Ebersole from her contract. She was offered the job and accepted.

Monday morning she was studying the script on an airplane to Toronto. Monday afternoon she was working with Lerner and music director Franz Allers to learn the songs.

Tuesday she knew 60 percent of her lines and was rehearsing with the cast.

Wednesday she was off-script and doing tech rehearsals.

Thursday she crammed the show from ten a.m. to one a.m.

Friday morning the pressure piled up and she nearly crashed, but on Friday evening she went on for the first preview at the 3,500-seat O'Keefe Center with some of her most troublesome words written on the back of her hand in blue eyeliner.

Saturday she played two more previews, honing her performance.

Sunday night, about two hundred hours after she answered the call from her agent, she stood beside Richard Burton and faced the opening-night critics, one of whom went on to call her "the evening's heroine." Comparisons with the plot of the 1933 movie *42nd Street* were rife. In that story, a chorus girl must replace the lead in her musical on extremely short notice. Ebersole later described the whole experience as being "like falling off a cliff."

She played the lovestruck queen for a year, 1980–81, including a two-month midsummer limited run at the New York State Theatre in Lincoln Center, technically a Broadway engagement. The fairy-tale (or perhaps boot-camp) circumstances of her accession made great copy everywhere the show played.

Her Guenevere from was very different from Julie Andrews's. Andrews's chiming voice had made the audience see the purity of soul inside the unfaithful wife. Ebersole gave Guen a more physically passionate dimension, but her aristocratic looks at last came fully into play. The actress had the command that comes with great beauty wedded to dignity. She looked like a princess, and then like a queen.

By late 1981, all the touring took a serious toll on her marriage to Bergman, and she found herself facing a second, less happy, wonder week. Within a few days in the fall of 1981 she separated from Bergman (they divorced in 1982), moved into a new apartment, and got the news that she was accepted into the cast of NBC-TV's late-night sketch comedy show *Saturday Night Live*. The revered original cast, including John Belushi, Gilda Radner, and Dan Ayckroyd, had left en masse after the 1979–80 season, and the intervening season, captained by producer Jean Doumanian, is today regarded as the nadir of the show's entire three-decade-plus run. For 1981–82, executive Dick Ebersol (no relation) retained comedians Eddie Murphy and Joe Piscopo and brought in a diverse new cast including Brian Doyle-Murray, Denny Dillon . . . and Ebersole.

At the time, Ebersol told *New York Magazine* that Ebersole was "the first 'Broadway regular' in the show's six-year history." "She s the first person we've ever had who can really sing and that opens up whole new avenues of musical parody."

Perhaps if they had actually followed that instinct, Ebersole might have done better. She was rarely given a chance to sing, or even to perform. In fact, the whole experience was painful for her, and her contract was not renewed for a second season. She told *TV Guide*, "I guess I never felt like [I] fit in. I think it was kind of overwhelming for me. My tendency was just to go shopping." When Tom Shales and James Andrew Miller published *Live from New York*, their 2002 oral history of *SNL*, no quotes from Ebersole were included.

For the next decade, Ebersole bounced from Broadway to Hollywood to Burbank. She stayed busy but made little in the way of a lasting mark. Perhaps her most notable project during this time was the Oscar-winning film version of the West End and Broadway play *Amadeus*, in which she played Costanza, Mozart's put-upon wife. She also appeared in the soap opera *One Life to Live* (earning an Emmy nomination) and in an embarrassing science-fiction film, *Mac and Me*, that slavishly imitated Steven Spielberg's *E.T.: The Extraterrestrial*.

She also tried a return to Broadway. In 1983 she took part in the debut of an original musical at the brand-new Norma Terris Theatre in Chester, Connecticut. *Harrigan 'n Hart* was the story of 19th-century Broadway stars Edward "Ned" Harrigan and Tony Hart, whose "Mulligan Guards" musicals reflected the roughhousing multiethnic street life of New York City at the time. The production was hailed in Connecticut and quickly moved to Broadway, with high hopes.

As performed by Harry Groener and Mark Hamill, respectively, Harrigan and Hart were shown as close-working buddies until suspicions began to circulate that Hart was gay. Hart marries English actress Gerta Granville, who turns out to be a pushy, homophobic nag who eventually destroys her husband's relationship with Harrigan and breaks up their act, despite Hart's obvious affection for his partner.

Gerta was an extremely unpleasant character, but Ebersole threw herself into it. "She's a total monster," wrote Frank Rich in the *New York Times*, "right up to the moment that a happy final curtain mandates her sudden, not to mention miraculous, redemption. It's not the least of the book's shortcomings that we never understand why Hart marries this woman—though we can certainly comprehend his desire to give her a good smack. . . . The strong voiced Miss Ebersole, who was Mr. Groener's feisty Ado Annie in the *Oklahoma!* revival, adds a crippling excess of humorlessness to Hart's mean spouse."

Faced with reviews like that, *Harrigan 'n Hart* collapsed after just four performances. It proved to be Ebersole's last Broadway appearance for more than a decade.

Instead, she headed west, where she enjoyed moderate success in TV sitcoms. The most successful of these projects was *The Cavanaughs* (1986–89), in which she played Kit Cavanaugh, a failed showgirl who was trying to endure the quiet life with her Irish-Catholic family after having kicked up her heels in Vegas. The series was created by Robert Moloney, who brought in his brother, Bill, to compose the show's theme song. Bill and Ebersole hit it off immediately and were married in 1987. They adopted three children, Elijah, Mae, and Aaron.

In the early 1990s, Ebersole and Moloney took stock of their lives and careers. Moloney had suffered a career-ending illness, and Ebersole was now the main breadwinner. She had passed her fortieth birthday and had survived both success and failure in so many areas of show business. But really, who was she? She admitted to the *New York Times* that maybe her career had been *too* eclectic. "There was never one thing that I did that made me identifiable."

Well, there was *one* thing. She had walked away from her budding Broadway stardom. She decided that it was perhaps time to reclaim it.

Her first try at a stage comeback ended in disappointment when *Paper Moon*, Larry Grossman and Ellen FitzHugh's 1993 musicalization of the Peter Bogdanovich film, closed after a New Jersey tryout. But the following year Ebersole appeared in two of the three productions in the inaugural season of the "Encores! Great American Musicals in Concert" series at the New York City Center.

Ebersole played Emily West in the rarely seen Rodgers and Hammerstein musical *Allegro* (singing "The Gentleman Is a Dope") and took the lead role of Liza Elliot (originated by Gertrude Lawrence) in the Kurt Weill/Ira Gershwin musical *Lady in the Dark*. The shows ran just one weekend each but convinced many in the audience that Ebersole had a glitter that linked her with divas of yesteryear.

Over the next few years she returned to "Encores" for *The Ziegfeld Follies of 1936* (1999) and *A Connecticut Yankee* (2001). She also appeared at New York clubs, performing show tunes and standards. She returned to Paper Mill Playhouse with a triumphant 1999 revival of *Mame*. She also moved her family to a house in New Jersey.

Once again she was attracting the notice of Broadway's gatekeepers, like casting director Jay Binder, who compared Ebersole to a young Elaine Stritch. "In the old days somebody would be sitting down writing a musical for next season for Christine."

Ebersole also appeared in several nonmusical plays, notably Stephen Sondheim and George Furth's short-lived murder mystery *Getting Away with Murder* (1996) and Gore Vidal's *The Best Man* (2000), a revival of his drama about back-room presidential politics, superficially about JFK and Nixon but having an added frisson in the year Al Gore was running against George W. Bush. Ebersole played a Pat Nixon–like would-be first lady. She also earned a Tony nomination playing tightly wound Millicent Jordan, whose opulent way of life is riding on the success of a party in a revival of *Dinner at Eight*.

The many roles gave Ebersole a chance to develop one of her trademarks, her ability to change the pitch, timbre, and accent of her voice the way Lon Chaney changed faces. In role after role, Ebersole's WASPy prettiness stayed the same, but the inner character was expressed through voices that could flute, growl, purr, or rasp.

The 2001 "Encores!" *A Connecticut Yankee* returned her to the world of King Arthur, which had been lucky for her in 1980 and proved lucky once again. Instead of playing Guenevere, this time she played the villainess of the story. And this time the *Times* gave its approval. "Ms. Ebersole, as the lusty, homicidal Morgan Le Fay, gets to sing this increasingly absurd catalog of the varied ways her character has dispatched her many husbands ['To Keep My Love Alive']. She does so deliciously, in an inspired operetta-ish style that suggests Jeanette MacDonald crossed with Carol Channing."

Even more to the point, the production was directed by Mark Bramble, coauthor of the stage adaptation of *42nd Street*, which was being readied for a major Broadway revival. "She had the look," Bramble said. "She had the style. She had the glamour. She has the uncanny understanding of the style of the 1930s. In another, time, in another era—not living in the world of Andrew Lloyd Webber and Claude Michel Schönberg—this would be a No. 1 star."

And that is how the actress whose career began in a *42nd Street*-like miracle of casting now found her stardom reborn in an actual production of *42nd Street*—though now at a stage in her life where it was time to play Dorothy Brock, the older actress who is unable to go on for opening night.

It's not a warmhearted part, and Ebersole voiced it with an icy, upper-class chirp. Brock becomes sympathetic only in her final scene, when it becomes apparent that the younger woman is the only one who can go on in her place, thereby saving the show. Brock proves that, in the end, she is a great lady of the theatre and a trouper. She passes her wisdom along to the newcomer and advises her to "be so good, I'll hate you."

The show is a treasury of show business traditions, legends, and superstitions (and clichés), and Ebersole played them all to the hilt—partly because she'd lived so many of them. On Ebersole's behalf, Bramble dared to make Brock a bit more sympathetic by interpolating the classic "I Only Have Eyes for You," which Ebersole delivered in a swanky gown on a hotel balcony. The witch was shown to have a human heart, and audiences ate it up.

At the 2001 Tony Awards, Ebersole won her first Tony as Best Leading Actress in a Musical—the only musical category not won by *The Producers* in its record-breaking sweep that year.

Around the World

But Ebersole found her greatest role to date in a highly unlikely place. In 1975, filmmakers Albert and David Maysles helped assemble *Grey Gardens*, a documentary about two odd-ball women living in squalor amid the wealth of Long Island's Hamptons communities. A mother and daughter stuck together in a once-grand mansion now overrun with filth and dozens of cats, they might have just wound up wards of social services organizations if it weren't for the fact that the pair—Edith Bouvier Beale and her daughter, "Little Edie" Beale—were aunt and cousin, respectively, of former first lady Jacqueline Bouvier Kennedy Onassis. Little Edie had come within an inch of marrying President John F. Kennedy's older brother, Joseph Kennedy (later killed in World War II). She might have wound up first lady herself if fate had been kinder to everyone involved. Instead, both Kennedy boys were dead and the Beales lived on, sharing cat food with their cats, in a sort of gothic-horror twilight formed partly of codependence and partly of madness.

In 2004, young writers Scott Frankel and Michael Korie turned their fascination with the film into a stage musical, also called *Grey Gardens*, which opened off-Broadway in early 2006, then moved to Broadway in fall 2006 with an unusual casting trick that gave Ebersole a unique chance to shine. Act I, set in the bright days of 1941, showed Ebersole playing Big Edie, with a younger actress as Little Edie. However, in Act II, which moved the action to the dingy and miserable scenes of 1973, Ebersole now played the grown-up Little Edie, opposite veteran actress Mary Louise Wilson in the role of the now-bedridden mother.

The *New York Blade* quoted composer Frankel as saying, "Christine was our first choice. She had so many gifts, so many styles. I've seen a lot of what she's done, on-stage and on-screen, I've seen her be tragic, funny, emotional, high-class, working class, so many different colors. Usually, though, any given role would only use one part of her talent, so we thought, how great to give this bravura performer a bravura role to play, something that uses everything she's got? She's one of those people for whom more is better."

It was a true coup de theatre, with Ebersole getting love scenes, mad scenes, breakup scenes, comedy scenes, dances, arias, and everything in between. Her Act II performance as Little Edie was a special achievement. Ebersole gave her a peculiar accent and cater-wauling delivery that mimicked the film. She played the part as obviously deluded and yet just self-aware enough to be tragic, living in a strange little hell that had her orbiting her needy and controlling mother forever. She clings to tiny shafts of brightness from her lost past, recalling that she was once known as "Body-Beautiful Beale." In one of the most quoted lines of the season, she explained, "It's my—what do you call it?—my sobriquet."

Ben Brantley of the *New York Times* wrote, "When she sings, skillfully layering softness with stridency, she takes familial ambivalence to an operatic level of eccentricity, yet becomes frighteningly easy to love, to understand and to identify with. She's every aging child with parent issues, and who doesn't that include? A blend of gentle compassion and acute observation, Ms. Ebersole's performance is one of the most gorgeous ever to grace a musical."

Opera News spoke of the song "The Revolutionary Costume for Today" with its distinctive trill, "Da-da-da DAH-dah," as being "to Ebersole's career what 'Adelaide's Lament' [in *Guys and Dolls*] was to Vivian Blaine's and what 'I'm Goin' Back' [in *Bells Are Ringing*] was to Judy Holliday's."

And the role won her nearly every laurel given for lead actresses in a musical: the Drama Desk Award, the Outer Critics Circle Award, the Drama League Award, and finally the Tony Award for Best Performance by a Leading Actress in a Musical, her second.

A quarter century after walking away from Broadway and fourteen years after storming back, she had reclaimed her crown.

In winter 2008 she encored at "Encores!," this time as yet another sort of queen: Queen of Broadway Margo Channing in *Applause*, the musical adaptation of *All About Eve*. Perhaps the royalty went to her head. Reviews were not kind.

Also in the election year of 2008, Ebersole went on talk shows expressing her eyebrow-raising belief that the outgoing administration of President George W. Bush was planning a coup and that the economic downturn of that year was part of an orchestrated government plot to compromise personal liberties. As history showed, her fears were misplaced. The night President Bush left office, Ebersole went on Comedy Central's *The Colbert Report* to perform a tongue-in-cheek version of "What I Did for Love" from *A Chorus Line* accompanying film clips of the outgoing administration's most risible public utterances.

Ebersole returned to Broadway a few weeks later, playing the ghostly wife Elvira alongside Angela Lansbury in a revival of Noël Coward's *Blithe Spirit*.

Like Elvira, Ebersole is a spirit come back to earth, a spirit of a special kind of glamorous stardom.

Donna Murphy as Anna Leonowens in *The King and I* (1996).
JOAN MARCUS/PHOTOFEST

DONNA MURPHY
Bright as a Penny

Donna Murphy came to stardom in the early 1990s with a combination of brains and talent that made her perfect for the kind of roles being created at the time by some of the most innovative writers. Murphy carved out a niche as the thinking person's sex symbol and one of the most admired stage performers of the baby boom generation.

Her abilities brought her two Tony Awards as Best Actress in a Musical for her first two starring roles on Broadway. By the early 1990s, both Stephen Sondheim and Michael John LaChiusa had written showcase roles for her.

Unfortunately, Murphy's career also offers a textbook example of the spirit being abundantly willing and able but the flesh sometimes being frustratingly weak. Her physical ailments were real, but they caused her to miss so many performances of even her greatest roles that both producers and ticket buyers became uncertain of her attendance at curtain time.

Murphy was born March 7, 1958, in the Corona section of Queens, New York, the eldest of seven children. The family moved to Long Island, and then to suburban Topsfield, Massachusetts, during her childhood. The performing arts provided some continuity for her. She asked her mother for singing lessons at age four. And in school she began performing and even writing plays and music. Her stage presence was recognized early. She performed in *Oklahoma!* (as Laurey) and *Flower Drum Song* (as Linda Low) at her high school in the 1970s. She wasn't shy about her desire to excel onstage. She watched every Tony Awards broadcast on TV and cherished dreams of stardom. When she arrived at Topsfield and found the school lacked a drama program, she helped organize productions herself.

She joined the undergrad theatre program at New York University's Tisch School of the Arts and was accepted as a private student of Method guru Stella Adler. One day while Murphy was performing a scene, Adler began criticizing the way she dressed, saying she looked like a whore. Murphy didn't miss a beat and continued with her scene through the tirade. When she was done, Adler allowed, "The girl's an actress."

Broadway producers obviously felt the same. In her sophomore year Murphy was cast to replace Debbie Gravitte in the tiny chorus of the Marvin Hamlisch musical *They're Playing Our Song*.

"I had fun doing that show," she told an interviewer, "but it was kind of a little detour off the path in terms of the training that I had been getting and what I wanted to do, acting-wise."

Murphy left school then, but her education has never really stopped. She is a self-described "research queen" who tries to learn all she can, not only about her characters, but about the worlds they lived in. During the researching of this book at the Lincoln Center Library for the Performing Arts, librarians would do a double take as I requested material on Murphy just moments after Murphy herself had requested material on Lotte Lenya, whom she was about to impersonate in the biographical *LoveMusik* on Broadway.

Murphy followed up her precocious Broadway debut with a 1980 trip to Goodspeed Opera House in Connecticut to appear in *Zapata*, a musical about the Mexican revolutionary. Murphy said the show itself didn't do much for her career, but she owes it one debt of gratitude. The title role was played by Shawn Elliott, whom she later married, bringing her a stepdaughter.

Murphy returned to Broadway briefly as an understudy in the short-lived Galt MacDermott musical *The Human Comedy* (1985) but made enough of an impression to be hired to understudy both Betty Buckley and Cleo Lane in the 1986 Rupert Holmes musical thriller *The Mystery of Edwin Drood*. She eventually replaced Buckley in the title role late in the run, achieving the distinction of starring in a major Broadway musical while still in her twenties.

The show gave Murphy a chance to hone both her comedy and drama skills and to play something very different from the chorus-girl or hooker roles that many young musical-comedy actresses are often handed. Looks were still important to casting directors, and Murphy's was unique. Part Czech, part French, part German, and part Irish, she inherited brunette hair, full lips, and penetrating, almond-shaped eyes, coupled with a rounded nose that gave her an intriguing look. In this early part of her career she also had curvy figure that helped earn her next role, playing a sultry nightclub chanteuse in the off-Broadway musical *The Song of Singapore*.

Set in the seedy Freddy's Song of Singapore Café on the Singapore waterfront, the show pokes fun at World War II–era film noir thrillers with its story of how the nightclub's happy-go-lucky house band helps solve the theft of some priceless jewels just as the Japanese are about to invade. Murphy played the daffy Rose of Rangoon, with frizzed hair and a slinky evening gown slit up to there. Her past is mysterious even to her. It's eventually revealed that she's an amnesiac who used to be . . . lost aviatrix Amelia Earhart!

The performance earned Murphy some of her first big-time notices for a role she created. Mel Gussow wrote in the *New York Times*, "Ms. Murphy is a terrific singer who can sing blues as well as barrelhouse and can move from an animated chorus of 'You Gotta Do What You Gotta Do' to a silky rendition of 'Sunrise.' As an actress, she is funnier than Rita Hayworth, Dorothy Lamour and other stars who ventured into movie Malaysia. She also plays a deft trumpet and kazoo."

Murphy earned some of her first award nominations. She'd gotten noticed. But some on the production felt she'd gotten a little too noticed. She stole the spotlight from, and did not get along with, her costars, who happened to be the authors of the show. And for the first time, people in the business began to call her "difficult" and "perfectionist."

She addressed the issue in an interview with *TheaterWeek* a few years later. "The issue of selfishness is a huge one for me," she said. "It pushes a button, maybe because when I was a kid, certain members of my family at certain times saw my aggressiveness and focused desires as being selfish."

Composer Mary Rodgers, who saw Murphy perform her songs in a revue *Hey Love: The Songs of Mary Rodgers*, told *TheaterWeek*, "She is a perfectionist. And nobody can help her. She's not the kind of actress who can have a George Abbott tell her exactly what to do and then at the end you realize he was right. She has to work it through for herself. By the time she's finished, she is very confident, and the result is well worth it."

In the paired *Song of Singapore* tunes "I Can't Remember" and "I Remember," onstage she managed to be heartbreaking and hilarious at the same time. Her performance, alas, was not saved for posterity, as she had left the show by the time the cast album was recorded. That's because during *Song of Singapore* Murphy also fell ill for the first time, seriously enough that she left the show and considered quitting acting altogether.

"I was not happy," Murphy told me in a 1996 interview. "I didn't know if I wanted to do this anymore—but I wouldn't have stopped if my body hadn't stopped." Unable to finish the run (and not for the last time), she withdrew from show business for a while. "During my health problems I did a lot of soul searching, exploration on a spiritual and philosophical level."

At that point, Murphy's career was modestly successful, with one or two enviable breaks, but not dazzling. She had appeared in a number of zany musicals, including off-Broadway's *Francis, Birds of Paradise, Privates on Parade*, and *Showing Off*, nearly always playing a sexpot. She had even made her Broadway debut in what ought to have been a big splash in the offbeat part in *The Mystery of Edwin Drood*. But something was missing.

She said, "I decided that if I was going to come back, I was going to come back on different terms. I had to be about what I could do in the work. How I could bring my own voice to it."

Hello, Again

Rising from her sickbed, she appeared in August Strindberg's *Miss Julie* at the McCarter Theatre in New Jersey, then in an acclaimed revival of *Pal Joey* in Massachusetts before being cast as in Michael John LaChiusa's groundbreaking *Hello, Again* at the Lincoln Center's Mitzi Newhouse Theatre.

Yes, it was another sultry role, and this time she played a hooker, the mysterious Leocadia, who sings the title song at the top of the musical. *Hello, Again* is based on *La ronde*, Arthur Schnitzler's uniquely structured drama that shows a pair of characters in the first scene, then one of that pair appears with a new character in the second scene, then that new character appears with a fourth character in the next scene, and so forth until the circle of encounters returns again to the first pair. Murphy was that first and last character.

It wasn't a huge part, but she brought an extraordinary quality to it. Leocadia wasn't just another streetwalker in a tight dress leaning against a lamppost (though she did do that, too). Leocadia seemed to be a supernatural emissary, one of those guardian angels like Mary Poppins or El Gallo who have been sent on a mission to teach a lucky chosen few a special lesson. She chooses a particular sailor to set in motion a round-robin of lessons in love and deceit. This remarkable quality signaled to New York's hardest-core theatre fans that a new star had arrived.

Passion

During rehearsals for *Hello, Again*, director James Lapine approached her to audition for a new musical he was developing with Stephen Sondheim. Originating a role for Sondheim was a sort of holy grail for musical comedy performers. The project was to be called *Passion*, based on Igino Tarchetti's novel *Fosca* and Ettore Scola's 1981 film adaptation, *Passione d'Amore*.

Murphy would play the central character, Fosca, a frighteningly ugly and sickly woman who conceives a monumental love for a handsome soldier, Giorgio. That the soldier already has a love, a stunning beauty, doesn't stop Fosca. She's terrified of this "love as pure as breath, implacable as death" but cannot help herself. She pursues her love with a profundity and single-mindedness that eventually wins the amazed Giorgio.

Murphy was given a fourteen-page chunk of the show to learn in a very short time. And, for a moment, she hesitated. "It was so fascinating and up my alley. I had always dreamed of doing a Sondheim/Lapine show. I had auditioned for *Into the Woods*. But I knew myself, and the way I worked. I knew it wasn't worth going into if I couldn't be really strong."

Ultimately she went into a workshop of *Passion* immediately after she wrapped up *Hello, Again*. It was to be her first major starring role, written especially for her.

It's worth taking a moment to focus on her vocal instrument: a pearly, oboe-like head voice and a woolly, growling chest voice.

Both are in evidence in the *Passion* song "I Wish I Could Forget You." She can be heard pressing her lips against the word "you" with that head voice every time she sings it (she does the same on "Loving You"), then plunges to Dietrichian depths on the words "unkind" and the second "my mind." The latter voice is also displayed in the line "They hear drums, we hear music" at the end of "Garden Sequence."

In the title song of *Hello, Again*, the voice purrs. In *Passion*'s "Trio," the line "I'm in love, hopelessly in love" is full of piercing pain of wonder. Her whispers are like razors; her sobs could break your heart.

But melancholy is far from her only mode. In the wacky off-Broadway revue *Showing Off*, she parodied the hard-bitten chorus girls of *42nd Street* in the number "72nd Street" and brought just the right snarling snottiness to the phrase "Move your ass!" in "S.I.P. (Self Important People)."

In *Passion*, she used this voice to illustrate the inner Fosca, the one that was lost behind her looks. The show's designers dressed her in black, crowned her with unbecoming hats, used make-up that accentuated her nose and made her eyes look sunken and hollow. She was also awarded a prominent mole. Audiences laughed at her entrance during early previews. But as soon as they heard that voice, they were able to see past the face to the complex woman within.

One critic called her an "icy princess," but Ben Brantley of the *New York Times* dubbed her the "First lady of musical tragedy."

Brendan Lemon in *The New Yorker* wrote, "While the show itself has been dividing opinion . . . the performance of its female lead, Donna Murphy, has brought uniform acclaim. Not since Holly Hunter in *The Piano*—which also featured an obsessed Romantic heroine with pulled-back hair—has an actress so excited serious audiences."

It all came down to whether you fell under the spell of that voice, and enough people did to win *Passion* the 1994 Tony Award as Best Musical, and Murphy won the Tony as Best Leading Actress in a Musical.

How did she come to understand Fosca so well? "I've had bouts of physical vulnerability as a result of emotional stress and stuff that have been key in my understanding of her," Murphy told Allan Wallach in *TheaterWeek*. "It's not hypochondria; you get sick."

Passion closed in January 1995 after a disappointing 280-performance run—the shortest ever for a Tony-winning Best Musical.

She drew comfort from Sondheim and Lapine, who "told me stories about other shows. After the intermission of [the Pulitzer Prize-winning musical] *Sunday in the Park* [*with George*], there would be barely an audience left during previews."

Passion, Murphy said, "divided people so strongly. Because, for the people who did take the ride, it changed their lives. I got letters from people who made major life-changing decisions after seeing the show. It's about recognizing what it is to be alive, and how important it is to feel passionate about what you do, about what you care for, about who you care for."

Perhaps it's just as well the show closed when it did. An old problem had recurred. She later told Alan Wallach, "I came home and my body was in pain all the time, I had blinding headaches, I was nauseous a lot of the time. I couldn't let go of her."

Fitting with her philosophy that "Nothing's a mistake, everything's for a reason," the closing of *Passion* led to the fulfillment of her dream to work in many different media. The year 1995 began with the final Broadway performances of *Passion*, which was taped as a TV special for American Playhouse, one of the best complete documents of Murphy's work. Later that year she created her first leading role in a Hollywood film, the erotic thriller *Jade*, costarring David Caruso and Chazz Palminteri.

Jade was a disappointing flop and helped push her back toward stage and TV work.

She played Dorothy Trowbridge in James Lapine's revival of his *Twelve Dreams*, though *New York Times* writer Vincent Canby sniffed that "the role makes use of approximately one-tenth of one percent of her talent."

She participated in a Toronto workshop of the musical *Ragtime* and shot the pilot of the TV series *Murder One*, on which she would play the recurring character of mysterious socialite Francesca Cross. She played the lead in an HBO special, *Someone Had to Be Benny*, which won her a CableACE Award as Best Actress in a Drama Special or Series, as well as a Daytime Emmy, and she recorded the CD *Leonard Bernstein's New York* with Mandy Patinkin, Audra McDonald, *Hello, Again* costar Judy Blazer, and others.

The King and I

After the experimentation of *Hello, Again* and the starburst of *Passion*, who'd have expected Murphy to do a revival of a seeming warhorse, *The King and I*?

At first Murphy said, she thought the same thing.

"When they first talked to me about it I wasn't exactly jumping up and down," she told me. "I mean it was wonderful—I was very flattered by it. And yet I wasn't excited at the prospect of doing a quote-unquote revival."

After all, how many different ways can you sing "I Whistle a Happy Tune"? At least one more, Murphy began to believe.

The Rodgers and Hammerstein Organization had gotten wind of an unusual and lavish, almost surreal, Australian production directed by Christopher Renshaw and toplining former child star Hayley Mills as Anna Leonowens.

"The R&H people didn't know much about the production but they went over to see it as a matter of policy," Murphy said. "Mary Rodgers, as I understand it, was blown away by this production. She then called [R&H president] Ted Chapin and said, 'Get over here!' She thought it was the most beautiful production she'd ever seen, both physically and interpretively."

Most importantly from Murphy's point of view, "Mary said it was so fresh, that the story was back to what its original intention was, which was to focus on Anna." And the Anna she wanted was Murphy.

The original 1950 *The King and I* is based on both the nonmusical film *Anna and the King of Siam* and on the central character's autobiography, *An English Governess in the Court of the King of Siam*. The latter title summarizes the culture-clash story, which was musicalized for star Gertrude Lawrence with a score that includes "Shall We Dance," "Something Wonderful," "I Have Dreamed," "I Whistle a Happy Tune," "Hello Young Lovers," and "Shall I Tell You What I Think of You?"

Most of the songs are sung by Mrs. Anna. Yet, somehow, when people think of *The King and I*, they think mainly of the *King*, and not much of the *I*. Those not familiar with the score will be surprised to read that the king has only one solo, "A Puzzlement," and shares a duet with Mrs. Anna on "Shall We Dance?" Yet such was the power of the original King, Yul Brynner, who repeated the role on film and for hundreds of performances on the road, that people still think of the show as the King's vehicle.

With no disrespect to her own Broadway king, Lou Diamond Phillips, Murphy said the production tried to shift the balance of power back to its narrator.

Murphy said she was also concerned with the show's racial issue, "of a Western woman going to the East and 'taming those savages.' The great white hope thing. It's really a tough issue."

She said Renshaw dealt with the problem by emphasizing the fact that "It's not just what she teaches them. It has to be things that she learns about herself."

Murphy said the real break came when Chapin gave her Leonowens's books to read. In addition to the source of the musical, there was *Siamese Harem Life*.

"As I read these books," Murphy said, "I was so blown away by this woman and the risks she took in that time—in any time. She seemed to be fearless. I was really very inspired."

The production opened in April 1996, and Murphy was hailed for her fresh interpretation of the well-worn role. She walked away with her second Best Actress in a Musical Tony for her second Broadway leading performance.

Wonderful Town

Murphy spent the next several years building a TV career but was lured back to the stage by the "Encores! Great American Musicals in Concert" series at the New York City Center, which was mounting *Wonderful Town*, a 1953 musical based on the play *My Sister Eileen*, with a score by Leonard Bernstein, Betty Comden, and Adolph Green. Comden and Green served as consultants on the production, which turned out to be their last, as Green died soon afterward.

Wonderful Town tells the story of Ruth and Eileen Sherwood, a pair of innocent Ohio sisters who come to New York, hoping to make their fortunes, but find themselves in a noisy, run-down Greenwich Village apartment surrounded by all manner of eccentric New York types. Murphy played the older, brainier sister who wants to be a writer and who is constantly amused, and sometimes exasperated, by the male attention paid to her younger and prettier sister.

Directed by Kathleen Marshall, the May 2000 production was a smash and became the second "Encores!" production to move to Broadway (in November 2003), with sets and costumes added back in. Marshall staged Murphy's numbers in a way that framed her strongest suites, her comedy on "A Hundred Easy Ways (To Lose a Man)" and "Conga," and her multidextrous voice on "Swing."

"On your knees, citizens of Broadway," *Times* critic Ben Brantley wrote about Murphy. "A superwoman walks among you."

Clive Barnes in the *Post* wrote, "Broadway belongs to Donna Murphy, she has the keys to the kingdom."

Murphy's fans were subsequently delighted to hear that she would be playing the wife of villain "Doc Ock" (Alfred Molina) in the big-budget film thriller *Spider-Man 2*, but when the film opened in summer 2004, the role turned out to be a microscopic one, and Murphy's character was killed off in an early scene.

Meanwhile, her real-life health was becoming an issue. Murphy's figure, which had been voluptuous in *Song of Singapore* and *Hello, Again*, became increasingly thin as the 1990s progressed. When I interviewed her before *Wonderful Town* opened on Broadway in fall 2003, she had become extremely pale and slender, even gaunt. She was determined to go ahead with the $5 million transfer but soon found her health had a way of overriding her will.

When she fell ill during previews of *Wonderful Town* and even missed several performances attended by critics, it made news. As the run progressed, Murphy began missing more and more performances. Flu was given as the reason; then hemorrhaged vocal cords. Her name remained on the marquee and in ads. But the box office began to suffer as news got out via word of mouth and the Internet.

The bottom line is that Murphy felt that if she was too ill to go on, her public should understand. A substantial part of her public, particularly *New York Post* columnist Michael Riedel, thought she was irresponsible, lazy, or outright faking her illness. One *Post* story, carrying the headline "Prima Donna," said Murphy's announcements triggered "long lines of angry theatergoers seeking refunds from the box office." A follow-up Riedel column headlined "Murphy's Flaw" said her absences would cost her a shot at her third Tony Award. He paraphrased "A Fine Way to Lose a Man," saying, "That's a fine way to lose a Tony." Sure enough, although she was nominated for the 2004 Tony as Best Actress in a Musical, she lost out to Idina Menzel of *Wicked*, though Menzel would have offered tough competition in any year.

That same month, the *New York Times* picked up on the theme in a story headlined "Broadway's No-Show Business," illustrated with a *Wonderful Town* production photo with Murphy's body cut out. It included the statement, "More and more, stars on the marquee aren't bothering to show up onstage" and berated Murphy personally. "Perhaps it's time for Ms. Murphy to rethink the whole musical-theater-star thing, since it seems to be proving so debilitating."

Murphy, who declined to be interviewed for the *Times* story, told her side to syndicated columnist Liz Smith. Murphy was quoted saying, "I am not cavalier about any of my absences, but the fact is, I have performed in *Wonderful Town* with severe back and neck injuries and series of colds and sinus infections like so many people this past winter. You can't believe what it's like to have a performance right in the middle of it because you can't get a sound out, and your vocal therapist and doctor are theoretically jumping up and down on the sidelines. It breaks my heart to hear I'm being called careless or disappointing theatergoers by not being there."

Murphy had been scheduled to play her final performance as Ruth in the Broadway revival of *Wonderful Town* on September 26, 2004, but left some time before that and never returned. The show closed at a loss soon thereafter.

In subsequent interviews, Murphy revealed the true reason behind her absences: a series of miscarriages. She had tried to maintain her privacy about such an intimate problem, but that proved impossible to do in the full spotlight of stardom. She finally got the sympathy she deserved.

In the years after the *Wonderful Town* debacle, Murphy focused mainly on her TV and film work, lending her coolly brainy visage to series like *Remember WENN* and *CSI: Crime Scene Investigation*; specials like *The Day Lincoln Was Shot*, in which she played First Lady Mary Todd Lincoln; and movies like *World Trade Center* and *The Nanny Diaries*.

After the battering Murphy had taken in the press, and the battering her image had taken among producers, it was widely assumed that her stage career (at least) was over. But Broadway needed someone with her qualities of intelligence matched with showmanship.

In 2007 she made two triumphant returns to the New York stage. The first came in February with the "Encores!" series' revival of another Sondheim musical, *Follies*, in which she played the astringent Phyllis Stone, a role originated by Alexis Smith. Murphy shredded the scenery on "Should I Leave You?" and her other songs.

Robert Hofler of *Variety* called her performance "the most fully realized interpretation of tough-as-diamonds Phyllis Rogers Stone in the show's complicated history."

There was talk of a Broadway transfer, but Murphy had already promised her spring to her other "comeback" project, playing real-life actress Lotte Lenya in *LoveMusik* opposite Michael Cerveris as Lenya's husband and collaborator, composer Kurt Weill. Directed by Harold Prince, the Manhattan Theatre Club original musical was based on the love letters between the German-born couple, who earned fame in *Cabaret*-era Berlin before fleeing the Nazis, first to Paris, then to New York.

Variety's David Rooney wrote that Murphy's Lenya was "all cool looks, gangly limbs and swaggering vulgarity . . . a brilliant caricature ennobled by truth."

Ben Brantley in the *New York Times* said, "Ms. Murphy demonstrates once again her singular gift for balancing intellect and intuition, research and actorly insight, in musical performance . . . Such is Ms. Murphy's attention to detail that her voice even ages as Lenya's did, becoming lower and grainier. When this Lenya takes the stage for the opening scene of the original *Threepenny*, narrowing her eyes in contemptuous assessment of the audience, you understand in a millisecond why the show made the impact it did."

Murphy seems determined to seek out new challenges despite her infirmities, and her fans seem determined to make every effort to see her.

Nathan Lane (circa 1990). PHOTOFEST

NATHAN LANE
Good Old Reliable Nathan

Nathan Lane has been Broadway's mask of comedy to the world, starting in the early 1990s. At the turn of the twenty-first century, he became the first Broadway star recognizable to the general public since Tommy Tune.

He has another distinction. He is the only musical-comedy star named after a great musical-comedy role.

Born Joseph Lane, he discovered, as many actors do, that there was already someone with that name in Actors Equity. He had to choose another. He named himself Nathan, after Nathan Detroit of *Guys and Dolls*, a role he would later play to acclaim on Broadway.

Lane has a pudgy body that resists diets and finely tailored suits. His dark hair frames a square face with a snub nose, a cleft chin, eyebrows drawn up in perpetual world-weariness, and a mouth that's usually tiny and withdrawn but that can wow out very wide when a comic effect is required. He has sometimes adopted a moustache or beard but usually appears clean-shaven.

In short, he looks born to be a vaudeville comedian. And that is another important part of Lane's appeal. He commands an arsenal of tics, expressions, and other vocal and physical bits of business—classic *lazzi*—that link him to a very deep comic tradition, like clown Bill Irwin.

And here's where things get complicated. Like many comedians, Lane is not exactly a lighthearted fellow offstage, though he is capable of hilarious flights when he's with friends. He continues to fight with serious demons, including a sense that success with comedy robbed him of the opportunity to play weightier roles. To a certain degree he is a Laurence Olivier trapped inside an Oliver Hardy.

But he also has enough perspective to realize that such a combination is hardly the worst thing in the world to be. He's rarely less than marvelous, whether on Broadway, off-Broadway, in films, making special appearances, subbing as host of David Letterman's TV talk show, or assuming other guest-starring roles. His Achilles heel appears to be TV situation comedy.

An out-of-the-closet gay man, Lane quickly wearies when the subject is brought up in interviews. He is convincing playing both straight and gay roles (except in one of the afore-mentioned sitcoms), finding essential truths (usually funny ones) in each.

Lane found himself following the late Zero Mostel into some of his classic roles, and some people called Lane the new Mostel. In fact, Lane's real spiritual ancestors are Bert Lahr and Bert Williams. All three were master comedians capable more serious work, who were adored for their masterful comedy chops.

★

Joseph Lane was born February 3, 1956, into what his brother later described to the *New York Times* as "a dark, nutty family" in Jersey City, New Jersey. His two brothers were sub-stantially older than he, and family legend had it that Lane was an accidental pregnancy. His father was an Irish-American truck driver whose failing eyesight caused him to lose his job. He became an alcoholic and drank himself to death when Lane was barely a teenager. His mother was diagnosed as manic-depressive and spent Lane's teenage years in and out of mental hospitals.

"Joe," as he was known to his family, was essentially raised by his brother Dan Lane, a New Jersey school administrator who was thirteen years older. It was Dan who began tak-ing young Joe across the Hudson to see Broadway shows. And he was the one who put the boy into St. Peter's Jesuit prep school, where he began acting.

Joe quickly realized this was what he wanted to do with his life. Despite his brother's background in education, he decided to skip college and go directly into showbiz. One of his early gigs was playing Nathan Detroit in a New Jersey dinner theatre production of *Guys and Dolls.*

Lane relocated to Manhattan and began the traditional grind of auditions. He began getting work with some of the major off-Broadway troupes, including Roundabout Theater Company and Manhattan Theatre Club, both of which earned his loyalty.

His personal life was less smooth. When he was twenty-one he resolved to come out as gay to his family. The *New York Times* reported that his mother memorably declared, "I'd rather you were dead." Lane replied with sorrowful bite, "I knew you'd understand."

It was through Circle in the Square that Lane made his Broadway debut on July 15, 1982, at the age of twenty-six. He was handpicked by master actor George C. Scott to ap-pear in a revival of Noël Coward's farce *Present Laughter*. Scott played Coward's semiauto-biographical role of preening actor Garry Essendine, who tries to handle constant interruptions as he prepares to depart on a trip. Lane played Roland Maule, an obsessed fan and playwright who is undeterred when Essendine insults him and literally tears up his play. In a cast that also featured Kate Burton, Dana Ivey, and Christine Lahti, Lane stood out as being an almost preternaturally gifted physical comedian, adding a skillful slapstick to the madness that at one point had the two of them wrestling on a couch.

By the time the limited run ended in January 1983, Lane was already preparing for his first Broadway musical, *Merlin*, in which he was to play Prince Fergus, the mousy son of a grandly wicked enchantress called the Queen, played by Chita Rivera. The campy show may have flopped, but Lane emerged with an excellent reputation in the business. He next played the heedless and comically self-centered (and spit-curled) Toad in a musical based on the children's classic *The Wind in the Willows*. It, too, flopped, further postponing Lane's Broadway stardom.

Still maintaining his links to the not-for-profit world, Lane appeared in two gentle comedies, the U.S. premiere of *Some Americans Abroad* (1990) for Lincoln Center Theatre and a revival of *On Borrowed Time* (1991) at Circle in the Square. Lane played Death, which comes in the form of a nattily tailored man named Mr. Brink. Lane played the Grim Reaper without gloating or seeming bloodthirsty; he was simply inexorable.

Working with McNally

Though in years to come he'd be identified primarily as an actor in musical comedy, Lane's most important collaboration in the late 1980s and early 1990s was with playwright Terrence McNally, who wrote a series of comedy-dramas, mainly with gay themes, in which Lane starred.

Lane played an obsessive fan of diva Maria Callas in McNally's 1989 play *The Lisbon Traviata*. Two years later, Lane starred with Swoosie Kurtz and Christine Baranski in McNally's *Lips Together, Teeth Apart*, playing the husband of a woman who is grieving over her brother's death from AIDS and has inherited his Fire Island beach house in his will. Lane was required to take a shower onstage, his midsection obscured by a small shower door. For this he earned the nickname "the Mary Martin of Off-Broadway," a reference to her hair-washing scene in *South Pacific*. Though the play had many comic moments, it was essentially about straight people's struggle to find healthy relationships with the gays in their midst—indeed, in their families.

McNally's 1994 play *Love! Valour! Compassion!* was again about gays and family, but from a very different angle. In this case, Lane was part of a circle of men who share a country house and eventually forge themselves into a new kind of family.

Lane also appeared in a supporting role as the neighbor of Michelle Pfeiffer in the 1991 film of McNally's *Frankie and Johnny in the Clair de Lune*—called just *Frankie and Johnny*—with Al Pacino.

The McNally series of roles gave Lane a chance to explore a variety of interesting and noncliché characters who also shared his sexual identity. Lane didn't advertise his homosexuality—he later told the *Times* that he was an old-fashioned gay who didn't march in parades—but he never denied it, either. He once flew into a rage when an interviewer tried to "out" him, when in fact he'd been comfortably out all along. The presumption of the interviewer pushed him over the edge.

That said, Lane soon found himself typecast to a degree as someone who played only gays. He has spent the rest of his career battling that, while still taking gay roles when he finds ones that interested him.

Guys and Dolls

In 1991, a consortium of innovative producers called Dodger Theatricals gave Lane the chance to play his namesake role on Broadway. Inspired partly by the success of a Royal National Theatre production in London, they decided to do a first-class revival of Frank Loesser's 1950 classic *Guys and Dolls*, directed by Jerry Zaks and featuring the young star Nathan Lane in the role originated by Sam Levene—Nathan Detroit.

The musical is set in Damon Runyon's neverland Times Square, where gamblers, gangsters, stripteasers, and Salvation Army uplifters talk in their own distinctive argot.

Lane infused the part with comic richness. He was less hangdog than Levene but seemed a lot more legitimate than Frank Sinatra had in the film. The whole production was directed as a sort of animated cartoon, with broad, brightly colored pinstripes on the suits for the gangsters by William Ivey Long. Nathan played Nathan as someone who looked always ready for the next blow to fall but who would meet that fate with a courageous comic belligerence. Here we first heard his gargled shout, his huh-huh-huh laugh, his ability to push his voice lower and lower to create a conspiratorial atmosphere, or to push it higher and higher to make some crazy point or other. Lane's Detroit followed a wonderful little arc from desperation to inspiration to collapse to comic surrender.

He played his relationship with his leading lady, Faith Prince as Adelaide ("the well-known fiancée"), with pure love and accepted her disapproval of his floating crap game as simply his cross to bear. There were moments of pure silliness throughout the show, such as when Lane (in a pencil mustache) battled his way through "Sue Me," and at one point he and Prince just held the note on the words "alriiiiiight already."

Although he lost that year's Best Actor in a Musical Tony Award to Gregory Hines for *Jelly's Last Jam*, audiences had fallen in love with Lane. Here was the first major new comic talent who might take his place with the Mostels, Lahrs, and Clarks.

Laughter on the 23rd Floor

Lane attained a personal landmark in 1993 when jokemaster Neil Simon (now a Pulitzer laureate for *Lost in Yonkers*) fashioned a play for him, *Laughter on the 23rd Floor*. The farce recaptured Simon's early 1950s work as a comedy writer for Sid Caesar's *Your Show of Shows* territory, already explored in the hit film *My Favorite Year*. Lane played the Caesar character, here named Max Prince, a crazed, insecure, demanding volcano of talent. Among his bullied writers were Ron Orbach, Lewis J. Stadlen, Mark Linn-Baker, and Randy Graff, many of whom would pop up again in future Lane projects.

The Lion King

Of all Lane's myriad shows, films, and recordings, it's very likely that the one performance experienced by more people than any other was that of Timon the meerkat in the animated 1994 Disney film *The Lion King*.

The plot, which borrows its outlines from Shakespeare's *Hamlet* and *Henry IV*, tells the story of lion cub Simba, prince of a stretch of African savannah called the Pridelands, who sees his father murdered and his wicked uncle seize the throne belonging to him.

He then goes into exile, where he's befriended by a Falstaff-like meerkat (Lane) and a warthog (voiced by pal Ernie Sabella), whose laid-back, "no worries" philosophy is outlined in the Elton John song "Hakuna Matata."

Lane did much more than simply supply a voice for the meerkat Timon. Lane's facial expressions, gestures, energy, and general attitude were captured by the Disney animators in the otherwise whiplike creature. He helped make phrases like "Tastes like chicken!," "It starts," and "Whadda ya want me to do, put on a grass skirt and dance the hula?" into tiny comic gems.

The success of *The Lion King* ricocheted on Lane, however. Everywhere he went, people wanted him to sing "Hakuna Matata." Others might find the creation of such a cultural landmark a blessing. To Lane, always striving for something new, it was a burden. Finally, in an appearance on the comedy show *Saturday Night Live*, Lane announced to the camera that he'd sing it *one last time*, and he did.

Forum

Hoping to duplicate the success of *Guys and Dolls*, producers Jujamcyn and Dodger Theatricals decided to reassemble the team for a major Broadway revival of the 1962 Stephen Sondheim/Larry Gelbart/Burt Shevelove musical *A Funny Thing Happened on the Way to the Forum*. Director Zaks sought Lane for the role of wily Roman slave Pseudolus, and Lane agreed—if they would wait for a year so he could shoot *The Birdcage*, a film based on the same source material as the musical *La Cage aux Folles*. Robin Williams played Armand, and Lane played drag goddess Albert. The film did modestly well—in fact, it's been Lane's most successful live-action film to date.

In the meantime, he fulfilled his promise to Zaks and the producers, opening April 18, 1996, in a rollicking production of *Forum* with sets and costumes by original designer Tony Walton and with a supporting cast of master comics, including his old friend Ernie Sabella as Marcus Lycus, Lewis J. Stadlen as Senex, and Mary Testa as Domina.

Inevitably, critics compared Lane with the original Pseudolus, Zero Mostel. And while many of them were comfortable with the notion that someone had come alone with the stature and old-fashioned showbiz technique to assume Mostel's mantle, the consensus was that he was a sort of Mostel Light, an impression that infuriated him. Perhaps more so because Lane has won the Tony Award as Best Actor in a Musical twice—both times for roles (in *Forum* and *Producers*) originated by Mostel.

But in reality, Lane never tried to imitate Mostel. He brought his own combination of determination and exasperation to the role, as the farcical plot threw roadblock after roadblock in front of his plans to win his freedom by helping his master, Hero, run away with the beautiful courtesan Philia.

Vincent Canby in the *New York Times* wrote, "Unlike the legendary Mostel, who delighted audiences by reportedly climbing all over the show and more or less taking it hostage, Mr. Lane succeeds by working with his colleagues. He insinuates himself into the consciousness with a kind of devious, hard-edged innocence."

Lane passed on an opportunity to play Tevye in a revival of *Fiddler on the Roof* because he didn't want to be perceived as simply following in Mostel's footsteps, though, as we shall later see, another former Mostel role proved too good to pass up.

He stepped into the shoes of another great comedian of the same era, Phil Silvers, for whom *Forum* was originally written, and who eventually played Pseudolus in a 1972 Broadway revival. One of Silvers's best Broadway roles was in the 1960 musical *Do Re Mi*, playing a former small-time crook who assembles his old gang to go "legitimate" in the jukebox business but winds up in trouble again. (The title sounds musical, but it turns out to be slang for money, as in "dough.")

The New York City Center's "Encores! Great American Musicals in Concert" series presented Lane in the Silvers role in May 6–9, 1999, performances of the Jule Styne/Betty Comden/Adolph Green/Garson Kanin musical, which featured Randy Graff as his long-suffering wife, with Brian Stokes Mitchell and Heather Headley as the romantic couple. In supporting roles were character actors who were becoming something of a repertory company for Lane: Lewis J. Stadlen and Brad Oscar.

It turned out to be one of the most delightful presentations of the entire "Encores!" series and was made into one of its best cast recordings. The show itself was still second-rate at best, but the stellar cast gave it as much of a high polish as it could take. Among the highlights were "Ambition," Lane's tempting of singer Headley into the swamp of the music business, and "The Late Late Show," in which Lane enacted every movie cliché from 1930s and 1940s film classics, then in rotation on television late at night. As it did for Silvers, the part afforded Lane a wide range of emotions to play and gave free rein to his underused gift for mimicry.

Wise Guys

In October 1999, *Forum* composer Stephen Sondheim chose Lane for one of two male leads in his long-awaited new musical *Wise Guys*. He and Victor Garber played real-life brothers Wilson and Addison Mizner, one a designer, the other a con-man. Despite the sterling credentials of all involved, the show didn't continue beyond its workshop. Sondheim and librettist John Weidman continued working on the project under a series of titles, including *Bounce* and *Road Show*, but Lane had moved on to other things.

Between Broadway projects, he appeared in more than a dozen films, including *Ironweed* and *Nicholas Nickleby*. He took a variety of assignments, from leading roles, as in *Birdcage* (1996) and *Mousehunt* (1997), to featured parts, as in *Love's Labour's Lost* (2000) and Terrence McNally's *Frankie and Johnny* (1991); and to voiceovers, as in *Titan A.E.* (2000) and the *Stuart Little* films, starting in 1999. He worked steadily, but Hollywood seemed to have no clear idea what to do with him.

Broadway did. He was a comic leading man. Lane had the privilege of inaugurating the refurbished American Airlines Theatre (née the Selwyn) on the reborn Forty-second Street with a summer 2000 revival of Kaufman and Hart's comedy *The Man Who Came to Dinner*, playing tart-tongued critic Sheridan Whiteside, who finds himself stranded in the middle of a middle-class home in middle America, which he proceeds to terrorize. He subsequently played the same role on a studio recording of a musical based upon the same play, retitled *Sherry!*, cowritten by James Lipton of BravoTV's *Inside the Actors Studio*.

The Producers

And now came Lane's greatest musical role: Max Bialystock in *The Producers*. Theatre fans had always loved Mel Brooks's 1968 movie *The Producers*, a ferocious parody of the 1960s theatre scene that turned on the notion that you could conceivably make more money with a flop than with a hit. The two main characters are down-at-the-heels Broadway producer Max Bialystock and his painfully mousy accountant Leo Bloom. After an exhausting search for a surefire disaster, they locate their grail: *Springtime for Hitler: A Gay Romp with Adolph and Eva at Berchtesgaden*, not only guaranteed to flop, but indeed to "close on page four." *The Producers*' black comedy—it was called "sick humor" when it first came out—had become much more mainstream in the ensuing thirty years.

When first rumors began to leak out that Brooks was adapting it to the stage, a kind of frenzy erupted in theatrical circles. But the consensus was there was only one actor who could fill Zero Mostel's shoes: Nathan Lane, because of his outsize persona and, of course, his inherent Jewishness. He played Jewish so well that many just assumed the Irish-American actor *was* Jewish.

Critics loved the show, and audiences loved Lane. Adding to his reputation as a vaudevillian reincarnate, Lane had warm chemistry with his costar Matthew Broderick and seemed to form a comedy team with him, just like in the old days.

Lines to get tickets for *The Producers* stretched down Forty-forth Street and onto Eighth Avenue. The like hadn't been seen since they started selling Broadway tickets over the phone and online. There was no need to come to the box office in person, but people did so anyway. They wanted to see the ticket in their hand.

On September 2, 2001, the *New York Times* published a story based on interviews Lane had given with Alex Witchel, titled "This Is It—as Happy as I Get, Baby." It chronicled Lane's rise to stardom, his troubled relationship with his parents, and his dour offstage persona, fueled by nearly crippling self-doubt.

Hopefully this helped: After Lane left the cast of *The Producers*, the box office subsided much more quickly than anyone had guessed. Producers now saw how much the success of the show itself depended on the charisma of its lead. Lane and Broderick returned to the show in late 2003, shooting the show back into the sold-out column.

Adventures in Burbank

After *The Producers*, people thought Lane would be perfect in a TV sitcom, but the industry had always had bad luck finding the right material for him. *One of the Boys* (1982) had faded away after just eight episodes, despite a powerhouse cast that also included Mickey Rooney, Scatman Crothers, and *Saturday Night Live* comedian Dana Carvey. It was quite a feat to have a flop with so much comic megatonnage at your disposal.

Encore! Encore! in 1998 had cast Lane as a womanizing ex–opera singer, perhaps vaguely inspired by Luciano Pavarotti. Lane was convincing as neither. It lasted twelve episodes. Reaction was so scorching he was quoted defensively saying, "It wasn't a war crime. It was a sitcom."

His big comeback show, *Charlie Lawrence* (2003), in which he was to play a Barney Frank–like gay congressman, fared even worse, expiring after a single episode. Lane has proven more successful as a guest star on shows like *Saturday Night Live* and *30 Rock*.

The Frogs

In 2001, Lane took part in a studio recording of a lesser-known Sondheim musical, *The Frogs,* written with Burt Shevelove in 1974 somewhat in the style of their *A Funny Thing Happened on the Way to the Forum*. It was based on the 2,400-year-old comedy of the same title by Aristophanes, about the god Dionysos, who grows unhappy with the political and literary state of Athens. He travels to the underworld to bring back a great playwright to inspire and goad the Greeks back to greatness.

The Frogs had debuted in a student production at Yale. A few of the songs surfaced in Sondheim concerts and solo recordings, but the entire score had never been recorded. Nonesuch Records sought to remedy that, casting Lane as Dionysus and Brian Stokes Mitchell as Xanthias. The project inspired Lane, who enjoyed the roughhouse fun of *Forum* but saw *The Frogs* as having a little something extra.

The Frogs, for all its bawdy humor and slapstick, had a political intention. It was about how to engage the polity—how to get people riled up and get them involved in correcting injustices in society and government. Like many at the time, Lane had grown increasingly upset with the direction America was taking under the administration of President George W. Bush. In his own way, Lane saw *The Frogs* as his chance to help rouse a largely supine public but felt it wasn't strong enough to stand alone on Broadway in its original 1974 form. Shevelove had died in 1982, so Lane conceived the idea of putting on a librettist's hat and expanding the book himself.

Accompanied by his *Producers* director-choreographer Susan Stroman, he approached Sondheim with the idea, which, they said, would require the composer to write some additional new songs. Stroman said Sondheim was skeptical at first, but Lane and Sondheim shared the belief that political theatre can have enormous power. The result, which opened at the Vivian Beaumont Theatre at Lincoln Center in 2004, reunited Lane, who again played Dionysus, with Roger Bart (the original Carmen Ghia from *The Producers*) as Xanthias. Whatever the intentions, *The Frogs* showed Lane's inexperience as a librettist. The tone of the humor was uneven, but the entire production was as heartfelt and inspiring as they could have wished. Smartly, Lane knew that most of the audience coming to see such a show would already agree with his political point of view. He makes it clear to his audience that having an opinion is not enough; even applauding *The Frogs* is not enough—you must act. Lane and Sondheim came together beautifully on new songs like "Think Big," "I Love to Travel," and "Hades."

Sondheim even wrote "Ariadne," a lament for Dionysus, telling the story of his love for the mortal Ariadne, her death, and how the constellation Corona was created when he flung her crown into the sky. In the song of heartbreak, Sondheim not only retold a classic myth and made it personal; he allowed a glimpse inside Lane, as well.

Nevertheless, *The Frogs* played out its limited run and did not extend into a commercial run. Lane hasn't written another show since.

Movie of *The Producers*

The movie readaptation of *The Producers* should have been a smash, but the 2005 release, which also served as Susan Stroman's film-directing debut, failed to hit the bull's-eye with the public as the show had done. Some compared it unfavorably with the 1968 original and saw it as excessively stagey. Stroman had reconceived the story so fully for the stage it was hard to put it back on film. Its stage artifices had become essential to its delight, and those just didn't land the same way when compressed into two dimensions.

The film also reunited the comedy team of Lane and Broderick. They cracked each other up and just seemed to enjoy working together. Their relationship was strained somewhat when Broderick appeared to have trouble memorizing his lines when cast as Felix in a 2005 revival of Neil Simon's comedy *The Odd Couple*. Lane employed his volcanic humor in his portrait of Oscar Madison, the slob half of the pair.

Lane, who had tried a more serious turn in the Off-Broadway solo show *Trumbo*, playing blacklisted screenwriter Dalton Trumbo, went to the Huntington Theatre in Boston to play a college professor at the end of his personal and professional rope in a revival of Simon Gray's *Butley*. It was filled with the kind of angry, witty humor Lane savored, and the performance was so powerful that producers moved the show to Broadway in 2006. Audiences may not have been fully prepared for the bitterness and self-loathing in their favorite clown—it ran just short of three months—but Lane had created a fine monster.

November

In January 2008, Lane finally got his chance to originate a role in a David Mamet play title *November*—but one that departed significantly from his earlier work. It was a high-speed farce about a deeply unpopular U.S. president facing a crushing reelection loss. Lane played President Charles Smith, who spends his day wheeling and dealing in the Oval Office to raise money for his presidential library—and maybe even find a way to swing the election around at the last minute. Along the way he tries to shake down everyone he can think of, from the turkey producers to the head of a casino-running Indian tribe.

Amid Mamet's traditional shower of f-bombs, Lane portrayed the flop-sweating desperation of the cornered con man with his usual dexterity. It was a deeply cynical view of the highest office in the land, but also hilarious.

As this book went to press, Lane was preparing to put his own stamp on one of Bert Lahr's greatest roles, Estragon, in a Broadway revival of *Waiting for Godot* opposite another master clown, Bill Irwin. Lane was still in the high tide of his career, still striking out in new directions, and still trying to find out if this is still really "as happy as I get."

Brian Stokes Mitchell as Petruchio/Fred Graham in *Kiss Me, Kate* (1999).
JOAN MITCHELL/PHOTOFEST

BRIAN STOKES MITCHELL
Wheels of a Dream

When Brian Stokes Mitchell arrived on the scene in the 1990s, he was exactly the kind of commandingly masculine (yet comedic) baritone leading man in the Alfred Drake mode that everyone was sure Broadway couldn't produce anymore.

As a bonus, the light-skinned black actor could play black, white, or Latino roles equally convincingly—something Drake could only dream of doing. He had enormous appeal to women. *People* magazine named him one of its "Sexiest Men Alive." Most people know him as an actor, but he's also a writer, as well as a composer whose credits include scoring for episodes of TV's *Trapper John, M.D.*

On top of everything else, the majestically three-named actor was humble and self-deprecating, insisting that everyone just call him "Stokes." The *New York Times* once described his laugh as sounding "like an express train just passed underneath on its way to Times Square," and people he worked with got to hear it often.

When Mitchell was fifteen years old, he had already done some semiprofessional work in theatres in San Diego, where he grew up, and was already deeply in love with live theatre. He recalls that he was up late one night writing a musical of his own when he suddenly felt the overwhelming urge to write himself a letter. He paraphrases it thus: "Whatever it is you are going through, don't give up. If you ever feel like giving up, read this letter."

Mitchell has never had to unseal that letter, but he absorbed its lesson.

Mitchell was born on Halloween 1957 in Seattle, the youngest of four children of a navy electronics engineer, George Mitchell, who had spent World War II as one of the legendary African American fighters the Tuskegee Airmen. His mother, Lillian, was a school administrator.

The Mitchells were a mixed-race family, predominantly black, with German and Scottish on his mother's side combining with "a smattering" of Native American. This rich ethnic legacy later created both problems and advantages for Mitchell as an actor in America. On one hand, it was hard to pigeonhole him. If a director wanted a certain combination of ethnic actors, where would he fit in? However, as resistance to such categorization began to melt (a little) in the 1980s and 1990s, Mitchell found he could get hired as almost any non–East Asian ethnic type.

He grew up in the Philippines and Guam, where he began playing the piano at age six. When he was fourteen, the family settled in San Diego, where he discovered musical theatre. Although his early inspirations were black singers like Ray Charles and Aretha Franklin, he found that his own developing orotund voice was not suited to soul or R&B. He searched the record collection at the San Diego Public Library and found the sound he was seeking in the likes of Alfred Drake and Richard Kiley on their original cast albums.

His affinity for musicals was immediate. He joined the San Diego Junior Theatre and at age sixteen in 1973 made his professional debut in a production of *Godspell* at the Old Globe Theatre in San Diego. During this time he also appeared in a production of *Man of La Mancha,* playing one of the Muleteers.

Although he'd been chubby as a child, puberty slimmed his waist, broadened his shoulders, and deepened his voice into a ringing baritone. Instead of comedy parts, he was getting romantic lead parts.

At age twenty he moved to Los Angeles to join the Twelfth Night Repertory Company as resident composer and actor. But being an actor in LA meant being an actor in TV and films, and Mitchell landed the role of John Dolan in the miniseries *Roots: The Next Generation.* At age twenty-two he got to see his name listed in the credits beside those of Henry Fonda, Olivia de Havilland, Ossie Davis, and Marlon Brando.

That led to a regular role as Dr. Justin "Jackpot" Jackson, the wisecracking intern on the TV drama series *Trapper John, M.D.,* which lasted from 1979 to 1987 and gave Mitchell financial stability. He might have settled into a career as a character actor in one TV show after another, but he missed the stage. That's why, in 1986, he took a supporting role in an obscure new musical getting its debut at the Pasadena Playhouse, *Mail.*

Still billing himself without his middle name (he added his just as his future costar Audra Ann McDonald was dropping hers), he played the friend of the leading man, Alex, in the musical about an author whose backlog of mail comes to singing and dancing life. The show was cowritten by its star, Michael Rupert, with Jerry Colker.

When *Mail* moved to Broadway the following year, Mitchell came along with it. The *New York Times* reviewed Mitchell's Broadway debut thus: "Alex's best friend (Brian Mitchell) is defined only by the fact that he is black (he sings a rap song)," which doesn't sound like it made much use of Mitchell's range or vocal skill. *Mail* ran thirteen performances and was forgotten. But Mitchell was just getting started. He'd been *noticed.* Casting directors got all sorts of interesting notions of what Mitchell could do. He fit so many niches.

Diversity

About his move to the East Coast, Mitchell later told Kathy Henderson in *Playbill,* "People in New York are a lot more creative and willing to judge actors on the basis of talent rather than on their 'look.' Los Angeles is very much into the blond, beach kind of look, and I'm not that. . . . I can slide into applying different ethnicities easily, and people accept it. I wish the whole word could be like that."

His next three Broadway shows illustrated that diversity.

First, David Merrick picked him to play Jimmy Winter, the romantic lead in a 1990 revival of the 1926 Prohibition musical *Oh, Kay!* Back in 1968, Merrick has been credited with the then-radical idea of replacing the entire white cast of *Hello, Dolly!* during its original run, with black actors, led by Pearl Bailey and Cab Calloway. Now Merrick decided to do the same racial switch, but do it from scratch, with an all-black cast playing hitherto white characters, though moving the action from Long Island to jazz-age Harlem. Critics mostly shrugged at Merrick's "innovation," which had since happened frequently enough to be considered a movement and to have acquired a name: nontraditional casting.

While the production ran only seventy-seven performances, it marked two important landmarks in Mitchell's life. It was his first leading-man role on Broadway and suggested that his shoulders were strong enough to carry a show, preferably a better show. Also, the production introduced him to dancer/singer Allyson Tucker. They married in 1994 and have a son, Ellington.

In 1992 Mitchell replaced Maurice Hines in *Jelly's Last Jam*, a musical about Jelly Roll Morton, the jazz pioneer ("inventor," to hear him tell it), born a Creole in New Orleans and who struggled for the rest of his life with his cultural identity.

Mitchell then, in 1993, replaced Anthony Crivello in Kander and Ebb's musical *Kiss of the Spider Woman*, playing Valentin, the imprisoned Brazilian revolutionary, opposite Chita Rivera and then Vanessa Williams as the Spider Woman, and opposite Howard McGillin as Valentin's cell mate, a gay window dresser who draws him into his escapist fantasy of colorful old movies—and falls in love with him.

David Richards of the *New York Times* found Mitchell an improvement on the originator. "Mr. Mitchell's Valentin may be a straight arrow, but he's not the categorical macho firebrand depicted by Anthony Crivello in the original cast. Characters who once faced each other from opposite ends of the sexual spectrum have been brought a little closer. While Mr. McGillin is playing up Molina's more exuberant charm, Mr. Mitchell is playing down Valentin's brusque condescension. As a result, the growing affection between them seems the more believable."

In addition to all the other constituencies Mitchell pleased, he was now a straight actor with appeal to gay audiences.

Wheels of a Dream

Mitchell next found himself drawn into an epic project that would allow him to create the defining role of his career. *Kiss of the Spider Woman* was produced by Livent Inc., a Canada-based producing company that was the baby of charismatic producer Garth Drabinsky. Drabinsky was a visionary and a risk taker, and while, in the end, Livent overextended itself and had to be sold amid fraud charges, in the mid-1990s it was riding high. Drabinsky was always on the lookout for interesting projects and artists. He later told the *Times* that when he saw Mitchell in *Spider Woman*, the actor became his first choice to play the lead in the biggest musical project ever attempted by Livent—a guaranteed monster hit, and one for which Livent was prepared to build an entire new Broadway theatre.

Drabinsky had obtained the rights to *Ragtime*, E. L. Doctorow's sweeping novel about the collision of class and history in turn-of-the-twentieth-century New York. The book mixed real-life celebrities like Harry Houdini, Booker T. Washington, Emma Goldman, and J. P. Morgan with fictional characters concocted by Doctorow. Among the latter was Coalhouse Walker Jr., a young black man—a piano player—who has earned enough money to put his family back together and to buy a little piece of the American dream in the form of . . . a car. A glittering new Model T Ford.

And in this sweet moment, *Ragtime* stops for a wonderful song by Stephen Flaherty and Lynn Ahrens, a song introduced by Mitchell and, as his wife, Sarah, a young African American actress who was appearing in her first Broadway lead, Audra McDonald.

There are national anthems far less stirring than "Wheels of a Dream." It's a soaring duet for two deeply cynical persons who allow themselves, for one moment, to be happy and hopeful—to *believe* something they'd heard about all their lives, like a fairy tale, and now suddenly hold in their hands. This once was the stock in trade of musicals, now rare in a cynical age.

They have a car. It's just a step to freedom and equality and respect for them and for their children. How will they get there? They'll "ride on the wheels of a dream."

The dream hits some big speed bumps in Act II. By the time he sings "Coalhouse's Soliloquy" in the second act, the car has been wrecked and Sarah has been killed (though the baby survives—a single ray of hope). Full of dissonant notes and clashing percussion, the song is an epiphany in which Coalhouse resolves not only to get revenge, but to die doing so.

Mitchell's youthful piano lessons came in handy for the scenes in which he played and sang "Gettin' Ready Rag" and "Sarah Brown Eyes." He gave the role a cocky physical presence, gazing slyly over his shoulder and under a tipped derby when he was playing and with his weight resting confidently back on his hips when he walked.

Director Frank Galati observed, "He moves with an extraordinary grace . . .yet he is very centered, able to be very focused and still. His voice is resonant and warm in color and very rich, and when it lifts up into the atmosphere it has a brilliance and a steady burning intensity."

Perhaps sensing an impending change in his status, Mitchell made a personal change, as well. Billed up to then as "Brian Mitchell," he added his mother's maiden name as his middle name, becoming Brian Stokes Mitchell and urging everyone, family as well as casual acquaintances, to address him not as Brian or Mr. Mitchell, but as "Stokes."

In his review of the show, the *Times*' Brantley said Mitchell "emerges as a sexy, charismatic star who finds a sinuous dignity in the persecuted Coalhouse."

In addition to being a great musical-theatre role, the part also directly addressed racism in America. Mitchell told an interviewer that playing Coalhouse was emotionally exhausting. It was like "riding a wave, it starts with the joy of falling in love, seeing your child for the first time, and then descends in to this utter hell. . . . I don't go to sleep until three or four in the morning."

It was in May 11, 1998, just a few months after the opening of *Ragtime*, that *People* magazine named Mitchell one of its annual "Sexiest Men Alive." And many felt he was sashaying to a Tony Award that might as well already have his name engraved on it. But it was not to be. Alan Cumming, who had rouged his nipples for his decadent take on the Emcee in Roundabout Theater Company's revival of *Cabaret*, snatched it away at the last minute. Ahrens and Flaherty won the Tony for Best Score, and Audra McDonald won for Best Featured Actress in a Musical. But Disney's *The Lion King* beat *Ragtime* for Best Musical.

Sexiest Man Alive

All the attention allowed Mitchell to see if prospects had improved in the TV business. He had recurring roles on the sitcoms *Frasier*, as grumpy neighbor Cam Winston, and on *The Fresh Prince of Bel-Air*, as egotistical TV personality Trevor Collins, memorable for his dramatic death while proposing to his girlfriend during a bungee jump that goes wrong.

He also arranged music out of his home studio and did a fair amount of voice work for animated cartoons, including *Batman* and *James Bond Jr.* But one of the few assignments that allowed him to sing was the 1998 animated film *The Prince of Egypt*, in which Mitchell played the white-haired biblical patriarch Jethro and sang the number "Through Heaven's Eyes," written for him by *Wicked* and *Godspell* composer Stephen Schwartz.

Mitchell finally won his Tony Award as Best Actor in a Musical for playing Fred Graham/Petruchio in the 1999 revival of *Kiss Me, Kate*. Mitchell was macho and ever so slightly oily as Fred, but he also showed real ability to laugh at his whole "sexiest man alive" image and constantly undercut his character's own ego with self-deprecating touches. Supported by Don Sebesky's pristine orchestrations, Mitchell put a soft sob behind "So in Love" and brought down the house.

These qualities were all noted by the critics. What they decided not to notice, or perhaps just *didn't* notice, was that a mixed-race couple held the leading roles of a classic American musical. (Though newer shows, like *Rent*, were born hip.)

Though none of the critics made a big deal over the fact that Mitchell's leading lady was the blond presence Marin Mazzie (with whom he had appeared in *Ragtime*), suddenly there was a big deal about the fact that there hadn't been a big deal. Was Mitchell playing the role as a white person, or had the whole idea of his race suddenly become completely irrelevant? Had society actually grown up a little bit? Talk about the wheels of a dream!

It was in this context that Actors Equity Association asked Mitchell to serve as keynote speaker for its November 14, 2000, seminar on diversity. In his speech, given to a crowd containing many African American professional actors, Mitchell was surprisingly cautious, urging the union not to rush the pace of nontraditional casting on Broadway. "We're all in this together," he tried to assure them. But actors who had not benefited as well from the nontraditional-casting movement tried to shout him down. They wanted firm action on the issue, and soon. Mitchell had become one of the most visible beneficiaries of nontraditional casting, and others now dared reach out for a piece of that pie, too.

Over the next few years he toplined three "Encores!" productions: *Do Re Mi*, as the suave record executive (in a company that included Nathan Lane, Heather Headley, and Randy Graff); *Carnival*, as the tortured puppeteer; and another Alfred Drake role, Hajj, the Baghdad storyteller in *Kismet*. All three were roles originated by Caucasians but fit Mitchell snugly and naturally. He also got to add "Arab" to his repertoire of ethnicities.

In 2001, Mitchell made his dramatic-acting debut, playing the title role in *King Hedley II*, part of August Wilson's epic cycle of ten plays about African American life in each decade of the twentieth century. *King Hedley II* covers the decade of the 1980s, set among an underclass left out of the "Reagan Revolution." The production was not a hit, but it gave Mitchell a chance to show his range. In a plot slightly reminiscent of *A Raisin in the Sun*, Hedley is trying to scrape together $10,000 to rent a video store so he can raise his family out of poverty.

The *New York Times* gave Mitchell a mixed review: "Mr. Mitchell, the charismatic star of the musicals *Ragtime* and *Kiss Me, Kate*, uses his firm baritone beautifully to modulate Hedley's speeches of longing and resentment. But there is no escaping the didactic feeling of these speeches or the sense that Mr. Mitchell is straining to create a hulking physical presence, with his open-legged stance and wide-armed gestures."

Mitchell is among actors who feel that they must know how a character stands and walks in order to get fully inside that character. He succeeded very well in doing that for both *Ragtime* and *King Hedley II*. When he was approached in 2002 to play the triple role of Cervantes/Don Quijana/Don Quixote in *Man of La Mancha* (something he'd dreamed of since his earliest days), Mitchell chose three distinctive walks. The one he chose for Quixote was stiff, deliberately so, and with back pain you could feel. But the physicality of the performance got in the way of the rest of the characterization, even with the show's climactic moment, "The Quest (The Impossible Dream)" rewritten to give him a key change and a second and bigger final verse.

In panning the "overscaled" production and Mitchell's performance, the *Times* observed, "There is a moment—and it really is only one moment—when Mr. Mitchell's gamble pays off big. . . . ['The Impossible Dream']. [A]s so many stars have before him, Mr. Mitchell takes those irresistible steps to downstage center and unleashes the old vocal cords, suddenly the theater is suffused with a hokey but undeniable grandeur that is peculiar to musical theater, Mr. Mitchell, drenched in what feels like the convergence of a thousand spotlights, lets his voice reach for the heavens. His eyes take on a fanatical gleam, his spine seems to grow at least a foot and a dusty ballad suddenly sounds as if it had never set foot in Las Vegas."

A feature on Mitchell in the same newspaper called him, in its headline, "The Last Leading Man." Looking back, the headline sounds a bit premature and hyperbolic, but it does express the way many Broadway observers felt about Mitchell at the time.

In 2002, Mitchell was asked to star in the inaugural production of a Stephen Sondheim festival at the Kennedy Center for the Performing Arts in Washington, D.C. Christopher Ashley's staging of Sondheim and Hugh Wheeler's Grand Guignol–inspired *Sweeney Todd: The Demon Barber of Fleet Street*, brought praise for Christine Baranski as the satanic baker Mrs. Lovett. The *New York Times*'s Ben Brantley took issue with some of Mitchell's acting choices as the murderously vengeful barber but added, "when he sings, he dazzles, infusing Sweeney with a Biblical fire."

While Mitchell was usually upbeat in interviews and never affected the self-involved scowl of many contemporary stars, Richard Corliss of *Time* noted Mitchell's affinity for characters who expressed the dark emotions Mitchell rarely expressed in his public persona. "In his stage roles," Corliss wrote, "Mitchell hasn't always played men with much to be happy about. Coalhouse Walker, Jr., the *Ragtime* character that made his Broadway name in 1998, must pursue his racial grievance into obsession and tragedy. Don Quixote, in a *Man of La Mancha* revival . . . , is the addled victim of scorn and abuse. Paul the puppeteer, in the City Center "Encores!" 2002 concert version of *Carnival*, is crippled and expresses his sensitivity in bitterness. The barber *Sweeney Todd*, whom Mitchell played the same year for a Stephen Sondheim season in Washington, D.C., kills his customers and sells their ground-up bodies as meat pies. As the put-upon petty criminal (a non-singing role) in August Wilson's *King Hedley II,* Mitchell plays a troubled man heading for tragedy. Even his roguish, blustery hero in *Kiss Me, Kate* (Tony Award for Best Actor in a Musical) is a sardonic sort, toying with the temper of his favorite shrew."

Just about the time Corliss was recounting Mitchell's gallery of roles, the ever-increasing demands on Mitchell's time from career and fatherhood led to him taking shorter-term projects and not committing to long Broadway runs. His stature enabled him to cherry-pick projects, like performing concert versions of *Porgy and Bess* with the San Francisco Symphony at Carnegie Hall, and *South Pacific* with Reba McEntire, also at Carnegie Hall (and subsequently broadcast on PBS). He sang with the Los Angeles Philharmonic, the National Symphony Orchestra, and the Boston Pops. He played Henry Higgins in John Williams's jazz version of *My Fair Lady* and created a one-man concert show, *Love/Life,* which he performed at Feinstein's at the Regency in New York and moved to the Vivian Beaumont Theater at Lincoln Center.

In 2006, Mitchell finally found a label for his long-aborning solo album: the newly created Playbill Records. The eponymous album, *Brian Stokes Mitchell* included show tunes and standards, mostly in his sunny mode.

Perhaps that's because, despite all the stresses of maintaining a career on such a high wire, the wheels haven't come off Mitchell's personal dream. He is self-confident and self-possessed. Seeing him with his family, he looks like the kind of guy who's had a lot of girls but now is happy with one.

Mitchell is proud of his ethnicity but seeks no more than to transcend it and just show the enormously flexible actor within—and perhaps thereby help create a society where such things will stop mattering. He seemed to feel the world took a step in that direction with the 2009 inauguration of Barack Obama as the first black U.S. president. Mitchell was preparing his latest nightclub act at the time and was quoted by BroadwayWorld.com as saying that idealistic songs like "Wheels of a Dream" and "The Impossible Dream" suddenly had new meaning to him. He told audiences that he had brought his then four-year-old son into the voting booth with him and let the boy push the lever for Obama.

"I'm so full of hope, joy and optimism," the website quoted Mitchell saying. He sounded not a little like Coalhouse Walker in Act I of *Ragtime*. "Even with all the other stuff that's going on, it feels like: Here's the light at the end of the tunnel."

I had spoken to Mitchell in 2007 and asked about that letter he wrote to himself when he was fifteen. He said he still knows where it is but hasn't yet felt the need to open it.

Audra McDonald in the title role of *Marie Christine* (1999)
JOAN MARCUS/ PHOTOFEST

AUDRA McDONALD
Is It Really Me?

Starting in the 1990s, Audra McDonald dynamited brick walls and glass ceilings that had held back actresses of color almost as long as there had been Broadway.

She may have benefited from the nontraditional-casting movement that had taken some baby steps in the 1960s and gathered momentum in the 1980s. But she also became its most visible practitioner in a series of major musical and dramatic roles. Sometimes she played traditionally white roles like Carrie Pipperidge in a 1994 revival of *Carousel*; sometimes she played black roles, like Sarah in *Ragtime*. Directors wanted to cast her not because of the color of her skin, but because she was just so plain old good in so many different kinds of roles. Which is what nontraditional casting is supposed to be about.

In his 1999 *New York Times Magazine* profile "Diva of the Difficult Song," Jesse Green summed up her nontraditional appeal to traditional audiences: "She was Julie Andrews, but black; Barbra Streisand, but trained; Ethel Merman, but svelte."

She won four Tony Awards for her first four Broadway performances and was nominated for every one of the others. Whether she can maintain that pace is a separate question; it will likely remain a tough record to beat for any performer for years to come.

★

Audra Ann McDonald began life as an army brat on July 3, 1970, in Berlin, where her father was stationed. He took her home to Fresno, California, and into the bosom of a highly musical family. Her grandmothers on both sides taught piano, and everyone played at least one instrument, if not a half dozen, and sang.

She began studying piano and dance at age three and soon was singing in the Episcopal church choir, where she recalls having had the loudest voice. When she was nine she had one of those early-life experiences that seem minor at the time but change everything that comes after. A friend gave her the cast album of *Funny Girl*, and McDonald recalls learning all the songs, singing along, imagining becoming a star like Barbra Streisand, and even practicing accepting a Tony Award (something Streisand never got to do).

McDonald described herself as "a very sensitive, very dramatic, very hyper child," to the point where she was taken to a doctor for treatment. Instead of medicine, the doctor suggested her mother find an activity to serve as a channel for young Audra Ann's energy. The chosen channel was a local theatre troupe, Roger Rocka's Good Company Players, which led her through the door into the world of musical comedy. In addition to book musicals, they staged revues that were tributes to the likes of Irving Berlin and George Gershwin, and sometimes to entire eras, such as the songs of World War II. It was fun, but it was also an education in the great show music of the twentieth century.

She landed the Patti LuPone role in its production of *Evita* at age sixteen, causing some protests from the parents of the white girls. It wasn't the last time her superior abilities would earn her a role usually played by a white actress.

After high school she moved east, applying for a spot at LuPone's alma mater, the Juilliard School in New York. McDonald wanted very badly to perform on Broadway but was told that her voice lent itself more to the classical repertoire. She auditioned with the Act IV aria from Mozart's *The Marriage of Figaro*, improvising the final passage when she went up on the notes. They accepted her anyway. The east side of Juilliard faces out on Broadway; she was almost there.

Enrolled in the music school as a singer, she developed her distinctive style: not pop, and closer to classical than a Broadway belt. It gave her the range and flexibility to tackle some of the most challenging scores that would be written during the next ten years. The *Boston Globe* said she had "a classical singer's breath support, but also a Jazz singer's sense of phrasing, a Broadway singer's theatrical intensity and a gospel singer's soul-shaking conviction."

Juilliard was far from a breeze, however. The high-strung young woman wasn't comfortable with the classical material she was given to perform. "I thought classical training was a little like eating broccoli," she told the *Globe*. "I didn't like the taste but I knew it was good for me."

McDonald increasingly felt alienated from the music. You can eat only so much broccoli before you start to get desperate. At the lowest point of her young life, she attempted suicide and wound up taking time off for a "mental vacation" before her senior year. The near-death experience forced her to focus on what she really wanted from life. She saw her destiny a little bit more clearly. Having nearly flung away all her talent and potential, she now resolved to embrace it.

She auditioned for and won the role of a nanny in the national touring company of the musical *The Secret Garden*. She was back at Juilliard that fall, in 1993, but already crossing Sixty-fifth Street to Lincoln Center, where British director Nicholas Hytner was auditioning American singers for the Broadway transfer of his hit Royal National Theatre revival of *Carousel*.

Lincoln Center's resident composer at the time was a young man named Michael John LaChiusa. When the *Carousel* casting director called him in to hear McDonald's audition, he was so struck by her talent he promised her then and there that he would someday write a musical just for her.

What did he see?

A slender, twenty-three-year-old woman with deep chocolate skin and curly black hair pulled back over a high forehead from a round, open face and a jutting chin. Classed as a mezzo soprano, she had a powerful lower register and a trained upper register that landed like an alto but could leap above high C and take those wide intervals at a single confident bound, making a three-point landing on even the toughest notes. She used her expressive lips to caress the sweet notes, and she had the ability to flare or narrow her nostrils to help make emotional points.

He also saw an actress who wanted the job so badly she fainted in the middle of her big moment in front of Hytner. Hytner eventually heard enough to make a bold casting choice. Instead of putting her in the chorus, he cast her as Carrie Pipperidge, friend of leading lady Julie Jordan. Richard Rodgers had written a major role for an African American actress, Diahann Carroll, in a romance with a white man in the 1962 musical *No Strings*. But this was going to be the first time on Broadway that a black actress had been cast in a traditionally white role in one of his classics.

Before McDonald appeared on the scene in the early 1990s, it was taken as an article of faith that there might be a few black actresses in the chorus and that all black female roles would be played by blacks. But simply handing a traditionally white role to a black actress—a practice that came to be known as nontraditional casting—was a novelty. Some argued that the practice harmed the verisimilitude of the storytelling and that traditionally black roles would never be given to white actors. But the sheer sunburst of McDonald's talent proved to be the most effective counterargument.

And *Carousel* was to have an interracial romance. Hytner cast white actor Eddie Korbich as the comfortably middle-class Mr. Snow. As it played out, McDonald was so natural and comfortable in the role, racial considerations were a nonissue for most audiences. They barely felt that particular wall coming down.

For her first Broadway performance, McDonald walked away with her first Tony Award (as Best Featured Actress in a Musical). She had dreamed of singing in a Broadway chorus, and it was the one dream she'd never get to fulfill. She went directly from college into featured roles, and eventually to starring roles.

And to go along with that, Audra Ann McDonald took the unusual step of changing her professional name after she had achieved success with it. She dropped the "Ann" and from there on out became just Audra McDonald.

Her next Broadway project was Terrence McNally's *Master Class*, virtually a solo show for Zoe Caldwell, who played opera diva Maria Callas. As the title indicates, the play is presented in the form of a master class on opera, with the audience as her student body. Much of the play is given over to narrations of Callas's tumultuous personal and professional life, but she also talks a great deal about stage technique—"You've got to have a *Look*!" became the show's catchphrase—and for that part of the show, Callas needed an actual student for demonstration purposes. And this is where McDonald came in.

Her stage time was relatively brief. She came on and sang Lady Macbeth's letter scene and cabaletta, piping out a high D. In the play, Caldwell-as-Callas listened and offered pointers. But McDonald turned the student Sharon into a miniature study of fear, talent, worshipfulness, and sass.

Master Class won the Tony Award as Best Play of 1996, and McDonald won her second Tony, this time as Best Featured Actress in a Play. Significantly, she won for a rare singing role in a nonmusical.

She got more out of it than that, however. McDonald and Caldwell may have come from different backgrounds (Caldwell was born and raised in Australia), but they clicked and became close friends, Caldwell gave McDonald advice about navigating the waters of stardom. McDonald was moved enough by Caldwell's efforts to name her first daughter, Zoe Madeline, after the elder actress.

Her advice was about to come in very handy.

Ragtime

For the inaugural production at Broadway's Ford Center for the Performing Arts in January 1998, charismatic Canadian producer Garth Drabinsky conceived the grandest production of his career, a musical based on *Ragtime*, E. L. Doctorow's epic of race, politics, and changing demographics in New York at the turn of the twentieth century. Terrence McNally would write the book, Frank Galati would direct, the songwriting team of Stephen Flaherty and Lynn Ahrens *was chosen to* write the score.

Galati and Drabinsky packed the cast with young talent just recently come to the fore, including Brian Stokes Mitchell as leading man Coalhouse Walker Jr., Marin Mazzie as Mother, Mark Jacoby as Father—and the dazzling-voiced Audra McDonald as Sarah.

Mitchell and McDonald were paired as the play's two main characters, Coalhouse and the mother of his child, Sarah. Here finally was a male lead with a voice and a presence to match hers. Here also was her first important role as a specifically African American character. The more Ahrens and Flaherty heard McDonald, the more clearly they saw how underwritten the part of Sarah was. In the novel she has no dialogue at all. But for a musical that would not do. So they sat down and wrote her a soaring, mournful soliloquy, "Your Daddy's Son," in which she tries to explain what drove her to attempt to bury her newborn child alive.

Ahrens and Flaherty wrote one of the most magnificent duets of the 1990s, "Wheels of a Dream," for McDonald and Mitchell. It's a moment of sparkling optimism written for a cynical story in a cynical decade, which makes it stand out all the more beautifully. Coalhouse has purchased a Model T Ford, and this act, for a black man at that point in history, makes him hopeful about his life, about his relationship with Sarah, and about America as a nation and a society. With two such powerful actor-singers, Ahrens and Flaherty filled the song with powerful emotions and long sustained notes. Here were two African American performers who had made the music their own, suffused it with their own passion, and minted it new. Members of the audience would sometimes hug each other at the song's climax.

A critic of the time wrote that *Ragtime* was the last great American musical. In fact, it proved to be among the first of a renaissance for Broadway in general that has continued into the 2000s.

For her performance as Sarah, McDonald won her third Tony Award for her third Broadway role. She was twenty-eight years old.

However, the show's godfather, Garth Drabinsky, would eventually overextend himself, just as he had done at Cineplex Odeon. The company went bankrupt, Drabinsky was indicted for fraud and removed to Canada where American law-enforcement officials couldn't reach him, and his grand theatre on Forty-second Street was sold off. For all the charges of financial chicanery, he had fostered the creation of a great musical and had seen enough in Audra McDonald to give her the part that made her a star.

And what did McDonald do with her newfound stardom? Help a new generation of songwriters.

McDonald has released four solo albums to date: *Way Back to Paradise* (1998), *How Glory Goes* (2000), *Happy Songs* (2002), and *Build a Bridge* (2006). All are filled with interesting song choices. But *Way Back to Paradise* was really revolutionary—the most influential theatre-based solo album of the decade. Where most celebrate the rich heritage of Broadway songwriting of the 1920s through the 1960s, McDonald completely turned her back on the old songbooks and instead chose only from the talents of her own generation. The album showcases the work of the group that came to be known as the "three-name" composers of the 1990s, Michael John LaChiusa, Jason Robert Brown, and Ricky Ian Gordon, plus Adam Guettel and Jenny Giering, who composed in a bold new style, an intellectualized and postmodern interpretation of show music that finally gave up trying for Top 40 airplay—show music wasn't going to get any anyway—and just served the text. It was all new and challenging stuff, and while it wasn't all embraced at the time, the album looks better and more visionary as the years pass.

Brown's song "You Don't Know This Man" previewed his upcoming Tony-winning score from *Parade*. Seven years before winning the Tony for *Light in the Piazza*, Guettel worked a comic poem by William Makepeace Thackeray into "A Tragic Story." And LaChiusa's work on the album included the "Mistress of the Senator" passage from *Hello, Again* and the title track, "Way Back to Paradise," from his then-forthcoming musical *Marie Christine*.

Which he was writing for McDonald. You see, LaChiusa had never forgotten the promise he made back at the auditions for *Carousel*—to write a musical just for her. And for her he was fashioning a quasi-opera based on no less than the Greek tragedy *Medea*. *Medea* is the story of a witch princess of Colchis who betrays her father and brother for the man she loves, Jason, of Argonaut fame, and helps him obtain the Golden Fleece—only to see Jason abandon her and marry another woman so he can rise politically in Greece. Not to worry, Jason tells her: their two children will be taken away and raised by the new wife as princes. In one of the great fits of high passion, Medea murders the children, both to punish Jason and to keep them from being taken from her.

It's one of the most disturbing of the classical tragedies, and the notion of it being turned into a musical seemed like a bit of a sick joke even in 1999. But LaChiusa had an idea for an approach that would make the story American and enable him to have his prize: McDonald as leading lady.

Relocating the beginning of the story to the 1890s Mississippi Delta, LaChiusa made it the story of Marie Christine L'Adrese, the black daughter of a voodoo conjure woman, who falls in love with a white man, the scion of a wealthy family. Turning her back on her own people, she follows him north to Chicago, where she discovers their interracial romance is not as accepted by her lover's family as she had expected. In fact, she is spurned because of her race, though he is willing to raise their two mixed-race children if she will relinquish her claim upon him.

The all-too-familiar tragedy ensues. It was the second major musical role in which she had attempted infanticide. In *Marie Christine*, she succeeded.

Along the way, LaChiusa gave her one soaring number after another, notably "Way Back to Paradise," which became the title of her solo CD. Nevertheless, many found the music ponderous and self-important. LaChiusa wrote in a postmodern idiom that rarely moved through traditional melodies but instead illustrated the text moment by moment, in a way that traditional audiences sometimes found difficult to absorb.

There was also criticism, mainly from white critics, that the story had lost something in the translation from Euripides, and that making it a parable of racial prejudice diminished it. McDonald herself, however, earned her usual glowing notices.

Marie Christine was presented by Lincoln Center Theatre at the Vivian Beaumont Theatre. It was LCT's practice to announce a subscription season of productions and then, if one clicked, either move it to another theatre or move the rest of the subscription season to another theatre. Neither happened with *Marie Christine*. It played its scheduled thirty-nine previews and forty-two regular performances and closed.

When time came for the 2000 Tony Awards, McDonald was nominated as Best Leading Actress in a Musical but lost to Heather Headley of Aida. It was the first time she'd been nominated and lost, and it broke her biannual Tony record that had held through *Carousel* (1994), *Master Class* (1996), and *Ragtime* (1998).

Through a quirk of scheduling, *Marie Christine* earned a historical note: Bowing on December 21, 1999, it was the last musical to open on Broadway during the 1900s. (The first had been John Philip Sousa's *Chris and the Wonderful Lamp* on January 1, 1900).

The failure of *Marie Christine* was an especially painful blow to McDonald. She had assumed that because she had embraced the younger generation of experimental songwriters, the rest of the theatre world had, too. That proved not to be the case, overall. She continued to do important work—in 2001 she earned an Emmy Award nomination for Outstanding Supporting Actress in a Miniseries or TV Movie for the HBO adaptation of Pulitzer Prize winner *Wit*, costarring Emma Thompson and directed by Mike Nichols—but McDonald has not, as of this writing, been as daring with her choices of subject matter again.

On September 24, 2001, less than two weeks after the terrorist attack on the World Trade Center, she joined in a benefit performance of *Dreamgirls*, in which more than a dozen stars took turns in the major roles of the musical. McDonald was among those who played the leading role of Deena Jones.

In 2003, McDonald tried her hand at the classics, playing Lady Percy, Hotspur's wife, in Lincoln Center Theatre's production of *Henry IV* (combining parts one and two), in which Kevin Kline played Falstaff.

In 2004, ambitious (and self-proclaimedly fearless) rapper Sean Combs, who styled himself variously and successively as Puff Daddy and P. Diddy, startled both the rap world and the theatre world by audaciously announcing his intention to add a Broadway credit to his resume. His chosen vehicle was Lorraine Hansberry's classic *A Raisin in the Sun*, about a black Chicago family battling "genteel" white racism and its own inner demons as it tries to pursue the American dream of escaping the inner city and buying a home in a safe suburb. Combs—he used his birth name in his Broadway billing—was to play the central character of Walter Younger Jr., who is torn between his family's desire to use a life-insurance windfall to buy the home, and his own dream to use the money to buy a share in a liquor store.

Combs's vanity project might have been easy to laugh off if it weren't for two things. First—props where props are due—it turned out he was a pretty fair actor. Second, he opted to share star billing with Phylicia Rashad of TV's *The Cosby Show* as his mother and Audra McDonald as his long-suffering wife.

McDonald and Rashad walked a fine, professional line. They never used their superior acting muscles to overwhelm Combs. They supported him and collaborated in their every scene together. This was a master class in ensemble performing. On the other hand, they were black women playing juicy roles written by a black woman, and they responded with burnished, aching performances that earned both of them Tony Awards. It was McDonald's fourth Tony, a track record surpassed only by Julie Harris and equaled only by Mary Martin, Gwen Verdon, and Angela Lansbury. Combs wasn't nominated, but he got what he came for: a first-class production with two of his generation's greatest actresses.

The production was filmed for broadcast on TV in 2008.

Except for some special events, McDonald was away from Broadway from 2004 to 2007 working on a whirlwind of film, TV, concert, and recording projects. Among the most notable of her stage works were productions of Stephen Sondheim's *Sunday in the Park with*

George and *Passion* at Chicago's Ravinia Festival (the latter of which aired on PBS), and a workshop of *R Shomon*, a musical adaptation of the film *Rashomon* by LaChiusa.

In 2007 she was lured back to Broadway with an unusual project, playing Lizzie in the first Broadway revival of Tom Jones and Harvey Schmidt's musical *110 in the Shade*, based on the N. Richard Nash play *The Rainmaker*. The *Music Man*–like story follows a traveling con man, Starbuck, who arrives in a parched little western town, promising to use his magical powers to bring rain in return for payment in advance. The town suffers from another sort of drought, too. Lizzie, the local rancher's daughter, is considered too plain to attract a man, even though she deeply desires a husband and family. Efforts to spark interest in the eligible local sheriff come to nothing until Starbuck's arrival starts to stir things up.

Lizzie was played in the 1963 original by Inga Swenson, a white actress. In director Lonny Price's new version, the whole town is multiethnic, with McDonald playing Lizzie and white actor John Cullum playing her father. Though there were some grumbles about the improbability of this scenario in that time and place, McDonald's sprightly performance made it easy to forget such objections. The song "Raunchy," in which she parodies the amorous strategies of other women in town, was hilarious instead of uncomfortable. Her big solo, "Is It Really Me?," in which she finally overcomes her negative self-image issues and accepts herself as a beautiful person, provided as much emotional relief as the onstage rainstorm that brings the story to a conclusion.

Another show, another Tony nomination. She lost to Christine Ebersole (in *Grey Gardens*) but got to perform "Raunchy" on the Tony broadcast (though it didn't work quite as well out of context).

At this writing, McDonald is nearing forty, still channeling her hyperactivity into many projects in different media, with a whole panoply of great roles still ahead. Who knows where the wheels of her dream will take her?

Sutton Foster as Millie Dillmount in *Thoroughly Modern Millie* (2002).
JOAN MARCUS/PHOTOFEST

SUTTON FOSTER
Show Off

Sutton Foster is the embodiment of the kind of quintuple-threat star (singer, dancer, actor, comedienne, acrobat) that Broadway treasured most in the early twenty-first century and, as such, the first full-fledged star to have achieved her stardom after 2000.

Born into a talented family in the hinterlands, the tall, slender, big-eyed, endearingly gawky actress followed the classic road up from school productions, came to New York full of dreams, got cast in the first show she auditioned for, and spent hard time in the chorus and in tours of big musicals before an insanely lucky break earned her the lead role in a big Broadway-bound musical that struggled, opened, and triumphed. She became the envy and hope of ambitious chorus kids everywhere.

And, so far at least, she's living starrily ever after.

Sutton Lenore Foster was born March 18, 1975, in Athens, Georgia, into a talented household. Her brother Hunter, who would help her get her first Broadway role and become a Broadway star himself, was nearly six years older and already a budding performer. Sutton began taking dance lessons at age four and remembers sitting in the audience watching her brother in a production of *You're a Good Man, Charlie Brown* and being "totally enamored" with the experience.

When Sutton was ten, her mother encouraged her to try out for a community theatre production of *Annie*. Foster told columnist Liz Smith, "I stood at the piano and sang 'Tomorrow' and the room went dead silent. My mother gasped in surprise. She didn't know I could sing [like that]. I didn't know I could sing. I got the starring role of *Annie*."

In the late 1980s her father, who worked for General Motors, moved the family to Troy, Michigan, a suburb of Detroit, and the Foster kids attended Troy High School. Sutton began thinking of college with the intention of becoming either an actor or a high school drama teacher.

Before *American Idol* became a TV landmark, the successor to Ted Mack's old *The Original Amateur Hour* was a syndicated show called *Star Search*. Like *Idol* contestants today, the fourteen-year-old Sutton Foster took a shot at its teen vocalist competition and made it to the finals. On March 15, 1990, three days before her fifteenth birthday, she sang "You Are My World" for host Ed McMahon and the judges but lost by a quarter star to Richard Blake, who sang the Whitney Houston song "One Moment in Time." Foster later told *Newsday*, "Not that I'm bitter, but I still won't listen to that . . . song."

When Sutton was seventeen and in her senior year, her mother encouraged her to go to New York and audition for the touring company of Tommy Tune's *The Will Rogers Follies*. When she was cast in the chorus, her parents and her school allowed her to finish classes by mail. The company manager gave her time off in 1993 to attend her prom and graduation. She told *Newsday*, "There I was this naïve innocent playing a sexy showgirl. I was on tour for a year and grew up fast."

Later that year, at the urging of her brother, she auditioned and won a chorus role in the original run of *Les Misérables*—her Broadway debut. She was named understudy for the featured role of Eponine, which put her in danger of having to play the lover to her brother, who was understudying the role of Marius. They never went on at the same time.

Hunter was next cast in the Broadway revival of *Grease*, or, as it was being billed, "*Grease!*" The production was known for casting crossover celebrities in featured and cameo roles, leaving the heavy lifting of the leading roles to hard-working newcomers. When Hunter heard they were casting the leading role of Sandy, he urged his sister to sing for it. At age nineteen, she was cast in the lead role of a Broadway musical.

And again, there was the possibility of embarrassment because, through a showbiz coincidence, Hunter was named understudy to Danny, Sandy's boyfriend. Once again it worked out that they never had to go on together.

Throughout the mid- and late 1990s, both Fosters worked steadily, though without getting special notice. She was one of "The Lovely Boylan Sisters" in the 1997 Broadway revival of *Annie* (also "Star to Be"), and sang in the chorus of Frank Wildhorn's swashbuckler *The Scarlet Pimpernel*.

Foster had the chops to be a leading lady, but there was an intrinsic perkiness to her that didn't quite jibe with the times in which she entered the world of Broadway. It was a fin de siècle period that preferred a dark edge not found in her freckled cheeks and corny manner. Slender and tall, Foster gave the impression (like Fanny Brice and Carol Burnett) of being gawky while actually being supremely graceful and athletic. She expended massive energy and pure old-fashioned musical-comedy showmanship on her work and had the tendency to flash glances at the audience as if to impart a Jolsonesque "You ain't seen nothin' yet."

Her style of showmanship had been out of fashion for a generation. But two events in 2001 joined to change that. In April, Mel Brooks's *The Producers* put traditional musical comedy back on the map. It was okay to be silly and funny. The terrible events of 9/11 that fall made the public long for something lighthearted to cheer them up.

During the summer in between, events were conspiring to transform Foster's career. She was cast in a new musical, a stage adaptation of the 1967 film *Thoroughly Modern Mil-*

lie, about a young woman from the Midwest who comes to New York during the flapper era of the 1920s. Millie was spunky and high-spirited, confident that she could meet any of life's challenges in the big city. The film role was originated by Julie Andrews, with Mary Tyler Moore and Carol Channing in juicy supporting roles.

The stage role of Millie was announced for rising star Kristin Chenoweth, who had all the right qualities for it. But as the show was preparing for its tryout at La Jolla Playhouse in California, Chenoweth announced that she would pass in favor of a TV sitcom offer (which subsequently evaporated). In her place, the producers cast Erin Dilly, who had claimed her place on the elevator to stardom with an outstanding performance in an "Encores!" revival of *Babes in Arms*. Headline writers loved the *Millie*/Dilly rhyme, and all seemed right with the world.

Barely noticed at this point was her understudy, newly moved up from the chorus, perpetual bridesmaid Sutton Foster. Just to make this story a little more dramatic, at this point the producers of Broadway's *Les Misérables*, then coming to the end of its long run, called and asked if she'd return to the role of Eponine, but Foster had made a promise to understudy Millie and declined. Good thing she did, because shortly afterward, things went sour between Dilly and the creative team, and just before Los Angeles previews were set to begin, producers decided to let Dilly go and gave the part to Foster.

In an age when Broadway musicals cost upward of $10 million, giving the lead to an "unknown" seemed suicidal to Broadway insiders. But the producers had seen something special. "We thought she was a little green," director Michael Mayer told *Newsday*, "but with a stupendous voice."

Foster knew this was her big chance. As one writer put it, Foster "leaped on the role with both hands, both feet and all thirty-two teeth and turned it into a star part. She stopped the show night after night."

In addition to the well-known James Van Heusen/Sammy Cahn title song, the new composing team of Jeanine Tesori and Dick Scanlan gave her a fervent love song, "Gimme, Gimme," the torchy "Jimmy" (written with Jay Thompson), and a part of a super-fast patter song, "The Speed Test," with a melody borrowed from Gilbert & Sullivan.

Mayer said, "We were blown away by the sheer brilliance of her performance."

Among those pulling for her was actress Shirley MacLaine, who made her name while subbing for an ill star in *Can-Can*. MacLaine sent Foster a bouquet with the note, "From one understudy to another."

Reviews in *New York* were mixed, with most giving Foster credit for her effort and energy. Ben Brantley wrote in the *New York Times*, "The evening is built less on style than on hard-driving enthusiasm, a trait perfectly embodied by its leading lady, Ms. Foster, who has the pearly toothed, clean-scrubbed glow of the young Marie Osmond and works like a Trojan throughout."

Looking back on the performance from 2004, *Time Out New York* put Millie in perspective as Foster's "breakthrough performance as a stubborn small-town girl," admiring her pratfalls, bobbed haircut, and "rubber-limbed physical shtick [that] seemed lifted from silent films."

Thoroughly Modern Millie launched into a 903-performance run at the Marquis Theatre.

That same spring, Foster's brother Hunter found himself in an unexpected hit. An odd little musical called *Urinetown,* which had begun life at the 1999 New York International Fringe Festival, not only found itself with a Broadway booking, but eventually earned ten Tony Award nominations, including Best Musical. Its main competition, with eleven nominations, was *Thoroughly Modern Millie.*

Hunter was not nominated for his performance, but Sutton was, as Best Actress in a Musical. Two actresses were contending in the same category from his *Urinetown,* but Hunter was unequivocal: "I'm rooting for my sister," Hunter told the *Daily News.*

Millie beat *Urinetown* in nearly all categories, including Best Musical. When it came time to announce Best Actress in a Musical, the name called was Sutton Foster's. The understudy had beaten the odds and beaten all competition. She stood where Channing and Verdon and Lansbury had stood and brandished the medallion.

When Jeremy McCarter profiled Foster in the *New York Times* he wrote, "When I saw *Millie* two years ago I didn't think Ms. Foster had the sheen of the born star—that indefinable something that allows, say, Kristin Chenoweth to walk onstage and instantly compel palms to start flapping together. Ms Foster impressed me—and almost everyone else—with a mountain of talent: a bold, colorful voice; a sharp sense of comedy; the ability to seem at once very hard-working and not working at all, *à la* Donna Murphy."

Asked what had changed in her life for the worse, Foster said, "The pressure of not being a one-hit wonder; 'Is she just a chorus girl who had a lucky break?' That's the hard part. . . . Now I know what it's like performing in New York City, having millions riding on you, the critical attention, sitting on your dressing room floor and crying. No one tells you that when you're 14."

But she had learned a few things. According to columnist Cindy Adams, producers (including Whoopi Goldberg) balked at giving her a substantial salary increase after a year. Foster was about to leave the show . . . until the producers "slyly" offered to give the romantic lead role [of Jimmy] to her boyfriend, Christian Borle. Foster accepted.

Little Women

Less than a week before she finally did leave the cast of *Millie* came word that Foster had signed to play what should have been a killer role in a hit show: Jo March in *Little Women.*

Somehow Louisa May Alcott's classic 1868 novel had resisted musicalization on Broadway. The role of Jo, a self-possessed, headstrong young New England woman bent on a career as a writer during the Civil War period, made a perfect star vehicle, as evidenced by having been played on film by actresses as diverse as Katharine Hepburn, June Allyson, and Winona Ryder. Foster was twenty-nine when she created the Broadway role of Jo, who ages from teenager to woman over the course of the story.

"After *Millie*," she told *Time Out New York*, "I wanted a nice, small part, preferably with a death scene early in Act II so I could have some time offstage." She was being ironic. *Little Women* called upon her to occupy center stage virtually the entire evening and perform a half-dozen big ballads and comedy songs by the Broadway tyro team of Jason Howland and Mindi Dickstein.

For the first time in her career, Foster didn't have to audition for a role. Director Susan H. Schulman said that when she saw Foster as Millie, she knew she had her Jo. Comparing Foster to contemporaries Audra McDonald and Kristin Chenoweth, Shulman said that Foster "goes the extra mile by being a superb physical comedian."

That quality came in handy on *Little Women*. In early 2005, I was among a group of journalists invited to watch Foster and the cast in an open rehearsal. They were working on the "An Operatic Tragedy" scene, in which Jo describes one of her swashbuckling early stories, gradually entering the action and finally embodying the hero by slashing, stabbing, leaping, and rolling around the hall, shouting out her narration and generally having an exhausting good time. It would have winded a teenager, but Foster seemed to be having a blast, coming up at the end with a big "ta-dah" grin on her face.

She had schooled her long limbs and big hands in how to achieve maximum comic effect. Her skill was to set her face in a look of determination, then struggle to make her coltish hands and feet do what she wanted them to. And then she would sing in her sunny, full-throated way. Her skill was showcased in the Act I curtain song, "Astonishing," Jo's anthemic promise to herself to fulfill her potential

Foster was hailed for her work on the show, but as it happened, they weren't the sort of bravura reviews one would have expected. *Little Women* felt like the kind of a show Foster ought to have been able to do *before* doing *Thoroughly Modern Millie,* not after. Despite Foster's dynamic performance, *Little Women* ran just 137 performances on Broadway, but it was captured in a recording on Ghostlight Records.

The Drowsy Chaperone

Demand for Foster's services was intense, but she found her next role after being invited to see an oddball new project that had been conceived in an unusual way: as a wedding present. Titled *The Drowsy Chaperone*, the show began life in 1998 when Lisa Lambert and Greg Morrison wrote a skit called The Wedding Gift for their friend and Toronto Second City actor Bob Martin, who had a large collection of vintage cast albums and loved playing them for friends. In *The Wedding Gift*, a character modeled on Martin started describing his favorite old show and, as he played the cast album, the show came to life around him. The result both glorified and poked fun at the ditzy musicals of the 1920s—and their fans.

Martin, Lambert, and Morrison liked the project so much, they developed it into *The Drowsy Chaperone*, which proved a sleeper hit at the 1999 Toronto Fringe Theatre Festival and moved to a commercial run at Toronto's Winter Garden Theatre. The narrator, called Man in Chair, was still central to the action, but the star of the play-within-a-play was a character named Janet Van De Graaf, pampered starlet of the mythical *Feldzieg's Follies*, who is giving up the stage to get married.

Foster joined the production as Janet in time for the U.S. premiere at the Ahmanson Theatre in Los Angeles. Janet appears in several comedy scenes full of the nonsensical plot devices and mistaken identities of 1920s musical comedies. But she has one showstopping number called "Show Off," in which Janet explains to the press that she wants to give up show business because "I don't want to show off no more," and she obliges by showing them all the things she *won't* be doing anymore. As he was staging the number, director Casey Nicholaw asked Foster what she could do. When she ran down the considerable list, Nicholaw decided to put them *all* into the song, including high notes, splits, high kicks, turning cartwheels, a bit of juggling, and even a little fancy ventriloquism.

At the conclusion of the song, another character wryly observed that she had done everything but a big encore. And, with perfect timing, Foster burst from the back of the set and did a not big but *huge* encore, reminiscent of Tommy Tune's star-making encore of "It's Not Where You Start" in *Seesaw*.

Foster threw herself into the role—perhaps a bit too hard. During rehearsals she broke her wrist doing a one-handed cartwheel during a song appropriately called "An Accident Waiting to Happen," but she recovered in time for the May 2006 Broadway opening night, at which she finally got the reviews she'd hoped for in *Little Women*.

Foster told *Parade* magazine, "Janet is unlike any other character I've played because she's an adult. Millie and Jo were teenagers with big dreams and gumption and high hopes. Janet is relaxed and glamorous."

She was again nominated for a Tony Award in 2006, meaning she'd been nominated four times in a row for her four major Broadway appearances. She settled into the same Marquis Theatre dressing room she'd inhabited for *Thoroughly Modern Millie*, and the show settled in for a 674-performance run.

"Relaxed and glamorous" described her perfectly at this time, though she still had the limberness to perform her trademark acrobatics. Offstage, however, she, like Janet, was looking to settle down. Every interview during this period mentioned her relationship with Borle, and finally, in fall 2006, she requested time off for a wedding.

Young Frankenstein

In her next show, *Young Frankenstein* (2007), Foster was technically the leading lady and wound up with the guy, but she found herself billed below squeaky-voiced TV star Megan Mullally. The musical was Mel Brooks's second stage adaptation of one of his old film comedies, a follow-up to his hit *The Producers*. For this plum assignment, Foster joined a group of young stars including Roger Bart (Tony winner in *The Producers*) and Shuler Hensley (Tony winner in *Oklahoma!*).

Foster made her entrance from under a wagonload of hay and was revealed as . . . a blonde! She played Inga, the randy Transylvanian lab assistant who helps Dr. Frankenstein (make that Frohnken-shteen) fulfill his destiny to create a monster. Foster's big number, "Roll in the Hay," was full of smutty double (and single) entendre, which she performed as she bounced around the wagon like an acrobat. But, apart from "Listen to Your Heart," a seductive duet with Bart in the title role, she didn't have a great deal more to do than to react and supply an extra dancer in the chorus scenes. It was something of a disappointment for those who recalled her work in *Millie* and *Little Women*, in which she was the show to a great extent.

During the early months of *Young Frankenstein,* Foster found herself in the tabloids for the first time, with rumors of trouble in her marriage to Christian Borle and the possibility of a romance with also-married costar Bart. Her career, however, still seemed to be on the upward part of its arc, especially after it was announced that she would leave Young Frankenstein for the lead role in DreamWorks' first Broadway musical, an adaptation of the animated film *Shrek,* as Princess Fiona. The marriage foundered in 2008, and Foster mourned it on her torchy debut solo album *Wish,* released in 2009.

Her troubles didn't stop her from taking the female lead of Princess Fiona in the 2008 Broadway adaptation of the animated DreamWorks film *Shrek,* with a score by *Thoroughly Modern Millie* composer Jeanine Tesori, working with David Lindsay-Abaire. Foster played a Rapunzel-like princess locked up in a tower for years, guarded by a hideous dragon, dreaming of the day her handsome prince will come and save her. When salvation does arrive, however, it's in the form of a gnarled but good-hearted troll named Shrek. His steadfastness (and a shared fondness for flatulence) causes her initial objections to melt.

It was her fifth leading role on Broadway in seven years, and not one of them had been in a revival.

The crashing economy made the family show a tough sell. Foster's career, however, still seemed to be on the upward part of its arc. She was in demand for exactly the kind of spunky and comedic musical leading ladies for whom shows were being composed at the end of the first decade of the twenty-first century. She could write her own ticket, and her fans stood by waiting to see what kind of ticket she'd write.

Kristin Chenoweth as Daisy Gamble in the "*Encores!*" revival of *On a Clear Day You Can See Forever* (2000). GERRY GOODSTEIN/PHOTOFEST

KRISTIN CHENOWETH
My New Philosophy

Kristin Chenoweth burst into stardom in 1999 and has lent her blond fizziness to a series of musical comedies in the early 2000s.

Petite, smiley, and curvy, she deployed a killer one-two talent punch. She had the Jim Nabors–like ability to distract you with one personality—for Chenoweth, a ditzy, piccolo-voiced lollipop—then sock you with another, a tough-gal interior with a "big" two-and-a-half-octave singing voice that aspires to Mermanhood. Critic John Lahr called this her "high-voltage interior."

One minute she could be Betty Boop, the next Joan Jett. One minute she'd be posing semiclad in a men's magazine, the next releasing an album of Christian inspirational music. People followed the twists and turns of her career and personal life in celebrity magazines; onstage they would follow her every move because her bag of tricks was so varied you wanted to make sure to see which one she'd pull out next.

★

Chenoweth was born July 24, 1968, in Tulsa, Oklahoma, and offered for adoption by her birth mother. The child, who was one-quarter Cherokee, was embraced by a Southern Baptist couple in the Tulsa suburb of Broken Arrow, who named her Kristi Dawn Chenoweth. Chenoweth described them admiringly as intellectuals who, along with a strict religious upbringing, encouraged her interest in performing. They placed her in the church choir, where her powerful voice was first discovered and developed, forever linking her performing with religious devotion. When she was seven they bought her a tape recorder and she began keeping an audio diary of her thoughts and hopes, plus her early performances on the flute. She said that from an early age she was determined to be on Broadway someday, even if she wasn't a hundred percent sure what that meant. Chenoweth attended Broken Arrow High School, where an entry in the 1986 yearbook pictured her future as a "famous singer." And why not? With training she was able to hit an E above high C, putting her in the 99th percentile of sopranos.

But it wasn't always easy for her to be taken seriously. First, whatever power she had in her singing voice, her speaking voice made her sound like a Kewpie doll. Everyone found this adorable, but it didn't do much to inspire respect. *Opera Today* would one day describe her as "a phenomenally talented helium-based Broadway life-form." Second was the fact that, despite the blossoming of some impressive feminine curves, she stopped growing when she was still quite petite. Reports put her height at four-foot-ten or four-foot-eleven, and Chenoweth herself claimed five feet in a *Newsday* interview.

Nevertheless, Lahr would later write in *The New Yorker*, "Size has been a defining issue in Chenoweth's life, and to some extent it accounts for the particular intensity of her talent. Her size cost her a career as a ballet dancer after fifteen years of training, and it got her pushed around in the halls of Broken Arrow High School. People seem to have an overwhelming urge to pick Chenoweth up, and throughout her childhood, shopping malls during holiday season were an emotional minefield. "'The Easter Bunny or Santa Claus—one of those people—had a tendency to yell at me, 'Come over here little girl!' . . . They'd follow me in the mall, and I'm like, 'Go away, I'm sixteen.'"

The condescension only hardened her resolve. Chenoweth graduated to Oklahoma City University, where she won the "Miss OCU" beauty contest and eventually earned a master's degree in opera performance. She also was second runner-up in the 1991 Miss Oklahoma competition. For the finals she sang "Art Is Calling for Me" from the 1911 Victor Herbert/Harry B. Smith comic operetta *The Enchantress*. The song about a princess who longs to be an opera singer may seem an obscure choice, but it also expressed Chenoweth's battle cry.

And so it was. In the 1993 Metropolitan Opera National Council auditions, she was named "most promising newcomer" and decided on an opera career. She won a scholarship to continue studies at the Academy of Vocal Arts in Philadelphia.

And here is where the seemingly straight line into the opera world zigged. On her way to the academy she stopped in New York, where they were holding auditions for a revival of the Marx Brothers musical *Animal Crackers* at New Jersey's Paper Mill Playhouse. She later said she did the audition just for fun, to see if she could land a job in a New York–area show on her very first audition.

Well, that's just what she did. And, in a breathless leap into the unknown, she took the limited-run job even though it meant she'd have to give up her scholarship in Philadelphia. The academy was very unhappy and warned her, "You're making the biggest mistake of your life."

Chenoweth was on the road to stardom.

Knocking on Doors

Despite her initial success with *Animal Crackers*, she spent the mid-1990s struggling to break in to Broadway itself. She ultimately didn't make her Broadway debut until she was nearly thirty. She did a stint as the Girl in the long-running original production of *The Fantasticks* at the Sullivan Street Playhouse. She made her debut in the Encores! Great American Musicals in Concert series at the New York City Center in a rare revival of the Gershwins' *Strike Up the Band*.

She also began to stock up on specialty material that would show off her skills. Marcy Heisler and Zina Goldrich gave her "Taylor, the Latte Boy," about a woman who fantasizes a romance with a Starbucks barista. Jeanine Tesori and Dick Scanlan wrote her "The Girl in 14-G," about a girl who moves into an apartment with a noisy opera singer living directly beneath and an equally noisy jazz singer living directly above. The narrator must imitate both arpeggios from below and the scat from above. This über-audition piece let her show she could sing in three styles (including Broadway), act, and play comedy.

Her years of struggle would later be used as grist for her short-lived 2001 TV series, *Kristin*. In that show, she played an actress hoping someone "big" in the business will notice her. In real life, that's just what happened. She was chosen by master New Vaudeville clown Bill Irwin to play the incontinently tearful Hyacinth in his self-directed January 1997 off-Broadway production of *Scapin*. Ben Brantley of the *Times* called her performance "delightful." Irwin liked Chenoweth enough to bring her along to create a "Mrs. Noodle" character to serve as a counterpart to his silent "Mr. Noodle" character on the long-running PBS series *Sesame Street*.

That fall, Chenoweth was tapped by director Susan Stroman for her Broadway debut, as one of the flinty-eyed dance-marathon contestants in the Kander and Ebb musical *Steel Pier*. Set in depression-era Atlantic City, the musical was the story of a marathon veteran (Karen Ziemba) who longs to quit the scene and the handsome flyer with a supernatural secret who wants her to dance one more time. Chenoweth's character, Precious McGuire, who was determined to win the marathon at all costs, was there mainly to provide contrast and competition for the leading lad.

This also marked the first time that one of the great songwriting teams composed a number specifically for Chenoweth, and she proudly introduced "Two Little Words" at the Richard Rodgers Theatre. The number, a travesty reenactment of her character's wedding, staged to show how low people will go to curry favor with the judge, showcased both her squeaky voice and her opera voice. Although the part of Precious was drastically cut in the final version of the show, and although the show itself ran just a few weeks, Chenoweth was named a winner of a Theatre World Award for outstanding Broadway debut.

In 1998 she appeared at New York's Lincoln Center in a project of the heart (or, more accurately, the head) for composer William Finn. The gifted composer of *March of the Falsettos* and *Falsettoland* had been diagnosed with a brain tumor, throwing his life and career into crisis. An operation to remove it was a success, and he recovered sufficiently to go on to write the long-running Broadway musical *The 25th Annual Putnam County Spelling Bee* (2005). But in the meantime, he turned his medical crisis into a musical called *A New Brain*, which had a summer's run at the Mitzi E. Newhouse Theatre. Chenoweth was cast as a waitress and his nurse, which raised her profile among a whole new stratum of Broadway elite and their audience.

Charlie Brown

In 1999 her old friend Andrew Lippa was engaged as musical director for a Broadway production of the "Peanuts" musical *You're a Good Man, Charlie Brown* and was given unusual latitude on how much he could tamper with Clark Gesner's long-running off-Broadway score. In addition to beefing up the tiny arrangements to give the show a fuller Broadway sound, Lippa was permitted to write new material of his own to augment the score.

Chenoweth was hired by director Michael Mayer for the new role of Sally Brown, Charlie Brown's opinionated younger sister, a part that drew material from dozens of "Peanuts" strips. These included a series in which Sally tries out a series of catchphrases. Lippa turned this into the song "My New Philosophy," which proved to be a showstopper. The revival had only a short run, but word got around quickly, and more than a few tickets were bought by Broadway musical fans convinced that if this wasn't another "Miss Marmelstein" (the character number that made people sit up and take notice of the nascent Barbra Streisand in *I Can Get It for You Wholesale*), it might be the closest thing they would see in their lifetimes.

It was the perfect role for Chenoweth at that point in her career. She was playing a five-year-old, but one who could bark orders, refuse to obey, and defy authority. It made the most of her elfin size while showcasing her talent. Charles M. Schulz, creator of "Peanuts," sent her flowers after seeing her in the role. She was named winner of the annual Clarence Derwent Award for promising young actor.

Chenoweth was asked to perform the number on that year's Tony Awards, in which she was nominated as Best Featured Actress in a Musical. However, those organizing the broadcast scheduled her number immediately before the category was to be announced, leaving not enough time for Chenoweth to change out of her polka-dot sundress and into adult clothes. Acutely aware of how much this exposure could mean to her career, Chenoweth went on the daytime talk show of former Tony Awards host Rosie O'Donnell to plead her case. In the end, the Tony producers assigned a platoon of wardrobe folk to help her make a lightning change immediately after the song.

It turned into a stressful night, as the show ran long and producers told her she had to sing the number at a crazed tempo. She did it, though it seemed terribly rushed. Afterward, she dashed offstage, dived into her gown, and, as expected, won the category. The whirlwind had a happy ending. She had a Tony Award, and millions had now seen who she was what she was capable of achieving under pressure.

In late 1999, just months after winning the Tony, she appeared in the Disney TV movie version of the Broadway musical *Annie*, playing dancing villainess Lily St. Regis opposite fellow Tony winner Alan Cumming as Rooster.

At the same time, back on Broadway, Chenoweth made a nonsinging appearance in the comedy *Epic Proportions*, playing Louise, an assistant director in charge of thousands of extras who are gathered under the broiling Arizona desert sun to shoot a biblical film epic. Cowritten by *Friends* scriptwriter David Crane, the play seemed to be satirizing a film world that disappeared many years earlier, and the show closed after just three months. But Chenoweth had proved she didn't have sing to make a strong impression.

Explosion of Work

She had made such an impression that she was at the point in her career where nearly everyone considering putting on a show envisioned Chenoweth in the role. "How about Kristin Chenoweth?" became the watchcry. There were detractors, too. Bloggers and posters on the Internet complained that she was excessively cute and they couldn't figure out what the fuss was all about.

As usual, Chenoweth plowed ahead. Like many of her generation, she wanted to try it all: stage, film, TV, recordings, et cetera. She appeared in a workshop production of a new musical based on the film *Thoroughly Modern Millie*, playing the role originated by Julie Andrews. Chenoweth turned down the chance to star in the Broadway tryout so she could make her short-lived sitcom *Kristin*, and the show eventually came to Broadway with Sutton Foster in the title role.

Chenoweth released her first solo album in 2001. Titled *Let Yourself Go*, it featured Chenoweth's take on standards from 1930s and 1940s like "My Funny Valentine" and "I'm a Stranger Here Myself." It wasn't her only CD that year. Mandy Patinkin invited her as a guest star on his *Kidults* album, and the two of them sang a duet on the *Fantasticks* song "Soon It's Gonna Rain."

Her mushrooming professional life took its toll on her personal life. She had gotten engaged to fellow actor Marc Kudisch in 1998, just as both of them were entering one of the busiest periods of their lives. In 2001 they broke it off.

Over the previous year Chenoweth had been working with writer John Markus to create a TV series not just built around her, but modeled on her early life as a singer who comes to New York hoping to break into Broadway. Its debut was put off again and again, and NBC canceled it soon after its first episode was aired in June 2001. In all, eleven episodes were shot and just six aired. She wasn't the first Broadway star to come to grief on the small screen.

If it was any consolation, on the 18th of the same month Chenoweth fulfilled the singer's dream to headline a concert at Carnegie Hall. She was subsequently offered a chance to play Marian the librarian in a TV remake of *The Music Man* opposite Matthew Broderick. As well as she did with the classic material, the production suffered in comparison to the original stage and film versions. It was time for Chenoweth to originate a role of her own—on Broadway.

Wicked

At the dawn of the twenty-first century, composer Stephen Schwartz picked up an unusual novel by author Gregory Maguire: *Wicked: The Life and Times of the Wicked Witch* of *the West*.

Maguire took *Wizard of Oz* stories of L. Frank Baum and recast the entire *Oz* saga from the point of view of the Wicked Witch, who in Maguire's version is the heroine of the entire affair. The book shows the early years of the young witch, dubbed Elphaba by Maguire, and how she turned her unusual birth defect (being green) into a political weapon to battle the dictatorial Wizard, who has begun using the clueless Dorothy and her cohorts as brainless, cowardly, and heartless cat's-paws.

This story would seem a dubious prospect for musicalization—as so many of the best ideas have seemed at first glance—but Schwartz pressed ahead with librettist Winnie Holzman.

For Elphaba, Schwartz and company picked charismatic brunette actress Idina Menzel, who had earned a Tony nomination playing performance artist Maureen in the 1996 musical *Rent*.

In Maguire's book, Elphaba's college roommate is the (literally) bubbly Galinda, a character who will morph into her enemy, her dearest friend, and finally her nemesis as Glinda, the Good Witch of the North.

The creators of the musical *Wicked* wanted someone who could play this part but also riff off the goody-goody image created by Billie Burke, in the 1939 *Wizard of Oz* film. They needed a blonde with a piping voice who was willing to be comedically cutesy-poo but at the same time develop a steely backbone for the later scenes. Oh, yes, and someone who could really sing.

Chenoweth made her entrance on a steel vehicle shaped like a bubble and riding through a cloud of actual bubbles, her crowned head cocked to one side. Looks were important, but to Chenoweth the key to the part was the voice. Speaking of Burke's performance in the film, Chenoweth told *Playbill*, "One thing I noticed . . . is that she never changed her tone. . . .It sounds like she's covering up something. I remember thinking, even as a child, 'What is she hiding?' In our show people find out what's behind that voice."

Noting that in Baum's novels Glinda is originally from the south of Oz, she said, "I use my own Southern inflection a little bit . . . my singing voice changes, as well. When I come on in the bubble—the best entrance I will ever have in my career—I sing in a very light, operatic style. My singing voice gets deeper as she gets more heart."

Schwartz also wrote her one of the great comic character songs of the decade, "Popular," a bouncy ode to superficiality.

"It became the story of these two women," she told *Playbill* in October 2003, "which I think makes it more interesting. I wanted to create a character that people think they know—the stereotype of the dumb blonde, the self-centered girl—and then have her turn out to be altogether different. It's something I relate to in my own life. Because I'm petite and have long blonde hair and a very high speaking voice, there are people who seem surprised that I actually have a brain and a master's degree. I wanted to play the dumb blonde to the hilt, but I also wanted to make her a little sassy and reveal her heart as the show goes on. I was interested in doing the show more for the acting than the singing. I love the singing, but it's a great acting piece."

In Menzel, Chenoweth met one of the few actresses of her generation with the talent, drive, and charisma to rival her own. However much the writers built up Glinda, Menzel was still playing the central character. Offstage, their personal relationship went through a *Wicked*-like series of transformations, from being friends to being rivals.

Perhaps cruelly, both Menzel and Chenoweth were nominated in the same category for that year's Tony Awards: Best Leading Actress in a Musical. The award went to Menzel, and while Glinda remains Chenoweth's signature role, she soon left it and moved on.

Religion

Only a handful of the stars in this book were as religious as Chenoweth. Chenoweth was red-state by birth but blue-state by temperament. And over her first decade beyond the borders of Oklahoma, she went through something of a real-life crisis of faith, though it played out not in the wilderness, but in tabloids, back stages, fan sites, blogs, and fundamentalist television.

Chenoweth had never been shy about proclaiming her faith but also never allowed it to upstage her career. In April 2005 she released an album of inspirational music emphatically titled *As I Am*. As part of her promotional tour she was a guest on my Sirius Satellite Radio show, *Radio Playbill*, saying she saw no conflict between her religious beliefs, which she would not characterize as fundamentalist, and her work in the popular media.

Not everyone agreed. As part of the same tour she also appeared on Pat Robertson's religious program *The 700 Club* and upset its audience by expressing support for her many gay fans, affirming that she was "an honorary member of the Gay Men's Chorus," a New York–based singing group.

Chenoweth found herself disinvited from a Women of Faith conference in Oklahoma. That was poor manners, and Chenoweth's publicist fired back with a statement saying, "She has been asked to withdraw . . . due to her public and heartfelt belief that God is accepting of all people on earth."

"I am a very liberal Christian," she wrote on one of her fan websites. "I think a lot of my songs and the roles that I play show that. I am Christian, but I am also a human who lives in 2006 and works in show business."

Not long after she brought out *As I Am*, she posed in a revealing bathing suit for *Hamptons Magazine* and also agreed to appear on the cover and in a cheesecake spread in a lads' magazine, *FHM*, wearing pink, white, and yellow lingerie and heavy eye makeup. The magazine dubbed her one of the sexiest women in the world.

She was welcome in pretty much any medium and soon was singing opera with Plácido Domingo in Washington, D.C., playing a recurring role on the TV drama *The West Wing* and costarring with Steve Martin in the film remake of *The Pink Panther* and with Robin Williams in the camper farce *RV*. All of these appearances helped spread familiarity with her face but did little to challenge her many talents.

The Apple Tree

In 2006 Chenoweth was lured back to "Encores!" to star in the musical *The Apple Tree*. Originally produced in October 1966, it consists of three one-act musicals, each of which has three main characters played by the same three actors.

Part one, "The Diary of Adam and Eve," is based on a Mark Twain story depicting the first man and woman as a pair of young marrieds. Part two, "The Lady or the Tiger?" is based on the Frank Stockton story of the same title, about a barbarian princess who must make a lethal choice that will either kill the man she loves or see him go to a rival. Which will she choose? Part three, "Passionella," is Jules Feiffer's retelling of the Cinderella story showing a mousy female chimney sweep who dreams of becoming a "beautiful, fabulous, radiant, ravishing" movie star.

Chenoweth seemed to be having a ball on the nearly bare stage, alternating comedy and tenderness, especially in "The Diary of Adam and Eve." Her "What Makes Me Love Him?" was especially lovely and touching, and it's a shame the production wasn't recorded.

After a delay for Chenoweth to complete an assignment on the last season of TV's *The West Wing*, *The Apple Tree* transferred to Broadway's Studio 54 in January 2007, with Brian d'Arcy James playing the Adam roles and Marc Kudisch, her onetime betrothed, in the Snake roles.

Back on TV again in 2007, she played Olive Snook in the ABC-TV series *Pushing Daisies*, about a man who finds he has the power to bring dead people back to life. As with *Thoroughly Modern Millie,* she turned down a Broadway role—the female lead in Mel Brooks's *Young Frankenstein*—to take the TV job. Once again, the Broadway role went to Sutton Foster.

Will Chenoweth, who has insisted to one interviewer after another that she is fundamentally a creature of the stage, come back to Broadway in challenging new roles, continue to sweep in and dominate revivals, or finally have a broadcast hit big enough to make her abandon the stage altogether? Her fans are waiting to see.

Sources

Special thanks to GoogleVideo.com, which enabled me to research film clips much more easily than I might otherwise have done. The Internet Broadway Database (IBDB), the Internet Movie Database (IMDb) were also valuable references for checking spellings and dates.

Bert Williams

American Musical Theatre: A Chronicle by Gerald Bordman (Oxford University Press).
Variety, 1969. "Bert Williams' Last Interview" by Ashton Stevens (reprint of 1923 story).
Journal of Popular Culture, Summer 1976.
Broadway: The American Musical by Michael Kantor and Laurence Maslon (Bulfinch Books).
Lost Sounds: Blacks and the Birth of the Recording Industry, 1890-1919 by Tim Brooks (University of Illinois Press).
Make Believe: The Broadway Musical in the 1920s by Ethan Mordden (Oxford University Press).
New York Times, February 21, 1986. This article covers Williams' salary and hard work, circa 1917.
New York World, September 6, 1922. This article describes Williams' funeral.
Undated letter in *The New York World*. This piece includes Ziegfeld's description of Williams as one of the "whitest men" he had ever dealt with.
Nobody: The Story of Bert Williams by Ann Charters (Da Capo Press).
Variety, 1969, reprint of 1923 interview. This article includes W.C. Field's memory of Williams as a sad man and other reminiscences of Williams' early career.
The Ziegfeld Follies: A History in Text and Pictures by Marjorie Farnsworth (G.P. Putnam's Sons).
The Ziegfeld Touch: The Life and Times of Florenz Ziegfeld Jr. by Richard and Paulette Ziegfeld (Harry N. Abrams, Inc.).
Undated clip bylined George Reason.

George M. Cohan

American Musical Theatre: A Chronicle by Gerald Bordman (Oxford University Press).
George M. Cohan: The Man Who Owned Broadway by John McCabe (Da Capo Press).
Lost Broadway Theatres by Nicholas Van Hoogstraten (Princeton Achitectural Press).
Show Music magazine, Winter 1999/2000.
Sing for Your Supper: The Broadway Musical in the 1930s by Ethan Mordden (Palgrave and Macmillan).
Twenty Years on Broadway and the Years It Took to Get There by George M. Cohan (Harper & Brothers).

Fanny Brice

The Great Clowns of Broadway by Stanley Green (Oxford University Press).
Fanny Brice: The Original Funny Girl by Herbert G. Goldman (Oxford University Press).
The Fabulous Fanny: The Story of Fanny Brice by Norman Katkov (Alfred A. Knopf).

Liberty magazine, August 20, 1938. This article deals with the private life of "Baby Snooks" and covers Brice's early years and relationship with Nick Arnstein.

The Ziegfeld Follies: A History in Text and Pictures by Marjorie Farnsworth (G.P. Putnam's Sons).

The Ziegfeld Touch: The Life and Times of Florenz Ziegfeld Jr. by Richard and Paulette Ziegfeld (Harry N. Abrams, Inc.).

Undated clip by David Martin and Peter R. Berlin.

Al Jolson

American Musical Theatre: A Chronicle by Gerald Bordman (Oxford University Press).

Broadway: The American Musical by Michael Kantor and Laurence Maslon (Bulfinch Books).

Jolson: The Legend Comes to Life by Herbert G. Goldman (Oxford University Press).

Make Believe: The Broadway Musical in the 1920s by Ethan Mordden (Oxford University Press).

Show Music magazine, Fall 1998.

Marilyn Miller

The Evansville Boneyard, September 2006. This article covers Miller's early life and unhappy romances.

Make Believe: The Broadway Musical in the 1920s by Ethan Mordden (Oxford University Press).

The New York Times, April 8, 1936. This piece is Miller's obituary.

The Other Marilyn: A Biography of Marilyn Miller by Warren G. Harris (Arbor House).

Show Music magazine, Fall 1998.

Sing for Your Supper: The Broadway Musical in the 1930s by Ethan Mordden (Palgrave and Macmillan).

The Ziegfeld Follies: A History in Text and Pictures by Marjorie Farnsworth (G.P. Putnam's Sons).

The Ziegfeld Touch: The Life and Times of Florenz Ziegfeld Jr. by Richard and Paulette Ziegfeld (Harry N. Abrams Inc.).

Eddie Cantor

American Musical Theatre: A Chronicle by Gerald Bordman (Oxford University Press).

Banjo Eyes: Eddie Cantor and the Birth of Modern Stardom by Herbert G. Goldman (Oxford University Press).

EddieCantor.com (The Eddie Cantor Appreciation Society).

Make Believe: The Broadway Musical in the 1920s by Ethan Mordden (Oxford University Press).

My Life Is in Your Hands by Eddie Cantor with David Freedman and Jane Kesner Ardmore (Cooper Square Press).

Show Music magazine, Summer 1999.

Sing for Your Supper: The Broadway Musical in the 1930s by Ethan Mordden (Palgrave and Macmillan).

The Spice of Variety by Abel Green (Henry Holt and Company).

Take My Life by Eddie Cantor with David Freedman and Jane Kesner Ardmore (Cooper Square Press).

The Ziegfeld Follies: A History in Text and Pictures by Marjorie Farnsworth (G.P. Putnam's Sons).

The Ziegfeld Touch: The Life and Times of Florenz Ziegfeld Jr. by Richard and Paulette Ziegfeld (Harry N. Abrams, Inc.).

Fred and Adele Astaire

American Musical Theatre: A Chronicle by Gerald Bordman (Oxford University Press).

Astaire: The Man, The Dancer by Bob Thomas (St. Martin's Press).

The Dance magazine, undated, 1927. This article describes Fred and Adele in their dressing room.

Fred Astaire: A Bio-Bibliography by Larry Billman (Greenwood Press).

Gershwin: A Biography by Edward Jablonski (Da Capo Press).

Gotta Sing! Gotta Dance! by John Kobal (Hamlyn).

Make Believe: The Broadway Musical in the 1920s by Ethan Mordden (Oxford University Press).

Newsweek, February 9, 1981. This article profiles Fred Astaire and features his reflections on show business and dancing.

New York Daily News, August 1, 1976. This article deals with Adele Astaire's life in retirement.

New York Post, January 26, 1981. This piece is Adele Astaire's obituary.

New York Times, January 26, 1981. This piece is Adele Astaire's obituary.
New York World Telegram, May 9, 1932. This article describes Adele Astaire at the height of her success and covers the "Rainy Afternoon" sketch.
Sing for Your Supper: The Broadway Musical in the 1930s by Ethan Mordden (Palgrave and Macmillan).
Show Music magazine, Fall 1998.
SR Magazine, December 30, 1987. This source discusses Adele Astaire's recordings and includes reflections on the Astaires from Irving Kolodin.

Bobby Clark

American Musical Theatre: A Chronicle by Gerald Bordman (Oxford University Press).
The Boston Globe, September 14, 1947. This article describes Clark's performances in various projects.
The Great Clowns of Broadway by Stanley Green (Oxford University Press).
Make Believe: The Broadway Musical in the 1920s by Ethan Mordden (Oxford University Press).
Morning Telegraph, November 23, 1926. This article covers the chemistry between Clark and McCullough, and their early years.
The New Yorker, September 27, 1947. This article features many details of Clark's early career and the content of his vaudeville acts, origin of his signature props, and measuring the sets.
New York Herald, February 12, 1960. This piece is Clark's obituary.
New York Journal American, February 16, 1947. This article claims "every drama critic has a pet" and that Clark is every drama critic's pet.
New York Times, January 14, 1942. This is Brooks Atkinson's review of Clark in *The Rivals*.
Show Music magazine, Fall 1998.
Sing for Your Supper: The Broadway Musical in the 1930s by Ethan Mordden (Palgrave and Macmillan).

William Gaxton

American Musical Theatre: A Chronicle by Gerald Bordman (Oxford University Press).
Boston Evening Transcript, October 15, 1938.
Gershwin: A Biography by Edward Jablonski (Da Capo Press).
The Great Clowns of Broadway by Stanley Green (Oxford University Press).
New York American, undated, 1937. This story calls Gaxton Broadway's "luckiest actor," and covers his record run at the Palace.
New York Evening Journal, undated, 1936. This piece deals with Gaxton's onstage jesters.
New York Herald, December 30, 1934. This article covers Gaxton's ancestry, his survival of the San Francisco earthquake, and his learning of Chinese.
New York Herald Tribune, August 18, 1935. This article covers Gaxton's introduction to theater by the priests of Santa Clara College, many other details of his early career, and his reputation as "new fashion in musical comedy heroes."
New York Journal, undated, 1935, bylined Louis Sobol. This piece covers the "Kisses" vaudeville sketch, and how Gaxton met his future wife.
New York Post, November 17, 1936. This article covers Gaxton's childhood and how he was frightened into becoming a comedian.
New York Times, November 22, 1934. This is a review of *Anything Goes*.
New York World Telegram, February 23, 1935.
New York World Telegram and Sun, undated, 1936. This article describes Gaxton as the wealthiest actor on Broadway.
Sing for Your Supper: The Broadway Musical in the 1930s by Ethan Mordden (Palgrave and Macmillan).
Variety, undated, 1919. This is a review of Gaxton's vaudeville act.
The World of Musical Comedy by Stanley Green (A.S. Barnes and Company).

Ray Bolger

Christian Science Monitor, February 7, 1980. This article deals with the shows *By Jupiter* and *The Runner Stumbles*, and the longlasting success of *Wizard of Oz*.
I Got the Show Right Here by Cy Feuer with Ken Gross (Simon & Schuster). Selections used from this book

deal with *Where's Charley?* and the audience reaction to "Once in Love with Amy."

Journeys in the Night: Creating a New American Theatre with Circle in the Square: A Memoir by Theodore Mann (Applause Theatre and Cinema Books). Selections used from this book deal with Bolger's appearance at the revival of *Where's Charley?*

Las Vegas Review-Journal, undated. This article covers the K.J. Evans story and Bolger's Las Vegas act.

The Making of The Wizard of Oz by Aljean Harmetz (Delta Books/Dell Publishing).

New York Daily News, January 16, 1987. This article describes Bolger meeting his future wife.

New York Post, January 16, 1987. This piece is Bolger's obituary and includes a description of *Oz* as an institution.

New York Times June 8, 1980. This article covers Bolger's politics and his appearances in *The Milliken Breakfast Show*.

New York Times, January 16, 1987. This is Bolger's obituary and explains Bolger becoming a dancer in self-defense.

Notes on a Cowardly Lion by John Lahr (Limelight Editions).

Not Since Carrie: 40 Years of Broadway Musical Flops by Ken Mandelbaum (St. Martin's Press). Selections used from this book deal with Bolger's final Broadway appearance.

Sing for Your Supper: The Broadway Musical in the 1930s by Ethan Mordden (Palgrave and Macmillan).

The World of Musical Comedy by Stanley Green (A.S. Barnes and Company).

Ethel Waters

Ethel Waters: Stormy Weather by Stephen Bourne (Scarecrow Press, Inc.).

Harold Arlen: Happy with the Blues by Edward Jablonski (Da Capo Press).

His Eye Is on the Sparrow by Ethel Waters with Charles Samuels (Da Capo Press).

Moss Hart: A Prince of the Theatre by Jared Brown (Back Stage Books).

Sing for Your Supper: The Broadway Musical in the 1930s by Ethan Mordden (Palgrave and Macmillan).

Uncredited newspaper clip, June 24, 1933. This piece covers how Waters scrubbed clothes for $1.35 a day, and other details of Waters' early career.

Undated newspaper clip by John Chapman. This piece covers how Waters decided to do *Mamba's Daughters*.

United Press International, July 1, 1985. This piece describes Waters as the "first black to break the super-star color barrier."

Bert Lahr

Broadway: The American Musical Michael Kantor and Laurence Maslon (Bulfinch Books).

The Great Clowns of Broadway by Stanley Green (Oxford University Press).

It Happened on Broadway: An Oral History of the Great White Way by Myrna Katz Frommer and Harvey Frommer (Harcourt Brace & Company).

The Making of The Wizard of Oz by Aljean Harmetz (Delta Books/Dell Publishing).

Notes on a Cowardly Lion by John Lahr (Limelight Editions).

Sing for Your Supper: The Broadway Musical in the 1930s by Ethan Mordden (Palgrave and Macmillan).

The World of Musical Comedy by Stanley Green (A.S. Barnes and Company).

Ethel Merman

Brass Diva: The Life and Legends of Ethel Merman by Caryl Flinn (University of California Press).

Ethel Merman: The Biggest Star on Broadway by Geoffrey Mark (Barricade Legends/Barricade Books, Inc.).

Gershwin: A Biography by Edward Jablonski (Da Capo Press).

The Great Clowns of Broadway by Stanley Green (Oxford University Press).

The Happiest Corpse I've Ever Seen by Ethan Mordden (Palgrave and Macmillan).

Just Lucky I Guess: A Memoir of Sorts by Carol Channing (Simon & Schuster).

Newsday, May 9, 1982. This article covers Merman's benefit for the Museum of the City of New York.

Show Music magazine, Summer 1994.

Show Music magazine, Summer 1998.

Sing for Your Supper: The Broadway Musical in the 1930s by Ethan Mordden (Palgrave and Macmillan).
Opening Night on Broadway edited by Steven Suskin (Schirmer Books).
The World of Musical Comedy by Stanley Green (A.S. Barnes and Company).

Alfred Drake
Bergen Record, December 16, 1973. This article deals with *Gigi* and Drake's career.
Los Angeles Civic Light Opera, press release, March 7, 1980.
Musical Stages: An Autobiography by Richard Rodgers (Da Capo Press).
New York Daily News, November 25, 1973. This article deals with *Gigi* and Drake's career.
New York Daily News, July 31, 1992. This article praises Drake as a consummate performer, calling him "versatile" and "dashing."
New York Post, March 29, 1978. This article desribes Drake in *Gigi.*
New York Times, December 26, 1973. This is a review of *Gigi.*
New York Times, July 26, 1992. This piece is Drake's obituary, and it describes his voice.
Opening Night on Broadway edited by Steven Suskin (Schirmer Books).
Show Music magazine, Fall 1997.
Sing for Your Supper: The Broadway Musical in the 1930s by Ethan Mordden (Palgrave and Macmillan).
Somewhere for Me by Meryle Secrest (Alfred A. Knopf).
Theater Week, August 17, 1992.
Variety, April 8, 1970. This article covers Drake's participation in the Players Club.
Variety, August 3, 1992. This source is Drake's obituary and discusses details of his early career and his place in theater history.

Mary Martin
The Days Grow Short the Life and Music of Kurt Weill by Ronald Sanders (Holt, Rinehart and Winston).
Diary of a Mad Playwright: Perilous Adventures on the Road with Mary Martin and Carol Channing by James Kirkwood (Applause Books).
The Letters of Noël Coward edited by Barry Day (Alfred A. Knopf).
Mary Martin on Stage by Shirlee P. Newman (Westminster Press).
Musical Stages: An Autobiography by Richard Rodgers (Da Capo Press).
My Heart Belongs by Mary Martin (Quill).
New York Times, November 5, 1990. This piece is Martin's obituary, and it discusses her dreams of flying and the shows Martin turned down.
Not Since Carrie: 40 Years of Broadway Musical Flops by Ken Mandelbaum (St. Martin's Press). Selections used from this book deal with *Jennie.*
Opening Night on Broadway edited by Steven Suskin (Schirmer Books).
Show Music magazine, Summer 1994.
Show Music magazine, Fall 1996.
Show Music magazine, Fall 1997.
Somewhere for Me by Meryle Secrest (Alfred A. Knopf).
The World of Musical Comedy by Stanley Green (A.S. Barnes and Company).

Danny Kaye
The Days Grow Short: The Life and Music of Kurt Weill by Ronald Sanders (Holt, Rinehart and Winston).
Gertrude Lawrence as Mrs. A by Richard Stoddard Aldrich (Greystone Press). Selections used from this book deal with *Lady in the Dark.*
Moss Hart: A Prince of the Theatre by Jared Brown (Back Stage Books). Selections used from this book deal with *Lady in the Dark.*
New York Daily News, undated, 1986. This piece covers Kaye entertaining at Buckingham Palace.
New York Post, February 25, 1986. This article covers Kaye's French honors.
New York Times, March 3, 1944. This is a review of *Up in Arms.*
Nobody's Fool by Martin Gottfried (Simon & Schuster). Selections used from this book deal with Kaye's

alleged affair with Laurence Olivier and many other biographical details.

On the Sunny Side of the Street by Deborah Grace Winer (Schirmer Books).

People magazine, November 17, 1975. This article describes Sylvia Fine as a force in Kaye's life and Kaye's candid attitude toward kids.

Saturday Evening Post, August 9, 1958.

The Secret Life of Danny Kaye by Michael Freedland (W.H. Allen/Virgin Books).

Show Music magazine, Fall 1994.

Time magazine, November 10, 1941. This is a review of *Let's Face It!*

The World of Musical Comedy by Stanley Green (A.S. Barnes and Company).

Carol Channing

Back Stage, January 19, 1996. This article deals with the renaming a Manhattan street Channing Way.

Diary of a Mad Playwright: Perilous Adventures on the Road with Mary Martin and Carol Channing by James Kirkwood (Applause Books).

Just Lucky I Guess: A Memoir of Sorts by Carol Channing (Simon & Schuster).

Maxim, January 2007. This article covers Channing's Super Bowl halftime curse.

Newark Star Ledger, June 11, 1992.

New York Daily News, August 3,1980. This article covers Channing getting her first laugh in grade school and her one week off from *Gentlemen Prefer Blondes.*

New York Daily News, June 13, 1983. This article deals with Channing's touring shows and her special diet.

New York Post, May 20, 1998, "Sex-starved Channing Demands Divorce at 77."

New York Times, November 29, 1995. This article covers the puffs eaten in *Hello, Dolly!* and Channing's *Looney Toons* accent.

New York Times, August 7, 1980. This article covers Channing on tour in *Sugar Babies.*

Not Since Carrie: 40 Years of Broadway Musical Flops by Ken Mandelbaum (St. Martin's Press). Selections used from this book deal with *The Vamp.*

Opening Night on Broadway edited by Steven Suskin (Schirmer Books).

Philadelphia Inquirer, November 2, 1976.

More Opening Nights on Broadway edited by Steven Suskin (Schirmer Books).

Playbill, undated clip by Sheryl Flatow. This piece covers the background of Channing's sensitivities to chemicals and the origin of her special diet.

Playbill, undated clip by Harry Haun. This piece deals with the composition of puffs eaten each night in *Hello, Dolly!*

Playbill.com, May 29, 1998. This source covers details of Channing's marriage breakdown and Lowe's countersuit.

Theater Week, July 1, 1991. This article describes Marilyn Monroe's visit to *Gentlemen Prefer Blondes.*

Time magazine, undated.

Vanity Fair, October 1995. This article covers Channing's relationship with her husband.

Variety, March 12, 1980. This article deals with her missing her first performance in *Hello, Dolly!*

Variety, September 12, 1994. This article compares Channing's voice to Tallulah Bankhead's and Baby Snookums'. It also has an account of George Abbott saying Channing was physically wrong for Lorelei Lee.

Yul Brynner

Gertrude Lawrence as Mrs. A by Richard Stoddard Aldrich (Greystone Press). Selections used from this book deal with the costar's view of Brynner in *The King and I.*

More Opening Nights on Broadway edited by Steven Suskin (Schirmer Books).

Musical Stages: An Autobiography by Richard Rodgers (Da Capo Press). Selections used from this book deal with how Brynner was cast in *The King and I.*

Opening Night on Broadway edited by Steven Suskin (Schirmer Books).

Somewhere for Me by Meryle Secrest (Alfred A. Knopf).

Yul Brynner: A Biography by Michelangelo Capua (McFarland & Company). Selections used from this book deal with how Brynner was cast in *The King and I* and his subsequent performances.

Yul: The Man Who Would Be King by Rock Brynner (Berkley).

Zero Mostel

Broadway: The American Musical by Michael Kantor and Laurence Maslon (Bulfinch Books).

It Happened on Broadway: An Oral History of the Great White Way by Myrna Katz Frommer and Harvey Frommer (Harcourt Brace & Company).

Jerome Robbins: His Life, His Theater, His Dance by Deborah Jowitt (Simon & Schuster).

Opening Night on Broadway edited by Steven Suskin (Schirmer Books).

Sondheim & Co. (second edition) by Craig Zadan (Harper & Row).

Zero Mostel: A Biography by Jared Brown (Atheneum).

John Raitt

Arizona Republic, March 18, 1962. This article covers Raitt's life on the road.

Drama-logue, Hollywood, October 24, 1991. This is a review that discusses the changing quality of Raitt's voice.

First-person interviews with the author.

It Happened on Broadway: An Oral History of the Great White Way by Myrna Katz Frommer and Harvey Frommer (Harcourt, Brace & Company).

Newsday, October 3, 1995. This article includes Raitt's claim to have sung more leading roles than any other actor, and in every state of the union; it also deals with Raitt being referred to as "Bonnie's father," turning down Daddy Warbucks, and other details.

New York Daily News, August 12, 1981. This article covers Raitt's early life in California.

New York Daily News, October 4, 1981. This article deals with Raitt's family and romantic life.

New York Daily News, March 25, 1994. This article covers Raitt's aborted film career.

New York Post, June 11, 1979. This article includes Raitt's self-description as a "workaholic."

New York Post, October 12, 1979. This article covers Raitt filing for divorce.

New York Post, October 16, 1979. This article covers Raitt's divorce.

New York Sunday News, February 29, 1976.

New York Sunday News, February 24, 1980. This article deals with Raitt as a leading man.

New York Times, October 5, 1988. This article covers Raitt's reunion with his first love.

New York Times, April 2, 1993. This article covers the anniversary performance of *Oklahoma!*

Musical Stages: An Autobiography by Richard Rodgers (Da Capo Press).

Not Since Carrie: 40 Years of Broadway Musical Flops by Ken Mandelbaum (St. Martin's Press). This book provides accounts of Raitt's flop shows.

OK! The Story of Oklahoma! by Max Wilk (Applause Books).

Opening Night on Broadway edited by Steven Suskin (Schirmer Books).

Parade magazine, August 2, 2000. This article deals with his relationship with Bonnie Raitt and how they got arrested together.

The World of Musical Comedy by Stanley Green (A.S. Barnes and Company).

Variety, February 28, 2005. This source includes Raitt's obituary and covers his audition for Oscar Hammerstein, along with many other career details.

Gwen Verdon

All His Jazz: The Life and Death of Bob Fosse by Martin Gottfried (Da Capo Press).

Colored Lights by John Kander and Fred Ebb as told to Greg Lawrence (Faber and Faber, Inc.).

Dance Magazine, July 1961. This article examines the inner workings of the relationship between Verdon and Fosse.

Dance Magazine, January 2001. This includes Vardon's obituary and details about her dance career.

I Got the Show Right Here by Cy Feuer with Ken Gross (Simon & Schuster).

More Opening Nights on Broadway edited by Steven Suskin (Schirmer Books).

New York Times, October 18, 2001. This article covers Verdon's talent as an actress and a tap dancer.

On the Sunny Side of the Street by Deborah Grace Winer (Schirmer Books).

Opening Night on Broadway edited by Steven Suskin (Schirmer Books).

Show Music magazine, Fall 1994.

Show Music magazine, Fall 1998.

Show Music magazine, Fall 1999.
Village Voice, Fall 2001. This article is Michael Feingold appreciation of Verdon as a performer, and decribes her performance as "lighter than air."
World-Telegraph & Sun, undated, 1954. This piece discusses the opening night of *Can-Can,* and how Verdon made the audience "spellbound."

Barbara Cook
First-person interviews with the author.
The Happiest Corpse I've Ever Seen by Ethan Mordden (Palgrave and Macmillan).
Opening Night on Broadway edited by Steven Suskin (Schirmer Books).
The Advocate, February 18, 2003. This article discusses Cook's experience in *Carrie.*
New York Observer, December 18, 2005.
New York Post, September 25, 1995. In this piece, Cook describes her preference for singing songs that are "triste" and how torch songs inspired her as a young girl.
New York Times, September 25, 1998. This article discusses Cook's three decades without romance, her issues with food, and her relationship with her mother.
New York Times, January 6, 2002. This is a review of *Mostly Sondheim.*
New York Times, August 15, 2002. This article discusses the contents of Cook's master class.
Playbill, July 2002.
Village Voice, February 26, 2002. This article explains the turning point in Verdon's career and how "she went deeper into her singing and found acting."

Robert Preston
Boston Post, May 10, 1941. This article covers Preston's discovery by a film company lawyer.
Cindy Adams syndicated column, March 23, 1987. This source covers Cary Grant refusing the movie role of Harold Hill, and Preston's plans to co-star in the aborted 1980s stage adaptation of *Victor/Victoria.*
Julie Andrews: A Life on Stage and Screen by Robert Windeler (Birch Lane Press).
Milwaukee Journal, June 13, 1943. This article describes Preston parking Barbara Stanwyck's car and later co-starring with her.
More Opening Nights on Broadway edited by Steven Suskin (Schirmer Books).
Newsday, January 11, 1965. This article covers Paramount's relationship with Preston.
Newsday, April 6, 1965. This article discusses Preston's affair with Ulla Sallert and how it nearly lead to divorce.
New York Daily News, March 22, 1987. This piece is Preston's obituary.
New York Daily Mirror, November 8, 1954. This article discusses Preston playing Julius Caesar at age sixteen and his Western films.
New York Mirror, September 4, 1960. This article describes Morton Da Costa seeing Preston in *The Front Page* and wanting him for *The Music Man.*
New York Post, May 16, 1963. This articles covers rumors of marital discord.
New York Post, November 16, 1964. This article covers Preston's affair with Ulla Sallert.
New York Post, January 10, 1965. This article discusses *Ben Franklin in Paris.*
New York Post, April 24, 1966.
New York Post, March 23, 1987. This article is Preston's obituary and covers his final illness.
New York World Telegram & Sun, March 2, 1962. This article discusses *Dark at the Top of the Stairs.*
Not Since Carrie: 40 Years of Broadway Musical Flops by Ken Mandelbaum (St. Martin's Press). Selections used from this book discuss *We Take the Town* and *Prince of Grand Street.*
Opening Night on Broadway edited by Steven Suskin (Schirmer Books).
Philadelphia Inquirer, March 22, 1987. This is Preston's obituary; it includes Preston's reflection of shooting the film *Music Man*—"the role is part of me."
Second Act Trouble by Steven M. Suskin (Applause Books).
Show Music magazine, Fall 1997.
Unidentified clip dated 1939. This piece includes extensive details of Preston's teen years, going on the stage, and early roles.

Richard Kiley

The Impossible Musical: The Man of La Mancha Story by Dale Wasserman (Applause Books). Selections used from this book deal with how Kiley was chosen to play in Don Quixote.

New York Post, April 29, 1987. This article discusses *All My Sons*.

New York Post, March 6, 1999. This piece is Kiley's obituary.

New York Times, February 6, 1959. This piece discusses *Redhead*.

New York Times, February 6, 1999. This article covers Kiley's mixed feelings about the role of Don Quixote.

Not Since Carrie: 40 Years of Broadway Musical Flops by Ken Mandelbaum (St. Martin's Press). Selections used from this book discuss *I Had a Ball*.

Opening Night on Broadway edited by Steven Suskin (Schirmer Books).

Playbill, May 1991. This article covers Kiley losing five pounds for every performance of *La Mancha* and never getting too old for the role.

Playbill, May 1992. This article discusses Kiley's vocal training during *Kismet* and provides background information about *Redhead*.

Time magazine, November 1, 1971. This is a review of *The Incomparable Max*.

TV Guide, December 26, 1987. This article covers Kiley's TV work and relationship with his family.

Variety, March 15, 1999. This article is a retrospective of Kiley's career.

Women's Wear Daily, March 23, 1983.

Chita Rivera

All His Jazz: The Life and Death of Bob Fosse by Martin Gottfried (Da Capo Press).

Broadway: The American Musical by Michael Kantor and Laurence Maslon (Bulfinch Books).

Colored Lights by John Kander and Fred Ebb as told to Greg Lawrence (Faber and Faber, Inc.).

Current Biography Yearbook: 1984 edited by Charles Moritz (H.W. Wilson Co.).

First-person interviews with the author.

Jerome Robbins: His Life, His Theater, His Dance by Deborah Jowitt (Simon & Schuster).

More Opening Nights on Broadway edited by Steven Suskin (Schirmer Books).

New York Times, December 24, 1981. This article discusses Rivera's club career.

New York Times, April 8, 1986. This article discusses *Jerry's Girls* coping with Rivera's injury.

New York Times, May 30, 2003. This article covers Rivera's return to Broadway in *Nine*.

Not Since Carrie: 40 Years of Broadway Musical Flops by Ken Mandelbaum (St. Martin's Press). Selections used from this book deal with *Bajour* and other shows.

Opening Night on Broadway edited by Steven Suskin (Schirmer Books).

Time magazine, February 2, 1984.

Show Music magazine, Summer 2001.

Julie Andrews

I Got the Show Right Here by Cy Feuer with Ken Gross (Simon & Schuster). Selections used from this book deal with *The Boy Friend*.

Julie Andrews: A Life on Stage and Screen by Robert Windeler (Birch Lane Press). Selections used from this book deal with Andrews' early life.

Moss Hart: A Prince of the Theatre by Jared Brown (Back Stage Books). Selections used from this book describe what it was like behind the scenes at *My Fair Lady* and *Camelot*.

Opening Night on Broadway edited by Steven Suskin (Schirmer Books).

Somewhere for Me by Meryle Secrest (Alfred A. Knopf). Selections from this book deal with *Cinderella, The Sound of Music*, and Andrews' relationship with Richard Rodgers.

Jerry Orbach

All His Jazz: The Life and Death of Bob Fosse by Martin Gottfried (Da Capo Press). Selections used from this book deal with *Chicago* and Orbach's friendship with Fosse.

The Amazing Story of The Fantasticks by Donald C. Farber and Robert Viagas (Limelight Editions).

Broadway: The American Musical by Michael Kantor and Laurence Maslon (Bulfinch Books).

First-person interviews with the author.

More Opening Nights on Broadway edited by Steven Suskin (Schirmer Books).
Opening Night on Broadway edited by Steven Suskin (Schirmer Books).
New York Times, December 30, 2004. This is Orbach's obituary.
New York Times, March 7, 2007. This article discusses renaming a Manhattan street for Orbach.
Washington Post, December 30, 2004.

Angela Lansbury
Balancing Act: The Authorized Biography of Angela Lansbury by Martin Gottfried (Little, Brown and Company).
Broadway: The American Musical by Michael Kantor and Laurence Maslon (Bulfinch Books).
First person interview with author.
More Opening Nights on Broadway edited by Steven Suskin (Schirmer Books).
Opening Night on Broadway edited by Steven Suskin (Schirmer Books).
New York Times, 2002. This article covers the role of Mrs. Lovett in *Sweeney Todd*.
New York Times, May 16, 2007. This is a review of *Deuce*.
New York Times, July 8, 2006. This is a retrospective of Lansbury's career.
Sondheim & Co. (second edition) by Craig Zadan (Harper & Row). Selections used from this book deal with *Anyone Can Whistle*, *Sweeney Todd*, and Lansbury's relationship with Stephen Sondheim.

Bernadette Peters
Andrew Lloyd Webber: His Life and Works by Michael Walsh (Harry N. Abrams Inc.). Selections used from this book deal with *Song and Dance*.
Bernadettepeters.com
Ever After: The Last Years of Musical Theatre and Beyond by Barry Singer (Applause Books).
More Opening Nights on Broadway edited by Steven Suskin (Schirmer Books).
Opening Night on Broadway edited by Steven Suskin (Schirmer Books).
Second Act Trouble by Steven M. Suskin (Applause Books).
Show Music magazine, Summer 1997.
Show Music magazine, Summer 1999.
Show Music magazine, Fall 1999.
Stephen Sondheim: A Life by Meryle Secrest (Knopf). Selections used from this book deal with *Sunday in the Park with George* and *Into the Woods*.
Sondheim & Co. (second edition) by Craig Zadan (Harper & Row). Selections used from this book deal with *Sunday in the Park with George* and *Into the Woods*.

Donna McKechnie
Broadway: The American Musical by Michael Kantor and Laurence Maslon (Bulfinch Books).
First-person interviews with the author.
On the Line: The Creation of A Chorus Line by Robert Viagas, Thommie Walsh, and Baayork Lee (William Morrow).
Time Steps: My Musical Comedy Life by Donna McKechnie with Greg Lawrence (Simon & Schuster).

Tommy Tune
The Advocate, October 28, 1997. This article covers Tune's life and career as a gay man.
After Dark, undated clip, 1970s. This piece deals with *The Patio Revue, Cloud 9*, and Tune's ethnicity.
Christian Science Monitor, August 31, 1973. This article covers Tune's early career.
Footnotes: A Memoir by Tommy Tune (Simon & Schuster).
More Opening Nights on Broadway edited by Steven Suskin (Schirmer Books).
Newsday, December 13, 1992. In this article, Tune compares static mediums such as film and recording to the stage and declares the stage as a more genuine and expressive medium.
Newsweek, May 24, 1982. This article deals with Tune's childhood nicknames, childhood dance work, *The Boy Friend*, "Famous Feet," and Michael Bennett.
New York Daily News, January 8, 1987.

New York Daily News, May 15, 1988. This article deals with Tune's concert shows.

New York Daily News, December 20, 1992. This article discusses Tune's height.

New York Daily News, September 17, 1997. This article discusses the love of Tune's life.

New York Post, June 24, 1978. This article discusses *Seesaw.*

New York Post, May 9, 1983. This article discusses Twiggy and Tune living together.

New York Times, June 1, 1980. This article covers Tune's childhood filmgoing, helping his father with horses, seeing *The King and I,* and other formative experiences.

New York Times, July 1, 1980.

New York Times, October 4, 1995. This article covers Tune's accident in *Busker Alley.*

On the Sunny Side of the Street by Deborah Grace Winer (Schirmer Books).

Opening Night on Broadway edited by Steven Suskin (Schirmer Books).

Second Act Trouble by Steven M. Suskin (Applause Books).

Show Music magazine, Fall 1996.

Show Music magazine, Winter 1997.

Soho News, July 2, 1980. This article deals with Tune and *Hellzapoppin'* and other shows—*The Dean Martin Show, The Legend of Sleepy Hollow,* and *Hollywood/Ukraine.*

Theater Week, May 13, 1991. This article deals with Tune's links with Will Rogers, and Tune's work on *The Will Rogers Follies.*

Variety, March 9, 1998. This article covers problems with *Easter Parade.*

Variety, January 11, 1999. This is a review of Tune's nightclub act.

The Villager, February 27, 1975. This is a review of Tune's nightclub act.

Patti LuPone

Andrew Lloyd Webber: His Life and Works by Michael Walsh (Harry N. Abrams Inc.). Selections used from this book deal with *Evita* and *Sunset Boulevard.*

Backstage, April 30, 2004. This is a review of LuPone's concert at Feinstein's at the Regency.

Cue, October 1979. This article describes how LuPone got the role of Evita Peron.

Ever After: The Last Years of Musical Theatre and Beyond by Barry Singer (Applause Books).

First-person interviews with the author.

More Opening Nights on Broadway edited by Steven Suskin (Schirmer Books).

New Yorker, July 5, 1993.

New York Daily News, October 21, 1975. This article covers LuPone working in The Acting Company.

New York Daily News June 10, 1980. This article includes contents from LuPone's high school yearbook.

New York Daily News, October 14, 1987. This article covers LuPone's time in London, her TV work, and her engagement.

New York Daily News, October 15, 1995. This article discusses the LuPone Trio, other amateur performances, and LuPone's relationship with Kevin Kline.

New York Post, January 1, 1980. This article describes how LuPone always knew she would be a star.

New York Theatre Review, June-July 1978.

New York Times, June 30, 1996. This article covers LuPone's conflicts with Andrew Lloyd Webber and her reaction to not getting the Broadway *Evita.*

New York Times, October 22, 1987.

Playbill, October 1995. This article covers LuPone's voice, her marriage, and how she did not get the Broadway *Evita.*

The Sondheim Review, Fall 2007.

Theater Week, October 9, 1992. This article covers LuPone's temperament, health, and career status.

Time Out New York, November 1997.

Christine Ebersole

Earl Wilson's syndicated column, July 14, 1980. This source covers Ebersole's first marriage.

First-person interview with author.

Gay City News, December 28, 2006. This article deals with Ebersole's politics.

The Happiest Corpse I've Ever Seen by Ethan Mordden (Palgrave and Macmillan).

New York Blade, November 6, 2006. This article covers how Ebersole was chosen for *Grey Gardens.*
New York Daily News, August 8, 1980. This article describes Ebersole's arrival in New York and her Broadway debut.
New York Daily News, December 1, 1982. This article discusses *Amadeus.*
New York magazine, September 21, 1980. This article highlights Ebersole's *Saturday Night Live* stint.
New York Post, August 5, 1980. This article covers Ebersole's early-career jobs.
New York Times, June 12, 1980. This article includes a timetable of Ebersole's wonder week.
New York Times,, August 21, 2001. This article features various perspectives on Ebersole's career.
New York Times,, March 16, 2006. This article deals with *Grey Gardens* and Ebersole's New Jersey home.
Not Since Carrie: 40 Years of Broadway Musical Flops by Ken Mandelbaum (St. Martin's Press).
People magazine, August 22, 1988. This article discusses *The Cavenaughs* and breakup of Ebersole's first marriage.
Pioneer Press, July 31, 1980. This article deals with Ebersole's first husband.
Playbill, November 2006.
Playbill, November 2006. This article describes Ebersole playing Edie Beale.
Show Music magazine, Fall 1994.
TV Guide, undated 1980s clip. This article describes Ebersole's feelings about working in television.
Village Voice, August 27, 1980.

Donna Murphy

First-person interviews with the author.
New York Daily News, undated clip 1994.
New York Post columns by Michael Riedel. These pieces deal with Murphy's health.
New York Times, December 2004, "Broadway's No-Show Business." This article discusses Murphy's missed performances due to illness.
New York Times, April 30, 2007. This article covers *LoveMusik* and Murphy's reputation for fragility.
Playbill.com. This source covers Murphy's premature departure from *Wonderful Town.*
Show Music magazine, 1996. This article covers *The King and I* and Murphy's early career.
The Sondheim Review, Issue 52.
Theater Week, April 25, 1994.

Nathan Lane

Ever After: The Last Years of Musical Theatre and Beyond by Barry Singer (Applause Books).
The Happiest Corpse I've Ever Seen by Ethan Mordden (Palgrave and Macmillan).
London Observer, November 7, 2004. This article describes Lane walking out of a magazine interview.
NathanLane.com
Show Music magazine, Fall 2002.
New York Times, letters to the editor, Fall 2004. These pieces deal with Lane's relationship with Matthew Broderick.
The New York Times Magazine, September 2, 2001. This article covers Lane's family issues, personal demons, and his coming out as gay.

Brian Stokes Mitchell

Amsterdam News, Mary 28, 1998. This article tells how Mitchell met his wife.
Gay City News, February 1, 2005. This article describes Mitchell's nightclub act.
First-person interviews with the author.
New York Resident, February 7, 2005. This article covers Lane's appearance in *Man of La Mancha* as a young man.
New York Times, January 11, 1998. This article discusses Mitchell's voice, childhood, and early career.
New York Times,, November 24, 2002, "Broadway's Last Leading Man." This article covers *Man of La Mancha* and Mitchell's career to that point. It also describes Mitchell as a guide for Broadway's leading men.

New York Times,, December 6, 2002. This is Ben Brantley's review of *Man of La Mancha.*
People magazine, May 11, 1998. This source highlights Mitchell as one of the "sexiest men alive."
Playbill, April 1977. This article covers Mitchell getting a role on *Trapper John M.C.* but dreaming of Broadway.
Playbill, January 1995. This article covers Mitchell's reception in New York versus his reception in Los Angeles.
Playbill, February 2000. This article compares Mitchell to John Raitt and Alfred Drake.

Audra McDonald

Boston Sunday Globe, July 18, 1999. This article discusses McDonald's Julliard training and "mental vacation."
First-person interviews with the author.
Author interview with Michael John LaChiusa on McDonald's audition and writing *Marie Christine* for her.
The Happiest Corpse I've Ever Seen by Ethan Mordden (Palgrave and Macmillan).
New York Times,, November 7, 1999. This article covers McDonald's upbringing and early career.
New York Times, October 27, 2002. This article describes McDonald's Carnegie Hall debut.
Show Music magazine, Fall 1998.
Show Music magazine, Spring 2000.
Show Music magazine, Summer 2000.

Sutton Foster

Cindy Adams' syndicated column March 6, 2003. This source covers Christian Borle getting hired for *Millie.*
First-person interviews with the author.
Liz Smith's syndicated column January 3, 2005. This source explains Smith's reaction to her audition for *Annie.*
Liz Smith's syndicated column April 9, 2006. This source describes the preparations for *Drowsy Chaperone.*
Newsday, April 17, 2002. This article covers how Foster got the leading role in *Millie.*
Newsday, April 30, 2006. This article discusses *Drowsy Chaperone* and Foster's plans for marriage to Borle.
New York Daily News, undated clip, circa June 2002.
New York Post, June 2, 2002. This article deals with Foster's relationship with her brother and the Tony Awards.
New York Times, February 13, 2004. This article covers Foster leaving *Millie* for *Little Women.*
New York Sun, June 16, 2004. This article is an overview of Foster's career.
Parade magazine, December 22, 2002. This article discusses Foster's family and career.
SuttonFoster.com
Time Out New York, December 30, 2004. This article compares Foster's shtick to that of silent films.
Time Out New York, undated clip. This piece mentions Foster's wish for a smaller role after *Millie.*

Kristin Chenoweth

Gay City News, February 8, 2007. This article describes Chenoweth's performance of "The Girl in 14G."
KristinChenoweth.com
Newsday, undated clip. This piece covers *Scapin* and Chenoweth's height.
New York Daily News, September 17, 2005. This article deals with Chenoweth's comments about gays and Christian fundamentalists.
New Yorker, June 4, 2001. This article by John Lahr discusses Chenoweth's voice and early career.
New York Observer, June 18, 2001.
New York Post, November 9, 1999. This article deals with producers bringing *Thoroughly Modern Millie* to Broadway with Chenoweth.
New York Post, October 8, 2002.
New York Press, November 3, 1999.
New York Resident, May 9, 2005.

New York Sun, September 8, 2004.

New York Times, March 5, 1999. This article covers the creation of Sally Brown in *You're a Good Man Charlie Brown.*

New York Times, June 12, 1999. This article covers Chenoweth's performance on the Tony Awards.

New York Times, June 5, 2001. This article covers the TV show *Kristin.*

New York Times, October 23, 2003. This article describes the upcoming debut of *Wicked.*

New York Times, June 6, 2004. This article describes Chenoweth's feelings about Broadway.

New York Times, January 22, 2007. This article discusses Chenoweth's Metropolitan Opera performance.

Playbill, September 1999.

Playbill, October 2003. This article deals with the creation of *Wicked* and Chenoweth being thought of as a dumb blonde.

Playbill.com, November 22, 2006. This source discusses *The Apple Tree.*

Playbill.com, May 14, 2007. This source covers *Pushing Daisies.*

About the Author

Robert Viagas is the founding editor of Playbill.com, host and program director of Playbill Radio, and founding editor of *The Playbill Broadway Yearbook* series. He was chosen by the original cast of *A Chorus Line* to tell their story of the show's genesis in the book *On the Line: The Creation of* A Chorus Line, with Thommie Walsh and Baayork Lee. He was chosen to tell the story of the creation of *The Fantasticks* in *The Amazing Story of* The Fantasticks, with Donald C. Farber. Among his other books are *The Back Stage Guide to Broadway* and *The Alchemy of Theatre: Essays on Collaboration* (working with the likes of Harold Prince, Edward Albee, Cy Coleman, and Chita Rivera), and he served as editor of Louis Botto's *At This Theatre,* telling the history of each Broadway theatre. He was drama, dance, and theatre columnist for Amazon.com. He wrote the theatrical history of Times Square used in the Broadway League's guided tours of the New York theatre district. He spent two years in the BMI Musical Theatre Workshop's librettist program and has written the books of two musicals, *City of Light* and *A Perfect World*. A graduate of Hofstra University, he was a theatre critic in Connecticut for fourteen years.

Index